The Men of the Old Stone Age

The Men of the Old Stone Age

(Palaeolithic & Mesolithic)

HENRI BREUIL
Membre de l'Institut, Professeur honoraire au Collège de France

and

RAYMOND LANTIER
Membre de l'Institut, Conservateur en chef honoraire des Musées Nationaux

translated by

B. B. RAFTER
Docteur de l'Université de Paris

GREENWOOD PRESS, PUBLISHERS
WESTPORT, CONNECTICUT

Library of Congress Cataloging in Publication Data

Breuil, Henri, 1877-1961.
    The men of the old stone age (paleolithic & mesolithic)

    Translation of Les hommes de la pierre ancienne.
    Reprint of the 1965 ed. published by G. G. Harrap,
London.
    Bibliography: p.
    Includes index.
    1. Paleolithic period. 2. Mesolithic period.
I. Lantier, Raymond, 1886-   joint author.
II. Title.
GN771.B7313 1980   930'.1'2   79-16777
ISBN 0-313-21289-9

To the memory of our friend

HUGO OBERMAIER

prehistorian and geologist
in remembrance of our long
and affectionate collaboration

Reprinted in 1980 by Greenwood Press, Inc.
51 Riverside Avenue, Westport, CT 06880

Printed in the United States of America

10 9 8 7 6 5 4 3 2 1

Preface to the Second Edition

T he rapid exhaustion of the first edition of this book seemed proof of public interest in a work that broke new ground, and has encouraged us to produce a second edition, in the belief that it may be a very useful introduction to early prehistory.

We were especially appreciative of the welcome given to our work by a number of educationists overseas, one of whom—the late Professor V. Gordon Childe—was kind enough to consider it valuable to students training for this field of research who wish to learn new techniques of investigation. These methods of pollen and quantitative analysis of ancient deposits and the assessment of their fluorine and carbon 14 content may be as yet far from infallible, but they give good results if properly controlled and can facilitate attempts to allot a precise date to organic remains.

It is not for us to guide researchers along these recently opened paths. Such specialization is outside our scope and reserved for a few experts.

The prehistory we unfold here is the result of the untiring work of the men of our own generation.

H. B. and R. L.

Foreword

Being absent from Paris when the first edition of this book appeared, I was unable to write an appropriate preface to explain its origins to the reader.

It is based on the manuscript copy of lectures given by me in the University of Lisbon between January and July 1942. Mme da Santa was kind enough to type it as I delivered the sections to her. Since circumstances obliged me (as in 1939 and 1940 at Bordeaux and Toulouse) to compress the whole of prehistory, up to but excluding the Neolithic, into about twenty lectures, it is not surprising that each subject occupies a somewhat restricted space. I ought also to mention that in Lisbon I was unable to refer to the works of authorities on the subject (except for J. G. D. Clark's book on the Mesolithic), and I had therefore to fall back almost entirely on facts I had remembered, or information acquired in the course of personal experience, which were fortunately extensive enough.

Then came my long stay in South Africa, from 1942 to 1951, with brief visits to France in 1945 and 1949. After my return to South Africa M. R. Lantier, to whom I had given a copy of my typed notes in 1945 to use as he thought fit, was kind enough to revise the text and add data not available when the original was written. Also, amplifying notes I had given him, he wrote the text of Chapters 18 and 19 (material for which was not included in the Lisbon lectures) and the paragraphs in Chapter 6 dealing with hunting and the abodes of men and their gods. I am deeply grateful to him.

In my lectures I had also given some space to dolmenic and rock-art in Neolithic times and later, but this will have to be left for another occasion.

H. B.

Contents

Illustrations

Introduction

It is not so very long since Copernicus and Galileo first proved that the earth is only a satellite of the sun. Yet to-day our conception of space is of an area so vast that all stars visible to the naked eye are but one single galaxy of the millions filling an expanded universe at intervals of millions of light-years. What an incredible change in outlook on the relative importance of our planet! It is now seen to be a mere speck of cosmic dust, and we crawl on it like micro-organisms.

Now, our total knowledge of the history of the earth and its crust has been acquired mainly within the last hundred and fifty years. Much patient toil has gradually revealed what remains of the crumpled pages of these records, written in folded rock strata, of which only the most recent have preserved the fossil remains of living creatures.

Set against the scale of human history, the durations of time calculated from studies of radioactivity are so gigantic that the most recent paragraph of the story, where mankind emerges, must perforce seem negligible. The formation of the pre-Cambrian strata, prior to any known fossils, must have occupied some 1000 million years, while the subsequent periods together total about 480 million, of which the Primary took 350 million, the Secondary 100 million, and the Tertiary 30 million, leaving only about half a million, or a little more, for the Quaternary, where man appears.

Prior to this astounding progress in recent research, nobody had any conception of the slow succession of changes wrought on the face of our globe, of the living creatures peopling it, or of the plant life of their habitat. Between the time when bacteria alone were active on the surface of the earth, preparing it for the arrival of more complex forms of life or transmuting its raw minerals, and the moment when, at the peak of mammal evolution, man made his presence and his intelligence known, how many living things—whole groups of fish and reptiles, often of enormous proportions—must have emerged, only to disappear again! One has but to think of the mammals, at first the size of mice and later to outstrip the noblest of our present species.

On this whole subject, as on the millions of years that such evolution presupposes, clear ideas are less than a century old. Even more recent is the notion, clarified by the gropings of endless research, of the modest part played by our species in the later scenes of this great drama. Some few minutes in the cosmic life of the planet are all the antiquity to which mankind can lay claim. Yet these few minutes, scaled against our time, represent hundreds of thousands of years of history. When, much later, man learned to fix in writing both his thoughts and his memory of the past, the race had forgotten, as do individuals, nearly all of its age-long infancy. The recollection of it, simplified like an adult's memories of early childhood, was now no more than a vague outline, a philosophical theory of Creation rather than an account of the true facts of history.

How did they come about, these new discoveries which so revolutionized our view of the past?

This is what our first chapter proposes to explain.

[1]

Proof of the theory of the great antiquity of man

First steps in the discovery—Geological and palaeontological methods

As we look back over the history of the Western world we come across peoples about whom little is known save the names given them by historians—Ligurians, Celts, Gauls, Iberians, for example. It is, however, certain that they used iron tools and weapons. Homer spoke of arms of bronze, not iron, at the time of the Trojan War. Lucretius, with a philosopher's insight, imagined an age when the first men used stone and wood for weapons, instead of claws and teeth. Herodotus noted that the Egyptians used flint knives when they prepared a body for embalming, and the Bible mentions blades of the same material used for circumcision. Ennius spoke of flints for cutting sails; while Livy, describing the ritual preparations for the combat of the Horatii and the Curiatii, related that the vanquished fell under a flint dagger.

A sixteenth-century scholar, Mercati (1541–93), had no doubt read these accounts, and saw that the European 'thunderstones' were identical with the polished stone axes and arrow-heads chipped from flint and obsidian by savage tribes. But his work, *Metallotheca vaticana*, was published from a manuscript in the Vatican Library only during the reign of Pope Clement XI, in 1719, in an edition by J. M. Lancisi and P. Assalti. Mercati had already visualized the existence, in the far-distant past, of a phase in human history characterized by the complete absence of metals. Man's first tools were a rough stone, a piece of wood, and, later, bones and chipped flints. "Students of history," he wrote, "think that these objects were split by a blow from very hard flint, to be used in the follies of war. The earliest men used flints for knives and made everything with sharpened stones."

During the eighteenth century discoveries made in Denmark showed that the Iron Age there had been preceded by a Bronze Age, which followed a Stone Age. About the same time the great call to adventurous exploration sent navigators to seek new lands in the Pacific Ocean, and they brought back with them weapons of stone, bone, and shell. This revived interest in 'thunderstones,' and put scholars and antiquaries into direct contact with primitive peoples. Jussieu, coming into possession of stone axes and arrow-heads of Canadian and Caribbean origin, was able to establish their similarity to those of the Old World. In his monograph *On the Origin and Use of Thunderstones* (1723) he concluded that our continent had, at some period or other, been inhabited by peoples whose need produced an industry similar to that recently discovered overseas, and that their tools had subsequently been buried. By close comparison of all the specimens, he proved that they had been shaped by rubbing, and were sometimes of local stone, sometimes from pieces brought from afar. Thus demolishing all previous, ill-founded notions about shaped stones being formed by lightning or the mere whim of Nature, Jussieu laid the foundations of comparative archaeology. The way was now open, and, following in his footsteps, Lafiteau, Majudel, Dampierre, de Frézier, La Condamine, and d'Ulloa were to make many revealing comparisons between the primitive cultures of the Old and New Worlds.

GEOLOGICAL AND PALAEONTOLOGICAL METHODS

Yet all these cultures, by now more or less fully understood, belonged to very recent geological periods—to our own times, in fact—and showed men as shepherds and farmers, living among flora and fauna similar to ours. The question now was: Had man ever known such vanished creatures as the great Pachydermata and Carnivora which, after Cuvier's work, were no longer considered quite so gigantic as they had previously been?

Schmerling in the caves at Engihoul, Belgium (1833), Buckland, Pengelly, and McEnery in Great Britain, Jouannet in the Périgord (1815), de Saussure, Tournal (1829), Dumas, and Christol in the caves in the Languedoc, and many others looked for human bones in close association with the remains of animals now extinct or migrated. Their findings were a mixture of fact and fancy. Their opponents, among them Cuvier, maintained that what they found were jumbled collections of the remains of many different ages, and in this they were frequently right. The result was that in this sector true knowledge made little progress.

It fell to a writer with no training as a naturalist, though helped by the experts of the Société Polymathique of Abbeville, a certain Boucher de Perthes de Crèvecœur, to gain professional scientific recognition for the discovery in the Quaternary gravel-beds of the Somme of implements made by 'antediluvian man,' in the form of simple chipped stones, closely associated and mingled with the remains of elephants, rhinoceroses, and hippopotami.

Similar discoveries had already been made in England—by Conyers in 1700 and John Frere in 1797. The former discovered in association, in old Thames gravel-beds, a chipped flint axe and elephant bones. It was too early for the true significance of the facts to be understood. Conyers thought that an Ancient Briton, wielding a stone axe, had stood up to an elephant from Caesar's army, but he wisely pointed out that since that time the Thames had changed its course considerably. His paper on the subject, published by the Society of Antiquaries in London, attracted no attention whatever.

Nearly a century later John Frere picked from a pile of pebbles extracted from a brickfield at Hoxne, Suffolk, not far from Ipswich, bones belonging to large Pachydermata and freshwater shells, which he mistook for seashells. Among the flints he recognized several pointed axes shaped by chipping, and at once grasped the full importance of his discovery. His report, published in *Archaeologia*, did not, however, succeed in attracting the attention of the experts of the time.

Then one day Boucher de Perthes, a distinguished man of letters and generous patron of local archaeological work, found himself looking at Neolithic remains dredged from the Somme Canal. There were broken bones, chipped flints, and polished axes, one of which still had its stag-horn handle. His friend Casimir Picard wrote a description of these 'Celtic' remains (as they were then termed), and Boucher de Perthes became deeply interested in this kind of research. They were still dealing only with remains of the late Stone Age, the period of the peat bogs, similar to those described by the Danes.

Theories concerning the early history of man and his world were still limited by the concept of the Flood as it is described in the Bible. To it were ascribed all manner of deposits, those in the caves and those gravel-beds left at various levels of valleys as the rivers had dug out their beds over thousands of years. It was the Flood, they believed, which had killed off the elephant, the rhinoceros, and the hippopotamus, remains of which were frequently found in gravel-pits at Menchecourt and Moulin-Quignon, just outside Abbeville.

According to the Bible, man had lived before the great catastrophe. Therefore his remains and the traces of his industry should be found in

B

layers formed in the cataclysm, mingled with the bones of such animals as existed at that period.

Boucher de Perthes, fascinated by the whole subject, decided to see if this assumption would be supported by facts, so he began to collect everything the workmen found in the gravel-beds. From this mistaken idea was born human palaeontology. From 1837 Boucher de Perthes devoted all his energies and talent to the search for evidence. Of course, he was often tricked by his workmen, who imported into the diggings Neolithic flints they had found on higher land near by, or had made themselves. They even borrowed a human jaw-bone from some burial-vault, and arranged for Boucher de Perthes to 'discover' it on the spot! Even so, there was no lack of genuine chipped axes in these gravel-beds, and, though mixed with more recent material, they provided a firm basis for the Abbeville scholar's conclusions. His own imagination was also another drawback. Not content with chipped stones, he sought artistic and religious objects, and imagined he had found them in the smooth knobs of virgin, natural flint commonly found in these gravels.

However, the real evidence was there: chipped stones were found in the same layers as the remains of extinct animals, and the persistence of the discoverer finally triumphed over the attempts of his opponents to discredit him. In 1854 one of his strongest critics, Dr Rigollot of Amiens, capitulated. Bent on discrediting Boucher de Perthes, he visited Saint-Acheul, a suburb of Amiens, where Boucher de Perthes was examining some gravel-pits. This was Dr Rigollot's road to Damascus, for there, too, chipped axes were found buried in the 'diluvian' gravels of the former course of the Somme. It was the first step along the road to complete success. In 1858 a group of English experts—Prestwich, the well-known geologist, Falconer and Flower, distinguished palaeontologists, and John Evans, a gifted young archaeologist—came to Abbeville and Saint-Acheul to check the truth of the statements made by their French colleague. They undertook their own diggings, and then stated categorically that the deposits of gravel and the pebble-strata left by the old Somme did indeed contain, in close association, genuine chipped stone axes and the bones of extinct animals. Back in London, they resurrected from the libraries where they had lain in unmerited oblivion the historic writings of Conyers and John Frere. They then visited the Thames gravel-beds, and there, in turn, made discoveries similar to those on the Somme. In 1863 Lyell, the great English geologist, published his epoch-making work *Geological Evidences of the Antiquity of Man*.

The words of the English experts echoed loud under the dome of the Institut in Paris. A brilliant young palaeontologist, Albert Gaudry, set out in 1859 to check by personal digging the discoveries at Saint-Acheul, and confirmed the findings. The discovery of fossil man, a contemporary of the great extinct mammals, was now to be classed with the great achievements of the human mind.

At about the same time, in the south of France, above Toulouse, Noulet had begun to collect from the terraces of the Ariège and the Garonne chipped quartzite pebbles, similar to the implements found at Saint-Acheul and associated at Venerque with the remains of mammoth and rhinoceros. The importance of this discovery was not lost on him.

In the neighbouring *Département* of the Gers lived an unassuming magistrate, Édouard Lartet, who had made something of a reputation as a palaeontologist by his diggings among deposits of Miocene mammals at Sansan. In 1852, following a chance discovery, he was asked to go to Aurignac, in the Haute-Garonne. A small slab of stone had been moved from the mouth of a little cave which was found to be packed with human skeletons. These were given decent burial in the local cemetery, but under this Neolithic charnel-house were found to stretch hearths full of bone and ivory implements, chipped flints, and the bones of reindeer, cave bear, hyena, and rhinoceros. Lartet investigated this layer, but thought it contained only the remains of funeral feasts held at the time of the burials. It was only later that it was discovered that they were very much older than the human bones in the cave above. Lartet then explored other caves in the Pyrenees, and at Massat brought to light, from hearths rich in reindeer-bones and chipped flints, barbed harpoons made from stag-horn, bone needles, and an antler tine with its point carved into a fine bear-head. A few years later a fossil-collector in Périgueux sent him a box of flints and bones picked up in the cave at Les Eyzies (Dordogne), and told him that the whole of the Périgord was full of such remains. Édouard Lartet reported this to one of his English friends, Henry Christy, who at once raised the money for a digging expedition to the now famous valley of the Vézère. This was in 1863, and the season's dig not only produced a remarkable collection of finds, but enabled Lartet to sketch out the first draft of a classification of prehistoric times. It ran thus:

1. The hippopotamus period, when man lived in the open air and made axes of the Saint-Acheul type. Layers of this were to be found in the old river-beds.

2. The cave bear and mammoth period. He rightly concluded that the site at Le Moustier was typical of this, but noted the appearance of reindeer. Towards the end came the Aurignac phase, represented, on the Vézère, by the Gorge d'Enfer rock-shelter, and in this period, together with finer flint chippings, came implements of ivory, bone, and horn, sharpened and polished.

3. Then came the reindeer period, where this animal, frequently found in the preceding phase, now predominated, at first mingled with many horses and bovines and later giving place to the common stag. Two types of industry were noted by Lartet, though he did not

indicate which came first. One, at Laugerie-Haute, was characterized by flint points and arrow-heads, delicately worked into leaf-shapes or else with a tang and notched on one side. The other, represented by the industry of La Madeleine, Laugerie Basse, and Les Eyzies, showed much simpler craftsmanship, but bone implements were much more common, including pierced sticks, arrow- and barbed harpoon-heads, spatulae, needles, and points, together with large numbers of works of art, such as engravings and carvings of animals and geometrical designs.

Such was the first rough outline of a classification of prehistoric times. It held the field until about 1880, and has been used as the basis for all subsequent methods. Its weakness was that being based on palaeontology, it could not, without serious modifications, be applied to regions farther south.

About this time the prehistorian Gabriel de Mortillet became assistant director of the Musée des Antiquités Nationales at Saint-Germain-en-Laye, and it occurred to him to replace the palaeontological terms by archaeological names based on the sequence of types of industry. At first this new classification was merely based on Lartet's, but the names are now derived from typical sites:

1. The period of the hippopotamus and the Saint-Acheul axes becomes the *Chellean*, named after Chelles (Seine-et-Marne), a site rich in remains of the *Elephas antiquus*, the *Rhinoceros Merckii*, and the hippopotamus. It yielded hundreds of almond-shaped axe-heads of the Saint-Acheul type. Mortillet called these *coups-de-poing*, and all the sites containing them were called by the above name.

2. A great part of the age of the cave bear and the mammoth becomes the *Mousterian*, typified by the industry using only chipping to form points and scrapers and as yet showing no fashioned bones. The people of this culture were Neanderthal men.

These first two divisions form the Lower Palaeolithic.

3. The Aurignacian level is incorporated, with the facies of Laugerie Haute and La Madeleine, into an Upper Palaeolithic where modern man begins to develop. Mortillet divides this Upper Palaeolithic into three stages: (*a*) *Aurignacian*, which he shortly afterwards suppressed and incorporated into the beginnings of the Magdalenian; (*b*) *Solutrean*, corresponding to the site at Laugerie Haute, named after Solutré (Saône-et-Loire), where H. de Ferry had recently made discoveries characterized by beautiful lance-heads, notched and shaped like laurel-leaves: Mortillet mistakedly stated, however, that this level bore no bone industry; (*c*) *Magdalenian*, from La Madeleine (Dordogne), notable, besides the simplification of the retouch working of the flints, for the profusion of fashioned bones and the progress in the art of engraving and carving small objects.

In the following twenty years some modifications were made in this classification, though it won universal acclaim. Its great merits were its clarity, simplicity, and logical order, though this was too rigid to give a completely accurate picture of reality, which is always much more complex than our concepts of it.

The first correction of Mortillet's classification was to be made by d'Acy and d'Ault du Mesnil, who introduced between the Chellean and the Mousterian a new phase with a mixed industry, the *Acheulean*, resulting from the discoveries of sites on the Somme and elsewhere in which, among the alluvium and loess overlying the river-terrace gravels containing Chellean flakes, were found lighter and more elegantly shaped coups-de-poing, associated with numerous retouched flints, very similar to those Mortillet classified in the Mousterian.

Then came the filling of the gap, due merely to lack of sufficient knowledge at the time, between the Magdalenian and the so-called Robenhausian, where Mortillet had placed the agricultural and pastoral civilization of the makers of dolmens, pile-dwellings, and fortified camps. It was then thought that France and part of Europe had at one time been abandoned by man. However, in 1887 Édouard Piette, the famous explorer of caves in the Pyrenees, found at Le Mas d'Azil (Ariège) a thick archaeological deposit subsequent to the Magdalenian, with fauna notable for the presence of stag and boar, containing also flat harpoons of stag-horn and pebbles painted with red ochre. This was the *Azilian*, the first stage of a new era in human history, the *Mesolithic*, when men still lived by hunting and fishing like their ancestors, but amid flora and fauna similar to ours.

Another facies denoted by small geometrical flints, the industry of a fishing and shellfish-eating community, was first brought to light in Portugal in 1865 by Pereira da Costa, in the *concheiros* at the head of the old estuary of the Tagus, when the sea-water went up as far as Muge and Carregado. Diggings by Carlos Ribeiro before 1880 and Paulo de Oliveira in 1887 made them more widely known, but it was only in 1896 that, after finding similar flints at Fère-en-Tardenois (Aisne), Adrien de Mortillet gave this industry the name of *Tardenoisian*.

Other modifications were still to be made to Gabriel de Mortillet's table, and these will be studied later in this work.

Geological evidence for the antiquity of man

Glaciers and fossil man—River terraces—Former sea-levels—Absolute chronology

This development of prehistory until about 1895 was little more than a work of classification based on palaeontology and, later, on archaeology. But these fields of study alone were inadequate for retracing the more remote stages of the history of mankind. Like so many other sciences, prehistory must call for assistance from its neighbours. The distribution over the globe of the various civilizations is a special department of human geography, and it is to this, to some extent, as well as to physical geography, that we must turn to understand the causes of such distributions, influenced as they are by climatic zones, the shape of the oceans, and the obstacles provided by seas, mountains, deserts, and tropical forests. Yet far more than any other science it is stratigraphical geology which provides the basis for prehistorical research, since it alone enables us, through the study of the soil layers, to place in correct sequence the bones and implements to be found therein. It can then furnish both the proofs of the antiquity of man's existence on the globe and, with the help of astronomy, some chronological assessment of the duration of those long-vanished ages.

The first question to arise is this: to be logical, how far back should we go? Man could certainly have existed alongside the pre-Quaternary mammals—say, from the middle of the Tertiary, among the mastodons and the *Dinotheria*, or at the end of the same period with the first southern elephants. Though none of his bones could be found—they are indeed rare enough in the Quaternary, where implements unquestionably indicate his presence—it was often thought that he had existed because of the discovery of chipped or split stones known as eoliths, dated as Tertiary. These were simple, natural pebbles adapted for gripping and somewhat crudely touched up and trimmed. The Abbé Bourgeois, at Thenay (Loir-et-Cher), in the Oligocene (1867), Desnoyers at Saint-Prest (Eure-et-Loir), in the Pliocene (1863), Rames at Le Puy-Corny (Cantal), Rutot in various parts of Belgium, especially on the Oligocene site at Boncelles, Prestwich and later Harrison in the Kentish Weald, Reid Moir in the Bone Bed both at the base and the summit of the Red Crag at Ipswich (Pliocene, 1910)—all thought they had found proof of the existence of Tertiary man. Others (Laussedat, for example) based their conclusions on finds of broken, incised bones at Billy (Allier) belonging to the Miocene; on rhinoceros bones with pebble impressions extracted at Pouancé (Maine-et-Loire); on the ribs of a *Halitherium* bitten by a *Carcharodon*, a giant Miocene dog-fish; on bones gnawed by a beaver (*Trogontherium*), at Saint-Prest, or scratched in moving soil by compressed flints.

We need not dwell at great length on finds which our more detailed modern knowledge of the causes of natural fracture enables us to reject. Yet even if they still leave open the question of man's existence at the end of the Tertiary, at least they clear the ground of much fruitless effort to prove his presence there.

What is important is to consider the position of the facts which are established beyond all doubt concerning man in relation to the sequence of geological phenomena of the Quaternary period—that is glaciation, the formation of river valleys, and the variation of the sea-levels.

GLACIERS AND FOSSIL MAN

At various periods of geological time, and not only during the Quaternary, but as far back as the Primary and different stages of the Secondary and Tertiary, the earth was subjected to the development of ice-fields which spread over vast areas in lands now free from glaciers. A complete glacial cycle comprised the following:

1. A period of very heavy atmospheric precipitation which, in mountainous and circum-polar regions, piled up enormous masses of snow, warped and packed into *névé* (granular ice) by its own weight. This then began to flow down the valleys, spreading across the neighbouring plains and ever farther, as long as the thrust of continued snowfall from behind maintained the movement. Such colossal snowfalls indicate a great increase in evaporation from the oceans, and therefore not a decrease but an increase in solar heat. This first phase of the accumulation and spread of ice-fields coincided with exceptionally heavy rainfall in the tropics.

2. As the sun's heat diminished a period of increased cloud led to a

considerable drop in the mean earth temperature, while sea-levels were lowered by the evaporation of water masses no longer able to return quickly and normally, since they had become ice. There followed a time of dry cold, causing the retreat, by slow thaw and wastage, of the glaciers. Tropical lands began to suffer drought and became semi-desert. Regions farther north developed a cold, dry climate in which the wind, scouring the surface of the bare silt left by the ice and the sandy beaches freed by the seas, piled up heavy layers of blown sand into loess and dune.

3. Then conditions improved. The sea-levels rose gradually, and rain began to fall in the temperate zones, affecting previous surface deposits. Thus began the interglacial period, damp in temperate regions, dry in the tropics.

4. The rivers, which, when the sea-level dropped, had scoured deeper, narrower beds, were now obliged to fill out and widen their channels as the sea-level rose again.

A mountain glacier produces a whole series of transport and erosion phenomena on and in its course. The walls of the gorges are scraped and polished, crest-lines are ground down to gentle undulations, the valley bed is dug deeper. On its back the ice carries boulders fallen from rocky spurs, and as they sink into its mass they act as scrapers, scooping out the bed, scratching it, and polishing themselves in the process.

Where the glacier stops it deposits all the material it was carrying, forming a semicircular ridge across the valley—the terminal moraine. Receding farther, it leaves behind other moraines, on the bed and sides of the valley—bottom and lateral moraines formed of piles or blocks of rock foreign to the locality. If the glacier reaches the sea, as it does to-day in sub-polar regions, it forms an ice-front or barrier which crumbles off into the water, forming great floating icebergs. These drift with the sea-currents and shed their debris far away.

From the study of the topography and the distribution of the boulder-clay, it is fairly easy to determine the area covered and carved by a given glacier of moderate age, the levels attained, the point reached before it retreated, and the stages of its recession. But it will be found that the torrent streaming from the glacier base has scattered far and wide moraine matter foreign to the plain below, thus forming glacial terraces.

An examination of the layers left either by glaciers or by their out-flowing rivers forces us to conclude that the glaciation processes were repeated several times over. Deposits containing temperate flora and fauna, gravel, sand and clays deposited on lake-beds, all indicate by their frequent interleaving the interruption of glacial conditions by other periods more favourable to life.

In high valleys of glacial ancestry the hollowing-out process still continues, even to-day, since the contour-line has not been reached as in the lower valleys of the plains. At various heights there can be seen fluvio-glacial terraces, linking up, at least for the three lower levels, with terminal moraines. This leads to the conclusion that the higher terraces must once have connected with similar moraines, now eroded away or destroyed by the later development of broader glaciers.

In low-lying countries like England, North Germany, and the Russo-Polish plain glaciers spread out over immense areas, running from Scandinavia down through Poland and Saxony almost to the Crimea. Farther west England was three-quarters covered by ice, Holland and Ireland covered entirely. At the height of glacier formation Switzerland was completely covered, and the Rhône glacier extended down to Lyon and the Saône. In Spain glaciers existed in the Central Plateau, the Pyrenees, the Sierra de Guadarrama, the Sierra Nevada, and extended even as far as the Serra da Estrella, in Portugal.

How does man fit into this picture of successive glacial and inter-glacial periods? Quite early it was possible to show that in fact man, in the reindeer age, or at least in the most advanced stage of it, the Magdalenian, had settled within the area of recent moraines, on the banks of Lake Geneva and of Lake Constance, in the deep valleys of the Pyrenees, and in England as far north as Settle (Victoria Cave), and even in the north of Scotland at Inchnadamph. In summer 'para-Magdalenian' men hunted reindeer on the very edge of the glacier, round Hamburg and Kiel. On the other hand, the first two-thirds of the reindeer age were lived outside the regions covered by this glacier: neither Solutrean nor Aurignacian is to be found there.

Of the older industries, the Mousterian, or rather a pre-Mousterian, has been found in bear caves high up in the Grisons, on the Wild-kirchli, on the Wildenmannlisloch, and on the Drachenloch, at 1477, 1628, and 2445 metres altitude respectively—that is to say, above the glacier-levels. Other Swiss deposits lie under moraines of the peak of the last glaciation and have blocked up the cave (Cotencher). Bouichéta, in the Ariège Pyrenees, is only just inside the terminal moraine of the last glaciation.

Thus the Mousterian, the age of the cave bear, was partly previous to, partly contemporaneous with, the final spread of the glaciers, and lasted until the beginning of their decline. At Taubach and Ehrings-dorf, near Weimar, it is found with *Elephas antiquus* and *Rhinoceros Merckii* overlying moraines of the penultimate glacial period and under-lying traces of the last.

As early as 1889 Marcellin Boule had reported finding an amygda-loid, heart-shaped axe near Aurillac (Cantal), in a layer above a moraine of the penultimate glaciation and under one from the last. He thought it was Chellean, but it was only Mousterian. He was the first to form the theory, based on collated details from various sources—mostly analytical observations by English experts—that man was at least contemporary with the last interglacial period. He also recognized three main glacial periods, instancing, among other rare direct contacts between human fossil remains and glacial deposits, the gravel bed at Hoxne, near Ipswich—first discovered by John Frere in 1797, and still worked to-day. Here a temperate layer containing *Elephas antiquus* and chipped stones covered the terminal moraine of a glacier, and was in turn covered by traces of another, not the last.

The difficulty was that human sites yielding chipped stones of great antiquity are generally found outside the regions covered by old glaciers, and this is particularly true of England and Germany, which were almost entirely covered by ice, as, indeed, of the sub-Alpine and sub-Pyrenean zones also affected by them.

In 1894 Geikie, the great English glaciologist, acknowledged that man had appeared for the first time together with the *Elephas antiquus* in the *second interglacial period*. He reached the conclusion that there had been four main glaciations, with a fifth, smaller glaciation in the north. In the first interglacial stage the southern elephant was still associated with the *Elephas antiquus*; but Geikie had as yet no proof of its coexistence with man. We now know that man did meet the southern elephant during this first interglacial time.

In the north of Germany, where the glaciers came from Scandinavia as well as from the east, a boring made at Rüdersdorf, near Berlin, revealed virgin soil at a depth of 178 metres. Above that were three moraines, separated by interglacial river or marsh deposits: the bottom moraine, named after the Elster, lay from 136 to 178 metres down; the middle moraine, named after the Saale, lay between 27 and 39 metres and the most recent one, named after the Vistula, was between 5 and 22 metres. The *Elephas antiquus*, then the mammoth, were found between the Saale and the Vistula, together with chipped stones, including a small Acheulean axe-head. Older chippings, thought to be Clactonian, had been found deeper down, at the Günz-Mindel level.

In the years 1901 to 1909 two great German glaciologists, Penck and Brückner, after very thorough study of glacial deposits in the Alps, of the surrounding fluvio-glacial layers, and of the interglacial formations occurring between them, published a chronological table based on four main Quaternary glaciations—Günz, Mindel, Riss, and Würm. They placed the appearance of Quaternary man in the intermediate Mindel-Riss period, and not in the Riss-Würm, as had been thought previously. All subsequent work on this subject has been derived from these remarkable studies.

However, in England, the Pyrenees, and Germany it has since been possible to find evidence of chipped tools dating from earlier still, prior to the second, or Mindel, glacial stage, and similar evidence has come from Morocco.

To take an example from France, in the Haute-Garonne worked

flints are found not only on and in glacial river deposits at 15 metres down (Würm), and at 30 metres (Riss), but at 60 and 70 metres (Mindel). They are no longer evident at a depth of 90 metres (Günz). But the districts richest in ancient industries had never been covered by ice. Northern France and Southern England were free of it. How, then, could data from these areas be connected with that from the glacial zones and also with the variations in sea-level associated with the glacial periods?

RIVER TERRACES

The basis of a solution to these problems lies in the study of the deposits stacked at various levels down the sides of river valleys, and an examination of their content in archaeological and animal remains. Throughout the long ages of geological time contemporaneous with the epoch of fossil man the waterways successively cut out their beds, then partially filled them up, only to scour them out again. Furthermore, down from the watersheds to the river and its terraces, left by previous scouring, came time after time great masses of jumbled gravel from the solifluxion caused by spring thaws or heavy rain. The action of wind and currents also piled up silt, loess, and dunes in the channels.

The general tendency of rivers to form deposits in descending tiers that were frequently covered over again is a phenomenon which, even before 1870, had attracted the attention of geologists. About that time Belgrand, working on the Seine, pointed out upper levels at about 50 metres, middle ones at about 30 metres, lower layers at less than 10 metres, and finally the bed buried under the modern talweg.

On the Somme, Commont, continuing the research done by d'Ault du Mesnil, did magnificent work between 1905 and 1914. He discovered, high above the deep bed of the present river (12 metres down at Amiens, 17 at Abbeville, and 35 metres under the sea at the mouth), an upper 'terrace' at some 45 metres, another at about 30 metres, yet another at about 22 metres (10 metres at least above to-day's level) which has produced two deposits. Continuing these studies, H. Breuil was able to show that on eleven separate occasions there slid down these slopes material produced by solifluxion, indicating near-glacial conditions of varying intensity, occurring at peaks of glacial humidity, the last four being contemporary with the final glaciation. Quite unintentionally a link was established with the figures given by Sörgel in his studies of the glacial periods in Northern Germany. It is therefore possible, while examining solifluxed gravels and the way they are interleaved with other river or open-air deposits, particularly with the loess formed in times of dry cold, to arrive, perhaps somewhat laboriously, at a correlation with the sequence of Ice Ages.

It is therefore clear that man appears for the first time—and the facts are seen on the banks of the Thames as well as on the Rhine—in company with fauna still including the southern elephant and the Etruscan rhinoceros; this is in the first interglacial period. The *two others* have only the *Elephas antiquus* and the *Rhinoceros Merckii.*

Upstream, quite a long way from the mouth, river deposits are loaded with matter from the estuary, since the rise in sea-level at the interglacial times made the rivers fill out their channels. On the other hand, during the ice phases the sea went down to more than 100 metres below the present level, and this explains why borings reveal, at un-expected depths, open-air surface features with easily recognizable watercourse and shore lay-outs, and pebble-belts similar to those on our own beaches.

FORMER SEA-LEVELS

Professor Depéret has attempted to give a coherent account of the peak changes in sea-level. His work reveals four levels, spaced in fairly regular tiers around the Mediterranean coasts and probably elsewhere. These four he named *Sicilian, Milazzian, Tyrrhenian,* and *Monastirian,* later renamed *Tyrrhenian II,* then *Grimaldian.* Between each of these levels, the last three of which at least were known to man, and closely following on the first, there occurred successive falls in sea-level by depths of 100 metres or more. These periodic falls are generally thought to have been caused by water evaporated from the oceans turning to ice over the land-masses and round the poles, during the glacial phases.

There are numerous points around the Mediterranean where Mousterian industries are associated with fauna first of warm-climate type, then cold, and overlying a sea-beach at about 10 metres which itself contains warm-water species, including the *Strombus bubonius* from Senegal.

It is obvious that if hippopotami, elephants, and Merck's rhinoceros could live on a site like Grimaldi, near Mentone, the continental shelf, covered to-day by more than 100 metres of sea, must have been clear of the water. This is the level with subaerial characteristics that is found at Gibraltar, at Romanelli (Taranto, Italy), and in the Adriatic.

Near Pisa, Baron A. C. Blanc recently studied deep borings into the coastal plain of the Versilia. He found 91 metres of sand, clay, and peat deposits, all of terrestrial formation and containing Alpine flora, except for a sea-level layer, about 19–20 metres, with present-day shells indi-cating a short period of temperate conditions, and a beach layer at 61 metres near Vitis, containing grape-seeds. Above the deposits at 20 metres come old dune sands containing all the final stages of the Palaeo-lithic, from the Upper Mousterian onward.

This shows that the Mousterian witnessed a fall in sea-level to minus 100 metres and a rise to minus 28 metres. At Peniche, in Portugal, the

Furninha cave scoured out by the sea at Grimaldi level has furnished similar data: the Upper Mousterian comes immediately after the lowering of the waters. At Monaco the Observatory cave, at about 90 metres above the Mediterranean, shows a human habitat of much earlier date. At the time when the *Strombus*-bearing sea was lapping the rocks at Grimaldi at about 10 metres down, man was forced to seek shelter at higher levels, as he was to do at various times such as the Abbevillian, Clactonian, and Acheulean epochs. He later abandoned the shelter of the cave and went down into the lower rock-shelters then freed, and it was only after the sea rose again that, seeking a change of diet and hunting ibexes, he returned to the old cave left for thousands of years to the bears, hyenas, and panthers.

Both in the English Channel and the North Sea lie old Palaeolithic deposits, off Le Havre and Clacton-on-Sea, and dredgings made by the *Pourquoi-Pas* revealed pebble-beaches at depths of 90, 60, and 30 metres below the Channel.

Probably the most interesting facts about the connexion between the changes in sea-level and the ancient industries are those observed some years ago round Casablanca by R. Neuville and A. Rühlmann.[1] They succeeded in locating ten levels of industry in coastal sites belonging, without a shadow of doubt, to the four great sea-levels—*Sicilian* (sea at 90–100 metres up), *Milazzian* (sea 55–60 metres up), *Tyrrhenian* (sea 28–30 metres up), and *Grimaldian* (sea 12–19 metres up). The industries are either worked into old beaches and rolled by the waves, or lie directly above such beaches and date from not long after the fall in sea-level; or else they are distributed within various layers of open-air formation, river gravels, hardened dune sands, crusty or crumbling limestone deposits, or red-clay silts.

As for the southern regions, sheltered, save for high mountain-peaks, by their latitude from any glaciation or its direct effects, and including not only all Africa but all Southern Europe, Southern Asia, and the East Indies, it has been observed that these vast regions were subject to *pluvial* periods of intense humidity, corresponding to the glacial periods in the north and more or less simultaneous with them. The rains alternated with semi-desert phases of extreme dryness occurring, as in our times, at interglacial stages.

For East Africa, E. J. Wayland and L. S. Leakey made a thorough study of the subject and suggested the following sequence of periods:

1. Pluvial, very early: industry with very primitive chipped pebbles named *Kafuan*.
   1st dry period: desert conditions.

---

[1] Their work was continued and completed by M. Biberson (1957–58), who found, in a cave used by Acheulean man, a cold marine deposit overlying the Tyrrhenian level.

2. 2nd pluvial: *Kamasian* = from the Abbevillian to the Acheulean, with some Clactonian and Levalloisian.
   2nd dry period: great seismic activity.
3. 3rd pluvial: *Gamblian* = Levalloisian and Aurignacian.
   3rd dry period: desert conditions.
4. 4th pluvial: *Makalian*. Industries of Upper Palaeolithic type with their transition from Levalloisian onward.
   4th dry period.
5. 5th pluvial: *Nakuran*. Neolithic industries, including *Tumbian*.
   5th dry period: up to the present day.

Thanks to these observations it has been possible to draw general parallels between the discoveries made in both northern and southern zones, where at least four pluvial periods have alternated with dry and semi-desert times, and industries comparable to our European types developed through these long ages spanning all the Quaternary.

ABSOLUTE CHRONOLOGY

Our own short span of life leads us to try to assess in years or centuries mankind's long journey. Except for relatively recent times corresponding to the last phases of the retreat of the Scandinavian glacier, we can soon get lost in astronomically vast conjectures.

Considering first some early attempts at evaluation, we find figures in the region of 10,000 years, obtained by studying the retreat of the Niagara Falls from the time when the last American glacier disappeared from the area after scooping out the basin of Lake Ontario. Another figure, produced by an assessment of the cone of post-glacial debris laid down by the Rhône under the level of Lake Geneva, is of a similar order. But into such phenomena of erosion and accumulation there enter essentially variable factors, such as the volume of water in the rivers concerned. The Scandinavians did rather better: de Geer noted that, from the time during the glacial retreat when the North Sea again invaded the Baltic, from which the glacier had so long cut it off, there were laid down each year two thin deposits, one of very fine black clay made in winter, the other of light-coloured sand put down in summer as the ice receded. Since each of these layers represented one year, it was convenient to work out the duration of this recession, the final phase of the glacier: it amounted to about 8000 years. The end of the remotest Palaeolithic time, the Magdalenian, may go back to 15,000 years, and, by deduction, the beginning of the Upper Palaeolithic to twice that number, or rather more.

More recent times can be estimated with much greater accuracy by pollen analysis. From 8000 to 5000 years ago pollen indicates a growth of silver birch and firs in Scandinavia; from 7000 to 4000 hazel and alder predominate, closely followed by the oak. Beech appears only from 4000 B.C.

Such time-spans, however, are almost within and on the same scale as history, which is but an infinitesimal part of the story of man. Over a considerable period attempts based on astronomy have been made to explain the glacial periods and their phases. Some thought that the solution lay in the precession of equinoxes and the rotation of the earth's poles in cycles of some 26,000 years. Starting from this basis, which is obviously too restricted, a final figure for the duration of Quaternary and human times would work out at the already considerable total of some 130,000 years. But even this is too short to accommodate the colossal phenomena, varying in length and scope, of which the earth was the scene during those times.

More intellectually satisfying is Milankowich's hypothesis. He worked a graph mathematically, showing the amount of solar heat received by the earth at each latitude over the last 600,000 years, taking into account the facts of precession and rotation, the dimensions of the earth's elliptical orbit round the sun, the direction of its axis of rotation in space, variations in its reflection of the sun's rays, and so forth. The graph for the forty-ninth parallel, valid for Europe, coincides fairly well, in the matter of perpetual snow, with the data of Quaternary geology. According to it, therefore, the final glaciation (Würm) can be dated at 120,000 years ago; the last interglacial period (Riss-Würm) must have lasted from 120,000 to 190,000 years ago; the Riss, or third, glaciation is to be placed between 190,000 and 240,000 years. Before that the long interglacial period, the second (Mindel-Riss), would cover from 240,000 to 440,000 years, and the second glacial age (Mindel) from 440,000 to 480,000 years; then the previous interglacial stage (Günz-Mindel) would date from 480,000 to 550,000. But as man in that age has left traces all over the Old World, it seems likely that he witnessed the first Quaternary Ice Age, dated from 550,000 to 600,000, and that he may have appeared even before that.

Such figures are indeed enormous in comparison with the total span of history, 4000 or 5000 years only, even for the most favoured regions. There has, of course, been, in the whole concept of the story of man, a profound change of perspective, similar to the reappraisals that have taken place in the domains of astronomy and geology. It was all too easy to forget the vast durations of geological time, the untold revolutions of the planet witnessed by ancient man, the constant and complete changes of scenery upon earth's stage, and the innumerable crowds of actors that have all played parts thereon. We are all inclined to suppose that the world has always looked as it does to-day.

Peering back along the deep receding lines of this perspective, meeting in a blur on the very horizon of Time, the eye of ethnic memory falters as it searches, for just as the individual recalls but dimly his early years and forbears, so the race seems to have lost the detailed recollection of its first steps forward and the concept of their immense duration.

To shed light on this distant past for us, we have but nameless remains, chipped flints, sharpened bones, skeletons or scattered relics of ancient man, buried in the soil of caves, the sand of beach or dune, or river silt; or perhaps a patch of rock-wall, decorated with paintings or engravings. Such are the data available to the student of ancient prehistory, by which the progressive stages of the human types and their civilization can be determined, from that vague time when man first emerged among the mammals at the end of the Tertiary, down to the more recent times that saw the foundations of our civilization being laid in the organization of agriculture and the domestication of animals. In those latter times we can see the setting-up of peoples and races to be met at the dawn of history. The curtain is still lowered at the front of the stage on which our times will be portrayed, but the scenery is being arranged, and the actors are taking their places. It is the end of true pre-history, and in spite of the absence of written documents it is the beginning of proto-history, history prior to the written word, but not to legend. At this point we are but some 5000 or 7000 years back, a short while indeed compared to the immense length of time taken for man's slow rise through nearly a million years.

[3]

Primitive man's implements

Wood and bone—Shells—Bones—Animal action on bones—Specifically human action on bones

WOOD AND BONE

It is usual when referring to the earliest periods of man's history to speak always of the Stone Age, and, indeed, chipped flints have been preserved for us in large quantities, but it would be a serious mistake to think that they were the only raw materials available to man for making tools: wood, bone, and shell were certainly equally important. Unfortunately, as these materials are not very durable, few examples have survived down to our times.

That there have been peoples using only *wood* is a fact revealed by modern ethnography: the Orang-Semang of Malacca use only wooden implements, mainly made of bamboo, and not durable enough to give fossils. Apart from white ants in the tropics and other wood-eating insects, wood rots and disintegrates in moisture, except in the very rare cases of charring by fire or preservation in peaty or salt surroundings. Sörgel has mentioned the existence, on the very old site at Mauer, famous for its ancient human jaw-bone, of the remains of wooden hunting-spears from the first interglacial period. In Palestine the hip-bone of one of the Neanderthal men found in the caves at Skul (Wadi-el-Murgaret) had been deeply pierced by the conical point of a spear of this type. The weapon itself had disappeared, but the dent left by the wound showed the conical shape of the strong point that had broken in it. To the old Palaeolithic, the last interglacial period, can be ascribed the extraordinary find at Lehringen (Schleswig) of a long spear (1·4 metres) made of yew, driven through the ribs of an *Elephas antiquus*, and

c

preserved thanks to the marshy conditions. The flints, including blades, resemble those on the Levalloisian site at Mecklenburg.

The conical point of a wooden hunting-spear, charred, was found in the site at Torralba (Soria, Spain) containing many *Elephas antiquus* bones and Acheulean coups-de-poing. Also dating from the same period, the peat-bed at Clacton-on-Sea yielded a strong cylindrical spear-head. Similarly, there have been reports from time to time, but no illustrations, of the existence of *woven brushwood*, looking like the remains of woven baskets, in interglacial peat deposits in Switzerland, and also in Northern Manchuria, in peat containing the mammoth and the woolly rhinoceros. A late date in the Upper Palaeolithic can be given to discoveries made by A. Rüst at Meiendorf (Holstein), of detachable wooden spear- and javelin-heads. In the late Magdalenian layer at Stellmoor were found wooden shafts of throwing-weapons, like those drawn on the sides of animals in cave decorations. We may also recall Perrier du Carne's publication of a drawing of a wooden bow found on the Upper Magdalenian site of the cave at Teyjat (Dordogne). Other fragments of bows were also reported at Meiendorf by Rüst.

However rare such finds may be, they should suffice to remind us how great is the gap left in our data for reconstructing the life of such early times by the disappearance of wood. In Switzerland the mud of lakes in Jurassic limestone has preserved, around the Neolithic and Bronze Age lake-settlements, a host of wooden and bone objects such as were destroyed in the acid waters of other lakes. In considering the preservation of wood and other materials we may also refer to the finds made in the rock-salt mines at Salzburg, in Austria, where large quantities of small pinewood sticks, used for lighting, and hods of skin on wooden frames were found in galleries worked in the Bronze Age. Among other media that will preserve any organic matter, including wood, mention should also be made of polar ice, which, during the brief summers, can yield, from pre-Eskimo sites, broken or carved bones, wooden implements, and the remains of skins used for clothing or containers.

SHELLS

Shells provide hard material, often with sharp edges, suitable without further treatment for shaping softer substances, for use as receptacles, even as spoons or lamps, then, in the Upper Palaeolithic, as ornaments. But in the tropics, where they reach considerable dimensions, and particularly on the coral islands of the South Seas, absolutely devoid of any hard stone and even of usable bones, beyond those of man and the pig (except, perhaps, for whalebone), the shell of the giant clam is the only hard matter that can be treated like stone—broken, and the fragments polished and sharpened. It is thought that in one of the layers

of a cave site near Algiers the equipment found consisted entirely of
implements made out of oyster-shells.[1]

BONES

It may be true, to some extent, that in certain parts of the world a
Bone Age preceded the Stone Age. It is certainly a fact that there are
vast areas of the globe in which usable stone cannot be found—Lower
Austria, for example, and China, where there are great tracts covered
with loess and sand-dunes. On the other hand, the carcasses of animals
that had died a natural death or been hunted were always and everywhere available. The same applies to subpolar regions, where there is
little if any stone, no wood except driftwood, nothing, in fact, except
the bones of seals or whales or of rare Arctic animals like the reindeer,
musk ox, and polar bear.

Furthermore, probably one of the first ideas that occurred to man
was to take from animals the weapons Nature provided in the form of
horns, antlers, teeth, and claws and to use these weapons against them.
It is a much more rudimentary idea than that of using a stone, especially
shaping it by chipping or rubbing into a tool or weapon—a complicated
process.

It is therefore reasonable to conclude that bone—and this includes
every single part of a skeleton up to horns and antlers—must have
formed part of primitive implements, and from the very beginning too.
It only remains to check the conclusion experimentally.

It should not be forgotten that Nature preserves bone, even in its
natural state, only in exceptional circumstances. A carcass left on the
ground is attacked by all sorts of living creatures, while buried bones
are bound to dissolve rapidly and disappear if they are not in a suitable medium such as limestone or fairly heavy clay. Plant roots corrode
them, seepage water loaded with carbon dioxide dissolves them; their
organic matter first, then their lime content, vanishes in a few years in
siliceous soil, unless they have been charred.

Fresh bone, hard, yet yielding, and not very brittle, was excellent
raw material for man, but it was also a vital food for all animals.

In soil which leaves its lime content immune, bone loses its organic
matter fairly fast. The first to go is its solidity, rendering it useless
as raw material. Animals now despise it, but roots, weaving over it a
hairy maze, corrode its surface. The bone then becomes porous and
tends to crack and scale. In this state it can absorb mineral salts,
principally ferrous, indeed silicate, which replace its organic matter.
It then petrifies and re-hardens, but it is rarely homogeneous enough
for man to have used it as he did stone. Examples of this have, however,

---

[1] Baron Blanc has informed me that in Mousterian times shells were used in caves
on the coast of Naples. (H.B.)

been found—fossil bear or swordfish teeth used more or less ornament-ally. So, in general, it is only in their first state, when fresh, that man or the animals have taken much interest in bones. It is therefore very im-portant to recognize the effects on them of mechanical action by animals, in order to be able to distinguish it from human action.

ANIMAL ACTION ON BONES

All animals are greedy for fresh bone, even ruminants in regions lacking limestone. In South Africa this eagerness for bones is one of the causes of the spread of epizootic diseases, since all sorts of creatures hasten to feast off the bones of the carcasses of animals which have died of disease on the veldt. Only traces of nibbling, however, remain on the bones.

Of greater interest are the rodents, the Carnivora, and man himself. The rodents eagerly attack a fresh bone, or even a sub-fossil or fossil bone, as they dig their burrows in soil containing them. Be they large or small, the beaver, porcupine, rat, and mouse all proceed in the same way: they firmly fix the points of their lower incisors on a surface more or less at right angles to the one they wish to attack. This gives a ful-crum for work with the upper incisors, as sharp as steel chisels, with which rodents produce double grooves. If they continue for any length of time without changing place, slowly rocking the head from side to side, this will leave a fan-shaped pattern of grooves, which may also run parallel to the edge of the bone and give a kind of frieze design. This is particularly true of small rodents. Such animals also often find a skull in the earth or in a cave and nest in it, getting in usually through the occipital cavity or some other natural or accidental opening; but they have been known to enlarge the access until it looks like a trepanation, with vertical, fluted sides, though quite different from such effects produced by Neolithic man scraping and grooving with flint.

Far more powerful are the teeth of the beaver, the *Trogontherium*, and the porcupine, the latter being in particular a great gnawer of bones. Since it preferred caves, traces of its work have frequently been well preserved, and the double impression of its powerful incisors can be seen on numerous bone remains. In the caves of South China, Tonkin, and North and South Africa it wrought terrible havoc among precious fossils, often devouring everything up to the roots of the teeth, leaving only the crowns intact.

Bone fragments found in many caves used by the porcupine have undergone strange modifications: at Capetown two human skulls, symmetrically gnawed into cups, can be ascribed to this animal, while at Port Elizabeth a fairly thin piece of bone was found similarly gnawed away into the shape of an 'Almerian' idol. Numerous scraps of thin, flat bone were gnawed into round or side scrapers and arrow-head wedges in South China and Upper Tonkin. Larger bones seem to have been given points, when the gnawing was confined to one end, or made into something like chisels.

Less is known of the fossil bones worked by the beaver and *Trogontherium*, but in a German cave were found the stumps of great-stag antlers transformed into polyhedral *bolas* by a porcupine. These, and probably other large tropical rodents, can devour even elephant-tusks, judging by the considerable range of incisions their teeth can make, with the precision of well-sharpened steel chisels. In South Africa stones even have not been immune from gnawing. Pieces oι certain lavas containing up to 18 per cent. limestone, sometimes cut by man, sometimes not, have been found to exhibit curious retouch working of non-human origin.

The Carnivora, with the exception of the hyena, are far behind the rodents in their skill in attacking bones, while the felines have never wasted much time on them, their teeth being unsuitable for the task.

The Canidae, especially the wolf and the dog, gnaw the ends of long bones they cannot break and destroy the spongy parts in an effort to reach the medullary canal containing rich fat. For this they use the incisors and the canine teeth, which leave parallel grooves. When they attack a bone at one end, or both, the result may resemble an implement with forked ends, sometimes taken, even by experts, to be of human origin.

Among the Carnivora, the hyena is the best equipped for cracking bones, as can be seen from its habits and its extremely powerful jaws. But it has its limitations. Such an animal cannot, except at the ends, crack open bones larger than the maximum opening of the jaws. Thus the largest Herbivora bones are beyond its capabilities, except at the epiphyses. Where such long bones are found split the hyena is not responsible. As for other marrow-bones, it breaks them by 'nutcracking,' seizing them full in the jaws in order to exert terrible pressure. But it cannot split them lengthwise, as man often does. If the bone has resisted —and this applies to other Carnivora—the double and opposite impact of both jaws can be seen to have formed dents under the stamp of the fang-points.

The Manchester Museum has a curious exhibit of this kind—a circular piece of the nose-bone of a rhinoceros. The head had been gnawed by a hyena while the horn still adhered, and this had protected the area of bone where it was inserted.

On certain thin bones, usually to be picked up in caves, strange circular perforations with no traces of splitting or teeth-marks or the use of either sharp or blunt instrument can be found occasionally. These are probably of animal origin, perhaps the work of burrowing larvae or, in other cases, of digging Hymenoptera, winged or otherwise (ants?).

Burrowing mammals not only use their teeth when making their dens; they make even more use of their claws. Rabbits, weasels, badgers, foxes, and at times bears, which have dug a great deal in the caves they occupied, have clawed into already fossilized bones, covering them liberally with curved scratches, usually of decreasing depth and roughly parallel. Cave-walls are also frequently covered with such scratches, ranging from the paw-marks of the cave bear, nearly 20 centimetres across, to those of bats, mostly located on roof-surfaces, and giving very fine, fanlike scorings only one or two centimetres wide.

In certain circumstances, however, man himself has gnawed bones, but only soft ones likely to be full of fat. As he can do this only with his incisors (numbering four, and not six, as with the Carnivora), and as his canines are not much stronger than his incisors, a human bite on a large, soft bone can be detected. In the Mousterian layers of the cave at El Castillo (Santander, Spain) and probably at Muge, in Portugal, in the Mesolithic level, such bones are by no means rare. They had, of course, previously been broken.[1]

SPECIFICALLY HUMAN ACTION ON BONES

Raw bones could be dealt with in the following ways: first they could be struck to break them open, usually in order to collect, either for food or lighting, the fatty marrow within, or, in the case of the joints, animal oil (neat's-foot oil). Then the fragments obtained were often so shaped as to be useful in various ways, as points, chisels, scrapers, and small cups. They could then be struck, either to perfect the shape of the piece for a particular task or to repair wear and tear sustained during work, making the tool less effective. In short, bone was used as a 'stone' of animal origin, generally shaped by breaking. It was only very, very much later that it occurred to anybody to cut bone with chisel or saw and polish it by scraping and rubbing on a hard object. In order to break a very, or fairly, large bone, it was usually struck full in the middle as it rested on a stone. The result was similar to that made by the hyena's jaws. But long, straight bones like the cannon- or shin-bones of small ruminants were split by end-blows breaking them lengthwise, a thing no animal could do.

The antlers of Cervidae were, from the very beginning, treated quite differently, like wood of animal origin. No doubt the lighter tines were often broken by blows or bending; but mostly a different process was used, mainly for the principal stock. The antlers were cut with a sharp

---

[1] Samples which the Abbé Glory and I sent to Dr Legoux confirmed this deduction, but he showed experimentally that only grilled bone can be cracked open in this way by a human bite.

stone used as a wedge, or with an axe-head or a reamer, or, very much later, with a chisel, to divide them, if too large, into sections of more manageable size.

As for young antlers, not yet, or only just, divided, they were detached from the skull for preference, leaving intact the pedicle feeding the horn, thus providing a useful handle, after trimming off the remains of the frontal bone.

The larger antlers had to be cut up. Tines could be broken or bent off, but even for this, and especially with the stouter stocks, the proposed cutting-point was burned, then laboriously grooved by repeated applications first of a stone punch and then a chisel, until finally the section weakened by the burn could be broken by bending.

While some antlers were used at once as implements or weapons, as can be seen from their points, blunted or scarred and then re-formed, often by scraping, pieces of the main stock with a stronger tine could be used as picks. Such tools are often found among deposits of Neolithic flints. The basilar portions were shaped into clubs or hammers, with the segment as the striking face. Very large bases, cut off short, seem to have been used as pestles.

Cylindrical sections, partially emptied of their spongy centre, were used as handles. The large blades of the *Megaceros* stag antlers, and perhaps of the deer, have been found with numerous slight incisions, as if they had been used as working surfaces or tables for cutting up meat or leather.

Horns of other, smaller ruminants (gazelles and small antelopes) were, and still are, used as daggers, their bony spikes being preserved. The edges of the frontal bone were also trimmed off, to afford a better grip. With the larger horns, all that can be seen is that the horny material has been torn away, for some unknown purpose. One can imagine their use as containers or as the basis of some luxury article.

When complete sets of antlers had to be carried from one place to another—and their weight was sometimes considerable—the dome of the adhering frontal bone was knocked off as far as possible. Then, by fairly laborious cleavage, the main wood was separated from the peduncle at the point of exit. The frontal bone, thus freed from its burden, then provided a well-shaped bowl or cup, and it would seem that the men of Chou Kow Tien, among others, used it as such, judging by the frequent burning or knocking off of awkward pedicles and the polishing of the chipped edges that is sometimes evident.

In the Solutrean and Magdalenian periods brain-pans were also made into cups, a custom familiar to ethnographers.

The ring round the edge of the occipital cavity was also at times chipped out, carefully enough to suggest some purpose of which nothing is known. The same goes for the rings of the first cervical vertebrae;

lower down the spine it was more frequently the vertebral disc, relieved of its accompanying arches and processes, that attracted man's attention.

Of the other parts of the heads of these animals hunted by man, it was, of course, the jaws and the teeth in which he was particularly interested. As early as 1869 Garrigou had reported finding, in the Pyrenees, numbers of half jaw-bones of the cave bear, still armed with the canines, the rising end shortened or missing. The parts suitable for gripping showed signs of the sort of wear left by a hand on a much used tool. The same observations were made at Chou Kow Tien on the jaw-bones of the giant boar, armed with tusks that could also have been useful independently. Several times in the same deposit jaws not only of boar but also of felines have been found, with the symphysis, complete with canines in the latter species but only the incisors in the former, broken off deliberately, to be used as a tool or a trophy. In the same region the upper jaw of a large feline with both incisors and canines intact was found.

Half jaw-bones of beaver, and, indeed, of hare, were certainly used in Neolithic times on account of their powerful incisors. Many have been found on dolmenic sites, pierced for hanging. The stag jaw-bones at Chou Kow Tien are unusual, at least those of the *Cervus pseudaxis pachyosteus*, which are especially hard. They were used without further modification, being ripped at the rostral part while the point was in use. The rising branch often shows slight wear.

As for the maxillary sections, both upper and lower, with their armament of molars, belonging to powerful Carnivora or Cervidae found on the same site, some seem to have been made more even by retouching the bone and then used, the smaller teeth having their points worn down as if by filing. The study of sub-fossil Eskimos has revealed this kind of usage. On the other hand, lower canine teeth of the bear, grooved at the neck and then split, are, with their derived fragments, to be ascribed to physiological sawing through by the stems of the plants these animals fed upon, and the subsequent break-up of the teeth.

Among trunk-bones can be found ribs from before the Mousterian period, worn at the ends by use, sharpened to a point by rubbing, or cut into sections of fairly regular diameter, and this cannot be accidental. The same applies to the long processes of the dorsal vertebrae of the large ruminants.[1]

Pelvic bones, particularly among the large Herbivora, provide a subcircular coxal cavity, a sort of natural cup. This was very frequently adapted by knocking off the three converging pelvic bones from it, and then smoothing off. Such bones, of Mousterian date, sometimes show traces of human scratches on the inner surface of the cup.

[1] Such fragments are still fairly commonly used in South Africa as castanets.

Medium-sized shoulder-blades were also quite often used as shovels, or, when the ridge had been levelled down, as knives or scrapers, the edge becoming worn and smooth in service. The larger ones were used as working surfaces, plates, or artist's palettes (Upper Palaeolithic). The joint formation at the base of the shoulder-blade allowed the round glenoid cavity to be used as a cup.

As far back as pre-Mousterian times, in different corners of caves on the Wildkirchli and the Drachenloch, hunters of the cave bear arranged groups of long bones from different animals, and set up, on a sort of altar, a row of bear-skulls, side by side, all pointing in the same direction.[1] A certain number of these bones had clearly been used, as the working surfaces were blunted. The rest had not been used. They were mainly fibulae and ulnae.

As for the ruminants and other Herbivora so common on most human sites, from Chou Kow Tien to Mousterian and even very much later, most of the bones were put to some use. The spongy proximal joints of humerus and femur, the terminal joints of these latter, as well as soft parts of the vertebrae, were often deeply hollowed out and also show broad rubbing grooves, as if they had been used to smooth down wooden tools. The knobs of other joints were made into *bolas*.

The terminal joint of the humerus in bulls and horses[2] was, in Mousterian times, used, after the diaphysis had been cut off, as a chopping-block or the fixed member of a press; when it became too dented it was scraped to smooth it off again. The blows sustained were often very violent, at times enough to break these very hard bones. It has also been noted that the same joint, from smaller ruminants, has been used as the handle of a tool, a spike or chisel, shaped up from the diaphysis. This is frequently found with the proximal parts of the radii, the terminal areas of tibias, and both proximal and terminal of cannon-bones (legs).

An unusual find was made in the Solutrean at El Castillo (Santander, Spain) of all sorts of long bones, broken down to one joint plus a part of the diaphysis, showing deep wear of the joint area and retouching of the diaphysis by striking. Another case, peculiar to the Upper Palaeolithic, is the making of phials or flasks from the rear-leg cannon-bones of reindeer, which have great capacity and thin walls. Some of these long bones, either their ends or their middle segments, may have been used as tool-handles.

Other bones may have served as punches or awls—for instance, the ulnae of any animal from the hare to the large ruminants, when

[1] I knew Baechler personally. He published his findings, and considers later criticism impugning the truth and objectivity of his work to be without foundation. H. Obermaier was of this opinion also. (H.B.)

[2] Dr Henri-Martin was responsible for extensive research into the use as chopping-blocks of such bones, knuckles, and various bone splinters from these animals.

detached from the radius, and those of large Carnivora, by breaking the terminal joint. The stylets or lateral metapods of horse and stag give natural spikes, often used from Chou Kow Tien onward, and blunted in the process.

Among the short tarsal bones of the feet the very hard ankle-bone is found from Chou Kow Tien and the Mousterian onward, and often shows signs of violent breaking action. Heel-bones often have the end where the Achilles tendon entered broken, perhaps to detach the tendon and use its fibres. Others, of suitable size for gripping, have been perforated along their spongy centre as if for use as a handle for a flint-point. The toe-joints of bull or horse were widely used as chopping-blocks in the Mousterian period at La Quina (Charente) and less frequently elsewhere. Many others were split open, not for their marrow, as they contain none, but for the oil and for the horny part, used for unknown purposes. This applies to the incisions found on hoof-bones from Mousterian times.

Many fragments of large and medium-long bones are usable, after mechanical fracture, without further modification, the only evidence being rare cases of localized wear found on them, from Chou Kow Tien until the end of the Palaeolithic Age. Those used were more often than not trimmed up like stones, by striking, especially the larger pieces. This touching up appears mostly on the concave faces, and sometimes, near the ends, it is on alternate faces. Points, side-scrapers, barbs, scrapers, and gravers were made from bones, just as from stone. Others were used as pressure chisels, very common in the Mousterian Age, but found after that. Narrow, thick splinters were used in particular as chisels for trimming stone or as punches for shaping long flakes or blades. It is obvious from the flattening of the ends and the lengthwise splits that one end was striking while the other end was being struck. They are identical with the 'fabricators' made of bone or schist by American Red Indians or Azilians in Scotland.

Thus a primitive bone industry always accompanied, where it did not precede, the use of stone implements, from the very beginning down to recent times, and even among modern savages. Verification is possible, for ancient times, only in places where the bone has been fairly well preserved—that is, in caves for the most part. Rarer and more difficult to recognize are the examples found in gravel-beds and other open-air deposits. This industry is more abundant and better developed in countries poor in stone, and much rarer in those with good-quality stone freely available. It is not characteristic of any particular level, since it appears in consistent forms (except for a few types) in all ages. It explains why, just before Leptolithic times, there flourished methods of working bone by sawing, graving, and polishing that were particularly widespread in the Upper Palaeolithic. It stands in the same relationship to that fine reindeer-age industry as the era of chipped stone does to the vast development of polished stone at the end of the Stone Age. Just as the rough Abbeville pebbles explain the fine Neolithic axes, so the bones chipped and shaped like stone and the stag-horn broken and cut like wood are the original ancestors of all the later and better techniques for working these animal materials.[1]

[1] Dr Dart, of Johannesburg, seems gradually to be confirming as a fact that in the Transvaal the bones of the animals killed and eaten were systematically used, in an industry called 'osteodontoceratic.' This dates from a level where nomad *Australo-pithecus* hunters lived in rock-shelters. See *Archaeol. Bull.* 1958 and the bibliography of his previous notes.

[4]

Natural causes of flint fracture

Mechanical fractures underground: tectonic causes; dissolution and compression of the surrounding milieu; cliff-face; tree-roots—Crushing in ground or surroundings moving laterally: cliff-falls; glaciers; landslides; static solifluxion or cryoturbation; sliding solifluxion on slopes—Fractures and crushing due to water movements: the sea; offshore bar; the part of the beaches uncovered only at very low tide; wave action in estuaries and lakes; rolling in rivers—Animal or human causes of accidental fracture—Causes of mechanical wear: the wind—Causes of thermal fractures: frost and sunlight; fire or very strong sunlight—Eoliths

---

Because most of the other materials have disappeared and left chipped flints a predominant position in the prehistoric industries of the Stone Age, it is absolutely vital for the student of prehistory to be aware of possible causes of error, which may, in many cases, seriously mislead him about the presumed human origin of angular flints lying in or on the earth. Misunderstanding of the causes of natural fracture in hard stones available as raw material to fossil man has on more than one occasion caused fragmentation to be ascribed to him, whereas in fact it was quite fortuitous.

Research into these fractures is mostly concerned with flint in all its forms, but can, to a lesser extent, be applied to quartz, quartzites, hard sandstones, fine-grained basalt or andesite lavas, hardened schists, and even dense conchoidal-fracturing limestone. However, since flint was the principal raw material in ancient industries and is most easily fractured by Nature and man, it is given first place in this study.

It is well known that the different sorts of flint are found in their natural state as nodules or thin slabs inside parent-rock, limestone, marl, clay, and even vesicular basalt where it has filled the holes; or may be it has solidified into twisted blocks of various sizes inside the rocks, or, on the upper level of a less permeable layer, has formed small veins or tabular slabs. From there all the agents of erosion that have worn down, dissolved, or split the virgin rock have freed nodules or irregular, thin slabs and transported them in the layers formed from the rest of the material. It is there, rather than in the original geological position, that fossil man, seeking something useful, picked them up and chipped them into implements, with the usual waste products.

Either in the parent-rock, or freed on the surface, or subsequently buried by mechanical displacement, the flint blocks underwent stresses tending to split them. These were of two kinds, some thermal, the others mechanical. One must also mention other chemical and geochemical actions which changed their very nature to a greater or lesser extent. In research into primitive human industries the study of such phenomena can explain the similarity between certain stones shaped by Nature and the results of human activity, sometimes in fact distorted by her. Moreover, since such influences affect all loose flints, including chipped implements, examination of them is vital if the history of an object, *in situ* or after various modifications, is to be established, as well as for a full understanding of the nature of the terrain where the surface will have preserved, more or less permanently, significant indications.

MECHANICAL FRACTURES UNDERGROUND

1. *Tectonic Causes*

The limestone layers in which flint formed were often subjected to subsequent distortions—folding or twisting—affecting the flint nodules buried in their mass. This resulted in mechanical fractures, but so long as the rock was not worn away the nodule remained intact and did not open into its various fragments. Once it was freed, however, under other mechanical or thermal influences, the cracks opened and presented special features. Whatever the shape of the piece, it shows, as in all cases of mechanical fracture, undulations running along the axis of propagation of the breaking force; but there are always present, and sometimes in great numbers, striations or keel-like ridges and fissures in deep, undulating, practically parallel sets, revealing the application of a torsional stress under which the resistance of the rock has produced splinters. In extreme cases the nodule has splintered into a mass of chippings of triangular section, fairly good imitations of those produced by human blows, though with no bulb of percussion. In the centre an elongated polyhedral prism is frequently found, 'peeled' around its parallel facets, as in an artificially cut laminated nucleus. But the keel-ridges and parallel splinter cracks are everywhere visible and reveal the true origin of the object, even when, after being carried away some distance, it has opened and undergone other changes (Campolide, Lisbon).

If the rock is a conglomerate or pudding-stone of quartz pebbles or quartzites, it may be that the separate stones, tightly compressed together, made impressions one on the other, denting slightly and forming cup-shaped hollows, together with splinter fissures that opened only after liberation and under the action of external agents.

2. *Dissolution and Compression of the Surrounding Milieu*

A layer of limestone dissolves, more or less slowly, under the action of rainwater filtering through. It thus partially frees insoluble matter it contains (flint nodules), which is then carried away into the space produced by the dissolving of the rock or of the more soluble sub-strata. Moved in this way, the nodules meet and sometimes clash, or more frequently are very tightly compressed together and chip into sharp-edged fragments. The larger pieces show, on their edges, the negatives of these chippings. Close inspection of the fracture surfaces will reveal, as for human chipping, a point of impact with an associated bulb of applied pressure, usually very small, though it may well be much larger and conical or hemispherical. The resemblance to human action is close enough to have deceived experienced prehistorians on more than one occasion.

3. *Cliff-face*

A cliff-face exposed to extreme variations of weather undergoes thermal action resulting in mechanical action: the surface, in sunshine and frost, expands and contracts, tending to detach itself in great slices and fall backward away from the general mass. For the flint nodules still embedded in the rock this means further stretching and twisting, which, combined with thermal effects, continue the development of pre-existing fissures and start the work of disintegrating the slabs into sharp-edged fragments.

4. *Tree-roots*

If, instead of thinking of a surface of rock exposed in vertica sections, we imagine it in horizontal layers, it is evident that similar, though less visible, phenomena take place. In addition, the presence of deep tree-roots causes other and different actions. Given time, roots can open a cracked rock just as they can rend apart pieces of masonry. It is obvious that when they worm their way into a thick, compact layer of flint, roots push it aside to make room for themselves, creating pressures strong enough to chip fragile edges with what looks like retouch working. No large flakes, however, are caused in this way.

Whatever their origin, compression movements in the earth are thus quite capable of imitating human action on stones: there is a bulb of applied pressure, and the breakage axis has directional wave effect, with secondary retouching. Yet there are differences: in pressure of human origin the plane of applied force is at an angle nearly always less than 90°, while in natural breaks it is mostly at an obtuse angle, at times extreme. This observation applies to all causes of mechanical fracture.

Under the normal earth pressures the fractured surface shows a very flattened point of impact—a cone that is nearly always very small in comparison to the size of the flake, with a trajectory curve impossible for a man to achieve, sometimes nearly completing a circle. This is due to the 'wrapped-up' position of the object in its fairly compact surroundings which absorb all undue vibration. A very careful search in layers where this kind of effect has occurred may sometimes reveal the actual nuclei still in contact with their flakes, these latter already trimmed by the following mechanical process. At the very instant when a flint, embedded in a semi-friable medium, breaks under pressure from another, the very fragile edges of the flake thus slightly raised are crushed back against the matrix by the resistance of the medium. This produces along the edge a series of tiny scallopings which are almost a perfect imitation of human pressure-trimming. Even when a buried flint is broken by thermal action, this also has the secondary effect of producing minute, or even at times fair-sized, flakes due to this mechanical pressure.

CRUSHING IN GROUND OR SURROUNDINGS MOVING LATERALLY

1. Among such movements should be mentioned *cliff-falls*. Their effects are probably considerable, but in any case they are unusual and not amenable to study.

2. *Glaciers*, carrying along pebbles embedded in their mass, rub them one against the other, wear them down, scratch them, and break off mechanically their weak corners. Flakes, sometimes of considerable size, are produced and, where flint is concerned, have the following characteristics—very splintery, very flat bulbs of applied pressure, stepped fractures, and numerous incipient fissures. The flakes frequently show very regular trimming, like that due to pressure underground. It has also been observed, particularly among flints with a previous patina, that they bore striations scored out by another stone, and that where these cut the edge, and on the opposite face, the retouch trimming formed a superb arrow-barb.

3. Near Aurillac (Cantal) the Puy-Courny volcano was subject during its destruction to *massive landslides* (M. Boule). Colossal sections of mountain-side slid several kilometres, dragging along and occasionally overturning river silt of the Miocene period trapped between the basalt

layers. During this vast transfer of material the flint blocks suffered intensive mechanical action, sometimes several times over. Their edges were chipped all round, giving fairly thin flakes with small bulbs of applied pressure, and often trimmed off as soon as they were formed. Some of them, if carefully selected, might be said to be the work of human hands. However, besides the fact that at Puy-Boudieu it is not difficult to find the flakes still associated with their pebbles, two facts are generally to be observed: firstly, the angle of fracture is nearly a right angle, which is quite impossible to obtain when chipping flint with a striker, the angle then being more or less 45°; secondly, the facets from which the chippings have come show greater patina on the top face of the stone than on the reverse, this being due to further displacement of the mass of material after a pause sufficient to allow the surfaces of the first natural fractures to assume a patina. Of course, higher up, among the gravels that have reshaped the flint slabs, the lighter flakes separated from them are all that remain, dissociated from the context that could explain how they were produced. This has been such a serious source of error in the district that many experts have been misled. Fortunately the situation is not common elsewhere.

4. A much commoner cause of flint fracture was *solifluxion*, glacial or not, but especially glacial. This process had several phases:

(a) *Static Solifluxion* (*Cryoturbation*). Water-sodden earth froze in the intense cold, its mass increasing and its surface rising; any flints it contained were raised and moved. Durng the thaw this mass fell back on itself, and as it did so the flints changed from their first position and tended to stack themselves vertically like books in a bookcase (emergence of old beach surfaces), or at other times just took up random positions.

When, after repeated frosts and thaws, the flints came into close contact with each other they rubbed together, and their fragile edges were chipped with tiny trimming marks, often very numerous. This process affected not only natural flints: chipped flints with their especially delicate edges were also markedly modified by it. Two cases of this, at Les Eyzies (Dordogne), gave rise to much discussion: the deposits at La Micoque and Le Moustier show layers of flint, now free of earth and looking as though they had been rolled in river-water. At one time it was thought that this was the result of the flooding of the Vézère. But this is certainly not so. If the current had been strong enough to fracture and wear these chipped flints so intensely it would have carried them down over great distances, which is not the case. Moreover, similar phenomena have been found at levels 100 metres and more above the course of the Vézère, never reached by the river since the middle of the Tertiary. Instead, through frost and thaw and static solifluxion the stones were thrown together, while the thaw waters took away the sand and clay, leaving behind in both cases only stones from archaeological layers destroyed on the spot and reduced to a layer of shattered stones made up of all the pebbles in the layer, chipped or not. The fragments of limestone were rounded off, while the angular flints had their ridges scalloped and their facets much worn away. Whatever the appearances, this was certainly not the work of a swiftly flowing river.

(*b*) *Sliding Solifluxion on Slopes.* When the subsoil remained frozen and for this or any other reason was unable to absorb the thaw waters or heavy rain the topsoil, during glacial periods and in regions near glaciers and nearly bare of vegetation, began to slide like flowing mud, and even on a slope as slight as five millimetres would slither over the contours to the bottom of a valley. Everything in its path was carried away pell-mell—boulders, stones of all sizes, and still-frozen slabs of friable earth. The whole mass, with its jumble of heterogeneous material, resembled a moraine formation, though without rocks borne down from afar, and it kneaded the pebbles it contained as in a kind of mortar, exactly like a glacier. Hence the scratching of surfaces, wearing-down of ridges, fracturing of delicate edges with pressure flaking, convincingly simulating human trimming and at times indistinguishable from it. The production of flakes of any size was, however, extremely rare. It was all the result of the stones rubbing together as they were borne down, or striking others still embedded in the frozen subsoil, which were also scored and chipped.

Such phenomena, still to be observed in action each spring in far northern and polar regions, were of enormous importance in the parts of Europe that bordered on the great ice-fields.

FRACTURES AND CRUSHING DUE TO WATER MOVEMENTS

1. *The Sea.* Besides destroying cliffs by causing them to collapse, the sea exerts two types of action through waves on beaches, with quite different results.

(*a*) *The offshore bar* of pebbles deposited by the waves at the end of their run is reshuffled by them at each tide. In certain districts most of the pebbles are of flint, and it can be seen that the sea not only rounds them by rolling, but, though less frequently, breaks them. It is well known that waves sometimes throw pebbles into the air with some force, since this 'bombardment' is one of the factors in cliff destruction and may even affect flints appearing on the surface of the exposed section. It can also happen that two pebbles thus thrown up meet in mid-air and break. A study of their fracture surfaces shows characteristic features: the very violent blow struck in the air produces a fairly deep cone of percussion and a plane of fracture heavily wrinkled, with sharply bent ripples centred round it. Of course, the fragile edges

D

of the broken pieces will be quickly shattered, but very roughly and irregularly.

(*b*) *The part of the beach uncovered only at very low tide* is little influenced by rolling. Here the undertow, the powerful current created by the rising or falling mass of water, is the main agent. At Cromer, just at this level, is to be found a great quantity of large flint boulders, some loose, some still embedded, subject to this twice-daily movement of water to and fro. The boulders clash underwater, and from time to time produce flakes very similar to those made by humans; they are long and thin, with very small cones and bulbs and very smooth, slightly curved fracture surfaces. These features are due to the fact that as the fractures take place underwater the water absorbs any extra vibration due to the blow. This is also the reason for the very fine regular trimming work resembling the work of human hands. Only the position of the bulb and the angle of fracture, different from human craft, enable us to determine that these are products, not of manufacture, but of the natural action of the waves of the present-day North Sea.

2. *Wave Action in Estuaries and Lakes.* Although far less constant in action, the waves of large sheets of water such as lakes or estuaries, tidal or not, should not be overlooked. Two cases may serve as examples: in earlier times Loch Earn (Perthshire, Scotland) stretched far to the east—about as far as Comrie at least. At one point along this great depression, at Kindrochat, the slopes of the valley show bare veins of milky quartz, while all around, at a given level, are to be found abundant quantities of small, angular quartz fragments, with edges that show much mechanical chipping of some regularity. They are not to be found in the present watercourse, nor farther up in the tarns and moraines where blocks of quartz and porphyry, etc., were 'chipped' by the glaciers. It is obviously a case of the wave action we have been discussing, marking an ancient beach. During the interglacial times the lower course of the Somme, at least as far as Bourdon, was flooded by a sort of ria several kilometres wide. In the interglacial deposits of this period (Mindel-Riss) are to be found actual sand-beaches, with horizontal strata, and offshore bars of subangular pebbles, without sand, where the corners have obviously been battered, detaching flakes of no great size very like those due to the action of sea-waves. Such mechanical actions were not the result of solifluxion, but of fractures due to rolling, and the phenomena are found again farther downstream, at the same level and in the Riss-Würm beach at Mautort. Similar examples have been noted in quarries in the Lower Seine valley, at Rouen and farther upstream. This source of error is thus by no means negligible.

3. *Rolling in Rivers.* Just as sea action has often been credited with chipping true craft-worked flints brought up by the tide or embedded in submarine fluviatile layers, so rivers have been allowed clastic powers of which they are practically devoid. Throw a pebble into a clear,

swift-running stream. It is carried along by the current for a few yards, then settles among the stones on the bottom, generally obliquely across the direction of flow. In normal times a stream or river does not break anything resting on its bed. Should a flood occur, however, all the stones on the bed are carried farther along, and are knocked together fairly gently. Only fragile points or thin edges, or the ends of pear-shaped pebbles, suffer slight chipping. Such a current, powerful enough to destroy walls across its path and, like a battering-ram, to carry the debris along for yards, will, when the flood is over, leave behind only a few mud pools, a little fine sand, and small gravel. No current is able to fracture stones in any way comparable to human chipping, or to split slabs of flint, still less of quartzite. But it can dent tiny chips out of sharp edges, giving a good imitation of intentional trimming, as the bottoms of glass bottles found in the mountain stream at Kindrochat have shown. Nevertheless running water—except where it caused river-banks to collapse, thus breaking stones by mutual percussion in the fall, or, less violently, at flood times, by knocking them together—can never remove flakes of any real size. There remains one exceptional case— waterfalls, especially of mountain streams, where it is not the current, but the fall of one pebble on another as they leap down the cascade, that can cause mechanical fracture of considerable size.[1]

All other broken stones ascribed to rivers or streams and discovered in their silt, ancient or recent, must be due to one or other of the causes already discussed.

One particular comparison, drawn from stones broken in the mixers at the Mantes cement works, is basically false, because it is not the whirling water in these mixers that breaks the flints so much as the steel flails producing the turbulence.

Undoubtedly rivers are capable of transporting even quite large blocks; but it is by a series of successive somersaults, due to sand being scooped out in front of the block and piled up behind, toppling it along. The main, and practically the only, effect of the current on the stones on the river-bed is wear from sand friction.

ANIMAL OR HUMAN CAUSES OF ACCIDENTAL FRACTURE

Long before man ever existed there were hooved animals moving about on flint-covered ground, and this has certainly been going on ever since. A herd of bison or elephants careering over a layer of stones cannot fail to break some, either directly by pounding with their hooves or else by the sudden clashes they produce between adjacent stones.

Near Bulawayo (Southern Rhodesia), on the way to Hope Fountain,

[1] I observed this personally downstream from the dried-up falls at Tsisab Ravine, Brandberg, S. W. Africa, a few months after a very violent storm (1950). (H.B.)

there is a ridge of a kind of flint, banded ironstone, which was worked heavily from the earliest times right up to a late stage of the local Stone Age. On the slopes, below a col over which herds of wild buffaloes and elephants must have gone on their way to the river, the ground is covered with edge-chipped flints, nearly all with fractures looking very like rough trimming. On the other hand, the chipped flints found at some depth nearer the col, where the Rev. Neville Jones carried out some excavations, all have perfectly sharp edges. It seems to me that the large Herbivora were the cause of these small fractures (podoliths).

Civilization has produced comparable examples on a much larger scale, since the time when the Gauls and the Romans first made, and then metalled with flint and quartzite, roads for horse traffic and chariots. A newly metalled road was filled with broken flints, and their edges went through a process of trimming, turning them into passable examples of awls, barbs, side- and other scrapers. Later, under excessive crushing, the likeness was destroyed, though country roads, subject only to light traffic in all seasons, are particularly rich in such pseudo-implements. Perhaps some day these roads will, in turn, be ploughed up, and their broken and trimmed flints will be scattered on the surrounding land. The only means of telling whether they come from old roads will be that the face struck by cartwheels and shod hooves will be covered with traces of rust. But as, in the first place, these side-roads would have been made up with stones from the neighbouring fields, this same characteristic rust will be found on real chipped flints mingled in such ballast. These are the features of the so-called 'Flenusian' Eolithic industry, ascribed to Neolithic times and so unfortunately described by Professor Rutot.

Passing mention may be made of the fact that a workman's pick digging out gravel or brick-clay, a ploughshare turning over land, virgin or not, can each strike flints or quartzites and, as it breaks or trims them, leave a trace of iron that soon rusts.

Mechanical stone-breakers, crushing flints for roads and other purposes, can also produce fine pseudo-chippings of unintentional human origin. Now that the high explosives and heavy transport of two wars have raged over North-west Europe there must be added a further unintentional cause of error, since military action has not only produced 'podoliths', but had important mechanical effects even at some depth. Shortly before the last War, in diggings going down to seven metres through the heavy gravels at Porte-du-Bois, near Abbeville, it was found (by Breuil) that flint nodules had been shattered into bundles of long, fresh splinters with extremely sharp edges, probably caused by the colossal compression of the nodules one against the other by a very violent shell explosion in a near-by crater during the earlier War (1914–1918).

CAUSES OF MECHANICAL WEAR

The Wind. Just as moisture-laden wind can corrode and pit the rock-faces it meets, mostly by dissolving softer parts, so a dry wind bearing grains of sand attacks them mechanically, giving them a high polish, covering them with vermicular marks, grooves, and striations, bringing out the harder parts, and finally creating considerable polished facets cutting, at dihedral angles, other faces made when the stone changed position. Among the most interesting shapes thus made out of such stones may be mentioned pseudo-coups-de-poing, pseudo-trihedral blades, pseudo-points. . . . One of the most curious is the long, spindle-shaped pebble with a high polish on all its long facets. Any citizen of Lisbon can watch the process at work, on Guincho beach, slightly north of the restaurant, at a place where dune sand has blown over the road. Here, hundreds of black basalt stones are lying about, beautifully worked and polished into multiple facets, and of all sizes, from tiny pebbles to pieces of several cubic metres. The latter are, of course, immobile and polished on one side only.[1]

When such action, taking place in certain conditions—in the Sahara, for example—affects prehistoric stones it can happen that their cut surfaces are so obliterated as to be difficult to detect. This is also found with many chipped flints in the Lisbon area and in Portugal generally.

CAUSES OF THERMAL FRACTURES

There are two: (i) frost and sunlight; (ii) fire, natural or artificial.

Thermal Fractures by Frost and Sunlight. Flint, quartz, and quartzite are poor conductors of heat, which, from the surface, penetrates but slowly into the mass. The result is that in cases of sudden cooling or heating the stones can fracture and break up into separate pieces.

Especially in desert areas, surface flints suffer a sequence of intense heating by day, followed by rapid cooling at night, with renewed baking in the sun next morning, and so on. When the surface cools, it contracts and can no longer cover the central mass, so that fine cracks appear, mere nail-scratches, giving a microscopic start to a semi-circular cleft that later becomes circular and deepens at every change of temperature. The time comes when the fragment bounded by the crack is connected to the main mass at one point only, a kind of umbilical cord. Then the slightest dilation of the inscribed surface will make it bulge a little and press its edges along those of the matrix; then, suddenly, with a sharp report, the fragment will fly off.

Fracture surfaces made in this way are, on the fragment, convex and

[1] A more recent visit to this site, in 1957, enabled me to ascertain that this phenomenon is not modern, but goes back to the Würmian era, as M. Guillot had pointed out in a more general study. (H.B.)

set in random directions, with the converse on the matrix. If the fragment is whole the umbilical point can be seen in the centre, most frequently in relief, with a corresponding hollow on the matrix; or it may be a tiny fossil, or a grain of harder material. If the flint is fairly pure the fracture surface is covered with tiny concentric zones, like the growth-rings in a section of tree-trunk. But these zones or rings, in flints split by frost or sun, stand out slightly in relief and progress inward from the edge, each one showing a sharp change in temperature that has meant a further stage in the development of the crack. Since thermal fractures of this type proceed in different yet simultaneous phases, it is not uncommon to find that fragments produced by their intersections are only segments of the whole break-away section. If the dividing face of such a segment, more or less at right angles, ran near the centre and the umbilical point it could easily create the illusion of a bulbed flake made by percussion.

The porous outer surface of flint nodules exposed to frost shows, in particular, a large number of tiny circular flakes of the same origin, and their multiplication produces a surface pitted with hundreds of tiny regular depressions that are characteristic.

Frost can also crack open flint nodules, but for a different reason. They often contain, embedded in their mass, geodes full of water. If this freezes it increases in volume, presses on the walls of the cavity, and splits open the block. Sometimes this action occurs simultaneously on two opposite faces, driving a hole through the piece, whether it be natural or man-shaped, or even at times in an implement already made, without any human intervention, the incident being subsequent to the craft-work and often of very much later date.

Other accidents of mechanical fracture accompany frost damage. A flint nodule fairly deeply embedded in the Ipswich Crag (Bolton and Laughlin's quarry) provides a good illustration: the two halves, fractured by frost as above, had remained in place, but at the critical time one had pressed against the other at the fracture surface, forcing off a fairly large flake, of mechanical origin, with a well-defined bulb.

Fire or Very Strong Sunlight. Fire applied to flint fractures it violently, with a loud detonation and fragments flying in all directions. This action proceeds in several phases.

In the first, the fractures remain relatively superficial. The surface, a poor conductor of heat, expands, but the internal mass, still cool, cannot follow, and the result is a split and breakage between the two. The fracture face of the fragment, which is convex and usually fairly round or discoid, and the corresponding concave face on the matrix show the following characteristics: on the outer edge is a smooth margin, mostly narrow, but at times quite wide, with fine, concentric rings; then comes the central breakage area, with numerous, random, and irregular facets.

If the heated piece is thick the fracture of the salient angles occurs concentrically with the centre, and the flakes that fly off will have their breakage surfaces concave in all directions, with very deep curvature. The matrix, its various angles roughed off, leaving very convex surfaces in all directions, will soon be reduced to a sort of spheroid polyhedron, with concentric fissures where the next fragments will fly off. At the same time, and this is equally true for all stages of fire action, the ferruginous elements in the surface or the body of the flint change from yellow or brown to red or pink.

However, mainly in hot deserts and the Tertiary regions of modern countries that have had this sort of climate at some time or other, hundreds of such spheroid polyhedra can be found, though with no reddening and no internal fissures. It must be supposed that these are due to the action of intense solar heat.

If such heating, either by fire or sun, affects the edges of a thin flake, this too will fracture concentrically, giving off narrow, sharply curved splinters. The edge of the flake will have a very convex plane, and this may spread all round, transforming the remainder into a smooth-sided flint disc of vertical section. In the body of this will be parallel, concentric fissures, deeper from the centre outward, showing where more splinters will be detached.

Subjected to further heating, flint, unless it contains ferruginous colouring matter, pales to a porcelain white as the organic pigments it contains are destroyed. Fire will completely crackle flint with fine fissures running in all directions, like the crackling on Chinese porcelain. A similar effect is obtained when very hot stones are plunged into cold water, as was done with English 'pot-boilers.' As is well known, among some primitive tribes with no pottery this method is the only one for heating water and milk, even to boiling-point. Prehistoric man used the same process.

Heating flint until it cracks is certainly not recommended, since it can be more easily chipped after moderate heating; but fierce heat was nevertheless used by fossil man to break large pebbles or blocks of quartzite or quartz that were hard to start splitting by percussion. It has been reported that the Mincopies on the Andaman Islands know no other way of breaking up the quartz they use as raw material for implements.

Fire action on stones does not always imply human action, although this is most frequently the case. Lightning or volcanoes can set fire to forests or savannah. Yet these are relatively rare natural occurrences, whereas man mastered fire long, long ago, and the flints, chipped or not, showing his influence are innumerable.

EOLITHS

All that remains of the many attempts to find traces of an Eolithic stage, Tertiary or otherwise, of human industry is a 'posthumous' list:

THENAY (Loir-et-Cher). Miocene: the cause of fracture was thermal and natural, similar to fire effect, acting on nearly all the flints, with intense crackling and frequent reddening.

BONCELLES (Belgium). Oligocene: compression of the flints *in situ*, causing chipping and trimming. Some have been reshaped, polished, and patinated in the Oligocene marine deposits.

PUY-BOUDIEU and PUY-COURNY (Cantal). Miocene: displacement due to mountain landslide and mutual pressure of the flints therein.

KENT and REUTELIAN (Belgium) and part of the Mesvinian: solifluxion type.

Another part of the REUTELIAN and FLENUSIAN (Belgium): flints crushed by carts and covered with rust. Some chipped flints have undergone the same process.

IPSWICH, Red Crag etc.: glaciers (striations) and pressure in older ground. But traces of fire and a certain number of flakes might be accepted, though their angle of cut is generally against it.

(Although we admit the existence of small pebbles with elementary marginal chipping in more than one cycle of the proto-Quaternary age in Africa and Europe, critical study of them still often remains to be done (Kafuan), especially in regions covered by the moraines, often subsequently reshaped, of the Permian glaciers of the Dwyka.)

[5]

Intentional chipping and its techniques

Methods of chipping—Two-element chipping: by manual percussion or on anvil; with wood, bone, or softer stone—Three-element chipping: bipolar, supported, by repercussion, by punch, by leverage—Methods of retouching flakes

---

If we admit that from his remotest origins man must have used the naturally sharp stones he found lying about, it is obvious that he must also soon have learned that use dented or blunted them, and then tried to restore their sharp edges, or remove them where they were a hindrance. This discovery of the use of breaking force must surely be the original source of stone implements. This is an abstract truth, but it must remain a theory, since the finds hitherto made have not allowed us to check it against the facts. We lack deposits that are completely free from misleading data due to the natural forces already discussed.

Moreover, the intentional chipping by man of craft-worked stones is, after all, only a special example of mechanical fracture, where the craftsman has used the properties of available materials and controlled the application of forces which observation had shown him to be effective. Samples of human chippings have, therefore, no absolute characteristic; each is an example of mechanical fracture by blows and natural pressures, where man has intervened to modify the process for his own ends.

There will be cases where there is legitimate doubt as to whether the stone was chipped intentionally or not; but once man invented his working methods he could produce thousands of specimens with ever-increasing technical precision and manual skill. The association of a large number of stones showing mechanical fracture, in conditions where they could not have been broken naturally, often with other material such as ash, charcoal, and broken or carved or burnt bones, is also often evidence of the human character of the site. It can also happen that the flint is foreign to the place where an implement made from it has been found, and that the only explanation of its presence is that it has been imported by the group using it.

The unmistakable outward signs common to all causes of mechanical fracture of flint and other breakable stone are as follows: a surface to which the force is applied, called the *striking platform*, forming a variable angle with the surface of the substance, this angle remaining about 45° for simple human percussion, but being very obtuse in cases of natural fracture. The point of application of the force on this surface, the *striking point*, is often marked in the matrix by a flattened point of impact. In human percussion—though not exclusively, however—it is often indicated by one or even several tiny circular cracks, ringing round, in the main mass, incipient cones of percussion due to blows which did not finally result in a fracture. They are found on all surfaces subject to rolling, and the plane of percussion may be the natural surface—the cortex of a nodule, or the surface of a pebble. In human chipping it is often due to a first rough trimming aimed at producing a proper percussion surface.

The fracture surface, or *splitting* or *chipping plane*, shows, both on the flake and on the piece from which it comes, fairly constant characteristics of very considerable variety. From the point of impact on the striking surface where the fracture occurs and the flake is detached, there starts the cone, of which a part is laid bare, known as the *conchoid*, or *bulb of percussion*, usually in relief on the flake and hollow on the matrix or original pebble. When the flake is the result of a violent blow this cone is large, and is proportionately smaller as the blow is lighter. The same applies if the flake has been produced by pressure from some hard stone, whereas if it is by pressure from softer material than flint there is neither cone nor conchoid, but merely a slight depression. This latter, especially when it more closely resembles a cone of percussion, is accompanied by a series of closely related features of varying intensity— a fan-shaped set of fine cracks, or slightly raised ridges (keels), due to excess elements of force being dispersed in the mass subjected to the blow. It is not uncommon for a splinter to be raised at right angles with one of these ridges. Again, the bulb or cone is sometimes partially removed by a secondary flake. Finally, it may happen that the blow itself breaks the flake it raises, depending on its axis.

A blow of sufficient force to produce a flake may yet encounter too great a resistance in the mass of the stone, resulting from increased density at a certain point; the energy is reflected back along its trajectory and produces a cross-break, sometimes called a 'hinge' fracture.

The surface of the splitting or flaking face varies according to the strength of the blow aimed, the material used for the striker, and the way in which the surroundings absorb a proportion of the vibrations, but it always shows concentric ripples round the cone, be they slight or deeply marked. The trajectory of fracture also varies considerably, being at times slightly convex and rising, but more often somewhat concave (the flake) and cambered, or in certain cases practically flat.

METHODS OF CHIPPING

Stone chipping refers to the various methods of applying mechanical force intentionally, in order to detach flakes with sharp edges and of different thicknesses, to be used either as they are or to be modified further; or else to give to a matrix or original stone, from which these flakes are removed, a particular shape which would make it into a more powerful or heavier tool than the flakes themselves.

Secondary chipping is a lighter form of the above, the aim being to remove smaller flakes so as to give a better shape to the edge of a roughed-out implement or of a crude flake.

Trimming or retouching is an even lighter technique, removing from the edge of the piece only very fine splinters, either to improve the shape or the cutting edge, or even to blunt or remove the edge altogether.

For these different operations various methods can be used, and it is likely that fossil man knew many more that are still unknown to us. Only by experience, and accidentally, was it found that slightly warm or gently heated flint can be cut better than when it is cold.

Chipping and allied processes can be carried out with a minimum of two elements and a maximum of three or four, and, as in natural fracture, by *percussion* or *pressure*; and softer stones than flint, quartzite, or quartz can be used for the purpose.

TWO-ELEMENT CHIPPING

For this the percussion is produced by a violent blow between two hard substances. If the two stones are of comparable hardness there are two ways of striking them together intentionally. The first has been tried out by every prehistorian, and it consists of purely *manual percussion*. A piece of stone, held in the left hand or steadied on the ground or on the thigh, is struck by another, swung in the right hand. This method uses a small mass, at a fairly high speed, with a relatively small expenditure of energy. It produces rather small flakes, with a splitting plane rising fairly steeply towards the surface of the matrix and a rather thick base, thinning out towards the other end. The striking platform usually forms an obtuse angle with the plane of fracture, complementary to the acute angle of the edge of the stone core. Since the blow is sharp, the flakes, in form of long, narrow blades, vibrate too much at the moment of separation and frequently shatter into pieces. In this regard, chipping a stone resting on the thigh or on the ground attenuates the excess breaking force of the vibration. The same effect would be obtained if the flakes were cushioned in a liquid at the moment of separation.

In view of the above, preference was soon given to another and much more powerful method of producing, quickly and with little effort, very large flakes—*anvil chipping*. In this case the piece of stone to be worked is brought down and guided as it drops so as to produce a blow, at the required angle and place, on the point of the stone being used as an anvil or passive striking platform. Provided that the raw material can be found in large blocks, this method is far superior to the former for producing very large flakes, which simply cannot be done by manual percussion. In addition, much less effort is required, since, in fact, gravity replaces the manual drive.

In flakes made on an anvil the striking surface is smooth and very oblique to the fracture surface, at times as much as 170°. A natural striking surface, or one obtained after preliminary chipping, frequently shows repeated points of impact, due to blows which did not produce the desired effect. The cone or bulb starting from the centre of the striking surface is well developed. It is always well shaped, often half surrounded at its rim by small flakings, which sometimes go so far as to dislodge it altogether by shattering all the striking surface. This cone is often double or triple, either because previously incipient cones, buried in the flint mass, have been brought out, or because the percussion has occurred on several projections of the anvil at once. The cone is at the centre of numerous ridges, scales, and splinters grouped fanwise all around.

The matrix block giving off these flakes will show that the fracture surface has risen steeply, extending only a short distance from its point of origin. The flakes are therefore short, stout, and with a thick base often lateral to their greatest length. Consequently the large implements, shaped by flaking in this way, are thick, with short, steeply rising faces.

Such are the characteristics found exclusively in the two most ancient industries of a large part of the Old World—the *Abbevillian*, with large implements made by flaking according to this method, and the *Clactonian*, an industry using flakes so obtained. Very large flakes, themselves reworked by this method, could give larger implements that would be much lighter.

Since this is the best technique for rough-hewing or trimming very large blocks, it never ceased to be used at any time during the Stone Age—concurrently with other methods, of course.

The blocks thus obtained soon underwent certain preparatory treatment: first, a flake was taken off one end to facilitate further flaking, this being especially necessary with large pebbles. Then, using as successive striking surfaces the newly made facets resulting from flaking, rapid progress was made towards producing subspherical polyhedra and, not much later, cores that were biconvex, subdiscoid, oval, or rounded, with flaking taken off from angular cutting edges.

Such flakes are smaller than those mentioned earlier—indeed, some are tiny—and their bulbs and cones show a much smaller expenditure of force than with the others. There are groups of industries where they predominate—for example, the *Tayacian* (from Tayac, in the Dordogne), generally more recent than the Abbevillian and Clactonian. It can easily be seen that in districts short of stone the Tayacian technique must have been developed earlier and forced upon man for a longer period. The striking surface in this technique is just as oblique as previously.

In what circumstances did man notice that by raising the striking surface until it was nearly vertical he could obtain much more regularly shaped flakes from well-prepared, biconvex cores? How, since in any case he used stone against stone, did he strike these cores? It is a technique that modern experimenters have not yet been able to imitate.

It is a fact that in the Acheulean industries, alongside the above method, are to be found quantities of flakes with a smooth, nearly vertical striking platform and a bulb-cone of modest size. On the contrary, in the Levalloisian technique (from Levallois, near Paris) and all industries deriving therefrom, including a part of the Mousterian (from Le Moustier, in the Dordogne), can be seen, on the edge of blocks shaped into rectangular or discoid cores, a special way of preparing the area of striking surfaces so as to obtain choice flakes. The others which merely serve to shape the cores are similar to the products of the aforementioned techniques.

Firstly the core, with its back face roughly squared by broad facets round the edges, shows on the front face flat chippings converging towards the centre and intended to form the back of flakes to be taken off later. Then, opposite one or more dorsal ridges, the rear edge of the core was very carefully trimmed down to a right angle. This produced tiny facets, and it was here that the blow to take off the flake had to be delivered.

An examination of the striking surfaces of flakes so obtained shows the presence of facets chipped from above downward, but split in the process so that the second half of the trajectory has remained still attached to the core. This enables them to be easily distinguished—if the flakes have not been worn by wind or rolling—from the products of previous methods, where, as a result of secondary trimming, the striking platform has been shortened by retouching it from above downward.

Among the Levallois cores, some are circular or broadly oval, and prepared to give broad flakes with very sharp outer edges, except at the base. Others, triangular in shape, gave pointed flakes of the same form, with double cutting edges. Again, others, intended to give blades, are rectangular of greater or lesser length, with striking surfaces at each end.[1]

Chipping the Wood, Bone, or Softer Stone. From the beginning of the Acheulean period another technique for chipping flint was introduced. Of course, percussion with hard stone continued to be used, without preparation of facets on the striking surfaces, for the production of large flakes and for roughly trimming blocks. But once flakes had been so obtained—or, if not flakes, then thin, selected slivers of flint—they were chipped in turn by a stick of hard wood, a bone, or a firm, though not rigid, stone, less hard than the flint. In this way, from the edges of flakes or slivers, and also from both faces, it was possible to remove thin, long blades or flakes, producing very flat facets that would reach up to or beyond the centre of the faces, almost without 'splitting back.' The same process was used to obtain, from long cores, thin, sometimes quite long, blades, and this method continued to be used in the Levalloisian period. It has been found possible to reproduce these long, fairly regular chippings experimentally, and the demonstration proved that work so executed proceeds very rapidly indeed.

Flakes made by this method show no cone of percussion, point of impact, or incipient cones, all of which are replaced by a slight bulge. The striker, being softer than the flint, affects it only by the transmission of vibration and is itself bruised in the process. Thus the striking platform remains intact except for the removal, from above downward, of a tiny, thin chip. On the splitting plane there is no cone, but again only a little bulge, rarely accompanied by the secondary effects of percussion. The resulting surface is smooth, scarcely and only slightly marked with weak ripples, with a very extended trajectory, barely concave on the flake. The facet of fracture is long, showing that the vibration was prolonged, 'drawn out,' instead of splitting back, as in preceding methods.

This technique represents an enormous step forward in working flint, and to it are due some magnificent specimens of perfectly regular, large implements. The blades, however, are always slightly irregular, and their edges lack the elegance of being absolutely parallel.

THREE-ELEMENT CHIPPING

Bipolar chipping was forced upon man whenever the raw material for his implements consisted of very small pebbles, from the sea or rivers, round or oval, which are impossible to work on an anvil or by manual percussion. The work becomes easy if, placed on a hard stone laid on

---

[1] Professor Bordes has rightly distinguished between the Levallois core, where the whole surface of the front face is prepared so as to give one single broad flake, and the other, more likely Mousterian, where the core is prepared for giving triangular flakes that are frequently pointed and have a median ridge, not usually going beyond the centre of the core.

the ground, the stone to be chipped is steadied by the left hand and struck a smart blow with another stone on its upper surface. This method is called *bipolar* because the flaking occurs simultaneously from above downward and from underneath upward. It can happen that if the two splitting planes coming from each end, or pole, coincide the flakes produced have a bulb of percussion at each end. The technique was used, among other places, at Chou Kow Tien (China) by *Sinan-thropus*, for working quartz; on the Mousterian and Aurignacian coastal sites at Monte Circeo and Nettuno (Italy), with thin quartzites and very small flint pebbles; and on the Mesolithic and Neolithic sites on the Charente and Breton coasts (small flint pebbles).

With flint and quartzite, the small stones are usually split, at the first blow, from end to end and into two or three segments. Each shows at either end a very small bulb, the one on the anvil side being the weaker, that on the struck side the greater. Between these two, along with minute scaling, can be seen a small, raised, transverse line marking the meeting-place of the shock-waves coming from each end.

Bipolar chipping of quartz is very much harder work when used, for example, on pieces as big as a fist. Prolonged and hard striking is required to produce anything more than quartz dust and crushing of the two ends of the stone being worked. At the points of contact of the anvil and the striker fairly deep bruise dents are formed, and at length flakes fly off, first obliquely, coming mainly from the lower part in contact with the anvil. These are splinters with no particular striking platform, or with an almost straight splitting plane; or they are very misshapen, being merely tiny incipient splinters and cross-grained, scaly irregularities. At a later stage the flakes fly off from end to end, with a flattened, scored bulb at each end and scale formation due to the meeting of two opposite forces. These flakes are thin and often tend to form long, narrow, almost straight blades or even strips. This method cannot produce large flakes, but it has the advantage, where other means of chipping cannot be used, of reducing an entire block of quartz to small pieces, since manual chipping or anvil work merely gives subspherical polyhedra on which ordinary percussion has no effect.

The other methods of three-element chipping do not seem to have originated in the West, though they developed there during the Upper Palaeolithic.

Supported chipping is similar, in more ways than one, to bipolar work, of which it is merely a specialized application. It consists of striking a flint, quartz, or quartzite object resting on something softer than itself. It was not, apparently, used to obtain large flakes but to effect secondary cuts, thin, long, and broad, such as are seen on large Solutrean points. Only later were the edges subjected to delicate pressure flaking. The secondary chipping was done by striking the blade on one of its cutting edges with a hard wooden stick, a bone, or a stone softer than flint, while the other cutting edge was rested on a billet of the same type as the striker—that is to say, also softer than the implement being worked.

The facets so obtained show, by their strong, lively ripples, that the blows used were fairly powerful. A great number of breakages were caused in this way.

Repercussion chipping consists of blows dealt squarely with a manual striker at an oblong pebble or stone, where the end to be worked is steadied obliquely on an anvil. This method is less brutal and affords greater control than direct striking and was widely used by coastal populations making implements from chipped pebbles in the Lisbon area. With this technique it is not uncommon to find that a median cone of percussion has been sunk in the mass of the specimen, on the upper surface, and brought to light by the flake taken off the end. This method of work is doubtless to be found in other regions.

Punch Chipping. From Acheulean and Levalloisian times the technique of chipping with wood had made it possible to produce thin, long blades, though rather irregular in shape. From before the beginning of the Upper Palaeolithic and down to the end of the Eneolithic these blades became remarkably regular, being taken from cylindrical or polyhedral cores with almost mathematical precision. This was due, among other new methods, to the introduction of chipping with a punch or intermediate striker placed between the core and the manual striker. When the core had been fixed in a suitable position and prepared by percussion the craftsman applied to its striking surface, after the fashion of a chisel, the end of some long object held in the left hand. Wielding a striker in his right hand, he dealt blows of suitable force on the other end of this object. This punch, or drift, could be made of various materials, preferably slightly brittle—a long piece of hard shale, a thickish splinter of bone, a tine of stag antler, or any kind of chisel made for the purpose. The end struck by the hammer was crushed and flattened, and if the material was shale or bone some splinters came off. The end applied to the core was crushed and flattened also, and often broke. As for the flake thus taken off, be it blade or strip, it usually had parallel edges and a very smooth splitting plane, only faintly rippled and with a very slightly curved trajectory, or even practically flat, though the curve at times increased towards the end. The striking platform was very small—sometimes a mere point—and might show preparation facets, generally oblique—that is to say, coming in from the side and not vertically, as in the Levalloisian and Mousterian techniques. If the punch was not of hard stone the cone disappeared and a slight swelling replaced the bulb. The back of the blade-flake would be the outer surface: cortex in some cases, but mostly, for the first layer of blades, a zigzagged ridge corresponding to the outer preparation of the core. The subsequent blades would be of trihedral section with a median ridge, or maybe trapezoidal with two ridges, usually parallel, or very occasionally three.

Chipping by Leverage. At the time of the discovery of America, and perhaps down to our times in certain districts, a further technique has been used. It was described by a Spanish monk who saw it in Mexico where a core of obsidian, held steady by the feet of the craftsman, was being chipped. To transmit pressure from the chest, a chisel made from a fragment of bone was fixed to the end of a long wooden handle. This produced very long, perfectly regular blades, similar to those made by the preceding technique.

METHODS OF RETOUCHING FLAKES

Basically, retouching is merely percussion of edges by gentle chipping, using the same technique as for large flakes. It is designed to give more regular shape to a cutting edge of the rough flake, or to remove an edge that might cut the hand, or to blunt too sharp an edge, or, again, to restore one broken or blunted in use.

Retouching on an anvil is possible, but it is neither delicate nor accurate. Work with a manual striker of stone, wood, or bone gives, in expert hands, very much better results. If the process is tried experimentally it is soon found that unless fragile points are to be broken off it is better to work from the point towards the larger base, and not the other way. A further discovery shows that it is preferable, in order to get a series of longer retouch chippings, to support with the finger the under side of the edge being worked, to absorb any excessive vibrations.

The trimming carried out by these methods, though rough-and-ready perhaps at the beginning of the old Palaeolithic in the Abbevillian and Clactonian times, and considerably improved thanks to the use of wooden and bone strikers during the Acheulean and Levalloisian periods, was refined during Mousterian times by the introduction of a new technique—retouching by repercussion, on an anvil of stone or bone. The edge of the flake to be worked was placed in contact with the anvil and held with the left hand, while the right dealt gentle or moderate blows on its upper face. After each blow the left hand slightly changed the position of the work, bringing on to the anvil the next part of the edge to be dealt with. By this method excellent results were obtained, with very regular, and fairly long, trimmed facets.

Corresponding to bipolar chipping, there existed a technique for trimming by taking splinters off each end, while a delicate form of supported chipping can also be noted here.

Similarly, pressure retouching, by hand or using chest pressure, corresponded to pressure flaking. The pressure, or compression, could be applied by holding a tool of stone or bone in the right hand and making it bear on the edges of a flake held in the left, which was generally

E

protected by a piece of leather or cloth. This method is found among the Eskimos and Redskins. The Australian aborigines use another: the craftsman sits and holds on the ground a piece of stone or bone, pressing down on it the different points of the edge he wishes to trim. From glass they can produce very fine points comparable to Solutrean work.

Experiments with pectoral pressure have given excellent results on small specimens. The object is fixed in a vice and the pressure brought to bear at successive points via a fairly short-handled pressure tool, so that a close visual check can be kept on progress.

In any case, it is to pressure retouching that we owe the master-pieces that have come down to us from the Stone Age, either from the Solutrean period or, much later, from the Neolithic and even as late as the Bronze Age—for example, Danish daggers, Egyptian knives, and the arrow-heads and throwing-sticks of prehistoric times.

These, then, according to the present state of our knowledge, were the various techniques progressively discovered by fossil man, enabling him to fashion weapons and implements for all his needs. It is, of course, obvious that his experience, so very much wider than ours in such matters, must have taught him many other 'tricks of the trade' still unknown to us, and likely to remain so.

[6]

Prehistoric sites

Water—Hunting—Fishing and gathering shellfish and fruit—Shelters—The living conditions of Palaeolithic man—Clothing and ornament—The life-span of Palaeolithic man

---

L ife, for primitive man, depended on a certain number of factors, all essential in varying degrees—water, food supplies, coming mainly from game, raw material without which he could not make weapons and implements or ornaments, and finally, protection against the weather, wild animals, and enemies.

WATER

Of all these factors or conditions the presence of water was the most indispensable and also the most varied in kind: the banks of streams, rivers, lakes, or ponds were all suitable, as was the neighbourhood of a spring. A study of the displacement, both laterally and in depth, of river-beds in prehistoric times shows that the traces of the oldest generations are to be found on the highest terraces, so that 'river-banks' must be understood to include the whole area between the foothills and the present banks.

In modern desert areas the water problem is complicated by the fact that long ago pluvial periods alternated with phases of dryness or complete aridity. In the Sahara rivers or lakes dried up or diminished, only to reappear or fill up again. This explains the wide diffusion of the Upper Palaeolithic culture and the times of diminished occupation, when the water-points, those meeting-places for human groups, gradually dried up. On the edges of some lakes (Moeris, Egypt) the stages in the regression of settlements can be noted by following, step by step, the fall in the ancient water-levels marked by traces of the old shore-lines.

Nature sometimes provided man with underground reserves of water, hidden in dark tunnels and deep caverns, where he came upon them one day. This allowed him to live, even in dry periods, in limestone regions where rain filters completely through the soil—as, for example, the cavern of La Pileta, in the Sierra Libar (Malaga, Spain), first used by Palaeolithic tribes.

Later, in Neo-Eneolithic times, man was not content to use merely the water from shallow basins or underground lakes. Earthenware containers, made and fired on the spot, were placed under runnels in cave roofs or in stalactites, so as to collect purer water, untainted by contact with the ground.

Food supplies for Palaeolithic man came mainly from hunting, fishing, and food-gathering. But for these early times we have little real information about vegetable foodstuffs.

This does not mean, however, that their use was entirely neglected. It is hard to imagine that man did not welcome the improvement in his flesh diet to be obtained from wild fruit, seeds, and, in the main, berries. In the milder climate of Southern Europe he was well supplied with walnuts, edible chestnuts, grapes, wild cherries, plums, beechnuts, and acorns, which, preserved by grinding or drying, made good reserve provisions. To these could be added herbs, certain kinds of fern, lichen, tubers, roots, mushrooms, and even the pulp of some trees when the bark had been scraped off. In times of famine man must also have sought out and eaten seaweed. In desert areas of South-west Africa and Somalia water-melons or river-crabs, rich in water, must have given him the precious, vital liquid. He certainly discovered, as is proved by finds of remains of flint sickles in the Magdalenian layers of the rock-shelter at Saut-du-Perron (Haute-Loire), the properties of certain plants for basket-making. Nevertheless it is true that only hunting, fishing, and food-gathering can be studied with any accuracy.

HUNTING

Hunting is still, in some contemporary primitive civilizations, the most effective way of obtaining not only food, but also the raw materials —bone, horns, antlers, ivory, and tendons—required for making weapons, as well as for fashioning clothing from skin and fur and producing water-bottles and bags. At certain times and in certain areas the whole life of the group was closely linked to an animal—for example, the reindeer in Eskimo civilizations.

An approach to the question of hunting, however, raises problems about the behaviour of Palaeolithic man in dealing with wild animals. It is a fact that man has not always been the hunter; he was, and sometimes still is, the hunted, in a world of large Carnivora—lions, panthers, bears, and cave hyenas. The skeleton of a young man who lived in Upper Palaeolithic times, found in the rock-shelter at Arene Candide (Italy), furnishes a reminder of the sort of dramatic encounter that cannot have been uncommon. A ghastly wound, probably inflicted in an attack by a wild beast, carried away part of the lower jaw, the collarbone, the shoulder-blade, and the top of the femur. The mutilations had been concealed, at the burial of the corpse, by plastering over with clay or yellow ochre. There seems little doubt that the diminutive hominid of early Palaeolithic times paid a heavy price, not only in bloody losses inflicted on him and his kind by wild beasts, but also in the share they stole of his booty. They ran off with animals he had wounded, raided his traps or his meat stores, and soiled them with their fetid urine—as did the glutton, or wolverine—and he was powerless to stop them, the only really effective weapon he had for keeping them out of his camps being fire.

Yet, on his side, this man had an advantage that should not be under-estimated—the animal's instinctive knowledge of the undoubted superiority of the human being, however weak his physical resources might be. Nor was there any great abyss separating man from the animal. The bonds between them were not yet broken, and man still felt near to the beasts that lived around him, that killed and fed like him. His experiments, at least during the early Palaeolithic times, were directed against animals. From them he still retained all the faculties that civilization has blunted—rapid action and highly trained senses of sight, hearing, and smell, physical toughness in an extreme degree, a detailed, precise knowledge of the qualities and habits of game, and great skill in using with the greatest effect the rudimentary weapons available. The wounds revealed on bones found in kitchen refuse, as well as many Upper Palaeolithic drawings showing wounded animals, seem to point to the fact that the hunter aimed for preference at the soft parts, this being even more clearly seen when harpoon or spear had been used.

The question of hunting cannot be separated from the problem of how man first began to feed on meat. The first stage was perhaps the use of dead carcasses, as has been noted in certain backward tribes and also at times of famine. It is, however, probable that man soon tried to obtain fresh meat by killing small, weak, or sick animals. This could hardly be called hunting, since it meant seizing, for food, any available prey, strangling it, or battering it to death with stick or stone. It was really a form of fighting, such as takes place between animals, and was merely a means of capture. True hunting presupposes methodical, reasoned pursuit.

However, it must be admitted that, in any attempt to reconstitute prehistoric hunting methods, whether it be of Mauer man pursuing elephants with sharpened stakes or the techniques of trapping and ambushing, one fact is absolutely vital. It is that the hunter must have had precise knowledge of the habits of his quarry.

Animals, or at least large game, need a drinking-place and somewhere to bathe in warm weather, and the neighbourhood of such water-points, particularly if water is scarce thereabouts, is especially favourable for hunting. In hilly parts it is the tracks leading to the water-points rather than the immediate surroundings that are of use—for example, the steep-sided ravines opening into the sides of deep valleys in the limestone plateaux of Aquitaine, between the uplands of woods and pastures and the narrow valleys.

Wild herds changed their pastures seasonally, just as their domestic successors were to do later in our own times. When summer came they went up into the hills and, as winter returned, came down again through the narrow valleys leading to the plains. The outlets between the high and low ground were especially favoured as hunting territory between the seasons, as were the unchanging routes used by reindeer in their seasonal migrations—much larger in scale, of course. To this very day Canadian reindeer, regardless of the traps and ambushes laid for them, make every year a round trip of almost 2000 miles in each direction. Les Eyzies (Dordogne) was certainly situated on one such route.

Some sort of elementary method can soon be noticed in hunting techniques, and discoveries made at various sites throw useful light thereon. A camping-site for elephant-hunters at Torralba (Soria, Spain) dates from the end of the Abbevillian period. In the last interglacial era the cave bear took to the mountain caves of the Alps and the Pyrenees, where the pre-Mousterians and Mousterians did not hesitate to attack their lairs, at altitudes of over 1500 metres on the Santis and over 2000 on the Drachenloch. At Myxnitz (Northern Styria) the Drachenhohle cave contained a narrow corridor, through which the bear could not avoid passing. At this point hunters would hide behind a boulder and fall upon the animal as it passed. This explains the large number of fractured bear-skulls, all showing damage on the left side, the one nearer to the hunter, who usually went only for young animals no more than two years old. In a cave near Trieste were found bear-skulls with the left parietal bone stove in, one still containing a Mousterian point. This means that the animal had been killed not by a spear, but by a club in which the flint spike had been set at right angles like the blade of a halberd. The cave at Tuteil (Ariège), set in the northern slope of the Roc de la Mousse, showed another method of bear-hunting. The great bear chamber runs up into a vertical chimney coming out into a narrow passage which ends in a kind of well. This was used as a trap, into which man got down to finish off and cut up any animals that fell in.

In some of these caves it has been claimed that the deep scratch-marks on the walls are evidence of attempts by the bears to escape from nets spread across their path. There is no foundation for the theory, since in all caves such marks are to be found where the beasts sharpened their claws on the walls. However, one has still to fall back on conjecture as to the methods used to capture large mammals that were difficult to wound seriously with the implements available. This leads to the theory that a simpler and less dangerous way was used—that of the pitfall, perhaps lined with sharpened stakes. The wounded animal, exhausted by efforts to free itself, was finished off with the coups-de-poing that had been used to dig the pit. Otherwise the hunters could just wait for death to supervene as a result of the wounds sustained when the animal fell into the pit.

If trapping, as a hunting method for use against large pachyderms, rhinoceroses, hippopotami, and the great Carnivora, seems to raise no improbabilities, the same cannot be said for interpreting as traps, pits, or nets a whole series of outline drawings found in cave art. Some writers with only book knowledge of cave-drawings have subscribed to the idea, not in itself absurd, that many of the tectiform signs represent drawings of traps of many different kinds. All this is based on an explanation put forward by Hugo Obermaier, who recognized, in certain tectiform signs in Franco-Cantabrian drawings—at Font-de-Gaume (Dordogne), and at La Pasiega, Altamira, Santander, Buxu, and La Pileta (Spain)—traps designed to attract evil spirits, similar to those used for the same purpose by some present-day tribes in Oceania. Even supposing that such a comparison, so far removed from the problems of Western Europe in the Stone Age, were valid, such signs could equally probably depict little houses prepared for these same spirits. Or one could say that in the Quaternary markings which were sometimes numerous in remote corners of the Spanish caves the lines showed places where the spirits of the ancestors were to be housed in these shelters.

In any case, such tectiform signs cannot possibly be interpreted as traps, nets, or hunting-gear, since they are practically never of the same age as the animals which lie under them or are superimposed. The connexion between them is unknown, and all theories about them are arbitrary. On the other hand, there is no possible doubt about the summer-huts found in most of these drawings.

Another hunting technique, not requiring perfected weapons or special equipment, was the beat: horses, bulls, stags, were all targets for organized pursuit, being at times driven down to narrow valleys or defiles, or at other times up on to promontories whence they were forced to leap over precipices or into marshes where they would be bogged down and unable to free themselves. Similarly, young animals or pregnant females were often relentlessly pursued until they fell, exhausted.

On flat ground hunting could be carried out as an encircling operation such as is still used by hunters in the American Far North. The
film *The Silent Enemy* gave an accurate account of the details of a
caribou hunt during the migration which probably differs very little
from reindeer-hunting in the Stone Age. After a more or less prolonged chase the harassed animals stop and huddle together in a
seething, constantly milling mass; on the outer edge a ring of hunters,
wielding bows, arrows, and small clubs, starts a veritable slaughter of the
panic-stricken beasts.

Snow also could be of great assistance to the hunter, making tracking
easier and preventing the rapid escape of bison, horses, and elks. When
it thawed mud into which they could sometimes sink belly-deep left
them an easy prey to their pursuers.

W. Sörgel has already pointed out the exhausting and imperfect
nature of these methods, as well as their poor results, mainly due to the
weakness of old Palaeolithic man in intellect and implements. The
axes and large points in his poor armoury were extremely inefficient and
had little effect on large animals. Yet elephants and rhinoceroses figure
prominently in the hunting bags, indicating, as for the larger Bovidae,
the use of pitfalls. In the Mousterian levels at El Castillo (Spain) the
high percentage of remains of swift-running species points to the use of
ambush tactics and certain throwing weapons, such as *bolas*, stones
covered with leather or net and joined by a thong. These could be
thrown at an animal's legs and bring it down. They were even used for
river- or lake-side expeditions, for when they were hurled into the water
they could stop swimming animals and cause them to drown fairly
rapidly. The progress in methods of attack during the Middle Palaeolithic period heralds new hunting techniques deriving from improvements made to throwing-weapons during Upper Palaeolithic times.
These enabled man to become more efficient in hunting from a distance swift-footed species like the Equidae, Cervidae, Capridae, and
birds.

The result was that subsequently, as seen in the distribution of bone
remains from game, zoogeography and topography were not the decid-
ing factors in the choice of animals to be hunted. Bags would now contain, besides the reindeer and horse, the mammoth, musk ox, bison,
giant deer, ibex, chamois, roebuck, saiga, boar; small mammals such as
foxes and polar hares, beaver, lemming, marmot; birds like ptarmigan,
swans, geese and wild duck, eagles, buzzards, snow owls, cranes, and
crows, hollow leg-bones from the latter being used as needle-cases or
small inkpots for ochre. Such variety came from the use of better
throwing-weapons—laurel-leaf javelin spear-heads, notched flint-heads,
split-base points, javelins of oval, flat, or slightly curved section, harpoons, and arrows with double or triple (Magdalenian) forked heads,
made of deer antler and fired from a hooked throwing-stick or a large,

triple-curved bow (Alpera, Minateda, La Cueva Remigia, in Spain). The boomerang, the hook, and the club were also part of the equipment for hunting small animals and birds.

Whole expeditions were carefully organized for hunting mammoth in Eastern Europe, at Willendorf, at Langmennersdorf, at Krems, on the lower Danube, in lower Austria, and at Předmost, in Moravia. Situated in the valley of the Becwa, on a track used by pachyderms, Předmost was the scene of the most spectacular of the great Pleistocene hunts. Its camping-grounds were used all through, from the mid-Aurignacian into a Perigordian period with faint Solutrean influence. These sites have yielded about forty thousand implements, flint, reindeer antler, bone, and ivory, as well as an enormous collection of thousands of mammoth bones, the remains of about five hundred separate animals. Contrary to commonly held opinion, these remains are not the result of some catastrophe, a gigantic blizzard that is thought to have buried whole flocks, nor did the men at Předmost merely have to help themselves to colossal heaps of frozen meat. Like the elephants at Torralba (Soria, Spain), the mammoths at Předmost were slain by hunters operating not far from their camps, during seasonal expeditions of which there are other known examples.

Very much later, in the Vercors district of France, the last of the Magdalenians and the Azilians used to go to Bobache and Méaudre to hunt marmot, probably for their skins, but also for meat. Seal jaw-bones found in the Dordogne, like the shin-, cannon-, and jaw-bones of reindeer found in the Cantabrian Mountains west of Bilbao, are probably reminders of some distant hunting trip. The Riviera tribes, great eaters of shellfish, must have wished to improve their diet after the sea rose at the end of the last glacial period, and, in search of meat, went into the uplands and rocky hills near by to hunt ibex and stag.

Now, at the very time when, by comparison and deduction, an attempt is being made to determine hunting techniques during the Upper Palaeolithic, rock-paintings in Eastern Spain and certain products of Franco-Spanish *art mobilier* have been found to provide interesting illustrations of these hunts of long ago.

In the light of such evidence, it can be seen that the trappers of the reindeer age, at La Cueva dels Tolls (Valtorta) and at Morella la Vella (Castellón) were skilled at tracking game, even using in the chase camouflage made from hunting trophies, like the bison-hunter at Laugerie Basse (Dordogne), with his body concealed by an animal's skin, a trick probably not confined to the Upper Palaeolithic. At La Cueva de la Araña (Valencia) and at La Cueva de los Caballos herds of stags, hinds, and fawns, pursued by invisible beaters, charge at full speed hunters waiting for them with volleys of arrows. At La Cueva de los Caballos the scene is shown developing from the top downward: one hunter, in the upper part of the picture, has used up all his arrows and is gesturing to this effect; the man behind him is using his last arrow; the third has just let fly, but still has three more shafts stuck in the ground at his feet. The last bowman is preparing to shoot and has a stock of arrows, three in front of him, two behind. The sweep of the game is therefore from left to right of the hunters. At the Villar del Huomo (Cuenca), the Val del Charco del Agua Amarga (Teruel), and at Mas d'en Josep (Castellón) can be seen the last stages of a boar-hunt: the animal is being pursued by huntsmen riddling him with arrows to hasten his final fall. At La Cueva Remigia (Castellón) a wild sow, with her young, one of which rolls over like a stricken hare, is rounding on the hunters.

In support of the evidence of such illustrations, discoveries dating from the late northern Magdalenian made at Meiendorf (Holstein) provide several remnants of bones, with reindeer shoulder-blades, a *Lagopus* pelvis, and the sternum of a crane, all bearing marks of wounds made by arrows or javelins and demonstrating the effectiveness of such long-range weapons.

Faced with the remains of hunting bags, the majority the remains of reindeer (79 per cent at the Kesslerloch; 75 per cent at Schweizersbild) and later of horse, bison, stag, and, in loess regions, mammoth, we cannot but consider the problem of how far the Palaeolithic huntsman contributed to the extinction of the major animal species. He cannot be blamed for the disappearance of prehistoric fauna, due to natural causes peculiar to each species. The mammoth and the reindeer survived by emigrating to the far north or to the east, following the retreating ice. Bison still survive in some parts of Eastern Europe. The cave bear disappeared only after the Middle Palaeolithic, and that as a result of disease. Man may, in certain cases, have accelerated the decline of a species, but he did not cause it. Changes in the climate, the diseases they cause, and the epidemics attacking organisms unable to adapt themselves to such changes—these are the real reasons for the disappearance of types of fauna. "But," as Hugo Obermaier writes, in *Der Mensch der alten Zeiten* (Vol. I, p. 110),

> besides the climate and man, before which the animal world could retreat, without disappearing, over a long period, inner causes must have come into play, causes of which we know nothing save that they acted on the most gigantic, at the end of their time. This very giantism of so many Quaternary types contained within itself some danger and marked the upper point of no return in their development and specialization. New lines of evolution usually stem from more modest forms that are less differentiated and still capable of development in many directions.

In any attempt to classify the animals hunted as game, consideration must also be given to the motives that led prehistoric men to go after one species rather than another. Though bone studies made particularly in Germany, Switzerland, and Central Europe enable a distinction to be made between the victims of man and those of wild animals and birds of prey, and to determine the period of the hunting season and the age of the bag, sufficient attention does not seem to have been given to the reasons for the choice of animal. Yet one can hardly fail to be struck by the relative disproportion, in some French sites, between bone remains of Bovidae, Equidae, and Cervidae. Similarly, in rock-paintings there is a notable predominance of the first group. This, therefore, raises the question: do these differences correspond to the fact that the Bovidae and Equidae were more or less what might be called butcher's meat, whereas the Cervidae were prized more for the raw material they provided in the form of antlers, hide, and tendons, all usable for tools and weapons, as well as for making clothes?

Research by L. Pfeiffer, in Germany, and Dr Henri-Martin, in France, has revealed details of how game was cut up and dismembered. The carcass, after skinning and disembowelling, was cut up with some skill, traces of which appear on the bones in the form of more or less deep cuts of remarkable sharpness. These have been found near joints and parallel or perpendicular to the plane of the joint. Specimens found at Meiendorf (Holstein) and at the Mousterian site at La Quina (Charente) show that the first part to be dismembered was the head, and then the trunk was cut up into several pieces, the limbs being removed, to be in their turn broken at the joints. Incisions affecting the joints and the tibiotarsal area had been made with remarkable skill. Traces of various aspects of such work are to be found also on the knuckle-bones of Bovidae, Equidae, and reindeer in the form of oblique furrows where the tendons were attached or oblique cuts elsewhere. On skulls they are found near the symphysis of the jaw-bones, around the protuberances, and above the antler exits in the Cervidae. Openings made in the thorax were part of the process of disembowelling. It is worthy of note that from Mousterian times man had found the most effective method of cutting up large carcass sections and already achieved some skill in disjointing and quartering, only resorting to fracture by brute force when seeking the marrow so prized for lamp-oil and as a delicacy. The marks of cutting and scraping visible on bones, except the epiphyses, and occurring in groups or separately on the diaphyses at places where the muscle passes through or terminates, all show how the flesh was removed. All the hoof-knuckles of the ox or horse were split lengthwise, probably to get at the highly prized oil. The Mousterians, for reasons unknown, always removed the hoof from the ungual phalanx (D. Garrod).

It would be strange if, in work of this kind, on which the life of the community might depend, certain general rules did not come to be established, to be obeyed by all if success was to be assured. In modern hunting laws a certain number of regulations always lay down the limits of the area reserved for hunting by a particular pack. Hugo

Obermaier considers that Upper Palaeolithic huntsmen were bound by similar rules, basing his assertion on the fact that certain types of weapon are confined to certain areas, like the throwing-spears with basilar holes found in Spain, but only in the interior. Differences found in the distribution of decorative techniques in Pyrenean art and in the Dordogne not only suggest the existence of regional art forms, but would seem to correspond also to actual, clearly defined hunting territories, with compulsory limits. According to the laws of primitive communities, the violation of hunting law may mean death, and we may well ask, with Hugo Obermaier, if, indeed, one of the rock-paintings found in the gorges of La Gazulla and at La Cueva Remigia, in Eastern Spain, does not portray the finale of one of these transgressions: archers are shooting at a man stretched on the ground. This would lead us to recognize, in Upper Palaeolithic society, the existence of a body corporate with judicial power which, for certain crimes, could exact the death penalty.

Still further problems suggest themselves in this connexion—the direction of collective beats, methods of sharing out the bag of game, control of the possession of weapons. Yet prehistoric archaeology is silent on these subjects, and all that remains is to base hypotheses on comparisons with what is known about primitive law among modern savages. However, the presence of marks of a personal nature on weapons seems to support the theory that there was some sort of regulation of their possession by individuals, and consequently the right to appropriate game, and to some extent to pursue it.

In concluding this study of prehistoric hunting it is not unprofitable to speculate whether the relationship between man and wild animals always took the brutal form of hunter versus hunted. One suspects other methods than the mere slaughter of game. An interesting case of discrimination is mentioned by Garcilazo de la Vega, in his *Comentarios*, concerning the Incas before the Spanish Conquest. A ceremonial hunt took place at a certain season of the year, after the young had been born. An enormous area was surrounded by beaters, and when the animals had been driven into an ever smaller space they were captured by lasso. Stray wild beasts or aged animals were destroyed, but not the llamas or vicunas, which were turned loose again after being sheared, together with the young females and the best of the young males. Even in antiquity Pliny relates (*N.H.*, X, 1) that in a part of Northern Greece men and hawks hunted to some extent in collaboration, the latter bringing down birds for the former.

Such observations open up new lines of thought and need to be collated with discoveries made on Palaeolithic sites. Dr Henri-Martin reported some time ago the presence, in Mousterian levels at La Quina (Charente), of reindeer hoof-bones with holes which are the result not of human boring, but of the bites of some carnivorous animal, probably the wolf. Can this mean that there was co-operation between the hunter and the wolf, the former taking advantage of wounds inflicted by the latter on their common prey? On the same site, but at Aurignacian level, the same worker found a heavy stone pierced by a hole. The edges of this were worn by friction, as if the block had been used to tether an animal, or at least to impede its movements, since the traces of wear had been made by the rubbing of a thong. Taming animals is a very widespread activity among primitive peoples, and there is no reason to suppose that such was not the case in Palaeolithic times. Who knows if the Aurignacians at La Quina did not try to keep, near their camps, female reindeer, for instance, as a source of milk, or their young as a reserve of fresh meat? There was no use of domestic animals before Neolithic times, but nothing prevents us from thinking that there was, in certain cases, some association between man and the wild animals. Many experiments were made, and many mistakes, before the use of domestic animals became fully established.

FISHING AND GATHERING SHELLFISH AND FRUIT

Except for Palaeolithic communities, mostly Mesolithic, settled near the sea, fishing was never as important as hunting in the daily search for food. This does not mean, however, that it was neglected, but rather that it remained confined within well-defined areas.

Fishing in the sea, in lakes, and in large rivers, requiring the use of boats and powerful tackle, seems not to have been within man's range before Neolithic times. There is no evidence in prehistory that whales, seals, or walrus were hunted at sea, the only traces of these being a few sperm-whale teeth and seal jaw-bones probably picked up, in the first case, from carcasses washed up on the beach, or, in the second, in some chance encounter on the rocks by the sea-shore or at the mouth of a large river. Since there is no direct evidence of the existence of fishing-tackle like nets or lobster-pots before Neolithic times and in lake-settlements, earlier methods of fishing must have been very crude. Trout-tickling was always carried on in mountain streams, as was the use of traps made from pebbles, quite extensive on the shores of ocean islands. The annual fishing expeditions for salmon, of course, are a special case, since the mass movements of these fish and others at spawning-time, in northern areas, are so vast that no equipment is needed to catch them. Use was made, however, of various sorts of harpoon, and fish-hooks of bone, antler, or wood, as well as lures or artificial bait designed to bring the salmon within range of harpoon or line. Such bait, made of thin blades of bone, sometimes decorated with diamond designs, oblique lines, or criss-cross patterns, and with a fixing-hole, were found in the Grotte des Harpons at Lespugue, at Le Placard, and at Laugerie Basse.

No less important a part was played, in the feeding habits of sea-shore dwellers, by shellfish gathered along the rocky coasts. The piles of seashells found in caves along the shores of Spain, quite far up valleys running down to the sea, and all along the western coast of Portugal in the *concheiros*, date back to various stages of Upper and Middle Palaeolithic times, and may be earlier. The species and sizes of the shells vary enormously: after molluscs uncovered at low tide come mussels, large gasteropods, and oysters, that never emerge and have to be fished by diving or from a boat. Some varieties, like the *Littorina littorea*, were very numerous in the Upper Palaeolithic, but disappeared in the Mesolithic, giving place to the *Trochus lineatus*, previously unknown, only to reappear in modern times on the same coasts, but slightly smaller in size. In the upper reaches of the estuaries of the Tagus and the Sado, now unaffected by sea-water, the Tardenoisians of Muge, like their fellows on the isles of Morbihan, piled up great heaps of shells, since the sea came up higher than in our times. Less sought after, except perhaps for their mother-of-pearl, were the fresh-water bivalves *Unios* and *Onodontes*, said to be the most tasteless food on earth. Even so, some tribes of South African bushmen used to come at certain seasons and feed on those they could fish in the lagoons near the estuaries of rivers running into the ocean.

On the other hand, land molluscs, like snails, were an important source of food—in relatively cool regions, of course, though North Africa can no longer be classed as such in our times. The main periods were Upper Palaeolithic, among the Capsians in Tunisia, and in the Azilian phase in the Pyrenean Mesolithic. Snaileries in Tunisia and at Constantine show that conditions were more humid than now in times towards the end of the last Ice Age.

An interest was taken in seashells for purposes other than food, since they are brightly coloured and beautifully shaped. From Upper Palaeolithic times they were used as jewellery and exchanged over great distances. Mediterranean species were carried as far as the Atlantic coast and vice versa. Small Tertiary fossil shells, the tiny ammonites, were also collected and exchanged.

In spring the collecting of marsh-birds' eggs and even the young from their nests played a far from negligible part in prehistoric food supplies, and the same can be seen even to-day among many primitive tribes. For those living near an enormous, shallow lagoon like the Laguna de la Janda (Cadiz) such collections must have been particularly useful, and the Neo-Eneolithic frescoes on the Tajo and La Figuras show the importance of this source of nourishment to contemporary tribes.

Palaeolithic peoples seem to have taken a similar interest in wild honey. In one of the rock-shelters at La Araña, near Bicorp (Valencia), a scene depicting the collection of wild honey shows two men, each with a basket in one hand, climbing rope ladders, which appear to be fixed to a wooden frame, up a rock-face, raiding the nests for honey while the bees fly round them in protest.

Always, everywhere, man, like the animals, has sought to protect himself against the vagaries of the weather, settling, according to the region, on sites sheltered from high winds, rain, snow, the burning sun, cold, and floods. Like the animals, too, he had to make seasonal changes of habitat so long as he was content to use natural shelter.

As we have seen, the sites he chose were connected with the food resources of the area, and were in localities it would be possible to defend, near a supply of water and usable stones and not far from hunting territory. Besides more or less permanent settlements providing proper bases for expeditions, we know he also set up hunting and trapping camps, to be occupied for a night or for a single ambush.

Conditions in the habitat varied considerably with the climate. It is certain that in warm weather the shelter was reduced to its simplest form: sloping wind-breaks, screens of furry pelts firmly lashed together, or domed huts of branches must have served most of the time. Other means must also have been known of obtaining protection against wild animals at night, such as hiding-places in trees or in hollow trunks, in ditches or in holes between rocks protected by branches.

Very early man must have learned from animals the protective advantages of open rock-shelters in fine weather and dark caves in winter. Such retreats can be found in various types of terrain. In any firm base of limestone, granite, shale, and other rocks the sea has dug out shallow caves along the ancient shore-lines, while shelters of all kinds can be found in hard rock eroded by rivers digging their beds, and in places by weathering. This latter process, even quite far from any running water, can eat away the softer parts of limestone and sandstone strata sufficiently to hollow out a shelter. Even layers of quartzite, basalt, and all the dense rocks can, as a result of local rock-falls or landslides, sometimes provoked by faults, produce small caves. Or, again, these can be formed, though they easily collapse or get blocked, where dense rock lies on soft subsoil, like the rough limestone set on sand around Paris and the Fontainebleau sandstone also lying on sand. Similarly, falls of very large rock on a slope can give rise to caves, of no great size but usable. However, apart from the Triassic sandstones and granites producing very large hollows by atmospheric erosion or the action of springs, it is mainly in limestone areas that rock-shelters and roomy caves are met with in any number.

Very cool in summer, most of these caves must have become very pleasant places in winter, with an average temperature of between 11° and 14° Centigrade, while it was perhaps minus 50° outside!

The direction in which a cave faced was also important. Preference was given to those facing south or east over those facing north or west—in our latitudes, at least. The choice was different in milder regions, or with rain-bearing winds, and in the Southern Hemisphere. Caves or shelters not very high above the valleys were favoured by hunting tribes, since war was uncommon, but in times of trouble those higher up were sought, since they were less accessible to an enemy, more difficult to detect, and easier to defend against surprise attack.

Once he had mastered fire, and soon afterwards more concentrated forms of lighting like torches and tallow lamps, man could then explore the darker cave labyrinths. Yet he nearly always set up his camps at the mouth of caves, round fires kept burning for warmth and to ward off the unwelcome attentions of large wild animals. In winter the smoke from the fires, drawn up by the draught of warm air rising away out of the cave, ensured ventilation. That is why at the cave mouth, and forward of it on the terrace outside, layers of ash and rubbish accumulated through the ages. When the gradual collapse of the front arch of the cave caused the hearths to be made farther back the later levels of human occupation retreated also, and are now to be found at some distance from earlier levels, on higher and higher banks of rock debris interspersed with thinner and thinner archaeological layers. The available living area was thus pushed farther back, gradually depriving man of sunlight and even daylight. The time eventually came when the cave entrance ceased to be used as a dwelling-place, though it could still be used as a cellar or temporary refuge, or for holding ceremonies, or for wall-painting.

The entrance to the cave or shelter was often modified, improved, or defended against wild animals by a fence of large rocks or thorn bushes. Sandy soil was reinforced by embedding river pebbles in it, as at Le Puy-de-Lacan (Corrèze), at the Dufaure shelter near Sordes (Landes), and at the Wildkirchli (Switzerland). At La Ferrassie (Dordogne) this sort of paving covers an area of some fifteen square metres. At La Font-Robert (Corrèze) an Aurignacian paving, entirely covered by the corresponding archaeological layer, covered fifteen square metres of the terrace outside the cave. It had been made of smooth pebbles, specially broken and arranged curved side uppermost, and covered with a mortar of grey ash. An even larger pavement was reported from the Knietgrote (Thuringia).

Recognizable improvements made inside caves are much rarer. In the Dufaure shelter (Sordes) the living space had been divided into two rooms by a party wall of dry stones. The most characteristic example comes from the finds made by D. Peyrony at the Fourneau du Diable (Commune of Bourdeilles, Dordogne), where there came to light, on the upper terrace, the remains of a Solutrean hut. The plan of this showed an irregular four-sided area, twelve metres long by an average seven metres wide, bounded on the north side by a bank one metre high on top of which was a row of large broken limestone blocks. To the east were other blocks, to the south a wall made of courses of large stones; to the west a side of the cliff-face and a rocky outcrop provided an underground shelter. At the south-east corner an entry 4·2 metres wide had been cut in the wall, probably being closed by skins or branches. The rough ground, which fell away steeply to the west, had been levelled up before the hut was occupied. Points where the stones were not close enough to give adequate protection had probably been reinforced by interwoven branches. D. Peyrony's theory is that "timbers must have been erected on the periphery of the rectangle, leaning together and joined at the top, so forming a roof of varying slope, probably covered with leafy branches. The occupants were thus protected from a disaster like the one which overwhelmed their predecessors on the lower terrace." Such collapses of cave entrances were common in Palaeolithic times. In this same part of the Périgord, in the phase known as Périgord II, an earth tremor caused the collapse of the Blanchard and Castanet shelters, at Sergeac, and at Le Ruth. At Laugerie Haute the victims of this earthquake lie in the layer known as Périgord III.

Palaeolithic peoples and their shelters were also in danger from the flooding of the rivers near which they so frequently settled. Occupation of the Bout-du-Monde shelter at Les Eyzies (Dordogne) depended on the state of flood of the river Vézère; after a short period of human occupation in Magdalenian II there can be noted, in Magdalenian V and VI, a fairly long stay continuing during the Azilian. The mixture of implements and river-sand shows that the climate was drier and river-flooding less of a danger. Even to-day, at La Madeleine, some water gets into the shelter every winter. The same applies to the history of the settlement at Le Mas d'Azil (Ariège), so closely linked to the variations in water-level of the river Arize. On the left bank the lower terrace was inhabited by Magdalenians; then immediately above the clay covering the first layer come the Azilian deposits. On the upper terrace a group of Magdalenians were driven out of their homes by flooding. A second group tentatively settled here again, but were again driven out by the rising waters. On the near-by river-silt, in a bed 85 centimetres thick, showing how far the Arize overflowed, can be found traces of the Azilians. In the period between the Mesolithic and the Neolithic the water-level fell, and the bank, now below the settlement areas, has dried up.

In all such dwelling-places the situation of the hearth was most important. There burned the fire that never went out, warming man, enabling him to cook his vegetable foods and give savoury taste to the meat grilled in the ash or on the embers. There were certain rules to be observed in setting up the fireplace: as far as possible it was in front of a rock, but far enough away for the flames to have free play; it had to be sheltered

F

from draughts and well in the light of the shelter entrance and easily controllable. It is rare not to find such conditions of comfort and safety constantly recurring in most inhabited shelters. In layer FI in the cave at Isturitz (Basses-Pyrénées), and in the upper part of layer E, the fireplaces show little difference. They were set up in depressions of medium size dug in the clay silt, then smoothed by hand and filled with very greasy ash containing little charcoal. The clay at the bottom of the depression was baked by the fire. Elsewhere, towards the bottom of layer E, we find built-up fireplaces. Flat stones and small slabs of sandstone formed a paved base, surrounded by pieces of limestone to keep the fire within bounds, while some of the larger ones probably served as seats. At this same level, forward of the great reindeer bas-relief, spread a vast bowl-shaped hearth, full of greasy black residue and surrounded by large pieces of rock, used as seats and also work-benches, as is shown by the considerable quantity of industry material and some very fine engravings found on the spot. Such improvements of interior arrangements were not uncommon and are to be found in the high-altitude shelter for bear-hunting on the Wildkirchli, made after the Riss-Würm inter-glacial period. Here a rough table had been made with stone slabs joined together. Elsewhere, at Bos del Ser and at Pré-Neuf (Corrèze), the fires had been made on a small paved area where some of the corners were protected by two stones on end. All around the hearth the dried, hardened earth had been trodden flat by the human occupants. Some fires were also made at quite a distance from the mouth of the cave. At the Drachenloch (Switzerland) traces are found 325 metres below, near burial-places and piles of bones.

The baking-oven was not unknown in prehistoric civilization. A dry-stone oven on the Drachenloch between 30 and 40 centimetres in diameter still contained, when found, a bed of pine charcoal 34 centimetres thick, and on top of that bones from the paw of a cave bear such as man came up to great heights to hunt at the end of autumn. At La Coumba, Pré-Neuf, Noailles (Corrèze) was found a braising-oven, built in a rectangle with flat stones set on end, slightly inclined inward towards each other, with the gaps at the corners carefully filled with smaller stones held in position by a mixture of clay, limestone, and sand. The small receptacle was completely covered with a thick layer of black ash from the fires that had been lit all around it.

Other interior improvements were designed to make this sort of shelter more comfortable to live in. Just as at Isturitz, certain places were reserved for the different activities of the community: at the Mousterian levels of La Cueva del Castillo (Spain) a collection of stone points marks the workshop where chipping went on. Cupboards of dry stones closed by slabs, as well as caches dug in the ground and concealed by flat stones, must have been used as food-stores or safes for precious objects.

In loess regions, where man dug his dwellings in the ground, seats cut out of the loess were provided (Langmennersdorf, Austria), and to protect the bases against damp the walls were lined with limestone slabs and the floor covered with a layer of flints.

So it was inside this kind of shelter that the small community lived its daily life, and since the place was both workshop, kitchen, and store, it was fitted with certain rough equipment. Yet, although he was aware of the properties of baked clay, Palaeolithic man made no pottery. He was a nomad, and so not to be encumbered with such fragile utensils. Baskets of wickerwork or woven fibre and leather or wood containers were sufficient. Of the former we have illustrations, such as the drawing of honey-gathering at La Araña (Spain), while the existence of the latter is proved by the nature of some sorts of kitchen refuse. In Northern Spain shellfish, such as *Littorina* and *Trochus*, were, of course, an important part of human diet in Upper Palaeolithic times. However, these creatures cannot be extracted alive from their shells, and since these show no sign of having been burnt or cracked, they must have been cooked in some sort of leather or wooden bowl. In the Basque country, even to-day, a similar technique is used for heating milk, red-hot stones being dropped into a wooden tub. Besides these utensils, one can imagine that extensive use was made of other containers borrowed from the animal kingdom, in the shape of small animal skulls, and, in warm climates, from the vegetable kingdom, in the form of calabashes.

When the ground was frozen other receptacles were made in it near the shelter, such as silos where meat could be kept for quite a time. In other places quarters of venison were placed on raised platforms out of reach of marauding animals, as is still done to-day among the Indians of the American Far North.

In Mesolithic times the climate changed and the sharp, dry cold gave place to a milder, damper period. This caused profound changes in the aspect of the landscape and the type of animals to be found there, the most dangerous then remaining being the wolf, the last of the lions, and the bear. This led to a great development of open-air dwellings, though caves and rock-shelters were not entirely abandoned. Men of the Sauveterrian and Tardenoisian civilizations, relying for a great part of their food resources on fishing and shellfish-gathering, usually settled along the shores of rivers, lakes, or the sea, where their kitchen refuse often collected in immense piles, called in Danish and Portuguese *kjoekkenmoeddings* and in English *kitchen middens*. The Mesolithic peoples lived in groups of huts, preferring to site their settlements on sandy soil, avoiding clays that became so muddy after rain, but in Denmark they had already, in peat-bog areas, laid down firm foundation layers of branches to build their camps on (Maglemose).

Some of the improvements made to living quarters during these times show the progress in organization made by certain human communities. In the Natufian cave at Mugharet-el-Oued, on Mount Carmel, Palestine, the rocky platform at the entrance to the dwelling had been trimmed with a pick and four cisterns hewn out of it, one of them with a circular, raised rim.

THE LIVING CONDITIONS OF PALAEOLITHIC MAN

Within the cave or shelter, then, the members of the group lived in very close community dictated by the vital daily need to find food and to help and defend one another. Their only bond was the family. Man in isolation was doomed.

There is as yet no sure way of determining with any exactness the density of such settlements, and thus of the population. The random manner in which areas then inhabited have been explored makes it impossible to produce reliable maps showing their distribution. Regions with caves and rock-shelters seem to have been the most thickly populated, but we seriously lack information about open-air settlements, discoveries of which have often been fortuitous.

The picture is still further blurred by the constant wandering of peoples, often random or on the spur of immediate necessity. Yet their movement went beyond the range of mere hunting trips, and through the ages some of these small groups of wanderers helped to spread their civilization over very large areas. It cannot be mere chance that accounts for close similarities in the equipment of sites as far separated as Le Placard (Charente) and Mammoutowa (Cracow), and one should not rule out the probability of great treks, over very long distances, taking Palaeolithic groups for a time far from their original homes.

The caves and shelters were not, in fact, occupied all the year round, at least in regions influenced by glacial climate. Evidence that they were in use from November to March has been found in the form of reindeer antlers, usually naturally shed, and young horns still attached to skulls. Now, young antlers are shed only in spring, while in fully grown animals, except females in foal, they fall at the end of autumn. Since the caves in the Pyrenees and the Dordogne yield neither the antlers of grown male reindeer, which were killed between July and November, nor shed antlers of young reindeer or even of deer, the conclusion can be drawn that during that part of the year the human communities had left their winter shelters and gone off to the hunting-grounds. They may have been following the reindeer migrating towards the Atlantic or Mediterranean coasts, or on their way back. On such trips they could have obtained seashells and met with the fauna of the sea-shore—for example, the sperm-whale teeth at Marsoulas and Isturitz and the pendant shaped like a flat fish from the Grotte des Bœufs at Lespugue.

The somewhat restricted living conditions of winter were followed by a season of wandering, of camping in shallow rock-shelters, preferably facing south or east in our latitudes, or in light huts made of branches and grass. They went wherever the flocks of Herbivora they were hunting took them, and it is thus obvious that any precise attempt to reconstruct the life of such nomads is impossible. Every trace of most of their camps has vanished, and, among the rare remains that have come down to us, important differences between specimens of weapons or implements make it difficult to interpret the facts correctly, since they represent various kinds of activity often quite unknown to us. It is difficult to believe that the only aim of these wanderings was hunting. The same group may for a time have gone on a hunting expedition, then stopped for a period to gather tubers, roots, berries, mushrooms, eggs, and wild honey (La Araña, Spain). Also they must have fished when the salmon came up the rivers to spawn. It would be quite natural, in all these varied stages, for the type of camp, the dwellings, and the equipment to be noticeably different in each case. Yet even the seasonal rhythm of Palaeolithic life was dominated by one constant, unifying factor: on the move or in camp everything was closely linked to the ceaseless search for food and raw materials (flint).

Dispersion in summer, concentration in winter—this is a form of symbiosis found among Eskimo tribes living after the manner of the animals they hunt. Summer opens up an almost limitless field for the chase, while winter hems it within the narrowest bounds, and these alternations explain the phases of expansion and contraction in the shape of the whole organization, men banding together or separating like their prey. The movements giving life to the group are synchronous with those in the ambient life of Nature, and social activity is not at a constant level throughout the year, but goes through regular, successive phases of increasing and decreasing intensity, of rest and action, of expenditure of energy and retrenchment (Marcel Mauss).

Such variations affected not only the material life of Palaeolithic communities, but also, as we shall see, their religious experiences and, in ways quite beyond our knowledge, their social organization and contacts between individuals. For Eskimos in summer life is, so to speak, secularized. On the other hand, their settlements live in winter in a state of almost constant religious exaltation. Then is the time for tribal rites, for initiating youths to tribal traditions and beliefs, and to the rights and duties of the adult state; time also for magic ceremonies aimed at increasing the number of useful animals, destroying the great predators, and casting spells over game. Advantage is taken of the stores of food laid in during the summer, weapons and tools are made ready for the next season, skins and furs made into clothes, and containers of leather, wicker, or bark prepared for gathering extra food. Might it not also be that in early times, during this close season, the work of decorating places of worship went on? Such activity, requiring skill born of long patience, in moments snatched from an exceptionally hard kind of existence during which the community must have guaranteed the artist some relief from material cares, can really be said to indicate a first attempt at specialization in work.

This division of society into tiny compartments, which limited the seasonal hunting migrations more than might at first be thought, still leaves room to suppose that there was some development of exchanges of raw material, like flint, or craft products, like stone lamps, and later probably seashells. Among the Mediterranean communities trade in these shells and in fossils during the later Palaeolithic and Mesolithic times caused men to move from inland towards the sea, or vice versa in Palestine and on the Saharan and Barbary coasts.

Such barter expeditions between Palaeolithic groups and the existence of defined hunting territories imply knowledge of traditional routes, rough tracks used by hunters and travellers and bound to pass through certain fording-places or over certain passes in the hills, usually following, as among primitive peoples to-day, the natural paths along river-lines and watercourses.

CLOTHING AND ORNAMENT

Though we can, to some extent, reconstruct the main stages of man's life in Palaeolithic times, his implements, and even some of his domestic equipment, we run into very serious difficulties when we try to describe exactly details of his dress and ornament.

Except in cold countries, all hunting peoples are more ornamented than clothed: belts, loin-cloths, headgear, are all more of a decoration than a covering. The source of this may be sought in the desire of the individual to distinguish himself from the group, for reasons as often psychological as material—desire to attract goodwill or attention, to show age or standing in the tribe, or whether he is single, married, or a widower. Or again it may be connected with religious ceremonies, war, or mourning.

Dating from early Palaeolithic times, in the Acheulean level of the rock-shelter at El Castillo (Santander, Spain), in the Mousterian level of the same cave and of La Cueva Morin (Spain), and at La Chapelle-aux-Saints (Corrèze) finds were made of colouring matter, red or yellow ochre and haematite, intentionally brought to the sites, while at La Ferrassie (Dordogne) there were stone palettes still bearing colour-stains and tubes made of bird bones or shin-bones of Cervidae or Equidae which had contained colours in powder form. These are thought to have been used for painting the body, a custom which may, at first, have been merely for hygienic purposes, but which persisted and spread during the Upper Palaeolithic and is seen also in funeral rites.

Similarly, and for the same reasons, prehistoric men practised tattooing and scarification. One of us (H. Breuil) has pointed out that on two naturalistic drawings of men in the rock-shelter at Minateda (Albacete, Spain) there are sexual deformations and mutilations, probably intentional in character. Cave art provides representations of tattooing in relief (statuettes at Předmost and Dolni Vistonice, Moravia, at Kostienki, Southern Russia, and at Isturitz, Basses-Pyrénées).

There remains, however, a whole group of perishable ornaments that we have lost for ever. These were decorations borrowed from the animal or vegetable kingdoms, such as wooden spikes or rods for the nose, lips, ears, or ankles, flowers, foliage, cloths of grass or bark, skins, and feathers. All that has come down to us are the many-coloured stones, rock-crystals, bones such as antelope hooves, rabbit knuckle-bones and claws, fishbones, and, of course, shells. These latter were often of very early origin, like the faluns of Touraine, Poitou, and the Gironde which provided shells for the peoples of the Dordogne, the Tarn-et-Garonne, the Puy-de-Dôme areas, and also Liguria. Besides these fossils, the Palaeolithic occupants of Laugerie Basse (Dordogne) also used species coming from the Atlantic and the Mediterranean. At Thayngen (Switzerland) a find was reported of Miocene fossils from the neighbourhood of Vienna (Austria).

Shells and teeth played an important part in what little we have been able to reconstruct of Palaeolithic costume—for example, in the pectoral chains, hair-nets, frontal diadems, necklaces, and bracelets made from *Nassa neritea* and found in the burial-places at the Grotte des Enfants, La Barma Grande, and the Grotte du Cavillon at Grimaldi.

The thousands of tiny, specially pierced *Nassae* found by E. Rivière in No. I burial-place at the Grotte des Enfants, covering the bodies from the waist to the knees, showed plainly that there had existed a sort of short skirt of strings or hair on which the shells had been threaded, to be fixed to a belt.

In the cave on Mount Carmel D. Garrod found other adornments gracefully arranged, in the form of complex nets with tastefully designed folds, draped over certain parts of the bodies buried in the Natufian period.

Some relics of French Palaeolithic art, such as the loin-cloth of the lady of Lespugue and the furs of the little dancers of the Mège shelter (Dordogne), are all too rare examples of these costumes.

The rock-paintings of Eastern Spain provide the most detailed evidence of this clothing and ornament. There are the cloche-skirts of the ladies of Cogul and Minateda, the skin breeches of the bowmen in the Abri dels Secans (Teruel), the fringed belt of Mas d'en Josep (Castellón), the garters, sometimes fixed to one leg only, bracelets on forearm and elbows, headdresses of feathers, shells, and teeth, caps with upstanding tassels like animals' ears, and the ring like a crown on the falling man at Barranco de Valtorta.

The women's hair-style was fairly varied: sometimes the hair was cut in the 'Nubian' style (Brassempouy, Landes), sometimes it was arranged in two little 'buns' (the walking child at Minateda).

Another source of detailed information is provided by the presence, in many deposits dating from the Upper Palaeolithic period, of a very varied range of equipment for dealing with skins, such as bone buttons with centre holes, often decorated with engravings, and spikes and sewing-needles made of bone, ivory, and reindeer antler. From these it can be concluded that clothes were made of skin or furs sewn with thread made from reindeer tendons or horsehair. The very range of this equipment seems to show that such clothing comprised a considerable number of separate items, and comparison with Eskimo costume seems valid. One example is the fur coat open over a richly embroidered shirt, of the same deep-red colour as the background, and the cap decorated with hanging tassels worn by the man at Angles-sur-Anglin (Vienne).

THE LIFE-SPAN OF PALAEOLITHIC MAN

In the light of all the evidence available from prehistoric archaeology the least that can be said is that life, for Palaeolithic man, seems to have been extremely harsh and precarious. That is why the life-span of fossil man was very considerably shorter than for us. Dr H. V. Vallois noted that

> out of 187 individuals of determinable age, more than a third (55 per cent of Neanderthal, 34·3 per cent of Upper Palaeolithic, 37 per cent of Mesolithic men) died before the age of twenty; most of the remainder (40 per cent of Neanderthal, 53·9 per cent of Upper Palaeolithic, 58·5 per cent of Mesolithic men) died between twenty and forty. Beyond this there are only 16 individuals, most of whom (relative proportions for the three types being 5 per cent, 10·8 per cent, and 15 per cent) died between forty and fifty. Only three lived over fifty years—the man at Obercassel, one at Hoëdic, and one at Montardit—and even these could not really be classified as old men, since, in all three cases, quite large sections of the cranial sutures were still open.

The further deduction can be made that there was a fairly large difference in the life-spans of men and women. Among the Neanderthal group the four who lived over thirty years were all men; in the Upper Palaeolithic out of eleven of determinable sex who lived over forty years ten were men; and in the Mesolithic the three who lived over forty years were again men. The proportions are exactly reversed for mortality between twenty and thirty years of age, so that mortality among women was very much higher before forty.

This short expectation of life was the inevitable result of the precarious existence led by Palaeolithic and Mesolithic peoples, totally dependent as they were on hunting and gathering what food was available. Before agriculture and stock-rearing were known it was almost impossible to store vital reserves of food, and the hunters lived under the constant shadow of danger and severe hardship.

A comparison between the life-span of fossil man and wild mammals seems to prove that such early mortality was not really abnormal. As in mammals, it is at the age when sexual activity diminishes—that is, about fifty for men or a little earlier for women—that most of the human organs show signs of declining vitality, and, as Dr H. V. Vallois points out, this was the age at which fossil men died. The longevity so common in our times is but the result of advanced civilization and could not be expected to occur in primitive societies.

[7]

Chipped stone implements and weapons

Their use—Stone used raw, or slightly modified, but not chipped—Chipped stone —Flake implements

---

THEIR USE

Prehistoric man made his implements of stone to meet the same needs for which we use iron and other metals. No doubt at first he just picked up sharp or pointed stones lying about on the ground, and later made them for himself by percussion.

With these stones he had to work on wood and bone, just as we do with choppers, chisels, gouges, files, saws, and punches. From animal carcasses he cut up he had to remove the fat and tegument attached to the skins, soften these, and make them into thongs and pieces usable for clothing. Other tools were required to strip, flatten and smooth bark from certain trees, to make personal ornaments, to pierce shells and teeth, and later to make eyes in bone needles. Then, when work on bone improved and it played, along with horn and ivory, an important part in human industry, still further implements became indispensable for cutting it into lengths to be scraped, polished, and made into spear-heads or engraved into *objets d'art*.

For hunting and war weapons were necessary, and wood must have been used prior to stone before serving merely as the handle or shaft. Such weapons had to be capable of piercing animal skins and penetrating deeply, or else, when used as axes or clubs, of cracking skulls and bones.

To fix stone war-heads to their wooden supports some kind of bond was required, and leather strips, unravelled tendons, or vegetable fibres were used, with resin as an adhesive. All this demanded a wide range of tools, some with cutting or jagged edges, others for grinding and rolling, the latter being river pebbles which were also useful for crushing seeds, tubers, and ochre and beating out bark or rushes.

Heavy tools were also vital for digging out tubers and flint, preparing foundations for huts, and making hunting pitfalls. For such uses the early equipment invented must have been simple, with improvements added subsequently and, once acquired, never forgotten.

The study, in recent or modern times, of primitive peoples so retarded that they can be considered as living in the Stone Age has, to a certain extent, given a more exact idea of how some types of stone implements were used. Even so, it is only by detailed examination of the actual specimens and the traces of wear on them that their real applications can be inferred, and then with only relative certainty, since the use by contemporary peoples of similar articles shows that such deductions should be treated with reserve. For example, what we call an 'end-scraper,' also often used as a chisel, serves in Australia as a sort of pen-knife.

Again, only deduction can suggest whether a particular implement had a handle, and, if so, how the stone was fixed to it.

Due account being taken of the foregoing considerations, we shall use, in referring to the various types of stone implements, a set of terms that has gradually been built up, since it is at least a working vocabulary of agreed meanings.

STONE USED RAW, OR SLIGHTLY MODIFIED, BUT NOT CHIPPED

Pebbles of tough stone like quartz, quartzite, basalt, or granite, either round or oval and of suitable size for a firm grip, occur in hundreds on Stone Age sites and even later. Some served unmodified as missiles, but others were used as grinders or rollers and show marks of crushing or localized wear due to pressure or friction against the larger, flatter surface of a nether millstone. From pre-Mesolithic times the latter shows not only radial grooves but general denting designed to increase its bite on the seeds and various kinds of ochre being ground. Frequently the colouring matter produced by the latter activity has been retained on the rough surface of the stone. The powder for colours, and probably also the grease, was also worked up on flat stones that have been found similarly stained and must have been used as palettes. Their surface is smooth with tiny lines running in all directions, made by the specks of quartz in the ochre powder as it was mixed, probably with a spatula. These colour palettes, often of raw shale in Upper Palaeolithic times, were, in Neo-Eneolithic and the late Stone Age in Africa, carefully

cut and polished into geometrical, or even animal or human, shapes
and embellished with sculptured, or more often engraved, designs.

Among the fixed implements, one of the most primitive is the *anvil*, an
unmodified block of raw stone, though the base was often trimmed and
chipped to bed it down more firmly. The upper part, roughly a cone or
pyramid, bears traces of the numerous blows that have scarred and more
or less blunted it. In bipolar chipping the lower, supporting billet re-
ceives a deep impact dent, and the active face of the striker has a
similar depression in the middle.

Flint strikers, which were too brittle and dangerous for the operator's
hands, were rarely used, save where it was impossible to get other stone of
adequate hardness and cohesion, like quartz, quartzite, basalt, and hard
sandstone, all of which were sought in the form of easily handled pebbles.

Basalt seems to have been particularly favoured in some Mousterian
sites. After lengthy use the strikers took on subspherical shapes, and
were so pitted as to be usable as graters. Softer specimens of this stone,
in particular, were used as *bolas*.

CHIPPED STONE

From the very dawn of human time jagged pieces of hard rock must
have been used because of the obvious applications for their spikes and
natural cutting edges, and it cannot have been long before percussion
was used to give a better grip or repair damage due to wear and tear.
Yet, though it is rarely possible to distinguish between minor adaptation
and natural modification, there is no mistaking, in the times when industry began, the improvements made to various sizes of natural pebbles
that were made easier to grip by rough chipping of one of their faces.
Such stones abound on sea- and river-shores, on beds of glacial material,
or old geological strata of similar origin. This elementary technique
was applied from the very beginning and has been called the Kafuan,
or Pebble, Culture, and, being the easiest and simplest, continued
through all subsequent periods.

No doubt it also happened that the chippings thus produced attracted
the attention of the worker by their very sharp cutting edges and their
light weight, so that he then tried to reproduce them by a more
methodical process with two different products: the block could be used
for itself or to make large implements, while the chippings gave lighter,
more varied, and more efficient tools like knives, picks, and slicers.
The former has been termed the *nucleus* (or core from which the
chipping comes) and the latter are known as *flakes*. We shall now give
some detailed consideration to the former.

Most nuclei, or cores, show numerous negatives where flakes have
been removed, and they have often been used for another purpose—
perhaps as stones for throwing, some of them being fairly regular sub-

spherical polyhedra, varying in size from a walnut to a large orange or greater. In Mousterian times their trimmed edges show that they were put to other uses, as polishers or scrapers, especially when they were fairly thin discs. In the Levalloisian period and mostly during the Upper Palaeolithic age the bevelled edges of their striking faces were used like chisels or choppers, or, in the smallest examples, as a core-scraper, similar to a plane.

Other, more powerful implements, chipped out of either blocks, large pebbles, cores, or slabs, were made with a view to immediate special uses. Some were chipped from both edges on both sides, either on both sides from both edges or from a single edge, or else on a single edge from either side, alternately. These are known as *bifaces*, either perfect or imperfect. If only one side has been worked on they are known as *unifaces*, the unworked side showing as pebble, core, or original flake. Their purpose, as well as the method of holding them, however, is shown by the two ends, the base, and the work on the edges.

Mainly during Abbevillian but also frequently during Acheulian times the base was thick and bulbous, with the smooth surface of the pebble or core, showing that the grip was directly over it. It does happen that the unworked part, instead of being at the base, is on one side, giving lateral grip. These are known as *choppers*.[1]

In other cases, particularly during the Acheulean and Levalloisian periods, the bases and edges are also sharp and would have hurt the user's hand unless intended for very gentle work. It is probable that some, at least, were fitted with handles of a kind, the base either being fixed on a short handle or covered with bark or skin. Others may have been fixed at right angles into the bulbous part of a club, making it a more deadly weapon.

The end opposite the base is usually pointed, and either thick enough to withstand use as a pick, or rounded and sharp enough to be a hatchet, or pointed like an auger or a dagger. Some, on the other hand, have retained part of the original cutting edge of the flake, square and running more or less right across, giving a powerful bevelled cutter, as wide as a small axe or as narrow as a chisel.

The lateral edges are no less varied. Some are straight, some concave, more often convex and so capable, if used as a hand tool, of cutting, scraping, or pounding. Observation of the lateral plane shows that they may be irregular zigzags made by taking alternate chippings from both sides, or may have a straight, more or less sharp, cutting edge. This indicates that at times (Abbevillian) the anvil work was imperfect, and,

[1] Before the War this term meant a biface with one cutting edge. Since then regrettably vague terms like *chopping-tools* and *choppers* have been made to designate almost any type of implement. In this case any tool not intended to cut, bore, or scrape could be so called, and the words then lose all clear and definite meaning. (H.B.)

at others the main importance was attached to the usable end, probably destined for a special purpose, while the lateral edges were merely roughly squared off.

Finally, the shapes and sizes of these objects vary considerably, showing the great variety of their uses. They may be disks, ovoids, short or elongated ovals (called *limandes*—'dabs'—in French), and ellipses; some are even shaped like spindles, hearts, pears (with globular bases), triangles, and spear-heads, all forming a complete range of instruments in the same style or of similar manufacture, and not at all to be considered as a single set of general-purpose tools. They were made, over the ages, according to the different methods in use at the time. Mainly in the Abbevillian period it was by rough chipping on an anvil with a hammer-stone, giving short, steeply rising facets. In the Acheulean period and later it was by chipping and long, flat trimming requiring percussion with wood and bone. Some are enormous, such as picks weighing several kilograms and needing two hands to wield them, while others, only four or five centimetres long, could be mounted on a handle or used in the bare hand for delicate work.

These implements, often called *coups-de-poing*, a generic and mostly incorrect term, were used at many archaeological levels, from the beginning of the Quaternary until the last Ice Age, which is more than three-quarters of the time man lived in prehistory.

FLAKE IMPLEMENTS

When flint cores were being roughly shaped during the first chipping they gave hundreds of usable *flakes*, of which only a few were in fact put to use on the work-site. They can usually be recognized by their irregularity and by the preservation, on the back, of the cortex of the original block.

In very early times, like the Abbevillian and the Clactonian, nearly all flakes look like this. Later, however, though they are always found in great numbers, they do contain special flakes removed from cores prepared for that specific purpose; and then these are either true flakes, where the breadth is more than half the length, or else they are *blades*, with a length much greater than their breadth. Such implements could be used directly, without modification or trimming, but, except for the chipping technique used, none can be said to be characteristic of an age or an industry. On the other hand, those which were trimmed for a special purpose could give rise to types which may be characteristic of a particular level and may have had a temporary vogue.

Flakes of the Clactonian, Acheulean, Tayacian, Levalloisian, Mousterian, and, to a lesser extent, later periods are to be distinguished by trimming on the base, at the point, on one or both sides, or all round the edges.

Base trimming may have been used with a view to eventual fixing on a handle or shaft, the bulb or part of the back nearest the striking platform being removed. The base could also, like the other end, be trimmed into a concave, straight, or convex scraper. The end could be made into a similar scraper, or could be shortened by cutting across, perhaps obliquely, and retrimming. Often it was trimmed into a more or less sharp point designed, according to the specimen, for making holes (punch or auger), digging (straight or lateral beaked graver), or piercing, like a dart or a lance-head, when the trimming was on one or both sides. More rarely this end, left with a broad, sharp cutting edge, was kept for use as a chisel.

The sides were left sharp enough to cut, but, very frequently, one was then trimmed down to reduce the sharpness, as for a backed knife, and left more or less convex, with the end pointed. In other cases one or other of the sides had its cutting edge notched by spaced indentations of varying depth, giving a saw-blade, though it was not used as such. Here again the edges were trimmed into convex, straight, concave, sinuous, or angular scrapers. Certain concave scrapers, less extensively worked and often multiple, are *scorers*, some meant for scraping wands or sticks, others as wedges for attaching implements to handles by thongs.

All these basic types could often be combined to produce a great variety of complex tools, usually trimmed on one face only, but sometimes with inverted or alternate retouching. Along with scrapers and points are to be found scraper-points, scraper-knives, point-knives, point-augers, scraper-chisels, beaked scrapers, scorers, punches, and knives.

Each kind of object, trimmed according to the technique prevailing at the time, appeared in shapes as varied as the random circumstances of the chipping that produced it. When blades predominated, in the Upper Palaeolithic, the outlines of the types derived from them were much less subject to capricious variation and could perform the same work, being meant for related specializations. Alongside them lengthy flakes, more or less intentionally cut, continued the old traditions, in spite of their different techniques, and were improved by the newly discovered ways of making special tools.

The lateral or terminal angle of one end (rarely the base) of a flake or blade, generally fairly thick, could be made into a graver, with the narrow cutting edge more or less vertical to the flake face. It was done by taking off, by one or more lateral blows, one or more pieces longitudinally from one or both of the converging lateral edges. This produced a very hard, sharp cutter. Such tools, used as gouges or very narrow chisels, occurred sporadically from early Palaeolithic times, but became very common and highly diversified as soon as bone and reindeer antler began to play an important part in the range of man's implements—that is to say, in the Leptolithic period.

[8]

Stratigraphy

Action by man—Action by burrowing animals—The nature of the strata

It is not sufficient to be able to recognize that a stone implement is the work of man. We also need to be able to classify it in at least some relative order, to consider it as part of a certain body of different objects, of later date than others or preceding another set of different groups.

Here reliable information can be obtained from the superposition of the layers or strata containing the objects, always provided that it is not the result of some later disturbance which may have upset or even reversed the order of the factors to be taken into account. Such study of strata, called stratigraphy, profiting by methods used in geology, geophysics, and palaeontology, permits classification in a fixed order of the finds made in the layers successively deposited by Nature one above the other. There will, of course, appear in each layer 'reshuffled' objects, but their 'physical' state will normally enable them to be detected. It is logical that only the most recent objects in a layer will enable its age to be determined, provided they have not been introduced by some secondary process.

The simplest case is surely that of a shelter or cave. It is generally known that these were usually filled by some underground watercourse, unless they were of marine origin. So the oldest layers, below all other levels, will be formed of sand or river gravel, or in the second case by the sea-beach. When the cave became free of water it was then accessible to large and small animals seeking dark dens, mainly bears, hyenas, and lions. A floor of mingled sand and clay will contain the remains of their skeletons and those of the prey they took there to eat. Even in these early times it did happen that man visited such places in the course of hunting expeditions. He may have eaten what he had caught and made brief stays there. Broken bones, a little charcoal, and a few stone implements left behind will bear witness to his first use of the cave, after which the wild animals again took possession of their den for a short time. But man then succeeded in driving them out for good and settling in the cave mouth, if not permanently, at least too continuously for the beasts to return. Then fires were lit and a more or less continuous layer of ash, with the remains of food and the debris of industry, was formed; this is called a 'hearth,' or level of habitation. Then, for unknown reasons, and on many different occasions, after periods of occupation running into centuries (seasonal excursions apart), the habitat was abandoned for thousands of years. Often the occupants were driven out by the threatened collapse of the roof, or by a harsher turn of climate, with winds that made the site uncomfortable. Whatever the reason, there was then laid down, over the layer of human occupation, a sterile layer of rubble, with even larger stones or sand and clay brought in by drainage-water or loess blown in by the wind. Only animals would then use the place from time to time—for example, owls that left layers of rodent-bone remains from their accumulated vomit pellets. The whole process would be repeated several times, so that successive 'horizons,' first sterile, then the traces of human habitat, then sterile again and so on, were laid one on top of the other, to a depth, in some places, of only 10 metres, in others 20 or even 50.

Such is the closed book of which the archaeologist and the geologist must gently finger the pages to separate them one from the other, yet paying constant attention to the causes which in certain places may have garbled the text and confused the message.

Causes of error can be both human action and the work of burrowing animals subsequent to the formation of the layers. Gullying out by water and subsidence in underground tunnels are also at times to blame.

ACTION BY MAN

Man may have brought from a distance older chipped flints already given a patina by silt or rolled in river gravel. He may also have noticed that the lower levels of the shelter he was occupying contained stone implements and have started to dig them out as an easy way of obtaining tools. Usually a sharp-eyed observer can pick these out from their physical state.

Of course, when the implement has been worked on a second time the double patina facilitates detection of its origin in another area or layer. Finally, stratigraphical inversions can be caused by artificial levelling, as at Le Mas d'Azil (left bank), or where the deposits on a plateau have been washed down a slope, so that the contents of the

G

affected layers, starting with the most recent, have been re-deposited in reverse order (Le Grand-Pressigny).

ACTION BY BURROWING ANIMALS

These animals, when digging their earths or lairs, have mixed up and intermingled the layers, so that the true stratigraphy can be determined only by comparison with the undisturbed parts of the deposit.

THE NATURE OF THE STRATA

A loose or soft layer can be penetrated by hard and relatively heavy objects, so that these, especially if there has been any trampling or cryoturbation, may have sunk more or less deeply below the level to which they belong. When water has gullied into an older layer (Hornos de la Peña, Spain) the more recent layer may settle into the depression, perhaps not filling it completely, in which case the older level will be found at the same height as, or higher than, the more recent. Objects belonging to the first layer may also have fallen into the second. All this would lead an unwary searcher to invert the true stratigraphy, whereas the skilled observer would be on his guard against such incidents. Even if no sterile, compact stratum separates two layers, some interpenetration, due to one of the aforesaid causes, is always to be found. Furthermore, successive 'horizons' of the same colour, but not very thick, are very difficult, if not impossible, to separate, and it is vital to check them against deposits from a single short and undisturbed occupation.

Hard frosts, followed by spring thaws, produced in shallow shelters and cave entrances cryoturbation phenomena, bringing up to the surface buried objects. During the thaws they sank again, assuming an upright position, but reaching different depths and not going back exactly to where they were before. This process may have brought up near the surface older and more deeply buried objects, while more recent ones may fall lower than their original level; hence an intermingling of two levels in direct contact. The stratigraphical structure of layers that have been disturbed or inverted thus makes it indispensable for the investigator to take these sources of error into account and to establish the true sequence and origin of his finds by comparison with layers undisturbed by cryoturbation.

By a contrary effect, layers and their contents may be drawn down from upper levels, through faults or shafts leading down into the earth, and intermingled as the fall occurs, through gravity or vacuum.

When all these sources of error have been allowed for or eliminated it nevertheless remains true that a sequence of deposits, laid down in a certain order, is permanent and can reveal, at one or more points in a region, the chronological succession of fauna, climates, and civilizations.

In Western countries, under the very recent humus of medieval, Gallo-Roman, or Iron Age origin, can be found layers with bronze or ceramic objects and, lower down, polished stone implements and pottery. Within these layers remains of contemporary or recent fauna mingle with those of domestic animals. Lower still the latter, except the dog, disappear, as does polished stone and pottery. The flints are often very small and chipped into geometrical shapes—triangles, diamonds, trapezes, or crescents. The boar, the stag, and the elk predominate. This is the Mesolithic period.

Farther down traces of the dog are absent, but an important series of layers yield fauna of which some examples have, in our times, emigrated to colder countries. For Northern Europe, the Pyrenees and the Alps, these are the reindeer, chamois, ibex, saiga, musk ox, wolverine, arctic hare, marmot, lemming, gopher or spermophile, and polar fox—all, moreover, associated with the horse, wild ox, bison, lion, hyena, and brown bear. The deeper one goes down through the layers, the greater the frequency of occurrence of the great cave bear, the mammoth, and the woolly rhinoceros, all now extinct. The last of them lived in the taïga of Siberia, but could not withstand the conditions on the steppe or tundra, and obviously lived in regions then subject to the Arctic climate of the last Ice Age.

Men and their industries show enormous variety. They lived entirely by hunting, but those on the steppe and tundra were craftsmen and artists, working not only flint but also bone and ivory into a great range of implements and weapons. They left behind beautiful works of art—sculptures, engravings, and paintings. This was the latest Chipped Stone Age, the Leptolithic, or Upper Palaeolithic.

In contrast, the men of the taïga, or northern forests, of earlier times were very different, with squat skulls, low foreheads, prominent ridges across the brows, and large faces with prognathous jaws. They used bones as tools, but did not modify them. Their stone implements, though skilfully trimmed, showed little variety and were mainly points, scrapers, and short knives. These were the last members of a very ancient race, the Neanderthal men.

Though they are very rare in Western countries, some shelters or caves contain even older beds revealing man's presence by his implements (Le Lherme, Ariège) and sometimes by his bones (Malarnaud, Ariège). These must be traces of very early hunters of the cave bear, men who sometimes also fell victim to their quarry. There is a quite exceptional case at Mentone where man hunted both the hippopotamus and the *Elephas antiquus*, late reminders of the last interglacial period.

Going back still farther, we find no trace of man in our caves, but there are breccias containing bone or seashells, indicating warm-climate fauna, adhering to the walls and forming part of them. If man existed at that time he must be sought elsewhere, on open-air sites demanding even more thorough research. Such studies would bring us nearer to a more complete general notion of the relationship, in time, of the various stages of human development, not only to one another, but to the geological history of the earth.

[9]

General stratigraphy and the Lower Palaeolithic Age

Sea-coasts—River deposits—The Haute-Garonne terraces of the Piedmont reaches—Industries of the Garonne terraces—Other valleys—The Somme terraces in the vestibular valley—Palaeolithic industries of the Somme and in England

---

The chronology of the Lower Palaeolithic Age and the order of its industries can be determined with accuracy only by studying the sequence of geological deposits in Quaternary times, and in three main sectors—firstly, on sea-coasts, by fixing the correlation between the formation of the beaches and the deposits from industries; secondly, by examining the river deposits in the form of terraces, descending in tiers, even, at times, below the lowest bed of the present waterway; thirdly, by research into the distribution of industries with reference to glacial deposits and the connexion between these latter and the rivers flowing from the melting ice.

SEA-COASTS

In Quaternary times sea-beaches were laid down, and can be seen in descending tiers from about 100 metres above the present sea-level down to very near it. There were four different levels, called, in descending order, the *Sicilian* (90 metres), the *Milazzian* (60 metres), the *Tyrrhenian* (30 metres), and the *Grimaldian* (10–11 metres), together with one last rise in sea-level, almost within our era, the *Flandrian*. To these 'invasions' by the sea must be added retreats of the order of 100 to 200 metres, revealed by observation of the sub-aerial topography of the sea-bed on the offshore coastal platform and by the existence of offshore pebble-bars—sunk, for example, in the Channel at depths of 90, 60, 30, and 19 metres approximately. Account must also be taken of tectonic movements in continental earth-crusts which in more than one place have disturbed the order indicated above. Little information is, of course, available on the deep strata under the sea. However, Baron A. C. Blanc carried out near Pisa drillings going down 100 metres under the Mediterranean. Here the boring went through non-marine deposits made in the second half of the last Ice Age, all containing cold-climate fauna and Norwegian pines. Only one marine deposit, of a temperate nature, was included—at a depth of 22 metres—after which dune sands with Mousterian and Upper Palaeolithic industries were found.

All along the Mediterranean coast, at a height of about 10 metres, caves scooped out by the sea, at Grimaldian level and containing warm-water shells, many of them *Strombus bubonius* from India, were occupied by Mousterian tribes after the sea retreated to a level of 100 or more metres below. Such are the caves of Grimaldi, near Mentone, of Circeo, of Devil's Tower at Gibraltar, and those along the coasts of Algeria, Tripolitania, Palestine, and Syria.

At a level some 60 metres higher, and older than the Tyrrhenian and Milazzian stages, the Observatoire cave, made by the Sicilian sea at 92 metres, was visited, then occupied by Abbevillian, Clactonian, and Acheulian tribes not found at Grimaldi.[1]

Outside the Mediterranean, exploration of the Atlantic coast in Portugal, between Cape Espichel and Peniche, has given results remarkable in every way.

At Cape Espichel a low Grimaldian level at 10 metres yielded fairly common, large shells from warmish waters, with a single chipped pebble, probably 'Languedocian' in origin. At Peniche, at a level containing shells forming the floor of the cave at Furninha, the accumulations of dune sand dating from the time the sea went down contained a fairly early Mousterian industry and temperate warm-climate fauna with striped hyena and *Rhinoceros Merckii*, which coincided at Furninha, as on the Riviera, with the first signs of the end of glacial times.

The Tyrrhenian sea-level, very constant over the level indicated and better developed than the others, contains sea-rolled industries and others a little later in date than the fall in level, mingled with clays or windblown river or sea sand of red or yellow colour. These implements belong to the very early Mousterian period and, deeper down, to the Acheulean. After them come a more recent Mousterian, some Languedocian, and then a little Upper Palaeolithic.

Higher up the sea-levels have been observed only at Magioto and Açafora with any certainty, but then reduced only to sloping beach deposits covered with pebbles. The Milazzian, being too sandy, has

---

[1] But the Acheulean and Tayacian peoples are amply represented at the Lazaret cave near Nice, at a height of about 28 metres. (Comdr. Octobon.)

yielded few implements, but the Sicilian, full of hard-cored stones, produced an abundance of very primitive chipped pebbles with very rare proto-Abbevillian coups-de-poing.

In Morocco important discoveries were made by R. Neuville and A. Rühlmann, near Casablanca, where the four sea-levels had already been observed, with maximal heights of about 90 metres (Sicilian), 60 metres (Milazzian), 30 metres (Tyrrhenian), and 18 metres (Grimaldian). The first two contained a shell, now limited to Senegal and Chile, *Acantina crassilabrum*, replaced in the last two by the *Purpura hoemastoma*, still extant on the coast of Portugal. Each level was covered, above the sea-beach, by a series of deposits. These were by nature fluviatile, lacustrine, or of dune sand (hardened into building-stone), powdery, scabby limestone, and red clay, and formed a separation from the next most recent beach. It was already known that large quantities of chipped stones were to be found in and on the Tyrrhenian and Grimaldian beaches, the former being considered until then as marking the time of the appearance of man.

However, Neuville and Rühlmann found in the quarry at Sidi Abderrahman (basic height 28 metres) a superb direct superposition of the three first sea-levels with their beaches. The Sicilian was separated from the Milazzian by sub-aerial deposits, and the Milazzian formed a cliff against which the Tyrrhenian sea had washed and hollowed out caves. The three levels contained man-made implements. The oldest, the Sicilian, had in its offshore pebble-bar a few chipped pebbles, with only two Abbevillian bifaces, rolled by the Sicilian sea. But right on the beach was found a very large chipping workshop and habitat, with hundreds of implements, together with hippopotamus and rhinoceros teeth, in an extremely hard phosphate breccia. The tools were large Clactonian flakes, rechipped into bifaces or especially into Abbevillian trihedra— hence the name Clacto-Abbevillian given by the finders to this industry.

It gives place, in the bar of small river pebbles a little higher up, to another industry with rare flakes of medium size—the Tayacian, showing a mixture of modified Clactonian chipping technique and Levalloisian, the striking platform having prepared facets. Then comes the Sicilian dune formation, followed by the Milazzian high-water mark, where the beach again reveals the small-pebble industry. After an enormous sterile deposit of sub-aerial river, lake, and dune material the Tyrrhenian sea is shown as having hewn, at its highest level, a cliff and caves in this already hardened dune and casting up pebbles and shells, including rare rolled Abbevillian specimens. Acheulean man lived on this beach and used the caves, leaving behind only a few implements.[1]

[1] Very recent observations by M. Biberson confirm the foregoing by establishing the existence, in one of these Tyrrhenian caves, of a level containing cold-climate marine fauna, *Littorina*, covering a previous deposit of Acheulean times containing human remains of the *Atlanthropus* type.

At El Hank, four kilometres from Sidi Abderrahman, stands the Martin quarry. Here only the Tyrrhenian level, from 19 to 28 metres, is being worked, giving a magnificent cross-section of these deposits. Its offshore bar has jumbled and rolled a vast work-site containing Abbevillian bifaces and Clactonian flakes made from pebbles and quite different from those found at Sidi Abderrahman. They are older than the beach, but it is difficult to place them exactly. On the pebble beach Acheulean man came in his turn to chip countless implements. He did not hesitate to dig into the shingle in search of good raw material, and some of his tools, unrolled and wood-chipped, became embedded in the beach as he turned it over.

This means that the Tyrrhenian beach is not Abbevillian, but only Acheulean, or very little earlier. The Acheulean period continues at various sub-aerial levels of superposed river, lake, and dune material, ending with red clay dating from the end of the Acheulean, or Micoquian, period.

As for the sea at the level of 18–19 metres, referred to as Mousterian, its waves hollowed out caves in previously hardened dunes, and Aterian man (Mousterian with tanged points), followed by Oranian man (Upper Palaeolithic), lived there in late Quaternary times.

All this highly valuable information was produced by well-organized study of the sea-levels round these coasts: man appeared in West Africa and in Portugal from the time of the Sicilian level—that is to say, on and in the beach laid down immediately prior to the lowering of sea-level during the first, or Günzian, Quaternary Ice Age (the industries being Clacto-Abbevillian and Lusitano-Abbevillian).

In Morocco the Acheulean period developed on the Mindel-Riss sands, during the Rissian drop in sea-level, following on other industries with more or less typical Tayacian or Abbevillian flakes.

In Portugal the Acheulean remains, and then an early Mousterian type, occur in the Tyrrhenian sands and always have a very marked Lusitanian appearance, being mainly very simple chipped pebbles. After the Grimaldian beach at over 10 metres comes a Middle Mousterian deposit with warm-climate fauna, at Peniche, as in the Mediterranean sites. There then appears a chipped-pebble industry, the Languedocian, developing and competing alternately with an advanced Mousterian into Upper Quaternary times. This marks an evolution towards the somewhat more recent Northern Asturian industry with *picks*, the last stage of the Lusitanian era before the Mesolithic in the north-west of the Peninsula and, in Asturias, following on the Upper Palaeolithic and the Azilian.

RIVER DEPOSITS

Every river valley can be divided into several sectors, each being under the influence of certain dominant physical conditions. Firstly, along its lower course, *vestibular* or even higher, the river may have been subject to rises in the sea-level. In the middle reaches, if the bed runs through a plain, these factors will have had weaker effects. Secondly, that part of the middle reach or main channel that is separated from the lower course by rapids or waterfalls is, by this very fact, sheltered from the aforementioned marine movements, and the rate at which it digs its bed is controlled only by the volume of water flowing and the nature of the terrain's resistance to it. Each stretch, between one obstacle and the next, perhaps a weir or lake, forms a base-level for the preceding one and must be studied separately, having dug its channel at its own pace. There may seem to be a link between the erosion terraces both upstream and downstream from a particular reach, but this is only apparent, not real. Thirdly, the upper reach of a river coming down from a mountainous area can itself be divided into two: (*a*) the *mountain reach*, where the water flows into a zone formerly covered by ice and, as the slopes are too steep, has itself left little in the way of ancient deposits, but merely washed the glacial sediments downstream; (*b*) the *Piedmont reach*, where the river flows out into a plain, either still covered, or not, by old glacial deposits, and *still continues to dig its bed in the rocky, pre-Quaternary subsoil*. This will have left, on the tiered slopes of its channel, almost horizontal accumulations of large fluvio-glacial gravels, often forming *very extensive terraces* resulting from the current's spreading fairly evenly fluvio-glacial matter brought down from the mountains. Upstream the link between these terraces and glacial moraines can, at least as regards the most recent two or three, enable us to determine that their accumulation corresponds to a given glaciation and that the digging of the next lower level of terrace took place in the subsequent interglacial period. In this part of the river, therefore, each terrace is the work of one single period, and bears on its surface the sub-aerial layers since deposited in the form of sand, loess, or silt by the wind or drainage waters.

For the fullest study we ought to consider from this point of view, in Western Europe, the Rhine, the Rhône, and their tributaries; the rivers flowing from the Central Plateau, such as the Loire, the Allier, and the Dordogne; and those rising in the Pyrenees—the Adour, the Ariège, and the Garonne. We shall limit ourselves to the latter.

THE HAUTE-GARONNE TERRACES OF THE PIEDMONT REACHES

Between the high Lannemezan plateau, a vast, fan-shaped area of fluvio-glacial Pliocene origin, and the narrows at Toulouse the Garonne, after a fairly narrow plain between Saint-Gaudens and Saint-Martory, spreads out its terraces in a great crescent, entirely on the left bank, their greatest width being 25 kilometres near Muret. Here can be seen:

1. Top levels, Pliocene again, 130 to 135 metres above the Garonne, with no traces of human occupation.

2. *Upper levels*, about 90 metres above the river, with no known human traces, dating from between Pliocene and Quaternary times.

3. An intermediate terrace, at about 80 metres up, with rolled chipped stones.

4. An *intermediate level*, at 55–60 metres up, connecting with *Mindelian* moraines (Second Ice Age), containing chipped implements in and on the gravels.

5. The terrace at 30 metres up (*top lower level*) connecting with *Rissian* moraines (Third Ice Age), rich in finds.

6. The *bottom lower terrace* at 10–15 metres up, connecting with *Würmian* moraines at Labroquère. The granites and shales are not rotted down, as in the previous levels.

7. More recent terraces, post-glacial, at 6–7 metres and 2–3 metres up.

Palaeontological Evidence. The gravels, except those at 15 metres, are sterile and contain none, but breccias with bone remains exist in caves which could have been used by animals only after their entrances were cleared by the deeper hollowing-out of the valley. Above the 60-metre terrace (Mindel) and below the 90-metre level (Günz, First Ice Age) and so belonging to the first *inter-glacial* period, the breccias at Montoussé, Montsaunès, and Montmaurin were found to contain remains of the macaque, the *Machairodus neogœus* (the sabre-toothed tiger), Merck's rhinoceros, an elephant that is not a mammoth, the striped hyena, the porcupine, the *Cuon*, etc. Above the 30-metre terrace (Riss) at Le Picon (Montréjeau) the complex breccia was formed at three different times, the lower level giving *Elephas trogontherii*, the large porcupine, the roebuck, the brown bear, a powerful panther, a large boar, a *Hyaena crocuta*, a small wolf, etc.; the upper level was penetrated in Würmian times by marmots and other glacial animals of the period digging their burrows.[1] Warm-water molluscs preceded these in an intercalated red silt.

In the Garonne gravels at the lower levels of 15–30 metres were found only rare elephant tusks, of *E. trogontherii* rather than of the mammoth, though the latter was found at the 15-metre level at the Jardin des Plantes in Toulouse. The silt of the Ariège, overlying the gravels, yielded bones of the mammoth, lion, woolly rhinoceros, and reindeer (Würmian fauna).

INDUSTRIES OF THE GARONNE TERRACES

Finds made on the *80-metre terrace* of genuine, if not very numerous, implements include, as far as can be ascertained, some Abbevillian work.[2]

[1] Including Carnivora, which brought in some reindeer.
[2] Breuil and Méroe, *Préhistoire*, Vol. XI, 1950: "Les Terraces de la Haute-Garonne et leur quartzites."

On the *60-metre terrace* (Mindel) finds *in situ* occurred in rifts in the plateau and the banks of streams. Here the deep, rough gravels of rotted granite produced several Acheulean bifaces that had not been rolled. The upper layer of gravels, broken down almost to sand, contained specimens subjected to various degrees of rolling; some, heavily affected, were Abbevillian, others, less heavily or not at all, were early Acheulean. Intact Acheulean specimens were also to be found, showing that the 60-metre terrace is Acheulean.

Of the two superposed silts the older, of red clay containing a ferruginous conglomerate base, also yielded, towards the bottom, Acheulean work often showing heavy wind erosion. All these specimens were heavily stained by rust. Under the recent loess the basic layer of hard-cored stones contained tools from the final Acheulean period (Micoquian), with little staining and heavy wind erosion, but with smoothed edges. Higher up an industry of pebbles, often flat and chipped round the edges, was sometimes associated with certain Mousterian shapes of the *Languedocian* type for which softer stone was preferred, and sometimes with degenerate Acheulean work.[1]

In the streams of the 60-metre terrace, which have not broken through the terrace layer, the gravel is pure quartzite, since all the other rocks have been reduced to dust. Any finds here are pure Languedocian.

On the 30-metre terrace the layers are represented by sections of paths or canalized streams, and finds are on the surface. In the bottom gravels, all of quartzite, are to be found few bifaces, but much chipping waste, that has probably come down from a work-place used by Acheulean men, embedded in the bottom of the old silt of the 60-metre terrace. Elsewhere heavily rolled Acheulean specimens come from the Garonne gravels. In the overlaid loess much Languedocian work is often to be found, mingled with some Mousterian examples. A small axe-head with notches for taking a handle was an outstanding find.

The 15-metre level, at times covered by recent loess, has yielded some older pieces—small numbers of Languedocian types, lightly rolled at first, then unrolled, and followed by Neolithic work.

OTHER VALLEYS

In the Rhône valley one of the rare Lower Palaeolithic sites, at Curzon (Drôme), in river sand covering the Mindelian terrace at 60 metres, is pure Clactonian and identical with the station at the Observatoire cave at Monaco dating from before the fall of the Tyrrhenian sea-level.

Near Aurillac, Marcellin Boule found *in situ*, in deposits from the last interglacial period, a heart-shaped axe-head, Acheulean in style, but

---

[1] Some Languedocian shapes continue throughout the Leptolithic and Neolithic periods and even later, as in Roman and Arab urn-stoppers.

Mousterian in date. A few odd finds in the Ain and the Jura show the same signs of Micoquian or early Mousterian work in the last inter-glacial span, and this is confirmed by discoveries, on the terrace at Villefranche-sur-Saône, of Micoquian and Mousterian flints, with re-mains of Merck's rhinoceros and buck, none of which had been rolled.

THE SOMME TERRACES IN THE
VESTIBULAR VALLEY

When, in the times we are considering, a river flowed out of its Piedmont reach, supposing it had one, and into coastal lowlands it laid down, at decreasing heights, steps or tiers, less accurately termed terraces. These occurred at fairly constant levels when compared with the very deepest part of the river-bed, now well below the present bed and water-level, and consisted of wave-battered pebbles over fine sand—of horizontal stratigraphy and repeating the order of the pre-vious terrace.

Detailed examination of the composition of these terraces shows how complex they are, even allowing for the superposition of sub-aerial deposits. Indeed, each one reveals a succession of interlocking cycles of phenomena repeated in the same order and connected with the rises and falls of sea-level as well as climatic variations of temperature and rainfall. Each cycle could be analysed as follows:

1. Following a fall in sea-level of about 100 metres, the river scoured out its bed very deeply, while, in a glacial period of savage cold and heavy snow, solifluxion and deep frost rapidly wore down the sides of the valley weakened by the almost total destruction of vegetation. The very deeply cut channel became choked with heterogeneous material brought down by solifluxion, and this the river was able partly to wash away down its bed, but left on the upper slopes it no longer touched. Thus each terrace begins by a thick layer of *lateral drift* due to soli-fluxion, jumbled and heterogeneous with masses of combe-rock at its base.

2. When the sea next rose again at the interglacial phase the river partly covered slopes it had left, depositing fine gravels and stratified sand. The thickness of these layers increased in a downstream direction and linked up with formations in the estuary, if not with the local sea-beaches. Over these deposits the estuary waves laid down bars of pounded pebbles and horizontally stratified beaches of fine sand which ran very far upstream, at times almost as far as Amiens.

3. When, after one or more of these stratifications, the river gradually abandoned a terrace at the onset of the next glacial period, though not before it had sedimented some final layers of flood material and peat that have not always survived, the process of sub-aerial depositing was again resumed. The lowest water-level of the cycle was marked by a

layer of solifluxed rubble, in thickness anything from a few centimetres to 10 metres, that the river never again washed out at this level.

Then, during the dry times of the prevailing Ice Age when the cold was most intense, the processes of solifluxion ceased. Layers thus formed were partly washed out by melting snow, while jagged pebbles, battered in the drift, split and cracked into small, sharp fragments, making scree. Next came the deposit of a mantle of loess of irregular depth, thickest at the foot of slopes facing the prevailing north-east wind, but replaced on leeward slopes by rough sand made of tiny grains of chalk or quartz, depending on the nature of the neighbouring plateaux. This covering by loess was sometimes interrupted by short damp periods giving a layer of solifluxed pebbles or a shallow dome of peaty humus.

With the approach of the next interglacial phase, a final, though not very intense, solifluxion took place after the laying down of a little peat containing temperate shells, and the loess slope started to form.

The surface of the limestone loess changed and was decalcified, weathering into red clay and brick-clay. Rain fell heavily in the north, streaming down loess slopes already eroded into watersheds, while in the south it gave way to warm, windy, dry conditions. Plant life resumed on these surfaces and laid down its own humus layers, of which the latest is our topsoil, while the valley bottoms filled with layers of silt or sand and finally peat or marshland.

Such are the processes to be taken into account in considering the formation of the river terraces of the Somme, the Seine, and the Thames, not forgetting the colossal and repeated draining-out of the rivers when the water-levels fall during the Ice Ages, nor the ponding-back as the sea rose again in the interglacial periods.

Since solifluxion phenomena are, over a particular area, related in character and may furnish links with the glacial and interglacial phases, it is vital to try to establish their order of sequence, working back from the most recent to the earliest. On the Somme eleven have been detected, corresponding to the same number of peak periods of damp cold, not all of the same intensity:[1]

Sol. 11: weak solifluxion at the base of the brick-clay.

Sol. 10: fairly weak solifluxion, interrupting the final deposit of upper *L.* 3 (ergeron).

Sol. 9: fairly weak solifluxion, interrupting the middle deposit of upper *L.* 3 (ergeron).

Sol. 8: strong solifluxion at the base of the recent loess (ergeron, Würmian glaciation I.) This solifluxion comes above, and has

---

[1] In this table, proceeding from the latest to the earliest, *Sol.* or *S.* = solifluxion; *F.* = fluviatile level; *L.* = loess layer, followed by a figure indicating its sequence number.

partly modified, the fissured red clay of the last interglacial Riss-Würm phase. It also went down the slopes and overlay *F.* 4.

F. 4: small gravels and stratified sand of the lower terraces [Montières, Longpré (Somme); Cergy (Basse-Oise)]. Often destroyed on top lower terraces by *S.* 8 and later, better preserved on the outer edge of the bottom lower terrace. Last warm fauna (Somme, Oise; and Crayford near the Thames).

Sol. 7: weak solifluxion at the base of the fissured red clay (pre-Würm ?) which destroyed nearly all the last flood deposit on the 30-metre terrace (peat with temperate shells) and the 30- and 45-metre terraces. So-called 'old' *L.* 2.

Sol. 6: solifluxion at the base of the so-called 'old' loess (penultimate). Found, partially washed out, on all lower terraces at 17 and 22 metres and down to the bottom of the sunken valley (Riss II).

F. 3*b*: reddish sand from weathering and loessic flood silt, with warm shells, on the 30-metres terrace. Also old *L.* 1.

Sol. 5: very strong solifluxion at the base of shell-bearing silt at 30 metres, not washed out. It goes down at least to the 10-metre terrace (Riss I).

F. 3*a*: deposit from the second part of the 30-metre river terrace.

Sol. 4: solifluxion, perhaps multiple, spread through the river deposits of the 30-metre terrace at least (Mindel II or III).

F. 2: river deposit of the 30-metre terrace, its lower part overflowing, at Abbeville, on to *F.* 1 (45-metre terrace), from which it is separated by *Sol.* 3*a*; the Somme overflowed (in the early stages?) on to the 45-metre terrace.

Sol. 3*a*: very powerful solifluxion at the base of the 30-metre terrace (Mindel I). It goes no lower, but naturally spreads higher, between the two fluviatile levels of the 45-metre terrace, where it divides the deposit containing *Elephas meridionalis* from that with *Elephas antiquus*.

F. 1*b*: 'Marl' deposit of small Abbeville limestone pebbles, with sand and small gravel from the 45-metre terrace, containing *Elephas meridionalis*.

Sol. 2: solifluxion dividing into two the layers with *Elephas meridionalis* (Günz II ?).

F. 1*a*: lower river deposits of the 45-metre terrace, with *Elephas meridionalis*.

Sol. 1: bottom solifluxion, perhaps double (Günz I ?).

Each one of these solifluxions, as it churned up less resistant river deposits, reduced them considerably, and in places it may have penetrated to previously solifluxed layers. On the other hand, the river deposit could wash out the solifluxed layers, removing their clay and sand. Even when not carried away the river material was often by-passed and the order of its component elements upset. With the thaw it was invaded by large stones sinking by their own weight from an upper solifluxion.

In solifluxion each layer raked down the slopes all the fairly loose material, so that thin sub-aerial deposits were destroyed and the chipped flints in them mixed with others, knocked about, and carried down the slope, where, washed along by the river, they may be found side by side with more recent, intact implements dating from the time the waters rose again. Solifluxion also frequently upset the order of elements in river deposits themselves.

Thus a specimen bearing traces of solifluxion is always older than the deposit in which it is found.

The *evidence of fauna* in the deposits can be classed as follows. The recent loess contained, together with solifluxion rubble of the last Ice Age: typical mammoth, woolly rhinoceros, reindeer, musk ox, and so on, with small loess shells such as *Pupa* and *Succinea*,' already extant in the stratified, loess-type silts of the deeper level that are not much earlier than solifluxion 8.

The fissured red clay yielded no fauna remains, but the contemporary river deposits at 17 and 22 metres contained traces of the last hippo-potami, Merck's rhinoceros, *Elephas antiquus*, and *Corbicula fluminalis*, all found in the Thames Valley in England as well as in Northern France.

The old loess has produced few bones, but the surface underlying the preceding layer revealed, at Crayford, Rissian cold fauna, with musk ox, reindeer, mammoth, and woolly rhinoceros.

Corresponding to the solifluxion of the base of this old loess (*Sol.* 6) are the chalky rubbles of the lower layers at Montières-Étouvy, giving remains of mammoth, reindeer, and woolly rhinoceros, possibly partly attributable to *Sol.* 5 (Riss I).

The river-levels all had warm fauna—*Elephas antiquus* and *trogontherii*, Merck's rhinoceros, hippopotamus—from *F.* 2 onward, and developed into terraces at 45, 30, and 22 metres above the deep-buried bed.

River-levels 1 *a* and *b*, only found on the 45-metre terrace, were alone in yielding *Elephas meridionalis*, older types of *Elephas antiquus* and *trogontherii*, the Etruscan rhinoceros, and the *Machairodus neogæus*.

This is the same fauna as in the Forest Bed at Cromer (Norfolk), a prolongation of the Rhine estuary.

The shells at all the river-levels were temperate or warm.

PALAEOLITHIC INDUSTRIES OF THE SOMME
AND IN ENGLAND

A very few Abbevillian bifaces were found in the 45-metre terrace, dating from *Sol.* 1, and some in the overlying river deposits (*F.* 1*a*). They are numerous in the bottom of the layers containing tiny limestone pebbles, known as 'marl,' that occur at the Porte-du-Bois, Abbeville (*F.* 1*b*).

Solifluxion 2 churned up the Abbevillian work and mingled it to some extent with a flake industry, the Clactonian, dated slightly prior to it. This stage corresponds, near London, to a terrace marked as 137 feet above the present level of the Thames. The Thames then continued digging its bed and again deposited a Clactonian layer, solifluxed in places or not, but later in date than *Sol.* 2, on the floor of the terrace at 90 feet (at its base), then, downstream, at a lower level, near Clacton-on-Sea, peaty sediment containing *Elephas antiquus.* At this period a loess (?) or shell-bearing silt extended at London to 90 feet, followed by the Acheulean river deposits of the same terrace.

The 45-metre terrace of the Somme shows a second river-level of early Acheulean date (I–II), perhaps preceded by a fall in the water-level to 22 metres, for at that level was found an even earlier Acheulean (I *a*) industry, chipped in great, flat flakes, and no doubt corresponding to the second half of the English Clactonian period, not found in Picardy.

At the base of the 30-metre terrace solifluxion 3 swept down the Abbevillian and Clactonian industries, together with the early Acheulean taken from the 45-metre terrace; this received two river deposits separated by a solifluxion (*S.* 3), containing a middle Acheulean III, with an incipient Levalloisian, similar to the same industry at the second river-level of the 90-foot terrace of the Thames.

On the Somme there followed a very strong solifluxion (*S.* 5), with more Clactonian flakes covered by loess-type, shell-bearing sands and reddish sand. It swept down, at levels of 22 and 15 metres, whole work-sites of early Levalloisian I from higher up. The shell-bearing silt of the red sands contains specimens of spear-shaped Acheulean-IV work.

Solifluxion 6 of the base of the so-called 'old' loess 3 swept down a fresh stock of Levalloisian II, and by mingling with *S.* 5 in its lower levels mixed up Levalloisian I and II.

At the bottom of the old loess (*L.* 2) appeared *in situ* the Acheulean VI and, on top, a second level of similar date.

The weak solifluxion 7 swept to a lower level (22 and 15 metres) work-places of Levalloisian III, a lighter and smaller industry with blades, often found isolated, and much less damaged than series I and II.

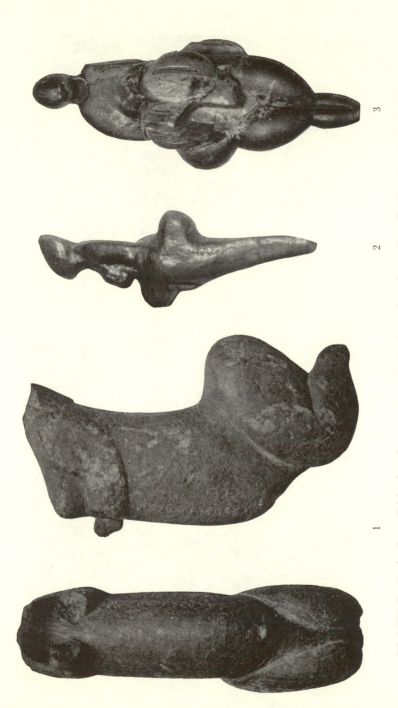

PLATE I. Early Leptolithic female statuettes. 1. Aurignacian, from Sireuil (Dordogne), in amber-coloured calcite. 2. Gravettian, in steatite, from Grimaldi, near Mentone. 3. Gravettian, in ivory, from Les Rideaux, Lespugue (Haute-Garonne). (1 and 2, Musée de Saint-Germain; 3, Musée de l'Homme, Paris.)

1

2

PLATE II. 1. Forepart of a feline, wounded with arrows. 2. Headless bear, also wounded. Clay models in the cave at Montespan (Haute-Garonne). Magdalenian IV.

Then came the fissured red clay, with Acheulean VI and VII at its base and on top, followed probably by Levalloisian IV, a blade industry, often isolated from Acheulean VI and interstratified in the river layers of *F.* 3, when not later mingled with them by solifluxion 8.

Levalloisian V, with many heart-shaped or triangular bifaces and large, wide flakes, appeared on the surface of solifluxion 8, with Levalloisians VI and VII on the surface of solifluxions 9 and 10.

The following table can therefore be set out, working from the top downward:

Biface Implements	*Flake Implements*
T. at 45 m. Abbevillian.	T. at 45 m. Clactonian.
T. at 22 m. Acheulean I*a*.	
T. at 45 m. Acheulean I*b*, II.	T. at 30 m. Thames: Clactonian II.
T. at 30 m. Acheulean III.	
	Levalloisian, swept by *S.* 5 at lower levels.
T. at 30 m. Acheulean IV (*L.*1).	
	Levalloisian II, swept by *S.* 6 and mixed with Levalloisian I at lower levels.
T. at 30 m. Acheulean V (*L.*2).	
	Levalloisian III, swept on lower terrace by *S.* 7.
T. at 30 m. Acheulean VI and VII in fissured red clay.	
	Levalloisian IV on low terrace only, where it is often mixed with Acheulean VI–VII by *S.* 8.
Recent loess (base) middle and upper.	Levalloisian V, partly Acheulean in tradition, then Levalloisian VI and VII and Leptolithic.

This table[1] refers specifically to the Somme, but could usefully be adapted for other areas, where a given level may be earlier or later than on the Somme. Thus in England the Clactonian is much more de-

[1] It must not be forgotten that this is still only a tentative working hypothesis. For one thing, east of the Rhine and even along the North Sea finds are beginning to be made of early industries belonging to either group—for example, in Hesse, which the glaciers did not cover, or from Flanders to Schleswig, where the sea is eroding levels underlying moraine deposits. It also seems that certain western industrial facies retreated before preceding advances of the glaciers, and so appear in these areas at more recent dates than where the industries started in the north-east.

Furthermore, the techniques described in this book are based mainly on the flint industries of Northern France and Southern England. They cannot have been strictly identical in other regions where the available tools must have been used for the initial cutting-up of large blocks of quartzite and other granular stone (Spain) and where all the tools, even the bifaces, had necessarily to be obtained by basic flaking in a more or less Clactonian manner. In the north-east industries with crude pre-Levalloisian flakes seem to have existed at a very early date. (J.-L. Baudet.)

veloped than in France, whereas early Acheulean is not common in the Thames Valley, though this does not apply towards Southampton.

On the other hand, though Acheulean IV–VII develop a more and more Micoquian facies in France, characteristic spear-head examples of this work, often quite roughly finished, at Swanscombe (Kent) become increasingly common as soon as one reaches the gravels[1] deposited over the shell-bearing silts which produced the remains of the Swanscombe skull, and yet which belong to the Mindel-Riss river terrace and were laid down by a rise in the Thames.

It was doubtless the onset of the great Russian cold that drove these industries south towards France when the Channel dried up. This may explain why our [French] later and final Acheulean work was influenced by their spearhead shapes, as it had previously produced few of them, whereas the oval *limandes* of the older French Acheulean were at their peak.

Similarly, while we can see the uncertain first attempts at Levalloisian cutting[2] occurring simultaneously in France and England, at the end of our French Acheulean III (Cagny) and towards the top of the river deposits at Swanscombe, in France we have, in the strong pre-Rissian development of our large, heavy Levalloisian I and II, an industry that is found in England only at Bapchild (Kent) and then even more battered by solifluxion. On the other hand, our series of Levalloisian III and IV, with increasing production of blades, partly during the Riss-Würm interval, are comparable to a very similar industry at Crayford, and there associated with a cold fauna previous to the last warm fauna of that area. Thus Crayford would be contemporary with the rather cruder Levalloisian III and slightly prior to our temperate Levalloisian IV of which it is probably the forerunner.

Further complications arise, however, when we consider territories farther to the east. The Saxon site at Markkleeberg is very much earlier and ascribed to the Mindel-Riss interval, being at times covered by Rissian moraines, although it closely resembles our French Leval-

---

[1] At Swanscombe the industries in the base of the old terrace were battered and scratched by the solifluxion that carried them there. A second industrial series of later date, chipped on the site and perfectly intact, was later mingled with the former by the river as it washed out the solifluxed gravels, and also by man in search of raw material for the work-place he had set up. The Clacton-on-Sea level consists of gravel followed by peat laid down at the time of the first drop in the Thames water-level. At Swanscombe the lower brick-clay (antedating the gravels overlying the Acheulean implements) reveals a level of silts, first due to flooding, then sub-aerial, where the upper part contains land-shells and considerable traces of temperate vegetation. I was present when a fine oval *limande* was found here. (H. B.)

[2] By this is meant a method of producing numerous flakes, usually untrimmed, seemingly derived from cutting up bifaces, but where the stump shows trimming facets round its edge. In France this would appear to have been the first stage in facet preparation, later to become systematic, of the striking platforms of flakes then produced for their intrinsic value by the true Levalloisian method.

loisian III and IV, which were Riss-Würm. As, in France, Levalloisian I and II cannot have given rise to Levalloisian III and IV, characterized by blades, it would appear that the spread of the Rissian glacier drove it out of Germany westward towards England and France.

But the difficulties with Levalloisian work do not stop there. Our Levalloisian V (at the base of recent loess), containing heart-shaped bifaces and broad flakes (more skilfully made and lighter than those of Levalloisian I and II), cannot be said either to be derived, on the same sites, from our Levalloisian III and IV, where blades predominate. It is very like the industries of the great English work-places at Northfleet, near London, lying under a very strong solifluxion which finished up there after crossing the 30-metre terrace, and which was therefore of more recent date than this terrace—probably Rissian. Again, we can consider that at the onset of the severe glacial conditions that brought down this mass of combe-rock the Levalloisians (pre-V, but not IV) crossed the Channel and brought their industry to France, where it was identical with our Levalloisian V.

It can now be seen that to the study of local stratigraphy must be added a geographical and climatic method of comparative stratigraphy, enabling further progress to be made towards a stage when we can understand lateral moves of industrial facies and the time intervals at which they took place, while at the same time taking into account certain local sequences and the small gaps in them.

So in Southern England and Northern France we find biface industries alternating with flake industries. The flakes come before and after the peaks of cold, and the bifaces in the interglacial periods. It seems reasonable to deduce that this alternation was due to movements of the human groups, which, as the glacial conditions came on, followed the animals they hunted to the south and west. It is natural that Central Europe, practically devoid of bifaces, should have been occupied earlier than Western Europe by people with flake industries—for example, the Clactonian type in Prussia in the Günz-Mindel interval; the Levalloisian III–IV in the Mindel-Riss at Markkleeberg, Saxony; and the Mousterian in the Riss-Würm at Ehringsdorf, Weimar.

Farther south bifaces and flakes are intermingled or often occur side by side, since the people who had fled before the advancing ice had no reason to retrace their steps. So a Clacto-Abbevillian type can be found in Morocco and many other places in Africa.

[10]

Lower Palaeolithic caves and rock-shelters

Chou Kow Tien—Makapan (Transvaal)—La Micoque—Fontéchevade—Coupe-Gorge—Combe-Capelle—Mousterian cave deposits

---

Traces of early human beings have been preserved in caves and rock-shelters, as well as in open-air geological deposits. Shortly after the last, Riss-Würm warm phase Mousterian groups settled on Grimaldian sands in southern caves at Furninha (Peniche), Grimaldi, Circeo, and Romanelli. Other proto-Mousterians, mountain hunters, had towards the end of the same phase visited caves frequented by the cave bear high in the Alps. Traces of them are found again at Cotencher, at the foot of the Jura, covered by moraines of the peak of the Würmian Ice Age and mingled with true Mousterian remains, showing that Mousterian man used caves at a precise geological moment in the sequence of glacial phenomena and variations in sea-level.

Other caves, less conveniently situated in the general succession of geological events, nevertheless show signs of human habitation at even earlier dates. In the Observatoire cave at Monaco, well above the 60–90-metre levels, first Abbevillian, then Clactonian and Acheulean men left implements, before the place was used again for a very short time by hunters of the cold fauna of the last Ice Age.

Chou Kow Tien, in China, Makapan, in the Transvaal, La Micoque and Fontéchevade, Coupe-Gorge, and Combe-Capelle, in the Charente, Haute-Garonne, and Dordogne *départements* of France, are all good examples of such shelters, filled with material of very great antiquity, though their very existence was often concealed by thick scree forming a smooth, regular slope.

CHOU KOW TIEN

Less than 60 miles south of Peking, in a limestone gorge running into the edge of the high Mongol plateau, is a succession of caves in which the deposits are some 50 metres thick and formed of levels of human habitation and debris from the roofs as they collapsed one after the other. The fauna is fairly consistent, from the bottom upward, as well as the human type (*Sinanthropus*) and the industry.

The fauna is quite different from that of the great stretches of loess in China, the home of the tiger, the spotted hyena, and *Cervus elaphus*. It still contains, towards the bottom, the *Machairodus* and the *Calicotherium*, animals typical of the site at Ni Ho Wan, to the north of Peking, where *Sinanthropus* probably already lived, and found in several other holes at Chou Kow Tien, where rare chipped stones, chipped and cut antlers, and charcoal have been found. The stags of these various sites are not of the same kind, which is evidence of considerable difference in age. The Chou Kow Tien industry consists, besides worked bones and split stag antlers, of great quantities of quartz, flaked small by bipolar chipping and often trimmed into scrapers, augers, beaks, points, barbs, and even blades and lamina, together with very rare flints, some chipped pebbles, and large flakes of more or less Clactonian style, roughly trimmed up.

Chou Kow Tien certainly dates from before the Mousterian at the bottom of the great loess deposit and the Moustero-Aurignacian in it. This civilization lasted a very long time in this part of the world, since the absence of glaciation did not force population movements. In Eastern Asia no trace of biface cultures have yet been found, though they exist in Asia Minor, India, and Java.

We can therefore distinguish two great archaeological areas, the second merely forming an eastern extension of the culture extending over Africa and Western Europe. Its western boundaries are on the Rhine, the Adriatic, and the Caucasus.

MAKAPAN (TRANSVAAL)

South Africa has also been found to contain caves and rock-shelters with very ancient contents, those at Makapan belonging to various ages. The oldest caves, completely choked by collapses, are Pliocene and have yielded enormous quantities of bones, with several important fragments of an *Australopithecus*. Another, Quaternary, cave was packed with chipped quartzites, including a fair number of Acheulean bifaces. Here a Neanderthal-type jaw-bone was found. Of more recent date and associated with the layer that contained the *Australopithecus* remains came, along with one of his jaw-bones, some very crudely chipped pebbles belonging to the 'Pebble culture.' Similar finds were made at Sterkfontein and Swartzkrans, other caves near the Rand.

In the Manaurie valley, quite near to Tayac (Dordogne), was found a rock-shelter that had completely collapsed and been levelled under a scree slope. It is known as *La Micoque*. The last habitat, in a red layer lying under limestone rubble, is remarkable for an industry rich in tiny spear-shaped bifaces of very careful workmanship, as well as for many implements made from flakes with smooth striking platforms and trimmed into points, scrapers, and so on. The fauna (horse, stag, and ox) is temperate. This horizon lies on top of a whole series of layers, separated sometimes by large scree, or by alluvial tuff-stone, or again by beds of limestone rubble rounded on the spot by solifluxion and mingled with flints, battered by the same process, coming from the partially demolished underlying layer. This breccia is about ten metres thick.

Five successive layers of human habitation lie one on top of the other and are older than the thin layer of latest Acheulean that covers them. The tools in most of these layers consist of an immense number of small flakes, with oblique striking platforms and small bulbs of percussion, in the Clactonian tradition, associated with a very small number of flakes with prepared, faceted striking platforms in the proto-Levalloisian manner. Finds of Acheulean axe-heads have been rare. The work, as a whole, is neither Acheulean nor Levalloisian nor Mousterian, but belongs to a special type of industry—the *Tayacian*. Many of the implements have been retrimmed into varied and impermanent shapes, such as beaked gravers, barbs, punches, and even crude gravers, points, scrapers, or side-scrapers. The chipping is rough, but the trimming is often excellent, qualities that are characteristic of this Tayacian work at La Micoque, with its hybrid technique. This is not found to the same extent in the penultimate layer, before the *Micoquian*, where more prepared cores occur, with thinner flakes with straight striking platforms or facets. This points to a Mousterian type that did not quite materialize or persist. The fauna remains temperate, with the horse, ox, and stag. The three glacial phases, intercalated between the layers and showing solifluxion *in situ*, do not appear to correspond to long Ice Ages, but to transitory peaks of one or perhaps two.

La Micoque provides proof of the existence, in that area of the Périgord, of a flake culture that was contemporary with a great part of the Acheulean, but prior to its last phase, the Micoquian, and all this occurred not far from Bergerac and the Charente, where the whole Acheulean period developed on a large scale.

The geographical spread of the Tayacian was considerable. It has been found in the Charente, in the Spanish Peninsula, and in Morocco.

In Palestine it occurs under the local Micoquian, at the bottom of various caves with deep deposits, as well as at El Castillo (Santander, Spain). It appears to be derived from Clactonian work, to have been influenced by Levalloisian, and to indicate a development towards the Mousterian, whose ancestors it probably is. It should not, however, be forgotten that the Tayacian technique is so simple that it may well have been discovered in different localities quite independently.

FONTÉCHEVADE

The station at Fontéchevade (Charente) consists of the porch of a vast grotto, nearly completely filled up before the Mousterian culture that came into it after the laying down of a stalagmitic deposit. Digging through the ten metres of this filling revealed a level of occupation of Tayacian facies, which according to research by Mlle Germaine Henri-Martin seemed to go back to a purely Clactonian facies lower down. All this was associated with a warm fauna, deer and boar being abundant, with Merck's rhinoceros and the land tortoise. Amongst these layers, but at a fairly high level, a brain-pan was found, resembling in many ways that of Swanscombe man, a completely different strain from the Neanderthal type.

COUPE-GORGE

The Coupe-Gorge site at Montmaurin (Haute-Garonne) was discovered when a quarry was opened immediately below a cave that had formerly yielded the remains of a *Machairodus*, found in a stalagmitic shelf. Under a rock-ledge on a level with the floor of the site previously explored M. Camas discovered, in the bottom of the quarry and connected with oblique rock-faults, a whole system of pockets containing bones of the cave bear, *Cervus elaphus*, etc., and leading to a series of cavities filled with deposits of quartzites and flints, some chipped into Micoquian bifaces. These came towards the upper layer, just under the reindeer of the Mousterian and Leptolithic periods. In one of the pockets was found a very fine pre-Neanderthal jaw-bone.

On the same level as the *Machairodus* cave, but to the right, can be made out the entrance to another cave, found to be rich in quartzite flakes, though it also gave several bulky bifaces of a rather more worn, Middle Acheulean type.[1]

COMBE-CAPELLE[2]

Another rock-shelter, completely collapsed and levelled into a slope, was found at Combe-Capelle, in the valley of the Couze (Dordogne).

[1] The whole of this site was very skilfully explored by L. Meroc and his pupils.
[2] Excavated by Dr Ami, of Toronto, under the direction of D. Peyrony.

This was found to contain an industry similar to the Tayacian, but rougher because of the Clactonian nature of its flakes, though a very few pieces are of well-executed Levalloisian technique, with prepared, faceted striking platforms. Rare attempts at Acheulean-type bifaces have also been found. Unfortunately, there was no fauna present. On top of this horizon came a layer of solifluxion, followed, after a very considerable interval, by a true Mousterian level, with fine heart-shaped and triangular bifaces in the Acheulean tradition, points, scrapers, side-scrapers, borers, and barbs, fashioned from thick flakes by a faceted striking-platform method not quite so advanced as in the later Mousterian phase. Temperate cold fauna indicate the end of the last interglacial period.

The solifluxion here noted is contemporaneous with the Riss glaciation, and this is confirmed by observations made in other caves—for example, at El Castillo (Spain), where reindeer was found above lower Tayacian and Micoquian layers with cave-bear fauna, and under successive Mousterian levels with temperate fauna. In Palestine and Italy there also occur similar industries of the warm Mousterian type from the Riss-Würm interval, preceding a colder Mousterian.

MOUSTERIAN CAVE DEPOSITS

Overlying the Tayacian deposits, with rare intercalations of other Micoquian layers, comes the great variety of the Mousterian, complex in its techniques and the range of its implements. At times it is a kind of advanced and perfected Tayacian, with few prepared, faceted flakes, but with fine tools trimmed into scrapers and points occurring in a very highly developed Mousterian level, as at La Quina (Charente). At others all the good flakes come from cores with carefully prepared striking platforms, as in the contemporaneous horizons at Le Moustier (Dordogne).

Then, again, some levels contain large quantities of heart-shaped bifaces or lance-pointed hearts in the Acheulean tradition, associated not only with scrapers and points, but with scrapers, borers, and scorers, often multiple. These latter are absent or rare in other sites lacking in bifaces,[1] but rich in knives with curved, blunted backs.

Furthermore, the implements in the Mediterranean habitats at Grimaldi, in Italy, North Africa, and Palestine show that points, or, indeed, triangular flakes and blades, predominate over the broad flakes and scrapers of the classic region of South-west France, which can be interpreted only as a direct derivation of the Mousterian work of these habitats from a Levalloisian precursor.

[1] M. F. Bordes has, for a number of years, concentrated on analysing the contents of a large number of Mousterian deposits, many of which he has excavated with great skill. He distinguishes several facies, some with a 'Charentian' chipping technique, others in the Levalloisian style, and still others, of more recent date, containing many implements with serrated trimming.

Thus Mousterian is very far from being a pure type of industry. It proceeds from the intermingling, in varying proportions, of three preceding types—the Acheulean, the Tayacian, and the Levalloisian.

In the classic region, Charente-Poitou-Dordogne, two and perhaps even three Mousterian levels can be traced, with triangular and heart-shaped bifaces, some spear-headed, and associated with the large range of tools we have already mentioned. One such level occurs at the bottom of the Mousterian cave deposits and, as at Combe-Capelle and at Laussel, has fauna that is still temperate. The other has been found almost, if not quite, at the top of the series of layers from the last Ice Age, and has abundant reindeer remains.

Between these two comes the typical Mousterian, where scrapers and scraper-chisels predominate over the less frequent points, and other implements are poorly represented. But the chipping, mostly Tayacian at La Quina, where the flint occurs in large blocks, was done with prepared striking platforms in the stations where the cores were smaller or rounder.

In the Cantabrian Mountains and the Basses-Pyrénées a comprehensive industry producing small tools such as scrapers, points, augers, and some gravers was interrupted about half-way by the addition of numerous flake bifaces, in the Acheulean tradition, made of quartzite, ophite, and even limestone, with choppers recalling those found in the Sahara and South Africa (Ohla rock-shelter, Basses-Pyrénées, before the cold fauna).

It would appear that the typical Mousterian, which existed in Central Europe from the time of the last interglacial period, penetrated Northern France as an influence increasing in intensity from west to east, at the time of Levalloisian III–IV and, when the waters of the Adriatic were at their lowest level, at the beginning of the Würm Ice Age. This influence then spread over the south-west of France and of Europe, combining there with the Tayacian and, farther north, with Levalloisian VI and VII.

Towards the upper levels of the Mousterian in the Dordogne area the dawn of Leptolithic cultures produced, on various sites, the level named after the rock-shelter of Audi, near Les Eyzies, and which is found again at Le Moustier and near by, characterized by curved knives with blunted backs.

The presence of many broad blades with skilfully blunted backs had already been noted in the advanced biface level of the lower shelter at Le Moustier. Very many more of these were found at the Audi shelter, at Le Moustier (Lartet shelter), and at Les Festons (near Brantôme) when they were excavated by Professor Pittard. They were there associated with even greater quantities of blades showing a tendency towards Aurignacian styles—scrapers, blades sometimes only partly trimmed at the end, crude gravers, and notched points. These must no doubt be considered as signs of the arrival of the newcomers. At the same time the last of the bifaces rapidly degenerate before disappearing completely, at least as coups-de-poing.

In the whole of North Africa the development of the Mousterian from Levalloisian origins took an original turn with the growth of the Aterian industry. Here the chipping was Moustero-Levalloisian, but it produced a range of tanged points and other such implements, as well as other new shapes. In the Sahara it gave many complex, Y-shaped, concave side-scrapers, generally in three sizes—large, medium, and small. In Egypt and in the Southern Sahara[1] came leaf-shaped Solutrean points, trimmed on both faces, which are much rarer in Algeria and the Northern Sahara. This is the last phase, in that part of the world, of the Mousterian series, but its technical influence continued to be widely felt in the later Palaeolithic in Egypt and in East and South Africa, where, at the height of 'Neanthropic' developments, the traditional Mousterian chipping went on alongside more recent techniques.

Recently Professor Zotz and his assistant, Fräulein Freund, brought to light the existence, prior to the Aurignacian in Central and Eastern Europe, of a Mousterian phase producing in fair quantities leaf-shaped points, very like Solutrean examples, particularly in a site at the Weinberg. This would lead us to prefer the name 'Weinbergian' to the term first used by the Abbé Breuil to indicate the Aurignaco-Perigordian complex that preceded the Solutrean in Western Europe.

These facts no doubt provide the explanation of the origin of the more advanced Solutrean facies found in the north of Hungary and in Bulgaria and suitably named 'Szelethian.'

[1] And in Northern Morocco (Abbé Roche).

[11]

Prehistoric men[1]

*Neanderthal—Swanscombe and Fontéchevade—Mauer—*Australopithecus—
Sinanthropus *and* Pithecanthropus—Homo sapiens *of Leptolithic times*

Although it is not usual to deal with a chronological series of events by going backward in time, it seems more objective, in the present case, to proceed from the known to the unknown. While it is true that we have a good deal of information about human types during the Leptolithic and final glacial periods (Mousterian), as well as during the preceding interglacial phase (Levalloisian and late Acheulean), we have infinitely less about them during the very long span prior to the third glaciation, and before that the second and first interglacials, the latter being the absolute limit of what can be gleaned, from the study of industries, about the presence of men on earth. The known number of human bones coming down to us from this immense stretch of time is so infinitesimal and they are in such a frustrating state of fragmentation that we must frankly admit that we have but the scantiest of data about these long ages that saw the development of the various human types and finally of man himself.

NEANDERTHAL

If we begin at the end and go back through the ages we find that the Würmian Ice Age saw the twilight of the ancient race of Neanderthal men, the undoubted source of the Mousterian industry in Europe.

Neanderthal man of the last Ice Age is represented by the following remains:

[1] Greater detail will found in books on this subject by specialists, which I do not claim to be. (H.B.)

In *Spain* the jaw-bone found at Bañolas, Catalonia; in *France* the jaw-bone from Malarnaud (Ariège), a skeleton from La Chapelle-aux-Saints (Corrèze), two adult skeletons from La Ferrassie and one from Le Moustier, a female skeleton, a child's skull, and a fair number of fragments of jaws and skulls from La Quina (Charente), a jaw-bone and a few other bones from Le Rigordou, at Montignac (Dordogne); in *Italy* the skull from San Felice de Circeo; in *Belgium* the two skeletons from Spy, the jaw-bone from La Naulette, a child's skull from Engis, and various small fragments; in *Western Germany* the discovery at Neanderthal; in *Czechoslovakia* the jaw-bone from Šipka.

Neanderthal men of the last, or third, Riss-Würm interglacial period are represented by:

In *Italy* the two skulls from Saccopastore, Rome; in *Gibraltar* two skulls, one of a woman, the other of a child; in *Croatia* numerous fragments of skulls (cannibalism) from Krapina; in *Germany* several incomplete skulls and two jaw-bones from Ehringsdorf, Weimar, and a child's skeleton; in the *Crimea* the lower extremities of a skeleton from a destroyed burial-site at Kik-Koba.

The Neanderthaloid man of the second, Mindel-Riss interglacial period is represented by the skull from Steinheim, found with a buffalo skull.

This gives a total of ten skeletons, twelve skulls, and six jaw-bones, with many fragments of jaw-bones and other bones. Neanderthal man, of medium height, stood about 1·6 metres, and probably held himself not quite so erect as *Homo sapiens*. His rather large skull varied in capacity within present-day limits—that is, between 1260 and 1650 cubic centimetres, with an average of 1490—with a high, well-developed face sloping forward from the top of the nose. The chin was straight and not prominent, or even slightly receding; the jaw-bone was very powerful in men and more slender in women, with strong teeth, the canines in men being a little longer than the others. The face had no canine fossa, though the nasal and orbital cavities were large, and among adults the superciliary ridges were very prominent. Dental development indicates that growth was quicker than in modern man. The forehead receded, the dome of the dolichocephalic skull was flattened. The occipital and parietal crests were present but not prominent. The legs were short and slightly bent, and the forearms shorter than in the European race. The back of the strong trunk rose in a single curve to a stout neck with powerful muscles. All these cranial characteristics are diminished in the human types at Saccopastore and Steinheim. Neanderthal characteristics became more marked as time went on.

Contemporaneously with Neanderthal men, there lived, in the caves at Mugharet-es-Sukhul and Mugharet-et-Tabun, in Palestine, from the last interglacial period onward, Neanderthaloids—that is to say, men combining certain Neanderthal features with others unlike them, and for this reason much closer to our human type in body, limbs, and facial characteristics.

Although it did seem improbable that true Neanderthalers could have given birth to any group of *Homo sapiens*, such a hypothesis becomes more credible after the Palestine discoveries, unless these were the result of cross-breeding, as more and more people seem to think.

SWANSCOMBE AND FONTÉCHEVADE

Older European human remains are exceedingly rare, and only three can be considered genuine. The occipital and parietal fragments of a skull found in the middle gravels (more or less Acheulean III) of the Barnfield Pit quarry at Swanscombe, near London, and dating from the second interglacial (Mindel-Riss) period, are neither Neanderthal nor Neanderthaloid, and, in spite of the great thickness of the bone, fall within possible types of *Homo sapiens*.[1]

To previous discoveries must now be added one made by Mlle G. Henri-Martin, in 1947, in the habitat at Fontéchevade, Charente. Here a brain-pan and a piece of the frontal bone belonging to another individual were found amidst Tayacian layers, but at a fairly high level, with remains of warm fauna. The brain-pan, small in size, belonged to a skull of notably smaller capacity than that of modern man. The dome is modern in shape, and the area above the brows shows no ridge. Considered in conjunction with the Swanscombe skull, this Fontéchevade fragment provides further evidence of the existence in Europe, before Mousterian times, of a non-Neanderthaloid type of man.

MAUER

The jaw-bone from Mauer, near Heidelberg, Baden, nearly as large as a gorilla's, was discovered under 24 metres of deposits laid down by the Neckar, in association with fauna including *Rhinoceros etruscus* and *Elephas antiquus*. This would date it at the first interglacial period. No chipped implement was found with it. Its stoutness and thickness, the complete absence of a normal chin and its replacement by a rounded, receding surface, together with the width and shape of the rising portion, all point to its being a purely human relic. The very strong teeth were well preserved, and the bone could be compared to the fossil

---

[1] Analysis of the bone fragments from Piltdown, Sussex, has shown that the supposed skull of a *Homo sapiens* from this site is of no great antiquity and that the jaw-bone is that of a chimpanzee, suitably faked. The whole deposit was thus a clever hoax, carried to extreme lengths, since fossil bones and teeth, with flints, were included.

remains from Chou Kow Tien and Java as having perhaps belonged to an ancestor of the Neanderthal stock.[1]

So, for Quaternary times, prior to the arrival in Europe of the Leptolithic culture, we have fairly satisfactory information about the last Ice Age and the preceding interglacial period, during which the Neanderthal race was dominant, but for the three first Ice Ages and their intervening phases, covering an immense span of some hundreds of thousands of years, we have only the very incomplete remains of four individuals showing no Neanderthaloid characteristics, the Swanscombe skull, and jaw-bones from Fontéchevade and Mauer, belonging to possible ancestors of the Neanderthalers. This is very scanty, and to find further evidence we must seek outside Europe.

Africa is less reticent concerning very early man. The fragmentary jaw-bone from Kanam (Kenya), difficult to date accurately, but nevertheless extremely ancient, has a straight chin and extraordinary depth and thickness, but there is not enough to allow a reconstruction to be made. In the north-west, after the primitive jaw from Rabat, found by Marcet in a beach-level cast up perhaps in the Mindel-Riss interval, came the three discoveries made by Arambourg at Ternifine (Oran, Algeria) in association with an ancient fauna and many early Acheulean bifaces, and the similar remains, post-Sicilian but pre-Tyrrhenian, found quite recently in the old beach at Abderrahman by Biberson.

In South Africa the skull found at Walfish Bay in the old dune sand, and associated with a rich fauna and advanced Acheulean work, bears a striking resemblance to another found at Broken Hill (S. Rhodesia). This latter, beautifully preserved and mineralized, but lacking the jaw-bone, is, by reason of the exaggerated overhang of the frontal bones and also because of other features, the most brutish of all the human skulls so far discovered. It is not far removed from the Neanderthal strain. The other bone remains described in conjunction with it did not come from the same level and belonged to an African *Homo sapiens*, but there was found with it, and in the same horizon, the middle section of a femur with the strong, harsh line of curve found in Neanderthal men.[2] In other characteristics this skull resembles the Java and

---

[1] In recent years the Coupe-Gorge site at Montmaurin, Haute-Garonne, has brought to light a Lower Palaeolithic complex of pre-Mousterian type, showing a Micoquian level overlying a quartzite flake industry that is probably Tayacian. Lower down still came a human jaw-bone—no accurate description is yet available —as primitive as that of *Sinanthropus* and similar to those from Abderrahman, from Rabat (Morocco) and Ternifine (Oran), all of which were associated with biface industries and, in the case of the latter, with a very early fauna, including the *Machairodus*. This evidence, with other examples from East Africa, confirms the existence, at the two extremities of the Old World, of a Pithecanthropian stage of human development to which Professor Arambourg has given the name of *Atlanthropus*, to designate his discoveries in the west and analogous types elsewhere.

[2] Seen by me in 1929 and wrongly considered by others as unimportant. (H.B.)

Peking skulls. If they are placed upside down, with the occipital foramen uppermost, the area contained between the foramen, the nape of
the occiput, and the occipital crests, which are here more marked
than in any other human group, stands out as an area contorted and
roughened by the attachment of very powerful muscles, in no way
comparable to the same place even in Neanderthal skulls. They have
one other peculiarity that is found again among the yellow race: the
cerebellum is very incompletely covered by the brain.[1]

AUSTRALOPITHECUS

Earlier than these human remains from very distant times in African prehistory comes the *Australopithecus* from Taungs, Transvaal,
dating from the Pliocene era. This was an anthropoid ape with teeth
closely resembling man's, with the canines only slightly projecting,
and it was certainly closer to man than any of the present-day anthropoids.

More recently, thanks to research by Dr Broom, numerous further
discoveries have been made in various bone-bearing breccias in the
Johannesburg area of South Africa. Those at Taungs, Sterkfontein,
Kromdraai, and Swartzkrans have yielded a very considerable number
of jaws and other bones of walking anthropoids with teeth very like
man's and many other human similarities in anatomical detail.
Though they were first dated as Quaternary,[2] they have now been
recognized as Pliocene, as were analogous remains from the Makapan
caves, much farther north of the Transvaal, where research was done
by Dr W. Robinson and his collaborators. Here the lower layers gave
several important remains of much earlier times than the Palaeolithic
deposits containing bifaces. As for the traces of fire and crude industry
thought to be associated with such remains, it is too early yet to be able
to draw any conclusion whatsoever about them.[3] What is certain is
that we are here dealing with anthropoids, possibly very closely related
to man, but with a brain of a size somewhere between anthropoid and
human volume, and undoubtedly walking on two feet. In any case,
these discoveries are closer than any other to human types and seem
to make it probable that man evolved in South Africa during the
Plaisancian period, though other strains seem to have begun in
Southern Asia from before the appearance of the *Pitheco-Sinanthropus*
group.

[1] We are indebted for these details to Professor Schellshear, a pupil of Elliot Smith.
[2] The recent inclusion by geologists of the Plaisancian in the Quaternary, though
it had hitherto been considered part of the Pliocene age, brings them back into a
much enlarged Quaternary.
[3] See notes in Chapter 3 on the considerable progress made on pebble implements
with elementary chipping and on the now probable use of bones.

SINANTHROPUS AND PITHECANTHROPUS

In that part of Asia only the eastern regions have given many vestiges of very ancient man, China with the *Sinanthropus* at Chou Kow Tien and Java with the *Pithecanthropus*.

We know already a good deal about the activities of *Sinanthropus*, the fire he kept alive, his life as a hunter, his implements of chipped quartz and pebbles, the stag antlers he worked on, and the bones he deliberately broke and retrimmed. His period seems pre-Rissian, since it was certainly prior to the great loess deposits in China, although subsequent to the very beginning of the Quaternary. We have three of his skulls, all fairly complete, about a dozen lower jaw-bones, one upper jaw with a large part of the face, but only three long bones in very poor state, a shoulder-blade, and a wrist-bone. In my opinion the supposition that the *Sinanthropus* remains were those of an anthropoid hunted by man was quite unfounded. It is inconceivable that during the very long period of occupation of the habitat at Chou Kow Tien two such closely related species could live side by side, considering the mutual exclusivism of natural species, or that there should never have come to light the slightest fragment of the remains of another man in all the enormous cube of earth that has been investigated.

The *Sinanthropus* skulls, with a capacity varying between 950 and 1200 cubic centimetres—similar to that of the smallest Australian skulls —appear to be human remains corresponding to a Neanderthal type of fairly small size, but with the frontal part narrower at the temples. The teeth are truly human, with no undue development of the canines, and the male jaw-bone is not unlike the Mauer specimen. The relatively small brain volume, though nearly twice that of a well-favoured gorilla (600 c.c.), must have corresponded to a smallness of stature, in which case it has no special significance, since the size of this organ must be considered in relation to the general bone structure—in other words, to the height.

The Java *Pithecanthropus* is so very closely analogous to the *Sinanthropus* as to suggest the existence of two very similar species or varieties.

In Java the Quaternary can be divided into three periods, distinguished by different mammals—Stegodons (very primitive elephants), hippopotami, stags, antelopes, and felines. The present-day orang, the *Elephas namadicus*, and a bear appear only in the second period.

In the oldest layer a child's skull, apparently belonging to the *Pithecanthropus* species, was discovered at Modjokerto. From the middle layer came the famous brain-pan, two teeth, a femur, a small fragment of jaw-bone, all found, in 1891, at Trinil by Dr Dubois; then two skulls, more complete than the first, part of an upper and a lower jaw, and various other bones, found twenty years ago at Sangiran by Dr Königswald.

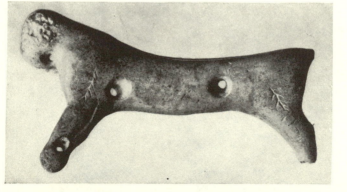

PLATE III. Round-carvings from Magdalenian IV. 1. Horse, ivory, from Les Espélugues (Hautes-Pyrénées). 2. Stag running and belling, part of an extended engraving on a reindeer-horn pierced stick from Les Hoteaux (Ain). Probably Magdalenian V. 3. Feline 'hoodoo' charm, base of reindeer-antler, from Isturitz (Basses-Pyrénées). (1 and 3, Musée de Saint-Germain; 2, Musée de Bourg.)

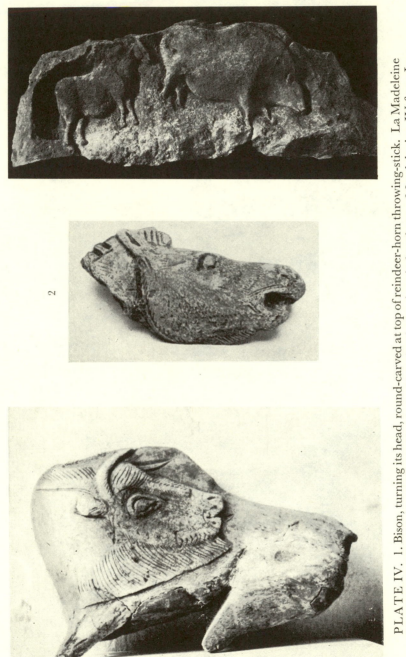

PLATE IV. 1. Bison, turning its head, round-carved at top of reindeer-horn throwing-stick. La Madeleine (Dordogne). Magdalenian IV. 2. Head of whinnying horse, in reindeer-horn. Magdalenian IV from Le Mas d'Azil (Ariège). 3. Fragment from rock-fall showing mare in foal and a quadruped with bison's body and swine's head, in bas-relief, Upper Solutrean shrine at Le Roc de Sers (Charente). (1, 2, and 3, Musée de Saint-Germain.)

The first skull, found by Dr Dubois, seems more of a fossil, since it is much more decayed than the typically human femur found near by. Its characteristics are approximately the same as those of the *Sinanthropus*, but the cranial prominences are less developed and the capacity is less, being more or less 900 cubic centimetres. This first skull is thought to be that of a man; a woman's would be 790 cubic centimetres. The flora in the Trinil deposit is to be found to-day at a higher altitude, between 600 and 1200 metres, showing that the temperature then was cooler than now, in a glacial or pluvial phase that was not the last.

More very old skulls and jaw-bones, though of later date, have been found in Java, some by Dubois, others later, at Wadjak and at Ngandong (eleven). They may represent a branch development of the *Pithecanthropus* type towards a proto-Australoid man, as the later finds seem to indicate fairly exactly. In many respects these skulls and jaws resemble Rhodesian and Neanderthal man. The Ngandong remains were found in a group, associated with a barbed bone harpoon, and therefore belong to the local Leptolithic age.

In spite of the absence of chipped stones on sites where *Pithecanthropus* remains have been found, chipped flints from Quaternary times have occurred abundantly at other points that can fairly certainly be connected with these bones. They belong to various industries, one of bifaces at Patjitan, the most eastern of this type and more or less Abbevillo-Acheuloid; others recall Clactonian work, but none looks Levalloisian.[1] In the most recent deposits, associated with the harpoons, broad, Solutrean, concave-based points have been found, but as yet no polished stone. This is the Javanese Mesolithic.

Thus, in the far east and south of the continent of Asia and in the Indian Archipelago, but recently detached from it, we can make out the line of an apparently continuous development, starting from the *Pithecanthropus-Sinanthropus* group and leading up to the pre-Australians and, probably by another ramification, to the early Mauer, Broken Hill, and Neanderthal men in the west of the Eurasian continent, including Asia Minor.

On the other hand, at least in Palestine, a group of less clearly defined Neanderthaloid character indicates an already notable transition towards *Homo sapiens*.

The dearth of information available on the very archaic human types makes it particularly difficult to propound, with any semblance of

---

[1] Professor De Almeida found, in an extensive beach deposit on the north coast of Timor, a refashioned industry consisting of several stages in significant ranges of large, Clactonoid flakes. In the more recent, mixed stages it evolved towards lighter shapes. This is clear evidence that the tide of Lower Palaeolithic humanity flowed as far as that. A flake fragment and the remains of a fossil elephant found at Flores confirm this. (H. B.)

I

probability, theories about their mutual relations, as well as about their connexions with the anthropoids, so close to them in anatomy and era. Yet it would be possible to imagine that at the beginning, in this vast, three-lobed continent of the Old World, there appeared simultaneously, towards the end of the Tertiary, in this group of anthropoid mammals and due to the internal spiritual urge of the power of the Creator, a whole series of branching strains coming very close to what we call man. The characteristics of these offshoots, and no doubt their mentalities, were a mixture, some features recalling the anthropoid background from which the new creatures sprang, others foreshadowing human reason in the birth of inventive intuition that gradually flowered into intelligence. This was the origin of *Homo faber*, but we do not know how he gave birth to *Homo sapiens*, who outlived him and profited by his discoveries and the acquired skills of his forerunners, those bold and courageous dwellers in a world of hostile and gigantic animals.

Perhaps it is with him, and with him alone, that we can mark the beginning not of zoological man, represented by the early races, but of man in the fullness of his graceful physique, of his inventive mind, of his soul that can contemplate the inner mystery of the world and moral life. It may be that nobody will ever know when or how man so defined was born and developed.

HOMO SAPIENS OF LEPTOLITHIC TIMES

The Neanthropic representatives of this new human race are mainly known through discoveries made in Europe, where they arrived not in the form of a people in transition, recalling their earlier Palaeanthropic phase, nor even resembling those pygmies who to-day are relegated to remote areas of continents, or to jungles, or the inaccessible heights of mountain-ranges, or islands lost in the oceans. The new arrivals in Europe all belonged to various types of the great modern races, in full flower and at the same stage of development as ourselves. They were therefore not 'ancient men,' as were their predecessors on our continent, but merely, as far as Europe is concerned, the most ancient of modern men and the first ancestors of the Europeans of to-day, to be joined later by other groups in the same stages of physical development.

Except for the very special Swanscombe–Fontéchevade group, an extraordinary homogeneity can be seen in the bone remains of the very ancient race of men. The Neanderthals are as alike as brothers, in spite of a few secondary differences, the most important being the contrast between the brachycephaly of the Krapina type and the long skull of all the others. This is no longer true of the new race, already very mixed—and, indeed, as Marcellin Boule put it, Upper Palaeolithic European man is a 'mongrel,' crossbred from various strains of *Homo sapiens*.

It is thought that this man may have preserved some characteristics of his predecessors. The frequently very prominent frontal ridge of the men from Brünn and Předmost is the only similar feature observable in both types, whose every bone, as well as the general organic structure, shows profound differences. So far only the men from Wadi-el-Murgaret (Palestine) and Florisbad (South Africa) seem to bridge the two groups, in a way rather similar to modern Australian aborigines, who also have a highly developed frontal ridge. Nevertheless the other characteristics remain very different.

Taking them in order of succession, the human types so far discovered are as follows:

The skeleton at *Roc de Combe-Capelle* (Dordogne), buried at the lower level of a series at the base of the Leptolithic, is that of a tall man with a long, well-developed skull, fairly prominent brow-arches, and powerful jaws. He could be compared to some members of the Ethiopian race, dark-skinned but not Negroes, and to the Capsian race of Mechta-el-Arbi (Tunisia) (Lacrorre and Vallois).

At the bottom of the Palaeolithic series at *Grimaldi*, in the Grotte des Enfants, a double burial-place revealed the remains of an old woman and a young man. From their prognathous facial structure and the comparative length of the limbs and their segments, these are thought to be remains of a Negroid type related to various modern Negro strains.

Another and much more numerous group, known as the 'Cro-Magnon' race, is very tall (1·79 to 1·94 metres), with elongated skull in the pure types and not very prominent brow-arches; the face, however, is short, the eye-sockets squarish, the nose straight and aquiline, and the chin prominent. Coarser examples of this race have been brought to light at Grimaldi itself and in Central Europe, at Brünn and Předmost. The brow is lower and the suborbital ridge more accentuated, recalling the older Wadi-el-Murgaret man, or being, perhaps, the result of probably complex cross-breeding, as shown by a certain amount of prognathous formation of the jaw-bones.

The three skeletons found buried at the base of a layer with horse-bone remains at Solutré (Perigordian Upper Aurignacian) are also cross-bred from Cro-Magnon with a short-headed element. They have kept the tall stature of the original race.

Remains of the Cro-Magnon race and its varieties are fairly well known, thanks to the discovery of a great many burial-places:

Cro-Magnon: at Les Eyzies (Dordogne)—five individuals.
Grimaldi (Riviera): in the Le Cavillon, Les Enfants, Baousso da Torre, and the Barma Grande caves—a dozen skeletons.
Soultré (Saône-et-Loire): three Upper Aurignacian skeletons and a Solutrean hut-grave.

Landes: the Duruthy cave, at Sordes—a skeleton from Magdalenian IV.

Dordogne: various other skeletons—men at Cap-Blanc, Laugerie Basse, etc., of Magdalenian date.

Charente: five skulls from Le Placard—Upper Solutrean and early Magdalenian.

Spain: skull from Camargo, a few remains from El Castillo.

Central Europe: Moravia—Brünn, two Gravettian skeletons; Předmost—twenty skeletons gathered together in one burial-place surrounded by stones, plus several others; Lautsch (Prince John's Cave)—one skeleton.

England: Paviland—Aurignacian.

In Spain, as in Southern France and North Africa (Berbers, and, in the Canaries, Guanchos), the Cro-Magnon strain has not yet died out in the population and can be traced as an important element through all later periods right up to modern times.

A third Upper Palaeolithic race is that of *Chancelade*, with the contracted skeleton from Raymonden, near Périgueux, as its prototype. Chancelade man was not very tall (1·55 metres), had a skull of great capacity (1700 c.c.), with a broad, high forehead, a ridged brain-pan, salient cheek-bones, and a narrow nose. His face was not short, as with the Cro-Magnon men.

Several Magdalenian skeletons (Laugerie Basse, Le Placard) seem to be connected with this type, which in some ways resembles the Eskimo, though in others it differs. It has been considered that the Laugerie Basse skeleton belongs to the 'Nordic race,' as may be the case with the mesocephalic-headed skeleton from Saint-Germain-la-Rivière (Gironde).

To sum up, then, during the Upper Palaeolithic period there is evidence of the existence of Negroid, Ethiopian, white, and probably yellow human strains.

Recent discoveries have provided further information about Upper Palaeolithic populations in other parts of the Old World.

North Africa has given a certain number of very tall skeletons with long skulls, of Capsian and Oranian strain. The Negroid type is rare, and comparisons can be made between the Berbers and the Cro-Magnon men (burial-places in the grottoes at Ali-Bacha, Les Hyènes, Afalou, and the snail-farms at Mechta-el-Arbi and Koudiat-el-Kerrouba).[1]

In East Africa the Oldoway skeleton seems attributable to this period.

[1] The Mechta type is constantly associated with the Ibero-Maurusian phase, and differs from that found in the Capsian deposits, belonging to the Aïn-Metterchen type (termed proto-Mediterranean by Vallois).

In the Southern Sahara the Asselar man, who lived at some time close to the microlith period of Mesolithic times, is connected with the Bantu tribes and the Grimaldi Negroid strain.

In Central Africa, in the Congo, the Likasi man can be compared to the Asselar man, except for the capacity of the skull, which is notably smaller.

East Africa has provided a fair number of skeletons also belonging to tall, straight-countenanced races with Negroid and Australoid affinities (Gamble's cave, at Elmenteita, Kenya). A pygmy strain appears somewhat later, in Mesolithic times.

South Africa has yielded the remains of a few Leptolithic fossil men: the one from Springbok Flats, near Pretoria, is of a well-developed type, said to have Negroid or Ethiopoid affinities. He reminds us of Combe-Capelle. The man at Fishhoek is considered to be Australoid, like the modern Korana.

In Asia Minor the cave at Antelias (Syria) contained various, more or less Aurignacian, human remains, but these have not yet been properly studied.

At Chou Kow Tien (China) the upper cave, of the same date as the great loess, contained a communal grave with skeletons of very different types, ranging from Eskimoid to Cro-Magnon.

Thus the Leptolithic races, formed outside Europe, invaded the continent about the middle of the last glaciation, coming probably from Asia, where, from the time of the last interglacial phase onward, there had been developing a human type that was less Neanderthaloid than the European Neanderthal men. These newcomers were of very diverse strains, but were related to races living at the time.

Their arrival in Europe was, from the racial point of view, an event of unique importance in the history of mankind. It meant the replacement, probably violent, by Neanthropic men of Palaeanthropic races that were wholly destroyed by the invaders. When, later on, Neolithic men, with agriculture and domestic animals, arrived they were still members of the Neanthropic group, though they had a social and economic life that had progressed farther under other skies. But it would seem that nowhere, either in race or civilization, were the Neanthrops a continuation of any known Palaeanthrops.

[12]

The Upper Palaeolithic, or Leptolithic

General remarks on Leptolithic and Mesolithic stone implements: Flint cores; flakes; implements derived from blades—General remarks on bone-working: bone; reindeer-horn; ivory; various ornaments—The stratigraphical subdivisions of the Leptolithic: Aurignacian; Gravettian; Solutrean; Magdalenian—The origins of the different Leptolithic facies

Some term other than 'Upper Palaeolithic' ought to be adopted to designate this new era of human history. *Miolithic*[1] has been suggested, but makes nonsense, since it means 'less stone.' The term should be *Leptolithic*, meaning 'light stone,' and referring to the implements based on thin, light blades used by the newcomers.

The various kinds of Leptolithic industry show important geographical and stratigraphical differences, but have certain common characteristics—the presence of well-defined bone implements, often of great number and variety, the existence of both figurative and decorative art, and the use of flint implements, most of the tools and weapons being principally developments of blades retouched in various ways.

[1] The term was no doubt derived from 'Miocene,' which does not mean 'middle of the Tertiary,' but 'fewer species now than later'! 'Eo,' 'Oligo,' 'Mio,' 'Plio,' and 'Pleistocene' designate the ascending order of appearance of species. However, although I reject this dreadful barbarism, I recognize the correctness of the idea of separating, by some more precise term than a simple adjective, the Neanthropic era and its culture from the whole Palaeanthropic conspectus known as early, or Lower, Palaeolithic. The word 'Leptolithic' was first proposed by E. Piette, but without success, and my suggestion that it should be reintroduced is gaining more and more ground among individual workers. (H. B.)

This latter industry has features common to all this period and to the Mesolithic, or epi-Palaeolithic, which, at the dawn of post-glacial times, carried on the nomad social conditions of the fishermen and hunters of the end of glacial times. Life and industry were still Leptolithic.

GENERAL REMARKS ON LEPTOLITHIC AND MESOLITHIC STONE IMPLEMENTS

Flint Cores

The *trimming-up* of cores, usually long in shape, was done with a stone striker or on an anvil, starting with a nodule of flint. A prepared core, whether large or small, was more or less oblong and showed along its length a series of zigzag ridges due to light transverse chipping. The ends, or an end, were sometimes oblique and smooth, or sometimes at a shallow angle to the surface to be chipped off. To this striking platform of the prepared core, when it had been wedged, was applied a bone, hard schist, or hardwood chisel, which was then struck with some kind of hammer. This detached a long, narrow blade, varying in size from 2 or 3 centimetres to 20 or 30 in length.

The first blade to be taken off showed on its back the zigzag ridging of the core, or simply the outer cortex of the nodule if such careful preparation had been omitted. Blades subsequently taken off would be triangular or trapezoidal in section, and on their backs would be long, nearly parallel facets, these being traces of the previous flaking. Such blades were ready for immediate use without further modification, though they were frequently retouched for special uses.

The core from which the blades had been removed was also often used as a powerful tool, the only implement of any size that the Leptolithic people made from this industrial residue. The angle of the striking platform, as well as that of the face from which the flakes had been removed, was often sharp enough to give a sharp cutting edge to one or both of the ends. If the core was of any breadth it then looked similar to an axe-blade or chisel, while if it was narrow and blades had been taken off all round the outside it looked like a stout graver. A shorter core, sometimes pyramid-shaped and giving tiny blades or shards, provided a kind of plane or core-shaped scraper. Evidence of such re-use is to be seen in the more or less delicate retouching of the cutting edges and the cracks made in them as they were wielded.

Flakes

The short, broad flakes produced when dressing cores, usually by rough-and-ready methods, were then often used as points, side-scrapers, beaked gravers, scorers, simple or multiple awls, stout plain gravers, and a whole series of scrapers, broad, thin, thick, discoid, keeled, with or without noses, or ogival. Although these shapes did exist at times from the Lower Palaeolithic onward, they continued to be made during the new phase, though mostly with greater care.

Only the keeled scrapers and gravers were of new types that had rarely been achieved before. The keeled scrapers were made with fine, shard retouching of fairly steep curve. They could be broad, more or less round, ovoid, triangular; or else long and narrow, with steep sides, or roughly chipped with broad, rising strokes, and end in a round or pointed nose. If they were broad and thick, with a base of plain nodule, they were to all intents trihedral hand-picks. If the two ends were narrow and not differentiated, which is rare, this gave a pick or rasp, according to whether the ends or the lateral angles were used. The typical keeled scraper, with curved, narrow facets, is characteristic of the classic Aurignacian sites. Other examples, with broad facets, have been found at various levels of the Magdalenian.

Implements derived from Blades

There are well-known examples of blades with retouched edges, on one or both sides, sometimes inverse or alternating; of pointed blades with sharp tips, or with ogival ends, symmetrical or not; of chisel-ended blades, though these are not common; of blades made into scrapers, generally quite abundant; of blades cut short by retouching that has cut off one end, either boldly, right across, or obliquely, the line being convex, straight, or concave.

When one cutting edge was removed, the other usually being left sharp, this gave points of the Châtelperron (Allier) type, which were retouched from the bottom upward on the generally convex back. In the Gravette points (from the Dordogne and elsewhere) the cutting edge is almost straight, or may have a slight projection in the middle. Trimming-up, only done near the base for fitting to a handle, gave notched points if done on only one side, or tanged points if done on both sides (Font-Robert, Brive, Corrèze).

Treatment of blades by pressure retouching and supported wood-chiselling permitted the production of the Solutrean points known as 'laurel-leaves' and 'willow-leaves.'

One of the most characteristic tools of the Leptolithic era is the graver, occurring in great variety. It might be made from a blade or a flake and is recognizable by its end bevel, more or less at right angles to the main plane of the instrument, a feature obtained by the removal of one or more thin strips from the end along one or both sides. The simplest kind was made from an angle of broken blade, or the single-blow type made from any end of flint. More typical is the graver made from an angle of blade where the end has been cut off straight, either square, or obliquely, or convex, or, more often, concave. Two varieties of angle graver show special features: the Upper Perigordian, known as the

'Noailles,' which was always made from a small, short, very thin flake, often with triple or quadruple cutting edges; the 'parrot-beak' graver of Magdalenian VI, fashioned on one side of the thin end of a blade or flake, with convex retouching of the underside. The surface of its cutting edge tends to curve sharply back and is oblique to the axis of the implement.

All these gravers were made by two sorts of cutting stroke: (a) the stroke giving a facet almost perpendicular to the flaking plane, and (b) the stroke forming an obtuse angle with the plane and more or less identical with it. This gave the plane, or flat-faced, graver.

Other kinds had simple or multiple facets on both sides. The commonest were the 'bec-de-flûte' gravers, simple or polyhedric, or prismatic when they were made at the end of a long core re-used for the purpose. Such a simple implement had but one facet on either side of the point, whereas the polyhedric graver had several, and all manner of gradations exist in between. These gravers had to be sharpened when blunted by use, and became, of necessity, more or less symmetrical. The number of little steps on their sides enables us to count the number of sharpenings they have undergone. The same is true where small strips have been flaked off. The strip removed at the first sharpening shows only one little step on its back; those with several steps reveal the number of previous sharpenings. Lack of steps means strips removed when the graver was first being made, and these often bear the marks of the retouching used to transform the blade into a graver.

Certain levels of the Middle Aurignacian are characterized by more elaborate types of graver. The 'hook-nosed,' or beaked, graver shows how, starting from a natural flat, or one made by a blow from another graver along one edge, a cluster of narrow, parallel, very curved strips has been taken off along the second edge, ending in a curved, convex gouge lip. Very often, but not always, as these lengthwise strips were taken off they ran into a notch cut into the same side so as to limit their spread. It did happen that some of these strip flakes tended to come off the underside rather than the top, thus producing a plane, or flat-faced, kind of beaked graver, similar to a derived shape that came in somewhat later (Charente and Palestine). Sometimes a 'miniature' beaked graver was fixed to the end of an awl (Le Trilobite, Yonne; Paviland, South Wales).

Making gravers is proof of a fairly special cutting technique that could be used more or less successfully, and with a little luck, in various ways: (a) with a hand hammer-stone (but this only gave broad facets); (b) by striking the end of the blade being worked upon an anvil-stone (here, in spite of successes, there was little control of results, since the blow had to be smart); (c) by indirect percussion (which gave good results). Other ways may well have been used also.

The graver was mainly used in working wood and bone.

Alongside the blades, there sprang up and developed in Leptolithic times a whole range of microlithic implements that was carried over into and increased in complexity during the Mesolithic. This was a result either of the intentional breaking of small blades, or of direct retouching of thin, narrow strips, some of which were no more than a centimetre long. Such tiny tools were, of course, not used in the hand, but mounted singly, or in sets in grooves or notches, on bone or wood tools. Some provided harpoon-barbs; others formed continuous cutting edges on knives of complex shape and on sickles.

Very early in the Aurignacian and the Perigordian stages of the Lower Leptolithic there can be found these thin strip flakes, with an edge carefully blunted by minute retouching, generally inverse. Later they formed a kind of micro-Gravette point with a more heavily blunted back, of the sort that went on into the Magdalenian and the Mesolithic. Their ends were retouched in various ways: some were made into very sharp micro-awls, used perhaps for making eyes in needles. Quite often, in certain levels of the old Magdalenian, they were pointed at one end and obliquely truncated at the other, with a blunted back between the two (scalene triangle). Some which had no doubt been intercalated in a set with others show ends cut off square or obliquely during the retouching process. The remaining cutting edge of these different pieces was frequently either wholly or partly serrated, with some delicacy. In other examples the blunted back forms an arc of a circle, the other edge being sharp for cutting (penknife-blade or bill-hook). In the Mesolithic especially the bill-hooks developed into triangles and then into trapezes, all with many variations. Later, towards Neolithic times, some of these pieces became tiny paring-knives, used as scissors or as arrow-heads with transverse cutting edges. A number of these geometrical shapes continued to find favour in the Neo- and even in the Eneolithic, showing evidence, no doubt, of the Neolithization of some of the Mesolithic tribes. In Ireland especially, in Neolithic times, very large pieces were worked probably as harpoon-barbs for hunting seals and whales, and deriving from these types.

In the Solutrean phase in the Iberian Peninsula arrow-heads[1] appeared sporadically, though they were abundant at El Parpalló (Valencia). In the Aterian culture in North Africa, from Upper Mousterian times, can be found rough, bulky, tanged heads, just as in the Mesolithic in Ireland and Scandinavia. Between the two, alongside the French notched Solutrean heads and concave-based heads, mainly Cantabrian, come elongated heads with fairly well-defined stems, rare in Aquitania, but abundant in Eastern Spain, and developing into the true flighted and tanged arrow-heads at El Parpalló. These were the forerunners of the extraordinary crop of arrow-heads, of infinite variety,

---

[1] With tangs and ailerons.

developed so superbly during the Neolithic, the Eneolithic, and the Bronze Age throughout North Africa, the Iberian Peninsula, and a large part of Europe and Asia.

GENERAL REMARKS ON BONE-WORKING

It would seem that at first the raw bone material was split up by striking it hard blows designed to break off workable pieces. This did not apply to Cervidae antlers, which were reduced by burning, boring, and bending, or by cutting through with a chopping-stone, before being split lengthwise. Ribs were often split into two sections along their thickness by rubbing down their edges as far as the inner trabecula, which was then generally levelled off by polishing.

The pieces thus obtained were then smoothed by scraping with flints (scorers or blades touched up laterally), and then polished and sharpened on a sandstone surface, according to the shape of the implement required. Secondary carving and incisions were then made to mark the base, the handle, the hafting-bevels, the sharp or blunt end, or the thin, curved edge, as each case demanded.

Rather later gravers were used for cutting bony material, especially true flat or long bones such as mammoth tusks or Cervidae antlers. By scoring to and fro with a bevelled edge a more or less straight groove was cut down into the spongy interior, where present, while another, practically parallel groove was made to join the first at each end, so that a long, slender wand could be taken out, the final separation from the matrix being accomplished by lateral pressure or blows. The piece was then fashioned as explained above.

Quantities of bone implements have been found at all levels of the Leptolithic, but others of a more specialized nature belong to a particular level.

Bone

Split rib-bones provided spatulae, flexible if they were thin, used for mixing ochre and fat or for trimming the tender skins of small animals. If they were thick they gave snow-cutters, chisels for blade-chipping, and, if long, levers. From shoulder-blades came centre-pierced discs, used, it is thought, as buttons in Magdalenian IV.

Long, pointed bones, or those easy to point by removal of the distal epiphysis, were made into punches by sharpening the pointed end. Splinters from long bones underwent the same treatment, and some were bevelled by use into chisels or drifts, the thick ends showing the marks of hammering. Lengths of reindeer antler or ivory were put to similar uses.

Very narrow shards were used in other roles—stout pins with heads, sprigs pointed at both ends. The smaller ones could be used as fish-hooks and the longer as combs or hairpins.

Some of these really fine splinters, taken off by gravers from very hard bones and having one end slightly flatter, were then pierced by a tiny hole, giving slender needles. They were rare before the Magdalenian, and their frequency during that period is proof of the development of sewing and the making of clothes from furs.

As is well known, tubes made from long, hollow bones (from large birds or reindeer hind-legs) were used as needle-cases or for holding paint in powder form.

Reindeer-horn

Those least subject to human modification were tines that were cut off and used as pointed tools, or daggers, while smaller segments were hollowed out for use as handles.

Examples exist where a long segment of main antler, often retaining the stumps of two tines branching off from it, bears in the centre of the crutch a large round hole. Sometimes other holes have been made along the main stem, or else a single hole at the base, often narrow, as if to admit a thong. The decorations on these objects have caused them to be considered as some sort of insignia—sceptres or 'leaders' maces.' Others think they were used for straightening arrows. The variations in their sizes, which range from a large 40–60 centimetres to a small 6–8 centimetres, show that they were produced for different purposes. These pieces, known from the Aurignacian onward, were not decorated with carving and sculpture until the Magdalenian.[1]

A very large number of thin shafts gouged by gravers from Cervidae antlers were, according to their size, designed to provide war-heads for hunting-spears, javelins, and arrows. During the Aurignacian their shapes varied widely; they could be flat, diamond-shaped, or triangular, with ends forked or plain; later they were longer, oval in section, and with a pointed base. Later still this base was carved with one or two bevels to ensure better adherence to the shaft. One or two grooves ran right up the length of the shank, being designed to contain poison or tiny barbs of microlithic flint.

Certain javelin-heads were of complex construction, in two parts, the outer end having a forked stem; others had three or more parts. Pairs of half-round rods were placed together by their flat sides, curved and highly ornamented;[2] they may have been used as handles for bags or bundles.

[1] An eminent Portuguese authority, Sr Ruy d'Andrade, has pointed out that similar pierced sticks, though of olive-wood, are still used in his country to-day, in rural areas where horses are bred, for making rope with horsehair. (H. B.)

[2] In the rare cases that have come to light (discovered by Begouen, Passemard, H. Pacheco) these rods were produced by splitting, with a graver, a single segment of thin antler into two lateral halves, the split being achieved by scoring two parallel and opposite grooves along the length of the segment. Such a delicate operation argues an important aim, though for some purpose unknown.

A large number of pieces of antler, either split into two or whole, and the remains of broken javelins were used as chisels or drifts for chipping flint blades. They were roughly bevelled at the working end, which was often blunted and remade, and hammered at the other. At times such punches were specially made from round or square rods and fairly roughly decorated.

Finally, reindeer antlers were made into hooked throwing-sticks for mounting on a long, wooden haft, to which they were fixed by a wedge-pin passing through a slender hole in the base, or, more rarely, by a bevel.

Ivory

In eastern regions, like Moravia, where ivory was more abundant than horn, polishers, javelins, awls, snow-cutters, and so on were made from this material, used mainly for works of art in the western areas.

Various Ornaments

Animal teeth, mainly the canine teeth from Carnivora and the incisors from horses and ruminants, together with an assortment of shells, fossil or fresh, were pierced for threading. Similar use was made of some of the hyoid bones of the large ruminants and horses, often threaded with beads made from bird or hare-bones, perforated scraps of ivory wands, and bits of steatite or other stones. Fish vertebrae were also made into beads. The arrangement of these different types of material was made with considerable taste, as is seen in the burial trappings at Barma Grande (Grimaldi) and Wadi-el-Murgaret (Palestine).

THE STRATIGRAPHICAL SUBDIVISIONS OF THE LEPTOLITHIC

In the classical area, South-east France and North-west Spain, H. Breuil had finally shown, in 1906, the necessity of dividing the Leptolithic into three main sections, each capable of further sub-division varying from region to region: (i) the *Aurignacian* and the *Gravettian*; (ii) the *Solutrean*; (iii) the *Magdalenian*.

Aurignacian

The Mousterian was followed by the Aurignacian (in the broadest sense), and this, at least in the main, had the same fauna, rich in mammoths, the woolly rhinoceros, and cave bear, and the hyena, later to give place to the horse and the great Bovidae. Always subjacent to the Solutrean, it can, in the classical area, be divided into secondary levels, as follows:[1]

---

[1] D. Peyrony created his Perigordian by separating from H. Breuil's Aurignacian all those levels showing blades with blunted backs. From the Châtelperron level he made his Perigordian I, which he connected with what H. Breuil considered to be

(a) *Châtelperron Level* (Allier). This is characterized by convex, blunt-backed blades retouched from the bottom upward, known as Châtelperron points. The remaining implements were still crude. The rather ill-produced blades were already being retouched into scrapers, points, and poor kinds of gravers. Bone industry existed, but little is known of it since the remains have not been well preserved in the known sites. At Châtelperron itself one might come across flat points with a split base, known as Aurignac points. D. Peyrony, following H. Breuil, compared this level with others where there are to be found, after a not entirely complete lapse, in the Middle Aurignacian, more advanced points and blades with blunted backs. This is Peyrony's Perigordian I, or D. Garrod's Castelperronian. No art has been found.

(b) *Middle Aurignacian* (= Peyrony's *Typical Aurignacian*). This is characterized, in the stone industry, by keeled scrapers with thin-flake retouching, at first broad, then getting narrower; by nosed scrapers, still rare at the beginning of the period; by different types of graver, angle gravers cut off obliquely, then beaked gravers, very common in the middle and upper layers; by stout blades with wide notches on one or both sides and then narrowed down, and very well trimmed (lower level); by pointed blades, or with their ends made into a scraper, or ogival, and with or without a combined graver. Microliths are very rare, as are blunt-backed blades.

Worked bones appear in quantity, being first split before the great spread of gravers. The leading fossil type is the Aurignac point made from reindeer horn, and it went through the following phases: (i) broad triangular; the base is not always split; (ii) nearly diamond-shaped, first with split base, then not; (iii) spindle-shaped, of oval section.

Art was developing, both *art mobilier* and wall-drawing.

(c) *Upper Aurignacian* (= *Gravettian* = Peyrony's *Advanced Perigordian*). Here the characteristic is the reappearance and multiplication of blunt-backed blades and laminae, occurring at many levels, the stratigraphical position of some being uncertain and probably variable.

1. *Bos del Ser level*, near Brive (Corrèze). This resembles the Châtelperron site by reason of the reappearance of quantities of that type of point, though they are better made and associated with a large number

---

the Lower Aurignacian. The other levels subsequent to the typical Aurignacian, the main one being La Gravette and its variants, were considered by D. Peyrony as successive horizons of the Perigordian that we shall call *Gravettian*, now definitively established as a result of the major excavations by Lacorre at La Gravette (Dordogne).

However likely an affiliation may seem between Châtelperron and La Gravette, these two groups are, in our part of the West, separated by the typical Aurignacian, and their continuity, though it may be possible elsewhere, is still merely an intelligent theory. It would therefore be better to speak of *Castelperronian* and *Gravettian*, and for the time being abandon the term 'Perigordian' as too vague and too ill-defined geographically. This initiative has, indeed, already been taken by many specialists.

of other tools like those of the advanced Middle Aurignacian. This horizon would seem to be a recurrence of the Châtelperron level, cross-bred with such a stage of the Aurignacian. Its position remains uncertain.

2. *Laugerie Haute level* (Dordogne). This is the lowest, underlying the series with Gravette points; it has fairly stout blades, truncated at the ends and developing towards large trapezes and triangles, together with angle gravers. There is no foundation for the statement that this layer is contemporaneous with a part of the typical Middle Aurignacian, although this exists in the neighbourhood.

3. *Bayacian level* (Lacorre). Occurring at the bottom of the Gravette deposit and sandwiched in between typical Lower Gravettian and the underlying Aurignacian, this contains many slender, dart-like points, generally with retouch working on both edges of the underside, in a horizon just below the levels with Gravette points. But such darts appear sporadically at other places with Gravette work, and their very short style of retouching is not at all Solutrean or Aurignacian.

This is the main level in the Pair-non-Pair cave at Marcamps (Gironde) and in similar deposits in other sites in the Corrèze (Font-Yves, at Brive) and the Dordogne. It contains splinter-blades with delicately blunted backs and small, multiple, semicircular scorers. There are still some keeled scrapers, beaked gravers, and serrated blades, but Gravette points are not present. This level is certainly subsequent to the typical (Middle) Aurignacian that is found mingled in it and with a heavy patina at Pair-non-Pair itself, and it is prior to the level containing Gravette work.

4. *Gravettian: the complexus of Gravette points* (Dordogne). This clearly belongs, by reason of its blunt-backed points, to the Perigordian facies. It can be subdivided into several levels, distinguished by: (i) very tiny gravers, named after Noailles (Corrèze), angle micro-gravers made from blades or thin splinters, usually cut off concave and often multiple; (ii) the long-tanged Font-Robert point, sometimes with inverse, proto-Solutrean retouching on the underside, together with other preliminary attempts at this type of trimming. It is to be noted that this point coming at the base of the 'Gravettian' series in the Charente, is found in the upper half in the Dordogne. On the other hand, at La Gravette itself the Noailles graver is not present in the classical level containing large Gravette points. It is more frequently associated with smaller versions of it and with pieces of blades, blunt-backed or cut off square. It would seem, therefore, that regional differences occur in the contents of the Gravette level.[1] Most of the gravers, often very stout tools, are of the angle type, with various terminations, but usually oblique.

[1] See careful monograph on the eponymous deposit at La Gravette, methodically excavated by M. Lacorre. Reference should also be made to the long thesis by Mme de Sonneville-Bordes, *Recherches sur le Paléolithique supérieur au Périgord*.

Among the great variety of bone implements, where ribs were used they were decorated with notches, but rarely split into two. The Pair-non-Pair level provides the transition.

The javelins were long, slender, and round-shafted.

In the Upper Perigordian should be placed the deposit at La Colombière (Ain), which, besides typical flints, including Noailles gravers and Gravette points, has yielded remarkable pebbles, engraved with very advanced artistry and showing horns and antlers free from the distorted perspective of the Western Aurignaco-Gravettian style.

Solutrean

Long, flat, Solutrean retouch work appeared tentatively in the Upper Aurignacian, at the advanced Gravettian stage, but it later developed in three levels in South-west France.

(*a*) A level with flat leaf points, distinguishable by blades with often incomplete retouching of the upper face, but also retouched at the two ends and on the underside. Bone tools are much rarer.

(*b*) A level with laurel-leaf points, with broad, powerful chipping of the large specimens, generally biface and complete. The dimensions vary considerably—from 30 centimetres down to 3 centimetres. At the foot of the Pyrenees can be found very long laurel-leaves with round or square bases, often associated with many asymmetrical types (points from Montaut, Landes), frequently developing on one side a sort of notched tang at the base; or found with prototypes of notched points, evolved from Gravette points, but, like them, without any trace of Solutrean retouching.

(*c*) The Upper Solutrean level with true, typical notched points, limited[1] to the south of the Loire and the west of the Central Plateau, is well developed at the foot of the Pyrenees, in the Cantabrian Mountains, and as far as Catalonia. The origin of the notched point is to be sought in the Dordogne, no doubt in the notched point of Périgord. Elsewhere (Pyrenees, Cantabria, Catalonia) it seems to derive from another type, a concave-based asymmetrical point abundant in those parts, but rare in Périgord. It is accompanied, mainly in the deposits in Catalonia and in South-east Spain, by fair amounts of small laurel-leaf points with a base developing into a stem and often provided with ailerons (El Parpalló, Valencia), and also by many blades with very skilful Solutrean trimming on the back. Lamelliform microliths are also very abundant.

This Solutrean chipping method did not come from a single source.

[1] We know of only two quite typical, sporadic sites in the region between Paris and Orléans; but there are others, atypical—that is to say, not of Solutrean technique—at various levels near the Pont du Gard, below and intercalated with local Solutrean levels and, indeed, mingled with some of them (as at El Parpalló, Valencia), and one at Rio Mayor (Portugal).

PLATE V. 1. Bison cut out of thin bone, from Isturitz (Basses-Pyrénées). Magdalenian IV. 2. Two men fighting a bear, engraved on schist, from the cave at Péchialet (Dordogne). Gravettian. 3. Gravettian wall-engraving of a family of great white owls in the Trois Frères cave (Ariège). (1 and 2, Musée de Saint-Germain.)

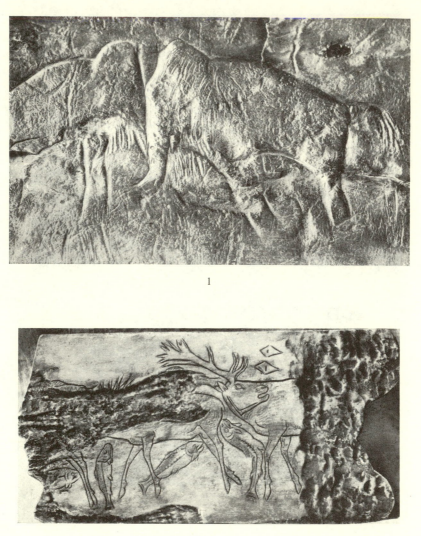

1

2

PLATE VI. 1. Two mammoths head-on, carved in light relief in a series on a reindeer-horn pierced stick, from the pre-Solutrean level called pre-Magdalenian by D. Peyrony, at Laugerie Haute (Dordogne). 2. Stags and salmon, from Lorthet (Hautes-Pyrénées). Magdalenian V. (1, Musée des Eyzies; 2, Musée de Saint-Germain.)

On the contrary, it appears to be related to various stages of trimming technique. The oldest centre, going back in time perhaps to before the cave bear, is to be sought in the post-Micoquian, Hungaro-Balkan area and in the same phase in Central Germany. It is now known that there was another training centre in Spain, where, in the sands of the Manzanares (Madrid) at Leptolithic level, an early Solutrean, with fairly crude biface leaf points, is associated with shapes that are rather Aurignacian, including beaked gravers. In France, in the deep-cut valleys of the Ardèche and the Gard, a technique for producing flat leaf points seems to have developed from an advanced Perigordian. At La Baume-Bonne (Var) these same implements, perhaps made a little thicker, could well come from an advanced Micoquian phase, as in Hungary and Bavaria, where the Germans call it Szelethian and Weinbergian. This zone stretches away to the east (Le Trilobite, Yonne) and to the north (Spy, Belgium). It is not therefore surprising that these shapes should have spread into the Dordogne, the Charente, the Pyrenees, and Catalonia. The single-sided, pointed blade of the Middle Aurignacian could easily have given rise to them, as we do possess Aurignacian specimens from Solutré which seem to bridge the gap.

Furthermore, in Africa, either in the Sahara and Ethiopia[1] or in the austral or southern regions, retouch work, at first on points, gave at the Stillbay site the leaf-like specimens of the Middle Stone Age.

It would appear that the same kind of industrial determinism led human ingenuity to invent and re-invent at various times, in Europe, North Africa, South Africa, and even Oceania, tanged implements and leaf-shaped points.

Bone tools were well developed, but while the industry in one part of the deposits continues the Upper Gravettian tradition, other, more advanced ranges of implements, with new forms of javelin and sewing-needles, are evidence of the approach of another culture, the Magdalenian, with which the *art mobilier* and the rock-art offer points of contact.

Magdalenian

The new culture was distinguished by the disappearance of Solutrean retouching, by the abundance of sewing-needles, and by the great variety of its numerous bone implements. Its flint industry, according to its subdivisions, shows affinities with the Aurignacian and the Gravettian. It added hardly any new tools to those already created; on the contrary, it abandoned many of them: beaked gravers, and keeled scrapers with the long, narrow, curved retouch work, all dropped out.

Even in the classical areas there can be observed, at different spots,

---

[1] There are many of these in certain late Aterian deposits in the north of Morocco and a few in the Southern Sahara, as far as Timbuktu.

K

notable variations in the first two phases of this Magdalenian civilization, revealing the existence of several training centres, where Magdalenian facies gave way to Solutrean. Starting from the Charente and Dordogne regions, where the basic complexity is greatest, we can subdivide the Magdalenian into six levels:

Magdalenian I. Lance-points, without grooves, but with a small-tongued base, gently bevelled, and frequently with fan-scoring, appeared in the Dordogne from the time of the Upper Solutrean at Les Jean-Blancs. Though very large at Le Placard, such points are smaller in Périgord, and they are found again in Cantabria, at the base of a local Magdalenian similar to type III. They are also numerous, but small at the base of the Magdalenian at El Parpalló.

The flint work varies: in Périgord there are many 'raclettes,'[1] or tiny scrapers with short, irregular retouching at the edges. Though rarer elsewhere, they are found with a range of well-trimmed implements, recalling a less skilled form of the typical Aurignacian, containing many multiple borers and gravers made from flakes, often cross-cut.

The *art mobilier* is crude, conventionalized, and barbaric.

Magdalenian II. This covers the area from Poitou to the foot of the Pyrenees, with an offshoot north of Cracow. The lance- or pike-points had conical or pyramidal bases. At Le Placard there were some examples of buckles made from reindeer-horn. In the Dordogne the flint work included many microlithic scalene triangles, some serrated, as well as small blades cut off obliquely with blunted ends. The art is not unlike that of Magdalenian I, but the small-tongued lance-points are lacking, though there are attempts at stem-grooving.

Magdalenian III. This industry spread over a very wide area indeed— from Poland, Moravia, Western Germany, and the Jura down to Cantabria. The bevelled points were smaller, and along their axis ran one or two grooves, for poison or the insertion of microliths, such as are found on other types of very sharp lance-heads, some being sharply curved. Half-round rods or wands appeared, and bevel-cut points became more numerous. Buckles of reindeer-horn were still used in the Charente district, and the first simple forms of hooked throwing-stick were introduced. In South-west France many of the bone knives, some with highly ornate handles, may have been used as snow-cutters. With Magdalenian III began the Magdalenian found in Cantabria, in which are mingled rare lance-points from Magdalenian I. Engraved stone slabs have revealed a very remarkable naturalistic art (La Marche, at Lussac-les-Châteaux, Vienne). Decoration of bone implements derives mainly from the same art form and is often of delicate geometrical de-

---

[1] 'Raclettes' is a term first applied by Dr A. Cheynier to types of irregular, small implements, with edges wholly or partially retouched, and found in many different forms. They look like combined scrapers, barbs, beaks, and so on, and the retouch trimming is 'nibbled.'

sign. Cantabria has been a source of many shoulder-blades carved with such figures, but they seem to have appeared at the end of the Solutrean. Saigas became common north of the Pyrenees from Magdalenian II onward.

The group of industries from Magdalenian I to III is, in many respects, so different from the group IV to VI that many writers tend to treat it as a separate industry, which they term 'proto-Magdalenian.' From the point of view of the fauna there are notable regional differences to be seen. In the proto-Magdalenian, saigas were fairly abundant from Poitou down to and including the Pyrenees. Then in Magdalenian IV the horse and bison predominated over the reindeer; in Magdalenian V the reindeer came to the fore, and in the second half of Magdalenian VI, particularly in the Pyrenees, it was the turn of the *Cervus elaphus*. These details had not escaped E. Lartet and E. Piette.

Magdalenian IV. The centre of the development of this phase is the range of the French Pyrenees, from Bédeilhac and Montesquieu-Avantès (Ariège) to Isturitz (Basses-Pyrénées), passing through Le Mas d'Azil, Arudy. In the Tarn-et-Garonne and the Dordogne it lies directly above Magdalenian III. It is not present in the Charente and Cantabria, but pushes out a weak shoot as far as Valencia (El Parpalló) and a colony in the east, on Lake Constance (Thayngen). The types of lance-point are very diverse, and the single-bevel javelin-head is longer and more slender than in Magdalenian III and rarely has a groove. The conical-base shapes often have protruding shoulder-stops at the end and deep grooves with oblique chequer-marking inside the undercut passage. The forked base is found only sporadically.

This level has yielded harpoon-heads[1] of various types, belonging perhaps to sub-levels. The barbs are usually small and do not stand out. Button disks, often decorated, were cut from shoulder-blades.

Half-round wands were also to appear. They were decorated with linear, pinhole relief designs or deeply cut spirals. The flat face had lengthwise striations—less commonly crosswise—and was often deeply cut out to form a gutter-like groove.

During this period *art mobilier* reached its peak, with superb sculpture in the round at the end of throwing-sticks, used only, perhaps, for ceremonial purposes, the stem being decorated with basrelief. Spatula-handles were carved to look like fish, pendants made from hyoid bones became horses' heads, and so on. Graphic art appears in a wealth of line-drawings, often in slightly cut-away relief, as in medal work. Conventionalization of figures or their parts continued in decorative art.

Magdalenian V. The sculptures, the worked bones, and the cut-away

---

[1] For convenience, we will call any barbed point a 'harpoon.' This does not mean that it was used purely for fishing. Many must have been used for hunting. As they evolved their bases were made in different styles, and there must have been many ways of mounting them.

drawings disappeared. The area covered was very extensive—from Cantabria, up through the Pyrenees to the Loire, over to Belgium and Switzerland, with some evidence of infiltration farther north into England and, in the east, into Moravia and Austria.

Throwing-sticks were no longer used. The lance-points were almost always double-bevelled, sometimes long and narrow, with the groove rare or absent. Other sticks, used as chisels or drifts, began to come in. Forked-base points became more common in certain deposits of the Basses-Pyrénées (Isturitz). The same can be said of the harpoons, usually with a single set of barbs. These developed into two successive types: the older had small, close-set barbs, the more recent bore stout, well-spaced barbs that were long and curved and lay back along the stem. Of this type, a few showed some barbs on the opposite side, being a transition to Magdalenian VI. Among the stone tools can be seen a return to the Gravette style of point with numerous angle or plain gravers.

The art of fine naturalistic engraving continued to thrive and was associated with a rich ornamental strain, derived from naturalistic figures modified for the purpose. There were many animal heads.

Magdalenian VI. This was a direct development from the preceding phase and covered the same geographical area. Yet it was complicated by the recurrence of other elements from the Aurignacian and Perigordian traditions, bringing back keeled scrapers, often large, but not so well finished as the Aurignacian; broad anvil-stones, biface-chipped from circle segments; and, in certain deposits, notched points that were not Solutrean, tanged points recalling Font-Robert shapes, and 'pen-knife-blade' crescents. A special, fairly thin graver, the 'parrot-beak,' was made from a blade or flake by cutting sharply back into it with another graver. Most of the other tools of this type were plain 'screw-driver' shapes.

Among the wood and horn work can be noted the disappearance of half-round wands, the abundance of round punches, decorated with conventional, deep-chiselled designs, and pierced sticks with engraving of strings of animals.

The harpoons had two rows of barbs, at first similar to those of the end of Magdalenian V, then with broad, angular ones, often decorated. Some had angular barbs on one side only. Others, not always sharp, were intended to be used in pairs like prongs or a '*foëne*,' but with the two heads laid laterally, instead of having only one fixed axially on the median line of the shaft. Becoming broader towards the end of the period, which has given some with angular barbs down one side only, they developed into the flat harpoons of the Azilian.

In Cantabria the development of harpoons was somewhat uneven. As Magdalenian IV is missing, there is no specimen prior to those of Magdalenian V; even the early kind, with small, close barbing, from the first part of this phase are also missing. As for the other sort, so common in the second phase, with long, curved unilateral barbing, they are often found with the base modified into a sort of pierced lug, forming a ring for fixing a line. This pattern is unknown in France, where a single specimen with double barbing from La Madeleine, dating from late Magdalenian VI, shows the same lug; the hole to be made in it is carefully drawn, but was never perforated. This fact is sufficient evidence that the inhabitants of La Madeleine had some knowledge of the Cantabrian type. The deposit at La Vache (Ariège) shows a perfect mixture of the two types of harpoon in an isolated spot at the bottom of a deep gorge in the Pyrenees.

THE ORIGINS OF THE DIFFERENT LEPTOLITHIC FACIES: MAIN AREAS

The industries of the Aurignacian and Gravettian groups cover a very wide area and are found from Gibraltar up to England, and across to Southern Italy; from the Rhine to the Vistula, and from Budapest and the Crimea to the Asiatic slopes of the Caucasus; in Syria, Palestine, Eastern Siberia, and in the great loess area of China (Ordos: Moustero-Aurignacian).

The Gravettian facies, less common in greater Asia, is well developed throughout Asia Minor, in North Africa from Egypt to Morocco as a series of derived industries, the Capsian and Oranian, which, with variants, penetrated all East Africa and probably the South. While the cradle of the Aurignacian must be sought far to the west, in the steppes of North China, that of the Gravettian seems to have been in Asia Minor, whence the parallel African and European branches sprang, to follow parallel, though not synchronous, developments.

On the Mediterranean seaboard, east of the Rhône and as far as Sicily, where they succeeded an ancient, typical Aurignacian (Grotte Fosselone—Monte Circeo) similar to that at Krems (Austria), the local 'Gravettians' produced the Grimaldian culture, increasingly microlithic in tendency, but persisting, while west of the Rhone and north of the Alps the Solutrean and Magdalenian were flourishing.

On their northern border the Gravettian, with the peduncled, Font-Robert points, had spread widely in Southern England and in Belgium,[1] with minor modifications—at first Solutrean, then Magdalenian, associated with an industry weak in art and bone work, yet with microlithic and even geometrical tendencies. This is known in England as the 'Cresswellian.'

Thus on the one hand the Grimaldian, and on the other the Cresswellian, were moving gradually towards the formula that was to over-

[1] In France Dr Cheynier found several of these at the Cirque de la Patrie, south of Paris.

run Europe in the Mesolithic with its microlithic and geometrical flint work.

The origin of the Solutrean is more obscure. Several centres produced Solutrean leaf-points. In North Africa the Aterian, which is an advanced Mousterian with short-tanged points and laurel-leaves, had no influence on French early Solutrean. Another apparent contemporary of the Aurignacian is the Hungarian and Balkan Solutrean, with leaf points—at first heavy and irregular and associated with short flakes, and later more regular and lengthened, with a greater quantity of blades that were very rarely trimmed into particular types of shapes, as in the Leptolithic. A final stage gave flat leaf points, and bone-working was more common. With the Gravettian at Předmost, in Moravia, came a few real laurel-leaves; others have been found in Bavaria and, more rarely, in Württemberg.

Professor Zotz and Fräulein Freund in Germany, and M. Bernard Bottet in the Var, have proved the existence, in Micoquian and Mousterian sites, of true, Solutroid, 'pre-Aurignacian' laurel-leaves in those parts. They proposed to call them 'pre-Solutrean,' a term that might better be replaced by 'Weinbergian,' after the name of one of the principal sites. 'Pre-Solutrean' has, in fact, already been used by H. Breuil, on the occasion of the 'Aurignacian controversy,' with quite another meaning, and the matter in question is not, really, a Leptolithic industry.

So it all looks as if an offshoot of a Micoquian industry in Central and South-eastern Europe produced the Solutrean technique, borrowed and later developed by advanced Gravettians.

A third source seems to have been centred in the Madrid region, where rather clumsy Solutrean leaf points were found associated, in the gravel-pits along the Manzanares, with round scrapers, nosed or keeled, and with beaked gravers with the typical Aurignacian facies. Their level is not Mousterian, as was wrongly thought.

When it died out in the west with the coming of the Magdalenian the Solutrean rose from its ashes, towards the end of the Leptolithic, on the banks of the Vistula, in the shape of the Swiderian and Swagolowitzian at the base of the dunes. In the Ukraine only minor Solutrean influence has been found at Kostienki; farther east some still persists, with Magdalenian characteristics.

The onset of the Magdalenian seems to have been caused by external circumstances of various kinds. Its early levels seem to be connected with little-known elements in the Aurignacian tradition, one level of these having come to light at Laugerie Haute, between the upper Gravettian and the lower Solutrean.

The arrival of some new influence from the north and the east cannot be entirely ruled out, and this may have been followed by several others. The appearance of the harpoon, in Magdalenian IV, may be the result of such an influence, and the recurrence of Aurignaco-Gravettian flint shapes in Magdalenian V–VI is further proof of this.

However, it does not seem at the moment that much more can be discovered about the population movements behind these facts, and the complexity of racial types in the Leptolithic shows us that we must be patient and wait until the missing information can be provided. Nevertheless, from this period onward, not only have we to study the industrial techniques of making stone, bone, and horn implements, another and absolutely unique set of facts must claim our attention—namely, the unparalleled and incomparable artistic development they reveal.

$\lceil 13 \rceil$

Leptolithic *art mobilier*

Carvings of humans in the round—Animal carvings in the round, in high relief, and in cut-out shapes—Bas-relief and chasing—Figured engraving on unworked articles—Engraving on unworked bones—Naturalistic engraving on worked articles—Decorative art derived from figures—Decorative art of technical origin: Decoration derived directly from bone-working technique; decoration derived from pictorial imitation of techniques other than bone-work; decoration based on copying artefacts—Schematic art in Leptolithic art mobilier.

This is the art found on small, easily transportable articles as opposed to the art on objects that might just possibly be moved, such as stone slabs or blocks, and to mural art on the walls of shelters and caves, whether exposed to daylight or not. Instead of studying them level by level, we shall examine the work according to its technical and artistic nature: (i) carvings of humans in the round; (ii) carvings of animals in the round, as cut-outs, in high relief, in bas-relief, or chased out; (iii) line-drawings on stone, unworked bone, and worked articles; (iv) decorative engravings based wholly or partly on figures; (v) decorative carving or engraving of direct or indirect technical origin.

CARVINGS OF HUMANS IN THE ROUND

From the time of the earliest typical Aurignacian, at Brassempouy (Landes), artists carved figures of women, perhaps of men, in ivory. Of these there are in existence: one head, with 'Nubian' hair style; three torsos, one incomplete and one corroded; two pairs of legs, one figuring a belt, the other with feet tapering down to a point; a fragment of bust, apparently wearing a cloak and with a folded arm, seemingly a part of the same object; and, finally, two little sticks, very lightly carved to render a minimum of head, bust, loins, and legs in the one case, the second being even more rudimentary. The fragment of broken torso is well preserved and finely worked; it represents a stout woman with plump thighs and detailed sexual organs; the corroded specimen must have been of the same type, with very full breasts, not hanging down as they do on the third, very flat fragment, where the hips spread laterally and the flat breasts hang down over the belly. The two pairs of legs are not as obese; the sex, only lightly indicated, might be male. An attempt has been made to connect these statuettes with others of advanced Gravettian date, but this falsifies their age. They were, in fact, found under the typical Aurignacian—at its base—but in association with a long, blunt-backed point, perhaps related to the Châtelperron type (Allier).

Only one other statuette, found at Sireuil (Dordogne), seems to have come from a Middle Aurignacian layer. Made of amber-coloured calcite, it represents a complete female body, arms and legs retracted, with the buttocks protruding behind; of the broken head there remains only a short tress of hair. The subject is quite clearly a young girl, as the breasts are not fully developed. Suspension-holes show that the object was worn, and the laterally flattened shape must have made it more suitable for this. Two small fragments of soft sandstone from the Mainz loess may also come from the typical Aurignacian.

All other Western statuettes belong to later levels or cultures. These are: the Venus of Lespugue (Haute-Garonne), made of ivory, very stylized but skilfully made, wearing a fibre loin-cloth behind, fixed very low; the hip-projections—if they are not lateral flattening of the buttocks, since the figure is flattened from front to rear—show very strong callipygia, as in the Brassempouy statuettes. The hair falls down the back; the head, with a striated, oval face showing no details, is small; the arms are brought across the upper base of the huge breasts, which fall very low. The shortened, rudimentary legs are without feet.

All other statuettes must be sought farther east; none seems to have been made in Iberia.

These consist of: the Italian group, of Grimaldian date, with the numerous specimens from Mentone—the caves of Barma Grande, Grimaldi, and so on; the larger figure from Savignano sul Panaro (Tuscany); and one other isolated fragment. All are made of steatite, except one of bone at Grimaldi. From the Grimaldi caves come seven small figures and one separate, Negroid head; four are complete, including the one in bone; one other, without a head, is of a man wearing scabbard and belt. The females can be divided into two groups: those flattened laterally, projecting the very stout, steatopygous buttocks to the rear; and those flattened from front to back, giving a steatomerous appearance. All have very enlarged sexual organs and very full breasts. They were turned out in quantity, crude, with no facial detail, except for the single head of Negroid appearance which has a low forehead, protruding brow-ridges, deep-sunk eyes, a flattened nose, and hair shown by criss-cross marking. In one other case the hair falls down the back. The arms are omitted or directed towards the breasts; the man's are directed towards the male organ.

Far more beautiful is the statuette from Savignano (Modena), which has the same pointed legs as one of the Grimaldi examples and displays a fine anatomical study of the thighs and trunk. It seems to be steatopygous, since there has been no flattening of the material in any direction. The breasts are also very full, and the head is completely hidden in an immense hood ending in a point.

The rest of these strange figures are to be found in the Perigordian deposits of Central Europe. There is the Venus of Willendorf (Lower Austria), carved from a limestone pebble, showing a fat, callipygous woman, with short legs and little arms folded over enormous breasts; the hair is piled up in knots and apparently frizzy. The balance of the masses is curious, as in those from Lespugue and Savignano, and shows an equally skilful conventionalization of the human form, although the final effect is very different.

The Venus of Vistonice (Moravia), modelled in clay mixed with powdered bone and lightly fired, is somewhat freer in style. Hence also come other, less complete, small figures of ivory or bone-filled clay; the only one of note is a small, finely styled head, with a regular, oval face, a long, almost straight nose, and a high forehead, apparently wearing a toque.

A grave at Brno (Moravia) produced a fairly large male figure, with no legs and only one arm (no question of breakages) hanging down alongside the torso, well modelled but too small. The head, seemingly unfinished, shows appreciable skill in technique.

The mammoth-containing sites at Předmost (Moravia) yielded a set of four mammoth metacarpal bones, partially stripped of their tough outer surface and roughly shaped into seated men. It is thought that some plastic material, such as clay or wax, adhering tightly to the exposed spongy matter, must have been added to finish the modelling of these little statues of which only the inner supporting core remains.

Farther on, in the Russian steppes of the lower Don and still in deposits with mammoth-bones in loess, came other, fairly numerous discoveries: at Kostienki a flat, severe, ivory Venus, without her head, and one other; at Gagarino seven highly detailed, ivory statuettes, with full bellies, slender limbs, and large heads. Much farther east, in Siberia, from Malta on Lake Baikal, came another eleven ivory statuettes, related to but differing (in lack of obesity) from their Western companions.

In the Ukraine, and again from the mammoth loess and in the

Gravettian phase—but, it is said, of much later date than our Western Aurignaco-Gravettian—it is worth mentioning the extraordinary conventionalized carvings from Mezine. All are of women (except one of a man), and they belong to two successive levels. In the older the statuettes are reduced to a kind of spindle split axially. On the flat, polished side of the most finished examples appear engravings of a few facial features, the breasts—or else the arms brought across them—a belt, a very large sexual organ, and the groin. The convex back bears some outline of the hair and a transverse mark for the belt; across the back too a very considerable, keeled relief shows protruding buttocks, decorated with very complex geometrical designs, like interlocking Greek key-patterns, which may represent tattooing.

Such a remarkable crop of statuettes shows that there flourished, from before our typical Aurignacian, a firmly established artistic tradition of which we know nothing, dedicated to serving purposes connected with the fertility cult. Only rare examples of this can be found after the Gravettian, and they are often very different.

As for the Magdalenian, only a single ivory figure is known, coming probably from Magdalenian III or IV at Laugerie Basse and known as the 'shameless Venus of Vibraye.' It is merely a plain, cylindrical torso, bevelled at the top, carried on two long, thin legs, with the sexual organ well developed. It is thought that neither the head, breasts, nor arms were carved from the same piece of ivory, but that it was completed by another piece, of perishable material such as horn or wood, on which were engraved the missing parts and which fitted on to the bevel at the top of the bust.

Two horse incisors from Magdalenian IV at the Mas d'Azil and Bédeilhac (Ariège) have their roots carved into a crude bust. One has conical, falling breasts and detailed but inartistic carving of the face; the other of indeterminate sex has the head wrapped up in a kind of round hood.

In Western Germany, in a Magdalenian that was probably IV, were found a whole group of statues of women made of jet. They are simplified, but recognizable by their accentuated posteriors (Petersfels).

Other human forms were carved in the round from reindeer-horn: a human head and a man stooping, with his single arm bent forward and the legs missing, come from Magdalenian III, or, more likely, IV, at Laugerie Basse, and are of not very advanced technique.

From Gourdan (Haute-Garonne), dating from Magdalenian III–IV, came a throwing-stick topped by two grotesque human heads, with monkey-faces or masks and deep-cut eye-sockets for the insertion of coloured beads or small pebbles. The crook was formed by the small lock of hair. Another pierced stick was found at Le Placard and dates from Magdalenian III. A third, from the same site and level, roughly carved on a small slab of stag-horn base, has very oblique, elongated eyes, a sharply hooked nose, merely notched out, and a 'sardonic' look on the face, like a kind of semi-animal mask. There are two other examples of these highly conventionalized masks that are engraved rather than carved—the first from Magdalenian III at Marcamp (Gironde) and the second from the Klause Magdalenian IV at Neu-Essing (Bavaria).

All the other human carvings are phallic versions of pierced sticks, sometimes also with a vulva, dating from Magdalenian III and sometimes IV, except for one human foot from Cap-Blanc (Dordogne) cut from a section of antler (Magdalenian III).

It is only in the Neo-Eneolithic, especially in the Balkans and the Middle East, that the series of female fecundity idols reappears.

However, in the Natufian Mesolithic in Palestine a few stone carvings of human figures were found, including one of a couple *in actu* in the sitting position.

ANIMAL CARVINGS IN THE ROUND, IN HIGH RELIEF, AND IN CUT-OUT SHAPES

So far none have been found from the Western Aurignaco-Perigordian. The oldest, really beautiful ivories come from the two typical Middle and advanced Aurignacian levels at Vogelsherd (Württemberg) and represent a hornless rhinoceros, a fine horse, and several large felines. There is also a bas-relief of a mammoth.

The other round-carvings are all Gravettian, from Moravia. They comprise a mammoth-tusk statuette from Předmost and a whole collection of bone-clay modellings from Vistonice, including a small mammoth, a lynx (?), a beautiful reindeer-head, and so forth.

It would appear that carvings of animals began very early in Central Europe, whereas none are known in the East or the West.

In France the oldest statues of animals belong to the Middle Solutrean at Solutré (Saône-et-Loire). There are two or three limestone cores, including a very unfinished bison, a reindeer with a broken head, the four legs raised under a fairly well-carved body, with the flanks full of point-pricks; the third, unfinished, also shows a reindeer in high relief, with pricked sides and only the hind-legs, shown stretching forward.

Next comes Isturitz, providing, from the very thin Middle Solutrean level, but running on into the Magdalenian IV directly above, a whole menagerie of small figures in soft sandstone—a well-finished bear, a feline with pricked sides, a bison, horses, and so on. There exist fragments of more than fifty small statues, many of them intentionally broken to be recarved.

Another similar workshop, though with less skilful artists, existed at Bédeilhac (Ariège) in Magdalenian IV. Two outstanding pricked carvings in stone were found in Magdalenian III at Marsoulas (Haute-

Garonne) and, similarly dated, in a rock-shelter beside the Vézère. They are thought to represent tortoises.

All the other carvings of animals belong to Magdalenian IV. They are sometimes in ivory, or in bone—but mostly in reindeer-horn, and rarely in jet or amber (horse-head at Isturitz).

The ivory ones are: the two reindeer from Bruniquel (Tarn-et-Garonne), the male following the female and magnificently carved on the tip of a mammoth-tusk; the superb Espélugues horse from Lourdes (Hautes-Pyrénées); the mutilated hindquarter of a ruminant, on the end of a pierced stick from Le Mas d'Azil; the splayed top of a hooked throwing-stick from La Madeleine (Dordogne) representing, possibly, a hyena. The mutilated body of a bear from Magdalenian III at Laugerie-Basse is perhaps of earlier date.

A carving in very high relief on a piece of ivory as big as a fist, found at Le Mas d'Azil, shows two very beautiful ibexes, but they are so smoothed away by being worn as charms—several holes enabled them to be sewn to the huntsman's clothing—that any detail that may have existed has disappeared.

Small carved reindeer-horn figures, or parts of them, are legion, and can be classified into three main groups: (i) broad-bladed throwing-sticks; (ii) throwing-sticks with a round stem; (iii) pierced sticks where the two antler stumps, or the end, have been made into parts of animals, usually heads.

The throwing-sticks made from an antler-tine splayed out palm-wise at the top usually have this latter part carved into a whole animal joining it to the stem—mostly by the legs, but at times by the head. About a dozen fairly complete specimens of these are in existence, showing four or five bison and as many ibexes, a single reindeer without the antlers, a grouse (Mas d'Azil), and a rather crude mammoth (Bruniquel). Most of the others are masterly adaptations of the figure to the material.

Most, about ten, come from the Pyrenees, the rest from Bruniquel (Tarn-et-Garonne) and La Madeleine (Dordogne). Examples of exceptional interest are the bison with head turned back, from La Madeleine, the bleating kid, again looking backward, from Le Mas d'Azil, the two headless kids at play, from Les Trois Frères at Montesquieu-Avantès (Ariège), and the headless ibexes from Saint-Michel d'Arudy and Isturitz. Many of these never had a head carved from the same piece, but can be considered as having been completed by heads made of wood or horn. Besides the living poses of the subjects, the tastefully stylized rendering of the skins and muscles speaks of the consummate skill of the artists—one might even say 'of *the* artist,' so close is the resemblance in technique.

Throwing-sticks made from young antler-tines or strong wands became common at the end of Magdalenian IV, and run on, perhaps, into the beginning of Magdalenian V, unless they were antiques piously preserved and considered sacred. Also they are fewer in the Pyrenees, but abundant at Bruniquel as at La Madeleine, and there were fragments of them at Laugerie Basse and Raymonden (Chancelade, Dordogne). Finally, a considerable number came from the Kesslerloch, near Lake Constance. The finest, and no doubt the oldest, from Le Mas d'Azil, shows an ibex reduced to its head (with the horns also curled round the top), its brisket, and forelegs. At Bruniquel, in the Dordogne, and at the Kesslerloch the subjects were horses, as well as a musk ox (Bruniquel) and a reindeer without horns (Laugerie Basse). The shaft of a throwing-stick from Le Mas d'Azil was turned into an eel pursuing a fish, of which only the tail remains. It is not uncommon to find the hook made into the beak of a bird of prey, with the head fairly conventionalized (Saint-Michel d'Arudy). Often these implements have several series of heads or forelegs following each other up the shaft.

Even more numerous are the pierced sticks topped, on one or more of the lateral stumps of the end, by animal heads. Although rare, they are found from Magdalenian II–III onward at Le Placard, the artistry being crude but naturalistic. The main examples are: a fox-head with a fine, long muzzle, on a stout stave, and a small hare on a very small stick. A few other broken specimens have also been found, in the same Magdalenian-III level, at Bruniquel and at Saint-Germain-la-Rivière (Gironde). But in Magdalenian IV such implements become more common: Isturitz (Basses-Pyrénées), Arudy, Lourdes (Hautes-Pyrénées), Gourdan (Haute-Garonne), Les Trois Frères, Le Mas d'Azil (Ariège), Bruniquel (Tarn-et-Garonne), Laugerie Basse, La Madeleine (Dordogne), and Kesslerloch (Lake Constance) have all provided large numbers, usually broken. They represent heads of horses, reindeer, ibex, oxen, bison, and musk ox (Kesslerloch). Many are real masterpieces.

It is not uncommon to find the body partially or wholly continued as a bas-relief on the stem of the object, where other figures may have been executed by the same technique or merely engraved. Heads, especially of horses, and either originating from repaired fragments of such implements or produced for the purpose, were made into pendants. Similar types exist in amber (Isturitz), ivory, and jet.

The use of the haft is rarer: one, from Magdalenian II at Laugerie Basse, is worked into a stag-hoof.

Bone was also round-carved, but in very flattened forms, like the Espélugues trout from Lourdes. Then we come to thin bone cut-outs, all from advanced Magdalenian IV. The largest (about 20 centimetres), from Isturitz, represents a big bison, with every detail engraved. Quite a number of spatula handles were also cut out into fish (salmon at the Rey grotto, Les Eyzies). Often hyoid bones from large

Bovidae were pressed into service for cutting out heads, mostly of horse and often very beautiful, and less commonly of ibex. Others represent whole animals—fawn, cat, and even a seal (Isturitz). Legs are also found and, like the heads, have holes bored for suspending.

The conventionalizing of the skin, and of the bone and muscle structure of these heads formerly and wrongly led to the idea that they represented banded head harness, which simply did not exist.

BAS-RELIEF AND CHASING

Magdalenian III gave some examples—one a large, fairly crude feline from Bruniquel. They occur abundantly in Magdalenian IV, often associated with the round-carving on the same object, as on the Mas d'Azil stick with two round-carved horse-heads and one figuring on the haft as an *écorché*, or anatomically accurate drawing of a stallion's head.

One throwing-stick top from Les Trois Frères is decorated with a round-carved goose and with two others in bas-relief.

Work in relief presupposes preparation of the design by tracing out the lines and not by deep cutting, as in round-carving. This is why most of the bas-reliefs are only very light chasings, obtained by simply scraping away the periphery of a fully detailed drawing. They are very common in Magdalenian IV, representing a variety of animals and even people—horses, bison, ibexes, fish, less frequently birds, and so on, or merely the heads of these animals. Among the human figures are to be noted the bison-hunter from Laugerie Basse, throwing a javelin at one of these animals, one of the very few scenic examples of the period, and, coming from the same sites and the same levels, an otter eating a fish. The pregnant woman from the same source is well known, and her placing is curious, in the background of a large, mutilated reindeer.

After fading out in Magdalenian V bas-relief work of a different, harsher stamp reappears in much of the worked-horn art in Magdalenian VI, often showing strings of horses, reindeer, ibexes or perhaps fish, all very deeply cut, crude, and turned out in quantity. The horse-heads are notably exaggerated in proportion to the size of the body.

Such objects, numerous though they are along the Vézère, in Dordogne, at La Madeleine, Laugerie Basse, Le Souvy, and elsewhere, are found only in isolated instances in the Charente, the Gironde, and Tarn-et-Garonne. Not a single one occurs in the Pyrenees. A few rare fragments have been found in the Gard, in Switzerland (Schweizersbild, near Schaffhausen), and along the Meuse (Pierres-Plates at Saint-Mihiel). This is evidence of an already fairly strict localization of tribes on well-defined hunting territories.

FIGURED ENGRAVING ON UNWORKED ARTICLES

Although the contrary was for long considered to be the case, representation by line-drawing appeared very early, at least in the West. Dr Henri-Martin brought to light, in the Lower typical Aurignacian at La Quina (Charente), a large slab of hard limestone covered with fine engraved lines, so tangled and shallow as to make interpretation difficult, but having certainly some pictorial meaning. Similar fragments of engraved stones, indecipherable because of their broken state, were found in the typical Aurignacian at Tarté (Haute-Garonne) and a few other sites. The frontal bone of a horse at Hornos de la Peña (Santander, Spain) bore the hindquarters of the same animal, deeply cut and of determinable age (typical Aurignacian). Mention must also be made of the bison drawn on a bone splinter and the tiny sketch of a human being from the same level at Cro-Magnon (Dordogne).

But it is only in the Perigordian that these articles begin to multiply. We find engraved schists at Gargas, a horse's hindquarters, two bison, and another animal in an advanced Perigordian level, with Gravette blades and Noailles gravers. Two or three animal engravings in the Planchetorte caves (Brive, Corrèze) were cut on small flat stones. Two similar drawings, one of which is a horse, come from the Perigordian in the Labattut shelter at Sergeac (Dordogne). The cave at Péchialet, of the same date, produced a small slab of schist with the drawing of a bear on its hind-legs attacking a man, with another man coming to the rescue.[1] Finally, a schist pebble from Le Trilobite (Yonne) bears on both sides very beautiful contemporary pictures of three woolly rhinoceroses and an indeterminate cavicorn. In this level at the Isturitz shelter were found a fair number of engraved stones, and the grottoes at Grimaldi have also provided several small, naturalistic engravings of animals (excavations by E. Passemard and R. de Saint-Périer). In Spain, at El Parpalló (Valencia), the Perigordian level is rich in drawings of hinds' heads of a very simple, individual facies, described by L. Péricot.

From the level Peyrony called 'pre-Magdalenian,' which at Laugerie Haute comes right on top of the Perigordian, but underlies the complete Solutrean complex, came a pierced stick bearing light-relief carvings of two mammoths attacking each other head-on, and it seems likely that another fragment found on the same spot by E. Rivière, also with two line-drawings of mammoths, is of the same origin. A fragment from Le Figuier (Ardèche) bears comparison with these pieces.

In England the same level has produced a human figure on a scrap of bone, from Creswell Crags (Liverpool), but almost nothing has

---

[1] Dr Pradel found a pebble with a horse engraving in the late Gravettian rock-shelter of Laraux (Vienne).

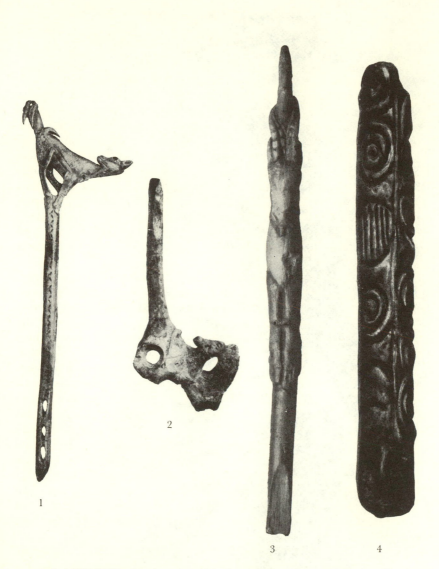

PLATE VII. Various carvings from Magdalenian IV. 1 to 3, from Le Mas d'Azil. 1. Fawn on head of reindeer-horn throwing-stick. 2. Horse's head on pierced stick in reindeer-horn palm. 3. Ibex on reindeer-horn throwing-stick. 4. Reindeer-horn wand with spiral decorations, from Arudy (Hautes-Pyrénées). (1, from Saint-Just Péquart Collection; 2, 3, 4, from Musée de Saint-Germain.)

PLATE VIII. Advanced Gravettian wall-painted frieze of brown horses, with arrows shown on the bodies, from the caves at Lascaux. Copy by M. Thaon, 1940.

hitherto come to light in Central or Eastern Europe, except two or three silhouettes of mammoths in Russia.

On the other hand, in the Grimaldian in Italy, on a small slab in the Romanelli cave (Otranto), Baron A. C. Blanc and H. Breuil were able to make out a fine feline, drawn by an unskilled hand, with the fore-paws showing extended claws and parallel-line shading. There, also, a boar and a goat, both rather crude, were found.

The proto-Solutrean level at La Baune-Bonne, Quinson (Basses-Alpes), revealed pebbles with deliberate line-engravings. With a good deal of imagination, some of the *graffiti* might possibly be understandable. The only unmistakable one is a fish, from Bernard Bottet's digging. A pebble found at Barma Grande, with herring-bone and other decoration, bears similar incisions, but these are absolutely impossible to interpret. Herring-bone decoration is the commonest, but Commandant Octobon found, in the Bonfils bequest of antiquities, two pebble engravings of mammals that are rudimentary but unmistakable.

In the shelter at La Colombière, at Poncin (Ain), underlying a fairly old Magdalenian level, stretches another, identified by Dr Movius as belonging to the Upper Perigordian, with Gravette points and Noailles gravers, and of great interest. It contains figured material and yielded to MM. Mayet and Pissot a set of pebbles with engravings of animals (to which Dr Movius added a further outstanding example) and an engraved bone representing two animal figures, a reindeer and a bear, so arranged that their backbones form the outline of a woman's body. This unintentional similarity prompted the prehistoric artist to add a man. The pebbles themselves are covered with a multitude of animal outlines, mammoth, rhinoceros, bear, musk ox, horse, Cervidae, Bovidae, and so on, all executed with remarkable skill. It is noteworthy that these drawings have got away from the distorted perspective of Aurignaco-Perigordian art and bring in the stylization that was to continue into the Western Magdalenian.

In the *Solutrean*, apart from the very advanced levels with Magdalenian influence, engravings are rare. There is an ivory fragment from the Klause, at Neu-Essing (Bavaria), with a mammoth outline lightly cut into it. At Solutré itself, in a high level of Solutrean with small laurel- and willow-leaf points, H. Breuil found in the middle of a hearth a schist pebble with an ugly drawing of a horse and a few other lines in no sense Magdalenian in character. Then come the very late Solutrean levels of the Dordogne and the Charente, where Magdalenian influence can be seen in the worked bones. At Le Roc de Sers (Charente) were found a few fairly simple but competent stone engravings of Magdalenian stamp. Many fragments of other drawings come from the deposit at Badegoule (Dordogne), where they were found by Dr A. Cheynier in a single level of the site, though it has

L

many of that date. The cave of El Parpalló (Spain) also yielded a large number, of very archaic workmanship, but in addition some painted slabs of a much better style.

It was in the Magdalenian, at all levels, that the art of figure-engraving with a point, either on unworked objects or on bone artifacts, flourished. Our information is unreliable when we are dealing with engraved stones found in early excavations, for they were not often seriously sought after. Similarly, it is not always easy when faced with old collections from deposits with several Magdalenian levels to know which of these horizons really contained them. The same can be said of unworked bones. The nature of engraved stones of schist, sandstone, and various kinds of limestone has also played a part in their preservation. Although several thousand have come down to us, their exact localization often leaves much to be desired. Some deposits have given hundreds of them, whereas others near by and of similar date have very few. Their accumulation thus constitutes a human phenomenon with social or ethnographical meaning.

Magdalenian III produced enormous quantities of engravings on thin limestone slabs, brought into the cave from beyond, many of such a size as to fall outside the category of *art mobilier*. MM. Péricard and Lwoff retrieved a large amount of decorated material from the cave of La Marche (Lussac-les-Châteaux, Vienne), and Dr Pales had the task of evaluating it. It is strange to find that many engraved slabs were used as hearthstones for fires that often split them into very small fragments. The cave was a well-lit, comfortable dwelling.

Bruniquel provided the British Museum with a magnificent set of small slabs, also of thin limestone and probably from Magdalenian IV, from the excavations by Lastic. Peyrony also obtained some from La Madeleine; but J. Bouysonnie's diggings at Limeuil in a pile of debris and rubble from Magdalenian VI produced a great quantity, on fairly thin limestone pebbles. In the Pyrenees they are very common, especially in Magdalenian IV, mostly on fissile sandstone and less commonly on schist. Only a few occur in the Cantabrian caves. One or two have been reported from the Bavarian Magdalenian V, at the Klause among other places. In Eastern Spain El Parpalló has given several thousand, from its bottom Perigordian level, throughout its Solutrean complex, and in its Upper Magdalenian level. They have little variety, however, and the artistry is mediocre.

On such flat stones the artist could trace out his drawings more freely, as on a book page. The fact that very often the surface has been used to cut several figures, and that at times they were so numerous as to make recognition of the multitudinous outlines impossible, shows that certain stones were used over and over again for long periods. It must be supposed that a layer of ochre or blood was used to mask the previous details before the new figures were cut.

The representation on stone of certain species of animal and of man himself is far from occurring in the same proportions in various levels and sites of the Magdalenian. In the Pyrenees, in Magdalenian IV, the bison, ibex, and horse predominate completely, though one does find stags, a rhinoceros, izards (few), Carnivora, bears, wolves, and felines (rare), as well as oxen (rare). Man, badly drawn and a mere scribble, is not as exceptional as has been commonly said. At Bruniquel, in Magdalenian IV (?), the horse is the commonest, then the reindeer, bison, and ibex. The izard appears only on three examples on fine stone, man not at all.

In the shelter at La Marche, Lussac-les-Châteaux (Vienne), slabs of often sizeable dimensions brought from a geological level just above the limestone shelf of the cave carry, alongside pictures of the animals usually represented, unusual numbers of pictures of bears and lions, together with human figures. Some of these are graphic transcripts recalling the obese Aurignacian women, others the heads of men with straight, hooked noses, of fairly attractive types and relatively large size. Such pictures are always rare in wall-art. They are not caricatures, but probably portraits, and often, because the artists were so used to drawing animals, the forward projection of the face is overdone. Another picture shows a man standing and shouting, arms above his head, surrounded by grotesque, grimacing faces, without other extra detail. It recalls some scene of spirit-raising or exorcism. On the other hand, in the early days, from such work many reproductions of human figures accompanied by abnormal detail were taken for use as illustrations. Without casting any aspersions on the undoubted sincerity of this abstracting, one cannot accept such casual elements without re-checking the originals, for they represent items, from a very rich crop of different engravings, that were not part of the undoubted portrayal of human beings extracted from them. In these images each artistic stroke corresponds to intentions and problems not externalized on other media. At Limeuil (Dordogne), in Magdalenian VI, the reindeer and horse have absolute priority, but there are also stags, bison, oxen, a few bears and Canidae, with very rare human figures—and those are artistically insignificant.

Fish are also frequently represented in *art mobilier* engravings at all Magdalenian levels, and, at times, snakes and birds.

ENGRAVING ON UNWORKED BONES

Few bones have wide enough flat surfaces compared with the stone slabs mentioned above, and this led to the use, mainly, of shoulder-blades, hip-bones, and the frontals of large Herbivora. Smaller surfaces occur on cut-up ribs of large Bovidae and big bone splinters, not to mention the splayed palms of the great male-reindeer antlers. One bison frontal, from Magdalenian II at Le Placard, carries a broad sketch of a very hairy horse. Stag shoulder-blades, hip-bones, and rib-sections from Magdalenian III at Altamira and El Castillo (Spain) bear many fine hind-heads, filled in with parallel lines that are not to be confused with the regular, parallel-line shading from El Parpalló and Romanelli used on silhouettes of a very different style. Nothing similar is known in France.

Magdalenian IV used a good number of reindeer-horn palms (Laugerie Basse, Le Mas d'Azil); for heads, particularly of horses, either singly or in series, it used sections of rib (Arudy, Isturitz, Gourdan, Le Mas d'Azil, in the Pyrenees; Bruniquel, in Tarn-et-Garonne; Laugerie Basse, La Madeleine, in the Dordogne). From Magdalenian IV at La Madeleine comes a superb sketch of a mammoth done on a large fragment of that animal's tusk.

With Magdalenian V and especially VI the intensive use of stag shoulder-blade comes in again, but this time for engravings of animals with fairly deep-cut contours (Laugerie Basse, Les Eyzies, La Madeleine, and so on, in the Dordogne; Le Mas d'Azil, on the left bank of the Arize, in the Ariège). The reindeer and horse predominate. The discovery, at Le Mas d'Azil, of a great number of well-engraved shoulder-blades in a confined space with very few other objects points to the conclusion that it was collected deliberately and formed a sort of 'art library,' an art school, or a small, easily portable shrine (Saint-Just-Péquart excavations on the left bank).

NATURALISTIC ENGRAVING ON WORKED ARTICLES

Most of the worked bones gave the engraver only narrow surfaces, either curved or flat, on their round, half-round, or rectangular sides. In this category come pierced sticks, throwing-sticks, lance- and javelin-heads, chisels, punches, and other articles in reindeer-horn. On the other hand, the polishers and spatulae, more often made of bone, were flattened like paper-knives, as were round, centre-pierced buttons and various oval pendants. Though slightly twisted, the sides of cannon-bones of the reindeer, stag, or horse (the latter with a smaller inner cavity), from which tube containers were fashioned, provided fairly broad flats. The figures to be engraved thereon had to be adapted to confined spaces and were, of necessity, distorted or even split into sections.

On the other hand, no careful engraving was done on articles likely to be lost or easily broken, such as projectile-heads or tools condemned, by reason of the violence of the work they were designed for, to be damaged easily or broken. Any sort of elaborate decoration was thus confined to articles of value to the owner, either as charms, or for their intrinsic beauty or their magic powers, or because they were used for work light enough not to disintegrate them too rapidly. However, most of these beautiful works of art, carvings and engraving alike, were, in the end, broken when the bone or horn was still fresh. It is certain that most were deliberately shattered, and the pieces were often scattered over considerable distances: for example, the two halves of the great contour-cut bison at Isturitz were found by a lucky chance several hundred yards apart. This leads to the theory of ritual destruction, perhaps following the death of the owner. The same goes for articles as useless in everyday practical life as the soft-stone statuettes from Isturitz and Bédeilhac, which were deliberately mutilated and the pieces used to make new and smaller figures.

For the reasons just explained, lance-points were rarely decorated—and then very plainly, with no very elaborate figures; this applies also to the functional chisels and throwing-sticks of Magdalenian III. Except for the pierced sticks, where the fairly voluminous round stem gave the artist more room to work, and on flat, narrow bone articles, pictures of animals had perforce to be small or confined to essential parts of their outlines, heads, legs, or parts thereof. Consequently, the component parts of a single drawing could easily become independent, and we shall see the results of this from the point of view of decorative art. The masterpieces of figurative art engraved on artifacts, nearly all of them from Magdalenian IV, V, and VI, are mostly to be seen on pierced sticks and on containers made from reindeer hind-legs, but they often occur on bone blades and disks, the latter belonging to Magdalenian IV. The most noteworthy bears a picture of a masked man capering in front of a bear's leg.

Of the pierced sticks[1] the oldest, a real work of art, belongs to

---

[1] There have been many attempts to explain the use of these pierced sticks—sceptres or maces, brooches for fastening cloaks, arrow-straighteners. Without rejecting outright such rationalizations or ethnographical parallels, other explanations might be preferable, and would not be exclusive, since the same object can be used for different purposes. 1. They may have been used for rope-making, as is done to-day among Portuguese horse-breeders, with pierced olive-wood sticks. This theory is due to R. d'Andrade and seems all the more plausible since the Abbé A. Glory found *in situ* at Lascaux (Dordogne) a piece of three-ply rope that is certainly Gravettian. Long ago it was noticed that the pierced sticks showed signs of wear due to the rubbing of thin rope on the stems, and there are Magdalenian representations of twisted-cord motifs. It is certain that the artists in Eastern Spain often depicted single ropes and rope-ladders with men climbing them, and the bow that occurs so frequently in drawings presupposes the use of other and finer cords. 2. According to another theory, also based on ethnography, they were used for propelling small, multiple projectiles held in place and coupled by strings, which were then passed through the hole in the main stem, laid flat along the handle, and kept in place by the thumb. In the act of throwing they were released, and this enabled the grouped missiles to be fired at small game, such as migrating birds resting on the ground after a long tiring flight. Such an instrument is said to exist as a children's toy among the peoples of Asia Minor. None of these uses excludes the others.

Magdalenian III at Laugerie Haute and bears three magnificent heads of *Cervus elaphus*. But special attention should be given to those examples where the figures are worked round the stem and not distorted when they move on to a flat surface: the stick from Montgaudier (Charente) dating from Magdalenian V, with two superb seals, two snakes, a fish, and so on; the stick from the cave at La Mairie at Teyjat (Dordogne), Magdalenian V, with a mare followed by a lightly drawn foal, around which caper figures with human legs, hairy bodies, and chamois heads, while the underside bears two figures of swans; the damaged stick from Lorthet, with a procession of male *Cervi elaphi*, one turning its head back, and salmon leaping among their legs, dating from Magdalenian V, probably; then, from Gourdan, an antler-tine with beautiful miniatures of the heads of some izards, a *Cervus elaphus*, a wild ass, and a marmot.

Among the tubes or containers, or fragments thereof, may be mentioned the two hinds following each other, found in the Le Chaffaud cave (Vienne), perhaps from early Magdalenian VI. On bone blades the following, among others, deserve attention: a wolf, from the shelter at Les Eyzies (Magdalenian VI); a fox, lying curled up, at Limeuil (Magdalenian VI); a cow with its calf, from Le Mas d'Azil, left bank (Magdalenian V?); and, from the Magdalenian IV at Isturitz, a man following a woman who is wounded in the thigh by an arrow.

All these superbly drawn animals have strong, sure outlines and are filled in with well-distributed hatching; the final product must have been smeared over with black or ochre. Among the impressive range of subjects depicted, the most frequent are horses and bison, mostly from Magdalenian IV, followed by reindeer; then come stags and ibexes; fish are also common, though they practically never appear in wall-art; human beings, or parts of them, are rarer than in free art on stone; bulls are not often depicted, nor are Carnivora, seals, rodents, and birds. There is even a cave-dwelling species of grasshopper (Les Trois Frères, Ariège).

DECORATIVE ART DERIVED FROM FIGURES

Primitive Schematic Art

Alongside naturalistic art, representing animals and man according to the conventions or *visual realism*, there can be found, especially during the Magdalenian, but occasionally much earlier, other pictorial elements drawn as abstract representations of *intellectual realism*. These are basically very simplified figures, reduced to a few essential features, and sometimes treated as decorations and grouped in motifs like geometrical designs.

Such diagrammatic drawing can be found starting with the Perigordian at Předmost (Moravia), the Rue Saint-Cyrille at Kiev

(Ukraine), and Le Trou-Magrite (Belgium). At these two latter sites we have, on the point of a mammoth-tusk and a reindeer-antler, long, slender, comb-toothed motifs, surrounded by other curves, also toothed, and these may equally well represent a fish, an eye, or a vulva. Only the artist knew what it meant. The Předmost tusk is much more complete, bearing the geometrically stylized figure of a woman, with a triangular head, ovoid breasts, a drooping arm, belly with navel-mark, jutting hips, and the beginnings of arms and legs. Mention ought also to be made of a Perigordian drawing from Le Trilobite (Yonne) of a branch, which might also be a feathered arrow.

In the early Magdalenian I and II many lance-points bear simple, usually intelligible, but carelessly cut designs, in which, at times, can be recognized a leg, a horn, part of an animal's head, or a face seen from the front or in profile. Sometimes on the same article three bull-heads appear, for example—one well executed, the second simplified, and the third reduced to a few lines and recognizable only from its proximity to the others. Such 'keys' occur at times throughout the Magdalenian and allow us to interpret graphic symbols that would otherwise be incomprehensible.

However, all through that same long period, alongside the constantly spreading features based on realist art, can be found simple ideographic symbols such as lunes, split or complete ovals, single or double Y's, facing chevrons joined by a line, and so on, and their meaning is uncertain or unintelligible.

A lune, often lined along its length or with points added at the ends, may be a fish, an eye, a vulva, or the sign for a wound. The Y-symbol may mean an arrow-head with forked base or point, a male organ, a horned head, and so on.

On the bone blades of Magdalenian III came a great flowering of these primitive diagrams, at first found singly on lance-points, but now organized into quite rich ornamental designs and associating, unmistakably, fish scales with wavy snakes; there were also horned-headed animal diagrams, a few of the clearer ones providing the key. In the actual chain of the Pyrenees, where there is no Magdalenian III —although it occurs at their foot—they are at first found, in small quantities, in Magdalenian IV. Were the articles imported from neighbouring areas? Later, in Magdalenian V and beyond, although these symbols persist, they give way to ornamentation directly inspired by the great realist art of the time.

Conventions and Ornamentation derived from Realist Art

In Magdalenian IV realist graphic and sculptural art, at its height, provided decorative art with a host of subjects that were depersonalized and turned into *motifs* freely adapted to the article in hand. Among them bison-horns, with their eyes, seem to be, at least *in part*, the source of the extraordinary ocellate and spiralled decoration found in certain areas in the Pyrenees. Some of this, in fine engraving, and not deep-cut as on certain half-round shafts (Arudy, Isturitz, and Lourdes), is already to be found on a pierced stick of Magdalenian III from Laugerie Haute and on a few lance-points of the same age. Only one object of this type emigrated to Hornos de la Peña (Cantabria).

The reindeer eye, with a large tear duct that tends to be exaggerated, is also a theme that occurs from the Pyrenees to the Dordogne; the knee of the ibex's foreleg, treated as a shaded-in square, is also found, with fringes of hair, as separate decoration. The swathes of hair on the flanks of horses and reindeer were similarly stylized and went on up to the end of the Magdalenian, combining with, or running alongside, bands of large dots that are a simplification of the markings on Cervidae hide. Engraving on narrower articles with less available space caused the dorsal and ventral outlines to be separated, or even reversed and elongated, this from Magdalenian III. The full-face view of Bovidae and Cervidae, mainly, but also of other animals, together with various fore-shortened views, full-face or from above, provided an inexhaustible source of subjects in Magdalenian III and IV, but even more so in Magdalenian V and VI. The whole head, well executed on half-round shafts in Magdalenian V, is elongated and simplified on other implements, especially lance-points and chisels, until it looks like a carrot or a beetroot. If the space is restricted in width the motif is reduced to one lateral half. Various parts may also be given individual treatment —ears and horns together, or separately. A similar method was used where the head of a horse is depicted as a trident: the ears are pricked up and the mane shows between them. Horns and ears may be reproduced at the other end of the linear axis, in bipolar symmetry. The fish, often a simple spindle shape, occurs as a graven ideogram on a large number of harpoons at all levels of Magdalenian IV, V, and VI, but it is during the last of these periods that it flourishes in various ornamental forms: on harpoons it gives strings of ellipses, alternate elliptical segments, rows of curves from semi-ellipses, or brackets placed back to back, which, as they keep on recurring, come to look like sets of vertebrae. On the chisels from Magdalenian VI in Dordogne well-shaped fish outlines give a succession of subjects that degenerate more and more until they are taken up again in various ways, either having another meaning superimposed on them or else turning into purely geometrical art.[1]

DECORATIVE ART OF TECHNICAL ORIGIN

Art of technical origin comprises two groups of objects: those *with decoration directly derived from the technique of bone-working* will be dealt

[1] These were formerly considered to be human arms, with the tails forming hands.

with first. Only then shall we consider objects where the engravings represent worked articles or were inspired by the desire to produce pictorial imitations of various crafts such as ropes, textiles, basket-work, and even jewellery.

Decoration derived directly from Bone-working Technique

The following processes were used in working bones: (i) cross-cutting; (ii) lengthwise-cutting, by grooving with a graver; (iii) boring holes for hanging, or for needle eyes, or the larger ones required for 'sceptres'; (iv) modifications to the base of lance-heads or harpoons for fixing to a shaft or adding an extension; or (v) for giving a better grip; (vi) production of lateral protrusions or transverse channels for fixing by binding; (vii) in Magdalenian IV and VI, graver-carving of harpoon-barbs.

Processes (i), (v), and (vi) produced encircling or transverse lines, or rings brought out in relief, that could be used as decorative motifs. Process (ii) gave long, parallel lines, sometimes with a point-marked hollow in Magdalenian I and II, and obliquely chequered in Magdalenian IV. With process (iii), during boring, the awl shoulders commonly traced arcs concentric to the hole, and these could be made into a single or several perfect concentric circles; on the pierced sticks in Magdalenian VI these circles, touched up free-hand, became squares, and if there were several holes near to one another gave rise to zigzags and wavy lines. In process (iv) the mounting-flats of the half-round shafts were, in Magdalenian IV, striped lengthwise with parallel lines, less commonly with flattened zigzags or criss-cross lines, or, especially in Magdalenian V, with parallel oblique lines with a slight wave in them. The flat surfaces of lance-point tips of Magdalenian I were decorated with radiating lines; sometimes, in Magdalenian III–IV, with St Andrew's crosses; later only by parallel, more or less oblique lines. It is not uncommon to see, near the point of a sharp lance-point, a mark which in Magdalenian IV and V is an imitation of the fork of a split-based point mounted on the end. In process (v) the base of the sides of awls, daggers, and pins was notched with regular, parallel cross-cuts, pleasing in effect and meant to prevent the tool from slipping in the hand. Here the craftsman achieved evenness and often an element of balance by grouping lines of different depth and length in regular alternations. From a useful article he made something pretty; from the unconscious, physiological rhythm of the moving tool in his hand he created something pleasant to look at and used his ingenuity to vary it.

This artistic feeling in the production of useful articles could already be found, in early Palaeolithic times, in the harmonious curve of re-touched flint edges or the regularity of the chipped facets of a coup-de-poing or a point or scraper. There is always an artistic element born in any technical process tastefully performed by a skilled crafts-man.

Once they had been realized as a basis of art these sets of lines were used to embellish other articles that were not tools or implements, such as pendants and pierced teeth. This occurred at all levels of the Leptolithic, especially in the first two Aurignaco-Perigordian and Solutrean levels of the three phases. It was still quite common in Magdalenian I–III, but fell away later, to remain only in the Western Mesolithic. In Central and Eastern Europe, probably under the influence of other techniques, it created a quite outstanding geometrical art.

In process (vi) graver-cutting of harpoon-barbs, turned out in quantity by a kind of cunningly standardized technique, became a work of really skilled carving. A fairly broad shaft of antler-horn was thinned down on one or both edges, leaving down the centre, or to one side, the stem or stout main axial rib. Then on this flattened margin were drawn the barbs to be made, and the process of cutting out began. The curved lines, intersecting one another at acute angles, left after designing the barbs were often used for decorating them and the stem itself, and were frequently transferred to other objects.

Decoration derived from Pictorial Imitation of Techniques other than Bone-work

There can be no doubt that Upper Palaeolithic men had string, thin ropes, small woven bags, baskets, and perhaps nets, either because comparative ethnography shows that such materials are known to modern savages nearest to their stage of development or even below it, or because some of these articles are abundantly represented in wall-frescoes in Eastern Spain.

In the typical Aurignacian at Brassempouy, the Dordogne, and the Corrèze there can often be seen hollow or relief cross-hatching of lines representing 'rope,' string, or other binding material, and often not far from the places where they must have been used. Magdalenian IV and V have stick-ends decorated with false bindings wrapped round in relief, in imitation of others that had been lost. On other sticks this appears as simple annular ridges, single or in series, with no useful purpose.

Imitations of basket-work, though always very simple, appeared in the typical Aurignacian in Aquitaine, either as open- or close-worked motifs—such as the ivory water-skin stoppers—from Brassempouy and the Dordogne, and show very close mesh. In the Upper Magdalenian and at Mezine (Ukraine) a needle or a lance-point bears a drawing of the thread or cord that in some cases must have been wound round it. Some zigzag markings may have been inspired by sewing, as among the Eskimos.

Engraved pebbles from the Grimaldian at El Parpalló and the Azilian

(Mesolithic) in the Dordogne seem in many cases to bear the representation of a narrow band wrapped round them.

In Central and Eastern Europe and in the Ukraine geometrical decoration, probably derived from basket-work, but later freely developed, produced a range of remarkable work. From Předmost came many ivories and worked segments of mammoth-rib ornamented with rows of tiny chevrons, sometimes covering them completely. Mezine (Ukraine), of more recent date, though in the same Perigordian tradition, reached a stage of very complex Greek key-designs, often cut on small, conventionalized statues.[1] These were possibly ancestors of the small figurines of the Neo-Eneolithic in South-east Europe, where this rich form of decoration is still carried on even to-day in the Ukraine and Rumania.

There are few examples—though some do occur in Magdalenian III on bone blades—of drawings that can be said to represent net meshes.

Decoration based on copying Artifacts

Only arrows are represented in any number, and they are, moreover, usually absolutely diagrammatic, mostly reduced to a V on its side. Others have a median line. The V is probably the simplification of forked-base heads of Magdalenian III–IV, but the sign both precedes and follows these phases.

In Magdalenian III at Le Placard we find drawings of two javelins with a cord throwing-handle in the middle. In Magdalenian IV at Isturitz symbolical arrows laid on the body of a bison and on a woman pursued by a man are drawn with a barbed line, although the double-barbed harpoon[2] made of reindeer-horn occurs sporadically only up to Magdalenian IV. A perfect reproduction of this type of harpoon was carved in bas-relief on a reindeer antler at Bruniquel.

Many diagrammatic arrow-heads are feathered on one or both sides and gave rise to motifs with bipolar symmetry. The point is not always shown with recurrent barbs; forked examples are known, but only from Magdalenian V.

It is doubtful, though possible, that the bow, common throughout Eastern Spain in the Leptolithic, is represented as in the possession of the little men shown near a bison-head at Raymonden (Magdalenian VI).[3]

---

[1] They may also represent elaborate tattooing.

[2] Antler-horn harpoons may have been preceded by others made of wood that have not survived.

[3] Fragments of reindeer-horn bows have been found by Rüst in deposits at Hamburg. A more complete specimen that could not be preserved had been seen by Perrier du Carne in Magdalenian VI at Teyjat (Dordogne). It is to be noted that the throwing-stick, even if merely decorative, disappears after Magdalenian IV.

The summer hut, either as a dome of flexible branches or of stronger framework with a triangular front, appears only very rarely in bone-engraving, though it is very common in wall-art. Nevertheless the first type is found on bone blades from Magdalenian III and IV and the second on javelin-points from Magdalenian III at Altamira.

The influence of jewellery can be seen in imitations, especially on carved ivory, of the canine teeth of the male stag and of decorative shells. A well-carved ivory cowrie shell was found in the fairly early Perigordian level at Pair-non-Pair (Gironde), and a *Cerithium* came to light in the Solutrean level (?) at Solutré.

Mention might also be made of lignite imitations of Coleoptera from the shelter at Le Trilobite (Magdalenian III) and a shelter in Belgian Luxemburg, at Juzaine (Magdalenian V). Various Coccinellae (?), or rather Chrysomelae, with metallic colouring, came from Magdalenian III at Laugerie Basse.

SCHEMATIC ART IN LEPTOLITHIC 'ART MOBILIER'

Primitive diagrams hold an important place in Magdalenian I–III, and odd elements from them crept into geometrical decoration. They still persisted into Magdalenian IV–VI, but in these phases decoration thrived on conventionalization derived from a degenerated, simplified realist form of art. Nevertheless in *art mobilier* from Magdalenian VI, particularly in the Pyrenees, there was a strong resurgence of elementary diagrams.

The Spanish shores of the Mediterranean, at El Parpalló (Valencia), show various levels of Perigordian date or later. There, together with many realistic engravings of animals on small slabs, quite a number of painted and even engraved geometrical motifs have been found, some of them recalling the curved-line style of the red wall-drawings at La Pileta (Malaga), and others are related to Grimaldian elements from Provence, Mentone, and Romanelli (Otranto).

Indeed, the Pont du Gard and another local cave yielded two massive pebbles with painted or engraved diagrammatic or geometrical symbols, some simple, others very complicated. A small slab from Romanelli bears a horizontal arrangement of red-painted diagrams. At Barma Grande there were also pebbles with purely geometrical engraved designs. All this is evidence that a centre of such non-naturalistic art gained supremacy east of the Rhône and made its influence felt from Perigordian times onward into their Upper Grimaldian extension.

When this influence reached North-west Spain, South-east and South-west France, and Switzerland the purely schematic, Azilian form of art, with painted pebbles, replaced Magdalenian naturalism. Often reduced to groups of lines and dots, it also went in for pure

diagram, mainly with human meanings. This latter form is limited to
Le Mas d'Azil, whereas the former type is much more widespread,
being found in the Central and Eastern Pyrenees, the Lot, the Dordogne, at Bobache (Drôme), and in Birseck (Basle, Switzerland).
Painted stones or small tablets have been found in Mesolithic surroundings as far apart as Victoria Cave (Settle, Yorkshire), Holland, and
Hungary.

【14】

Cave art

General considerations—The first phase of cave art—The second phase of cave art—Schematic art

GENERAL CONSIDERATIONS

At first nobody realized that the Upper Palaeolithic peoples were not merely content with engravings or carvings on small objects. Yet the first discoveries of rock art were either too humble (Chabot cave, in the canyon of the Ardèche) or too beautiful (Altamira, Spain) (1879), and so little publicized by their finders that they passed unnoticed or roused understandable scepticism.

It was only with the discovery of La Mouthe, at Les Eyzies (Dordogne), in 1895, published by E. Rivière, that the 'battle' of the painted caves began, for some of the figures actually went down below the clayey filling. The publication of the engravings from Pair-non-Pair (Gironde) by F. Daleau in 1896 was more important and authoritative, for the figures on the walls were entirely covered by Quaternary archaeological deposits. Daleau had noticed the engravings as early as 1881, but had not understood what they were. When he heard of the discovery at La Mouthe he washed down the walls with a vine-sprayer and brought the figures to light.

The two discoveries at Les Eyzies in 1901, by Capitan, Breuil, and Peyrony, of the shelter with engravings at Les Combarelles, and then of one with frescoes as complex as those of Altamira at Font-de-Gaume, marked the triumph of the new idea that limestone concretions did, in fact, cover drawings of animals now extinct or migrated, such as the mammoth, rhinoceros, and reindeer. E. Cartailhac came to Les Eyzies in 1902 with the A.F.A.S. Congress and was converted, as were many others—and that in spite of the attempts, now seen to be ridiculous, by

Élie Massénat and Paul Girod to gain credence for the idea that they were either modern forgeries or the doodlings of political refugees.[1] E. Cartailhac and H. Breuil then fought the case for the defence in the struggle to vindicate Altamira, and that cave was finally recognized for what it is—the 'Sistine Chapel' of rock art (the expression is Joseph Déchelette's).

For more than sixty years now discovery has followed discovery, so that the total of caves and rock-shelters decorated with paintings, engravings, or carvings, mostly situated in South-west France or North-west Spain, not counting open sites where rock masses have collapsed on to hearths, has now reached the impressive figure of 112. All are limestone caves, except one in the Permian sandstone, near Terrasson (Dordogne). Their geographical distribution is as follows: France: 32 in the Dordogne, 1 in the Gironde, 2 in the Charente, 1 in Vienne, 2 in Seine-et-Oise, 1 in the Yonne, 2 in the Tarn and in Tarn-et-Garonne, 7 in the Lot, 16 in the Pyrenees, 1 in the Hérault, 8 in the Ardèche and the Gard. Spain: 25 in Cantabria, 5 in Old Castile, 4 in Andalusia, to which might be added about 35 painted rocks in the Levant. Southern Italy: 1. Sicily: 3, one of which is on an island. Czechoslovakia: two small red spots at Sloup, near Kulna. Yugoslavia: the well-lit mouth of a large cave, near Cattaro, where a large fish was seen by Dr Absolon. England: Bacon's Hole. Besides these, falls of debris from painted walls and carved blocks have been found in the Dordogne, at Sergeac (three sites), at La Ferrassie, at both Laugerie Haute and Basse, at Laussel, at the Fourneau du Diable, and at Cap-Blanc, and these provide evidence that paintings and engravings did exist on open sites and have now been destroyed, but that carvings in the living rock *were made only where daylight was available.*

The state of preservation of the figures in dark caves is more remarkable than is commonly realized, and is generally related to the draughts of warm air coming in from the mouth, bearing water-vapour that later condensed. This is the commonest cause of the destruction of decorated walls in a wide-mouthed cave that has never been closed.

The reindeer-, bison-, and mammoth-hunters, at various times in the Leptolithic, penetrated deeply into these dark recesses, carrying lights—either tallow lamps or, farther south where wood was more abundant, torches or resinous sticks. Since they were so bold in exploring everywhere, they must have been capable of quickly relighting a lamp extinguished by dripping water, an earth-fall, or a strong draught, and for this they no doubt used a fire-bow or 'drill.' There they used flints or sharp bones for engraving or carving the rock, while in the dark galleries they modelled statues from the earth or clay. Many a time

---

[1] This explanation was unfortunately revived, in 1956 and later, concerning the fine animal figures at Rouffignac (Dordogne), and has also been surreptitiously applied even to Lascaux. (H. B.)

they painted, using different techniques—sometimes with charcoal, but usually in a range of ochres from yellow to purplish red, sepia, brown, black and blue-black (from manganese), and sometimes white (from pipeclay or slaked lime). The ochre was scraped or ground into a powder, pounded with a pestle in cups, then transferred to saucers or hollow bones and mixed with fat or some other fixative; or, as the case required, it might be applied by blowing, either by the mouth or through a tube.

All such works of art are not contemporary, but belong to successive periods of the Leptolithic. They can be dated by reference to geological time. It is obvious that drawings of animals that are now extinct or have migrated are either of the same age as those animals or are modern forgeries. If the work was buried, partially or wholly, by floor material at the spot, or was covered by stalagmitic sweating, that would be evidence sufficient to rule out fraud and might at times give indications firm enough to date them in antiquity, even with some precision. This is, however, by no means generally the case.

They can also be dated by reference to the different levels of the Leptolithic, in the following circumstances:

1. When a fragment of wall is found where it fell into an undisturbed archaeological deposit it may be older, but cannot be more recent, than the layer containing it. It is certainly considerably older than the undisturbed layers covering them both. We can thus be certain that such drawings are not later than, but prior to, given periods of the Leptolithic.

2. When, in a cave floor, there are found, *in situ*, bone engravings similar in style and make to the undated wall-decorations we can be morally certain that the same artists were responsible for both. Fairly rare examples are: Altamira, El Castillo, Hornos de la Peña, and Gargas. Such observations provide a definite criterion for considering —approximately, of course—whether engraved figures are earlier or later than others cutting into or covering them.

The study of these rock palimpsests enables us to determine the sequence in time of works of wall art; first by direct analysis of their physical contours, which will show the order in which style succeeds style on a particular site; then by comparing the resulting groups with single, unmixed series of figures from other places. This will lead us to see which groups are forerunners of others and which are opposed by different conceptions of drawing and pictorial technique. Using such lines of approach, and combining them, H. Breuil succeeded in establishing that there were, in Leptolithic wall art, two separate and successive phases. The first undoubtedly covered all periods previous to the Solutrean, while the other started about the middle of that period and went on until the end of the Magdalenian.

Such a conclusion, applicable without any important difference to all

PLATE IX. Large black bull, 5·50 metres long, superimposed on a red cow. Upper Gravettian wall-painting, Lascaux. Copy by M. Thaon, 1940.

PLATE X. The 'unicorn,' a black figure superimposed on a small red line-drawing of a horse (Aurignacian, not very visible here) and another horse of later date. Cave at Lascaux. Gravettian. Copy by M. Thaon, 1940.

the various areas with decorated caves, strongly suggests that they are to be explained quite as much as social and religious phenomena and not merely as art. Indeed, it is difficult to imagine such uniform development in the Dordogne, the Pyrenees, Cantabria, and to some extent in Southern Andalusia without a certain spiritual unity, even without some artistic orthodoxy, rooted in actual seminaries of artists or probably magicians. This leads on to a consideration of the place of such wall art in the life of these hunting peoples and also of what can be called the problem of the origin of such art.

There has been much discussion to determine whether the artists created these works from love of their art, for the mere subjective satisfaction of having produced them, or whether they painted and engraved in order to gain magic powers over the animals they hunted. The two views are not contradictory, or mutually exclusive, but really complementary. It can hardly be claimed that each line, each figure, had a magic purpose, and one can well imagine that, in many cases, to dash off an outline may have had no more significance for the artists than an expression of their personalities to themselves or to subsequent visitors to the sites, just as modern sightseers have a tendency to scribble their names on things. On the other hand, it is obvious that many of the figures must have taken a considerable time to produce, as well as real understanding and skill in drawing—a technique that would have required long practice in time freed from the exigencies of everyday living and hunting—and they demonstrate, firstly, that the artist took real aesthetic pleasure in his work, and, secondly, that the society in which he lived attached some importance to his productions and guaranteed him a living more or less free from daily cares, because his works had a bearing on the satisfaction of needs his fellows considered vital for their existence.

Nobody will deny that in Egypt art was sacred to the cult of the dead or that in the Middle Ages it was placed almost entirely at the service of the Christan ideal. Similarly, in the reindeer age our painters and sculptors, of no less artistic skill than Egyptian priests and the craftsmen responsible for our cathedrals, found, thanks to belief in the magic of hunting, of reproduction, and of destruction, a social basis for practising, developing, and teaching their art. They were both artists and magicians, creating for love of art, but also to increase and multiply the game they wanted, to make the hunt fruitful, and to destroy harmful beasts. Art, particularly in little-developed societies and cultures, could survive and grow only by becoming part of some activity they looked upon as essential.

Yet before it could be adopted and live in and on practices based on sympathetic magic this art, the oldest of all, had to be born, for although magic may have adapted art to its own ends, it did not originate it. Its origins were very humble. In the first place, man's faculties at that

M

time were in no way inferior to our own and were in many respects superior. A highly retentive memory, fed by an active life and visual training without which survival itself would have been doubtful, could analyse in most minute detail the shapes of game animals, providing an indispensable mental basis for any creation of animal art. Then he had to think of drawing, of interpreting in two dimensions creatures living in three. This was a matter of sheer luck and a spark of genius. For reasons unknown, man collected clay from cave walls, rubbing it on his body or plastering over cracks in the daub or branch walls of his hut. Accustomed as he was, like any hunter, to observe the tracks of game, he noted with interest the marks made by his fingers in the clay and repeated them for the pleasure of seeing the results of his acts, making them into meanders or swirls or trellis-patterns. With them he changed natural reliefs into shapes suggesting a figure, and then he began to try to interpret the lines and give them meaning. Then suddenly, nobly, out sprang the free outline of a horse or a bison, traced after a few first attempts with a steady, sure hand. Thus 40,000 years ago was born the first drawing, done first with a finger on clay, then with any bit of wood or bone, and finally with flint or rock.

The origins of painting were similar. Already in Mousterian times man used colouring-matter for daubing his body, varying from red iron ochre to charcoal or manganese black. He put an ochre- or charcoal-smeared hand on a smooth rock-wall, left a print—and gazed at it. This was the first wall-painting. He varied it, made negatives of it, then imitated it by tracing in colour. He trailed his colour-dipped fingertips across bright walls and was delighted to see the arabesques of parallel lines he produced. He could see that they waved like snakes, so he sometimes added a head. As with the silhouette drawings on clay, the lines were first triple fingermarks, then came the single line, and coloured drawing had been discovered—that humble forerunner of the magnificent works that were later to be the pride of mankind.

There, at the end of long, dark passages, ill lit by a few small lamps, when the deep, Ice Age winter became more savage and hunting was impossible, the tribe would go to ground in the relatively warm recesses of the earth. For weeks, like the Eskimos, they carried on ceremonies that the fine weather had interrupted, living on smoked meat, using for illumination the fat or resin stored in the better weather, listening to the priests or magicians as they told of their traditions and the teaching of their forebears on their origins and history. Young men, on the threshold of adult life, were initiated into the duties and knowledge required in their new estate. There were ritual dances in grotesque or animal disguises. Then came the magician, the artist engraving or painting figures of the animals they wished to see multiply, or to possess or destroy. Sometimes they drew, in shapes similar to the ones they knew, half-human, half-animal beings, spirits who control the breeding of animals and give victory in the chase, and prayers would go up to them or to Him whose benevolent creation could bring comfort into the lives of the assembly.

Through each phase run, in parallel currents, pictorial art, with coloured figures, and the art of carving or engraving. It is rare in the first phase to find the two techniques associated in the same figures, though this double process is frequently met with in the second phase.

Engraved or Carved Figures

Alongside the clay daubings and irregular 'macaronis' that gave rise to the first firm outline drawings of animals and are always cut into by other figures, there occur, on free stone blocks sunk in the Dordogne deposits and certainly early Aurignacian in date, carved figures of vulvae and less commonly of phalli, crude tributes to the elements for perpetuating the race. With them come line drawings, on the same stones or others, of animal tracks and rudimentary shapes of quadrupeds, done freehand in a very simple style, or carved adaptations of natural outlines.

The art of flint-engraving on walls quickly developed, with, at first, a fine line that soon became deeper. This recalls the 'wiry,' continuous lines of the rare figures in *art mobilier*, only giving way to hatching for depicting the bodies of long-haired animals. The legs are sometimes, but not always, reduced to two and are very stiff. Bison- and bull-horns are shown head-on and not in profile outline. Much later only a single horn was shown on bison, those on bulls being three-quarter view. With ibex, sometimes the two horns can be seen, rarely full-face; at other times there is a single horn swept back. The first style is much commoner in the South-east Rhône area, and very rare elsewhere.

The hooves were at first ignored and then drawn with the same *twisted perspective*—an oval or circle for horses and a centre-split oval for cloven-hooved species, principally the Bovidae.

Yet as art develops in the Gravettian period horns and antlers, as well as hooves, tend to come nearer to profile (Lascaux), though they never really lose the twisted perspective of the three-quarter view. At this advanced period of the first phase the four legs are usually shown quite independent of one another, as is fairly general throughout the second phase.

All these observations apply equally to painting, and it is only important to study its development after the initial stage of finger-drawing. It ought to be pointed out, however, that triple-line yellow or red finger-drawings have so far been found only at La Pileta (Malaga, Spain) and at La Baume Latrone (Gard). In this latter cave there are not only bears (?) and rhinoceroses, but in particular elephants with tusks in distorted perspective, pointing up and down. At La Pileta alongside wavy snakes is a picture of a long-horned rhinoceros, a bull, and an ibex, each with a single horn and in the most archaic style of finger-drawing. The large snake at La Baume Latrone has a strange head resembling a bear-skull.

Mostly, the old figures drawn subsequently are in yellow, and then in thin, red lines. Later the line, often red, rarely black, appears as a broad or a thin stroke, before becoming thicker and more blotchy. At that stage it was produced by rows of dots run together, at first made as if with a pencil or brush, later with a pad. The horns are nearly always in pronounced false perspective, though this decreases later still.

As early as the Upper typical Aurignacian rough silhouettes appear in plain red, black, or sepia, subsequently with black outlines for other colours. The legs are stiff and, in horses, very short. They already alternate with outlines rubbed in black, and then the broader lines of deep-black liquid paint. At Lascaux, for applications of black, red, and even sepia, an air-brush, or blowing-tube, was used. There the silhouettes in plain red, then in plain black with the horn perspective less distorted and nearer to profile (with only one exceptional example), are the peak of Gravettian artistic development, together with the very skilful black line-drawings of heads of *Cervi elaphi* with an almost Magdalenian flavour. An attempt can be seen to bring the two antlers together by changing the shape of the tines on the head shown behind the other. This is the latest stage of Aurignaco-Gravettian art, which, in the Lascaux cave, reached an extremely high level and a very remarkable range of expression. Its connexions with paintings of animals in Eastern Spain cannot be denied and are, indeed, confirmed by the practice—here unusual, but common in Spain—of composing the figures into scenes: a man dying between a disembowelled bison and a rhinoceros that was presumably responsible for the slaughter.

Already, five years before the discovery of the Lascaux paintings, one of us had written:[1]

> Didon's finds at Sergeac are far more important. At the Blanchard rock-shelter he came across a broad fragment of wall that had collapsed into an advanced level of the Middle Aurignacian. It bore two drawings of bison done in broad black outlines on a plain red ground; the legs, all four being depicted, are extraordinarily stiff in style, but the detail of the hooves (seen from the front) is fairly carefully conveyed.
>
> A large animal in the same style, of which no reproduction is yet available, can be seen on a vast block that collapsed between two Upper Aurignacian levels at the Labattut shelter, quite close to the above. Didon sent it to the Saint-Germain Museum. On the same block, but

[1] Abbé Henri Breuil, *L'évolution de l'art pariétal dans les cavernes et abris ornes de France,* a paper from the Congrès préhistorique de France, 11th Session, 1934, p. 12.

seemingly of later date, appear several small animals done in blue-black, and one, better preserved than the others, represents a stag that is far better drawn than might have been expected at such an early date. The distorted perspective of the antlers is identical with Cantabrian figures of stags, and also with all such subjects in Eastern Spanish art. Together with the thin painted slabs from the pre-Magdalenian levels at El Parpalló (Valencia), the stag from the Labattut shelter, hitherto an isolated example in French wall art, forms the bridge between Franco-Cantabrian, Perigordian art and that of Eastern Spain, which seems to continue and develop it in the Solutrean and Magdalenian.

Another fallen block from the roof of the Labattut shelter showed a hand outlined in red. It is obvious that painted blocks that have fallen into hearths and been covered by them enable us to state with absolute certainty that such drawings are prior in date to the levels that contain them, but nothing more precise can be expected from such facts; the antedating may be so slight as to allow them to be considered, to all intents and purposes, contemporaneous, or else the difference may be considerable. Personally, I am of the opinion that the small, single stag is from the Upper Perigordian, while the red-lined hand and the large animals in two colours are from the end of the Aurignacian.

At that time we were right to expect new discoveries to confirm these early conclusions, but we were far from suspecting that the Lascaux cave-paintings would reveal an era when the techniques followed one another with such speed and variety, reaching the first peak period of wall art, and at least equal in value to the products of the artists at Altamira and Font-de-Gaume many thousands of years later.

THE SECOND PHASE OF CAVE ART

After a break in the continuity of the available information, covering the first two-thirds of the Solutrean, we find wall art again appearing, though very different, according to the nature of the rock used as a base. Between the very high Solutrean of Le Roc de Sers (Charente) and Pey de l'Aze (Dordogne) and the early Magdalenian of Cap-Blanc (Dordogne), Mouthiers (Charente), and Isturitz (Basses-Pyrénées) a very fine style of accentuated bas-relief was practised, with quite modern artistic conventions, on walls (Reverdit shelter at Sergeac) and on blocks (Les Jean-Blancs, Laugerie, both Basse and Haute, in the Dordogne).[1]

---

[1] In 1956, in the vast Cro de Granville cave at Rouffignac, an enormous collection of engravings and paintings was discovered by MM. Nougier and Robert, who called me in to identify them. There I saw a large number of engravings and many paintings done in black lines with hardly any modelling and beautifully economical in style. Besides a few horses, bison, and ibexes, there were enormous numbers of mammoths, often shown face to face, and a few superb woolly rhinoceroses. These figures, one in age and style, reminded me of the two mammoths, also face to face, in

Quite recently, in a shelter near Angles-sur-Anglin (Vienne) at the 'Louis Taillebourg Cave,' under a large mass of debris from a roof-fall, were found fragments of a large frieze that had fallen in blocks and smaller pieces on to a layer of Magdalenian III covering the rocky floor. They show mainly horses, reindeer, bison, an ibex, an izard, a mammoth trunk, and a human head. Further excavations brought to light at the downstream end of the same shelter, some 60 metres long, a continuous frieze of the same animals—in particular, a family of ibexes. This frieze seems to have been joined to the upper, ruined section found first. The most remarkable figures are three nude Venuses, standing side by side. These underline the importance of the discovery made by Miss D. Garrod and Mlle S. de Saint-Mathurin. In 1952 M. Bessac found in the shelter of La Madeleine at Penne (Tarn), which is well exposed to daylight, not only a beautiful horse in light relief, but the more deeply cut figures of two women, astonishingly graceful in general appearance and symmetrically arranged face to face on either side of the entrance. They are stretched in a sensual pose, the bust slightly raised and supported by a bent arm, keeping the head almost invisible. This confirms that there was a custom in Gravettian and Magdalenian times of confining the portrayal of realistic female figures to well-lit, inhabited caves, to the exclusion of dark ones.

Elsewhere such bas-relief becomes attenuated into deep-cut lines with chasing or into vigorous engravings (Commarque, Bernifal, Las Combarelles). But in the Pyrenees area—except Isturitz—and Cantabria the rock was too hard for high relief, and the artists had to be content with shallower cutting for the outlines, filling in with parallel hatching, like the engravings on shoulder-blades in the final Solutrean and the early Magdalenian at Altamira and El Castillo (Santander, Spain).

In any case, from the Pyrenean Magdalenian IV the technique of clay-modelling (bison at Tuc d'Audoubert, bears, horses, and felines at Montespan, Ariège) was widely practised. In that period engraving in the Pyrenees reached a high state of perfection, especially in the Trois Frères cave (Ariège), where the drawing attains modern conventions in its representations of antlers, horns, legs, and hooves.

For rendering surfaces 'cameo' engraving was invented, bringing meaning out not only by line, but by the yellow-ochre tint of thin clay

the pre-Magdalenian level at Laugerie Basse (below the whole Solutrean complex). In its perfectly corrected perspective this art is also comparable with that at La Colombière (Ain), dating from the end of the Perigordian. It would seem that after the expansive flourish of the magnificent frescoes at Lascaux a phase of severe reaction led to more austere tastes, just as in Western religious history the Protestant reaction followed the rather excessive Humanism of the Roman world. Other passages contained huge ceilings with extensive clay drawings, which, though related to our Aurignacian, are notably different both in their total lack of animal figures—except for snakes or sinuous lines—and because the purely abstract motifs do not overlap. (Seen by H. Breuil, August 14, 1958.)

surfaces, the white of rotted rock, and the black of the living rock underneath.

Yet soon engraving ceased to hold pride of place, and apart from a few light *graffiiti*, charming though they are in their pure outlines (Marsoulas, Teyjat, Font-de-Gaume), it became the handmaid of painting, either for outlining beforehand the picture to be painted or for obtaining highlights in the colours. However, about Magdalenian V the hard sand floor of the shelter at Niaux (Ariège) was being engraved while the walls were only painted, or else medium-sized blocks were used, as at Limeuil (Dordogne, Magdalenian VI).

Alongside these engravings and carvings, painting continued to develop. Strange to say, at first it had forgotten everything about the advanced technique of the late Gravettian and started again with modest *graffiti* of black lines as in charcoal, and rarely very ambitious. Then the line soon thickened and grew firmer, with thin and thick strokes. Some rendering of hair began to look like hatching. But this was only about Magdalenian III (Cantabria). Some clumsy attempts were made at quite plain, partial filling in, accompanied by very discreet use of engraving (Le Portel, Ariège). Then came hatching to mark the indentations of flanks and bring up curves into relief. Finally black, modelled as in charcoal-pencil and stump work, became generalized; dark brown was used plain on engraved backgrounds, and black or red stippling for filling was attempted, but did not spread (Marsoulas, Laugerie Basse). Later, at the beginning of Magdalenian VI, true polychrome work came in, first as discreet touches to eyes, hooves, and ears, and then boldly, outlining figures with strong black lines, or encircling modelled areas with different tints ranging from sepia to vermilion through purple and orange tones.[1]

Engraving, light in the Pyrenees, bold and deep in the Dordogne until it almost became bas-relief, was used to prepare the painting and to trim up various details. This was the summit of such Magdalenian art, and it was suddenly to die out. Hardly any light *graffiti* help to model the polychromes at Font-de-Gaume and Marsoulas, and in this latter cave they are not quite obliterated by wide rows of red barbs, preceded by tectiforms and pectiniforms. At Niaux, at Les Églises d'Ussat (Ariège), on the threshold of the Azilian Mesolithic, are to be seen, besides rare, small red line-drawings of horses and ibexes, rows of ladder-work signs. These were the last fitful struggles of an art that was dying as it took up again shapes that had been out of date since the Aurignacian.

---

[1] All such wonderful developments are unknown in the Andalusian caves (La Pileta, Ardales). Pictorial art, starting from the same finger-drawing, stopped after the 'wire-line' stage (with one horn) at the black line-drawing with the distorted perspective. No trace of the influence of true advanced Gravettian or Magdalenian art can be seen.

The influx from the Mediterranean that was to give birth to the Azilian had begun. The newcomers, more fishermen, snail-collectors, or shellfish-eaters, no longer had the powerful imagination that was the source of the great art of the hunters of the mammoth, rhinoceros, stag, reindeer, and horse. That fruitful source of violent emotion so liable to be expressed in great pictorial art was gone for ever. It would take tens of thousands of years before humanity again found the power— in other ways, and then only after an infinitely long development of intellectual and social life—to rediscover that vigorous view of living things and identify itself with them.

Only in remote corners of South Africa did other peoples—the Bush-men—continue to draw on the same springs of searing emotion, at first in pursuit of no less powerful and agile game, and later in a savage struggle against foreign invaders. This gave them the sacred inspiration for great animal art, for pictures and frescoes of the hunt and battle into which, in their moments of leisure or anxiety, and unaware of the splendour of their work, they sublimated the overflowing energies of their wild lives.

SCHEMATIC ART

In *art mobilier* as well as in wall art there existed, at all stages of de-velopment of the Leptolithic, an original schematic art which though perhaps modest in comparison with the great naturalistic forms, was nevertheless quite definite. In the Magdalenian caves of the Dordogne mention need be made only of the tectiform markings (huts), usually quite clear, which belong to the various stages of that culture.[1] At Lascaux, which goes back to the older Perigordian, alongside arrows and throwing-sticks there appear barred rectangles and polychrome chequer-patterns, perhaps of heraldic significance. One of the caves at Cabrerets (Lot), probably dating from the very end of Magdalenian VI, contains a panel of red signs in the form of shoe-soles, seemingly derived from Cantabrian tectiforms. In the Pyrenees the Magdalenian IV paintings and engraving at the Tuc d'Audoubert and at Les Trois

---

[1] During the last war Kurt Lindner attempted to read these signs as traps or hunting-nets, and many writers subsequently subscribed to this opinion. None of them realized that the animals they presumed to have been caught in the traps are not in the same pictorial layer as these objects. Thus, although it is ingenious and by no means absurd, this explanation is false, in spite of its unwarranted success. Hugo Obermaier had interpreted the signs of Buxu (Asturias) as spirit-traps, similar to the kind of cricket-cages, veritable midget houses, set by the inhabitants of the Celebes to capture evil spirits. The fact that many of these signs are grouped in remote corners away from the other figures leads one to think that they are 'little houses' made for the use of the shades of the dead, often in the farthest reaches of the caves. (See the comparative series of huts of all countries and ages listed by H. Breuil in *Font-de-Gaume*, pp. 235–246.)

Frères (Ariège) show quite a number of club figures and strange signs derived from a lion head, as well as others from bats, which again may be tectiforms. The most recent elements, probably from the end of Magdalenian VI, at Niaux (Ariège) and mostly drawn in red, show many groups of 'punctuation' marks, with tectiforms, claviforms,[1] ramiforms, feathered arrows, and diagrammatic arrow-heads. Others are to be found at Les Églises d'Ussat (Ariège), while Marsoulas (Haute-Garonne) has given, overlying the polychrome animals of Magdalenian VI, two successive layers of grouped punctuations with symbols that are at first pectiniform (hand diagrams) and tectiform, then ramiform. It is doubtful whether these signs still belong to the Magdalenian, since the Azilian in the Pyrenees in general, and at the Mas d'Azil in particular, has provided many Mesolithic painted pebbles with punctuations, bars, and signs.

The Cantabrian caves, however, are rich in schematic art and, from the Aurignacian and Gravettian up to the end of cave art, have yielded great quantities of tectiforms, more varied than elsewhere, ramiforms, feathered arrows, claviforms, and pectiniforms. The frequency of occurrence of diagrammatic art thus increases from north to south.

The cave at La Pileta (Malaga, Spain), both in its stage with red, then yellow figures and in the more recent black phase, contains a great number of symbols: yellow serpentiforms,[2] testudiforms, and tectiforms in red; black tectiforms[3] and rectangles with erased corners, similar to those at Altamira (Santander, Spain, Magdalenian III);

[1] In the 'sex-maniac' interpretation we have already mentioned the claviforms are made to look like female profiles with prominent posteriors, comparable to the small jet Magdalenian amulets from Petersfels (Baden) and, though not so closely, to the unusual *graffiti* with the same meaning from La Roche (Lalinde, Dordogne). I was inclined, though to the best of my knowledge I never said or wrote anything to that effect, to agree with this view, and I turned it down only because there are too many missing links in the comparison, both as regards *art mobilier* and wall art, and we were therefore proceeding *de genere ad genus*—always a deceptive method when dealing with conventionalizations. It was, however, the least absurd of the comparisons invoked by this generally deplorable method. Claviforms (club-shaped) do not exist in Dordogne, are very common in the Pyrenees, and are fairly rare in Cantabria, except in the early period (Altamira, Santian, Pindal), all of which is very far from Baden.

[2] These red serpentiforms in complex arabesques, of later date than the triple-line 'macaronis' and often interpreted as snakes, form a special group. As for those which slash so strangely into the animals on the engraved pebbles from La Colombière, others can be found cut into the flanks of mammoths in the cave at Rouffignac and on small Gravettian bison at Les Trois Frères.

[3] Among the red drawings at La Pileta (Malaga), in one of the most inaccessible corners of the cave there occur several nearly circular, comb-toothed motifs enclosing ruminant tracks; one encircled a yellow ibex of earlier date. H. Obermaier and H. Breuil considered it possible to interpret them as enclosures for keeping live wild ruminants.

and even completely diagrammatic human figures in black. The size is quite considerable.

In these decorated caves the often quite numerous figures relate almost exclusively to animals it was particularly desired to catch, and in any given site they are of one particular species rather than any other. However, the drawings are not exclusively of one kind, and pictures of other animals, some common, others rare, can be found on the walls. Thus in the cave at Les Combarelles (Dordogne) they are more particularly of the horse, then of the mammoth, bison, reindeer, ibex, and stag—but the wolf, bear, lion, and rhinoceros do also occur. At Font-de-Gaume (Dordogne) bison predominate, with reindeer and a few horses. The mammoth also takes first place at Bernifal (Dordogne); at Rouffignac it is absolutely predominant, followed by the rhinoceros, ibex, bison, and horse; there are no Cervidae or bulls. Niaux (Ariège) is characterized by the predominance of the bison and the absence of the reindeer, while at Les Trois Frères (Ariège) the bison is more frequently represented than the horse, ibex, stag, reindeer, and wild ass. Here are also to be found drawings of a few bears, a rhinoceros, a mammoth, two owls, and, as though they were guarding certain approaches to the cave, several lions.

It is very difficult to distinguish, in such collections of figures, those contemporaneous with a particular colder or temperate geological phase, or to determine which can be ascribed to some tribal fashion, or to a certain season of the year, or to the preference shown by some animals for a given locality or area.

Interesting analogies can, however, be noticed in the presence or absence of particular subjects in wall art or *art mobilier* at certain times in their history. For instance, fish, very abundantly represented in Magdalenian *art mobilier*, hardly ever occur in cave art. There is a salmon at Gorge d'Enfer (Dordogne), two trout at Niaux (Ariège), a pike at Cabrerets (Lot), an indeterminate fish at Les Combarelles (Dordogne), and a few others (giant flatfish) at La Pileta (Spain). Birds are even rarer, with owls at Les Trois Frères, a wader (ibis?) at Gargas, and a penguin at Pendo (Santander).

In wall art engraved hinds are much commoner than stags—except at Lascaux and Rouffignac where the former are lacking; and there are more stags than hinds in the Cantabrian caves. The opposite is true of the open rock-shelters of Eastern Spain, but not in the specimens of *art mobilier* in that area (El Parpalló, Valencia). This is quite different from Lascaux (Dordogne), where horses and wild bulls occur in great numbers, with a moderate number of bison and ibexes. The single male stag with vast antlers is, on the other hand, often represented at Lascaux and in Cantabria. At Pair-non-Pair (Gironde) horses, stags, bulls, and ibexes dominate in the kitchen refuse of the early Gravettian. At Les Combarelles II engraving of the saiga occurs, its bones being those most commonly found in early Magdalenian kitchen refuse on the plains of the Gironde and neighbouring regions (Saint-Germain-la-Rivière, Marcamps, Le Placard, Le Roc de Sers). Repeated finds of it had already been reported in the Upper Solutrean and early Magdalenian levels in the Périgord.

Though it does not figure in the repertory of the cave artists, the wild sheep did live in France in early Palaeolithic times, being met with in the bear caves and at Grimaldi. Similarly with the thar (the Nepalese goat-antelope), whose presence was reported in bone-bearing breccias in Central and South-east France.

The human figure is fairly rare in Aquitano-Cantabrian wall art in dark caves. Though mostly absent, when it occurs it is nearly always in semi-animal or grotesque shapes, as at Les Combarelles, Font-de-Gaume, Bernifal (Dordogne), Cabrerets (Lot)—fat women in clay—Marsoulas (Haute-Garonne), La Bastide (Hautes-Pyrénées), Altamira, Hornos de la Peña (Santander), and Candamo (Oviedo). Those at Lascaux call for some comment: a semi-schematic man, lying stretched on his back, has a bird's head; his throwing-stick has fallen on the ground near a symbolic bird perched on a stake; a disembowelled bison, with intestines hanging out from a long spear-wound, stands motionless, but threatens him with its horns. This scene is set at the bottom of a well. Is it symbolic or the portrayal of a hunting accident? A second figure, engraved in another place, is completely covered by a large grass cloak.

At Les Trois Frères (Ariège) there are engravings of tiny human faces and two small mixed characters (a man with the head and body of a bison, but human arms and legs, and a broad, Perigordian face of earlier date), together with an extraordinary figure, painted and engraved four metres above the floor in an apparently inaccessible position. This represents a creature with tall stag-antlers on its head, a long beard but no mouth, a long, bushy tail, and a male organ, apparently dancing a kind of cake-walk. It really dominates the whole collection of engraved animals represented in this shrine, since it is the only one both painted and engraved, and portrays the god that gives increase of game and success in the hunt.

In Aragon the Casares cave revealed a whole range of engraved sketches passing from humans to fish and frogs. Could this have been connected with a water-rite?

In Sicily the Adalura shelter, near Palermo, contains a strange scene, very carefully engraved and in full daylight; the actors are male figures, some with bird's-head masks. Two of them are lying on the ground with their legs bent back and held in that position by a thong tied to their necks in such a way as to produce gradual strangulation. As Baron A. C. Blanc has shown, they are being subjected to ritual sacrifice with intense sexual stimulation. Associated with this highly artistic tableau are fine animal figures, buck and horse, in the Magdalenian manner.

Apart from this site in Sicily, all the other previously mentioned figures were produced in dark caves. In France a series of shelters, open to daylight and mostly preserved by fallen debris, have revealed some remarkable carving of human figures of quite a different character. In the Vézère district, at a much earlier date—from the Aurignacian onward—in shelters well exposed to daylight carvings were made on loose blocks of many sexual symbols, mainly feminine. In the Laussel shelter, of Gravettian date, three small slabs bear figures of tiny Venuses; a large block is carved with another, fatter and more elaborate Venus; another small slab bears the image of a slender-limbed man in what seems to be the position of a spear-thrower. These bas-reliefs are similar to the ivory statuettes of the same date or earlier, and such human motifs have sometimes been found on these sites in association with fairly numerous animal figures in the same style as the animal engravings in dark caves. Yet nowhere, at any time, is deep-cut bas-relief work to be found in dark passages. The reason for this lies in the enormous amount of fuel it would have taken to provide the light for such work, so that up to that time bas-relief was confined to daylit shelters. Another, psychological factor may also be considered to underlie this contrast: perhaps the tribes considered that the subjects themselves were not suitable for these underground shrines, just as some rather too worldly pictures would seem out of place in our churches. This is no doubt the reason for the presence, in a daylit outer chamber of the rock-shelter at Penne (Tarn), of two women in high relief, stretched out in sensual poses, and the same could be said of the similar trio at Angles-sur-Anglin (Vienne).

[15]

Leptolithic rock art in Eastern Spain

Leptolithic rock-paintings in Spain—Rock-painting and -engraving in the Forest of Fontainebleau

---

LEPTOLITHIC ROCK-PAINTINGS IN SPAIN

From the beginning of the Aurignaco-Perigordian period the Cantabrian fauna kept its temperate aspect. Merck's rhinoceros and even the *Elephas antiquus* finally disappeared. A few reindeer came down into the region. Arctic seashells developed on the coasts (*Chlamis islandica*), and the *Littorinae* reached very large sizes. Prior to this it had been possible to get over the cols in the Cantabrian Mountains, which were thus open to migrations towards the high plateau to the south, pushing on as far as Central and Eastern Old Castile and Andalusia. The narrow tracks along the shores of the Mediterranean were always open to the movements of Solutreo-Magdalenian peoples, and their industries filtered mainly along the Catalan littoral, from Alicante and Almeria into Andalusia and Portugal.

The cave at Casares (Guadalajara) shows how Aurignaco-Gravettian art pushed on as far as Guadalajara and kept its Aquitano-Cantabrian style. Bulls with their horns in distorted perspective are very common; rhinoceroses and lions are present, while strange human figures, also engraved, are more numerous at this site than in all the others of that date.

Three hundred kilometres farther east, in rock-shelters on both sides of the Sierra de Albarracin (Teruel), bulls are again to be found, drawn in the same style, but painted at different periods in various colours. The only variants are a few human figures, rare at Los Toricos d'Albarracin, more numerous and varied at El Tormón.

From the Ebro to the province of Almeria, all along the coastal chains that form the eastern edge of the Spanish *Meseta*, is to be found an open-air wall art spreading under the shelter of rocky overhangs and carefully avoiding dark caves. This Eastern Spanish art is at least contemporaneous with everything which, in the classical Leptolithic area, comes after the typical Aurignacian, and it is a sector containing at present about fifty known sites, of varying importance. The most noteworthy have been found at Cogul (Lérida), Cretas, Charco del Agua Amarga, Albarracin, El Tormón (Teruel), La Araña, Morella la Vella (Tarragona), Barranco de Valtorta, La Gasulla (Castellón), Alpera, Minateda (Albacete), and Los Cantos de la Visera (Murcia). There are about four in Catalonia, ten in the Teruel region, two in Tarragona, two or three in Cuenca, two at the end of the Sierra Morena (Aldeaquemada), and two in each of the provinces of Murcia, Almeria, and Valencia.

Under these Mediterranean skies, in an infinitely milder climate than that of the Aquitano-Cantabrian regions farther north, lived various peoples both Leptolithic, Gravettian, Solutrean, and Magdalenian. Having apparently given up using dark caves in such temperate conditions, and being separated from the lands of their origin by high plateaux and the Pyrenees, they developed their own form of art based on a conception that was at the same time different from yet related to the main current.

The relationship can been seen if the animal figures are considered in isolation: the stags and bulls show the same artistic conventions of distorted perspective as our [French] Perigordian and none of the Magdalenian. They have the same graceful silhouette, the same lithe, accurate outlines. The stags at Lascaux and on the block at Sergeac (Dordogne), as well as those at La Pasiega (Santander, Spain), look as though they had been painted in Eastern Spain. Apart from the scale, the same applies to the bulls and cows. But the fauna, as the latitude demands, is different: at Cogul there are two bison, one in poor preservation, the other, a young one, unmistakable; the Equidae,[1] though not numerous, are somewhat different from Northern types. There are a fair number of elks, one at Alpera, at least two at Minateda, and three at La Gasulla; quite a few boars and a large number of ibexes, with the horns in profile; some birds and very few rabbits, though these are abundant in the Palaeolithic deposits in these areas. The scale of the figures is small, at times minute, and rarely equals the

[1] Most seem to represent a form of large-headed, maneless horse, found also in the cave at Levanzo (Sicily) on a small island off the coast at Palermo—an *Equus hydrontinus*, now extinct.

size of the medium figures found in our caves, though a few of these—
at Le Portel (Ariège), at Lascaux (Dordogne), and at Le Mas d'Azil
(Dordogne)—have yielded miniatures as small as their counterparts in
Eastern Spain. Poorly worked representations of insects, bees, spiders,
and flies(?), have also been found.

Among the most outstanding examples of this art may be mentioned:
a boar, wounded but still running and hotly pursued by a loping hunter, at Charco del Agua Amarga; a hunter, at El Tormón, rushing
towards the young stag he has just brought down; an archer at Tor-
tosilla, calmly approaching a wild goat(?) lying, no doubt, mortally
wounded; a herd of boar, at La Gasulla, surprised by a group of huntsmen who are riddling them with arrows as some flee at full speed and
others roll over with arrows sticking into them; a herd of four hinds,
a stag, a brocket, and two small fawns being pursued by a team
of beaters towards a line of huntsmen in ambush. The arrangement of
this scene shows evidence of a remarkable attempt at composition: the
herd is passing from right to left across the front of four huntsmen in
echelon one above the other; the first and highest is gesturing that he
has no more arrows left, the second is firing his last, the third is in full
action, and the fourth is just beginning to loose off his first shots. At
Alpera a string of ibexes is running away to the right, pursued by a pack
of wolves shown on either flank and in the rear. Even more outstanding
is the honey-harvesting scene from La Araña: the collector has climbed
to the top of a three-ply rope-ladder, his companion holding the bottom. He has reached the hole—a natural opening in the rock-face—
representing the hive and has taken out the honeycombs and put them
in a basket, which he is showing to his companion while the bees swarm
furiously around him. Among the scenes from everyday life it is worth
mentioning the following: at Minateda a young man seems to be courting a girl wearing the traditional short skirt, and a mother, similarly
dressed, is walking along holding the hand of her naked small son. At
Alpera there are two tall dancers with aquiline profiles and feather
headdresses, holding in one hand three arrows, point downward, and in
the other the end of a drawn bow with the string turned outward. Battle
scenes are also portrayed: at Morella la Vella a group of archers, very
simply drawn but full of life, move around in a very restricted, subcircular space, keeping up a lively fire at one another. At Minateda
the scene is more artistic: a band of archers with lithe, striped bodies
and armed with huge, triple-curved bows charges down on another
unarmed group and riddles it with arrows.

The great difference between this and Franco-Cantabrian art is the
abundance in the former of anecdotal drawing of human beings and
the frequency of more or less crowded scenes taken from the hunt, war,
and family and social life.

In Franco-Cantabrian art the figures are, indeed, rarely grouped into tableaux. In the Gravettian wall art at Lascaux the semi-schematic scene with the dead man between a bison and a rhinoceros is most striking, as is the rearing bear bringing down a man while his companion rushes to the rescue, in the engraving on a small slab of contemporary date at Péchialet (Dordogne). The bison-hunter at Laugerie Basse (Magdalenian IV) and the processions at Raymonden and Le Château des Eyzies (Magdalenian VI) are most unusual examples of such compositions in Magdalenian *art mobilier*.

Other differences are very important. The use of the ceremonial mask, common in the Franco-Cantabrian world, was rare or doubtful in Eastern Spain, and in the conception of how human beings should be represented two absolutely opposite views can be seen. In Aquitano-Cantabrian art human figures are clumsy or schematic, but in Eastern Spain they become, in spite of their inaccuracy, full of life and at times overflowing with movement. The representation may reach a kind of expressionism in its methods, but, though it lengthens the limbs somewhat, it preserves the reality of their shapes and also keeps them subservient to the proper portrayal of the action, slipping occasionally into conventionalization of certain parts not involved in the activity of immediate interest to the artist. The torso is linear and cramped and the arms simplified.

There is another, profound difference: Aquitano-Cantabrian art never represented a garment, a weapon, or an ornament. In Eastern Spanish art, on the contrary, women wear short skirts and the men, though generally naked, sometimes have 'overalls'[1] and breeches. They often wear feather decorations, perhaps arranged as headdresses, and garters; and they carry bows, arrows, and quivers—rarely spears— while in Aquitaine the throwing-spear and stock were alone sometimes shown.

The fact that the Eastern Spanish artists were Palaeolithic is attested by the kind of life depicted in their scenes—pictures of hunters with no knowledge of domestic animals—and by the presence in the frescoes of the elk, bison, and rhinoceros. Confirmation comes from the discovery of the indisputably Palaeolithic deposit at El Parpalló (Valencia), with its three levels—Gravettian, Solutrean, and Magdalenian, not later than stage IV—and the great quantities of small slabs, some engraved with stags, often with antlers in distorted perspective similar to those in the cave paintings. Further finds were made there of painted tablets, not entirely unknown in the French Magdalenian, showing animals to be found in the wall-paintings.

The next step is to seek the origins of this art in the Spanish Levant. The inhabitants of the region had probably long been familiar with the almost purely geometrical art of the other Mediterranean lands, the

---

[1] A kind of short, wide trousers used by hunters for walking through thorns and scrub.

1

PLATE XI. 1. Frieze of stag heads, black, in twisted and semi-twisted perspective. 2. A prehistoric news item: near a bison, wounded by a lance and disembowelled, lies a dying man. In the centre, a bird on a pole. Going away to the left is a rhinoceros, presumably responsible for the massacre. Gravettian. Lascaux. Copy by M. Thaon, 1940.

2

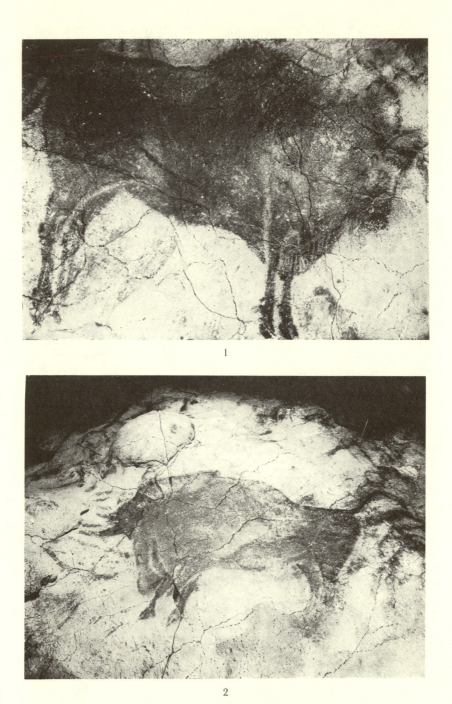

1

2

PLATE XII. 1 and 2. Bison painted in polychrome on the roof at Altamira (Spain). Very late Magdalenian VI.

Capsian from Africa, the Grimaldian from the north and south of Italy; flints and certain geometrical-art products bear this stamp in the Gard sites and are found again at El Parpalló in the form of engravings and paintings. At Minateda the oldest layer of pictures wavers between conventionalization of the figures and the feeble beginnings of naturalism. Then a current of naturalism spreads over the area, either through the Castiles via the Casares cave or along the Mediterranean seaboard, and becomes predominant, bringing in that Gravettian animal imagery which remains the basis of the local art until the onset of its decline.

Can we see in these human figures, so full of humour and action, a spontaneous development springing from the initiative of those tough hunters who carved Laussel, painted Lascaux, and engraved Casares? Or was some other influence at work?

In spite of the enormous distances separating them, there is an undeniable family resemblance connecting the art of the Saharan and South African huntsmen and the tableaux of their Iberian counterparts. The question therefore arises: was it African influence in Europe, or Spanish influence in Africa, or a convergence of the two?

However, between these two complexes, so far apart in space, the Sahara appears as a connecting zone. There is no comparison between Eastern Spanish art and the heavy, powerful figures carved by shepherds and hunters on the rocks of the Fezzan and the Southern Oran mountains. Yet in the rock-shelters of the Fezzan, of the Tassili-n-Ajjer, the Tibesti, the Hoggar, and the Libyan oases the herdsmen at an early Neolithic stage developed the art of drawing scenes and animals, and this spread sporadically as far as the mountains of Algeria. Now, all these domestic bulls are very similar to the wild ones of Eastern Spain; both display the same treatment of the horns in false perspective, and this is found again, later, in the carvings on Egyptian tombs.

Another undoubted connexion between the two groups lies in Africa, in the frequency with which humans are portrayed grouped in pastoral, family, or social scenes, in the liveliness and expressiveness of the poses, in the bows with which the figures are armed, and in the type of dress of some of the women. Could it be that the resemblance between the Solutrean arrow-heads from El Parpalló and the types discovered in the Neolithic at Ouargla, or the obvious connexions between the bone harpoons from the Southern Sahara and those of the Magdalenian, all indicate a migration towards the south where, meeting other shepherd tribes less skilled as artists, the Iberians taught them more perfect forms? One may also wonder whether the origins of South African art may not have sprung from this source during the migration of pastoral peoples who, having lost their flocks through the ravages of the tsetse fly, became hunters again and spread their art among the aborigines. It may not

N

be possible to answer such questions, but they certainly ought to be raised.

Some complex problems arise when we come to study the development of rock art in Eastern Spain. Mostly the colours used by the artists were black, brown, red, and ochres of all shades from yellowish brown to sepia with intermediates of purplish red and vermilion, the use of white being only very exceptional. This is the same range of colours as was used in the caves in France. Sometimes, though very rarely, the silhouette was prepared by a very lightly engraved line. Usually the colour has become part of the rock, having no doubt penetrated by capillary creeping of the grease used to mix the colour. However, where it was applied to a particularly impermeable surface with a stalagmitic or naturally bituminous crust the colour has not sunk in. It may then (as at Los Lavanderos de Tello, Almeria) have been sealed between two calcite layers, and the top one can be pricked off to bring it out. Special precautions must be taken when moistening such figures to revive the colours, since the pigments are not fixed and some, particularly the flaky black, come away very easily. At Los Lavanderos de Tello, a light black outline came off completely at the first wetting, and would probably never have been preserved but for the top layer of calcite.[1]

Another difficulty arises from the passion these artists had, as has already been seen at Lascaux, for restoration of earlier work. This makes it hard to determine the true sequence of techniques and even the true meaning of the figures. One particular drawing of an elk at La Cueva del Queso (Alpera) was based on an erased ibex. On the same site the bulls at La Cueva de la Vieja replaced stags and were themselves restored to stags by the later addition of antler extensions to their horns. The dancing scene with the little satyr at Cogul is the product of several successive contributions: of the nine women two are much earlier work, other similar forms were then added and then a final group, and it was only very much later that the little satyr was fitted into the centre of the scene by the last artist, who certainly was not acquainted with his predecessors.

Many of the rock-paintings of Eastern Spain show superposed layers of work of different tints and colours, obviously belonging to different phases of artistic development. From this point of view the most characteristic and most complicated example is the great rock-shelter at Minateda (Albacete), where about thirteen layers were detected by

[1] Moistening, though it may be necessary, has serious disadvantages, not so much because it may destroy the figures as because the water available locally has a high limestone content. If the operations are frequently repeated the figures are overlaid with a fine layer of chalk which may finally mask them completely. Their original lustre could be restored by washing with absolutely pure water containing a trace of acid.

H. Breuil. This does not mean that there were only thirteen phases during the period concerned: some which do in fact exist on other frescoes are not represented at Minateda.

The first series is characterized by very small figures in pale red, often human, in the proportion of about sixty of the latter to about twenty animals only. The drawing is very simple and wavers between pure convention and the beginnings of very vivid realism. Recognizable animals are a stag, a horse, a hare, and a stork. Among the human figures males predominate. There are numerous archers, armed with fairly small bows, usually single-curved. The arrows are very rudimentary, and many of the bowmen also hold a curved object—perhaps a boomerang. They are often formed into small groups, and one single set seems to represent a joust or a fight.

The second and less abundant series consists of fairly large figures outlined with broad red strokes or filled in completely. A stag in the most elementary style already shows all the general characteristics of such silhouettes. Notable are three rhinoceroses, one unmistakable. Among the rare, fairly complete human figures can be seen a woman in a dress and an ithyphallic man.

The third series shows very tiny black figures, eleven men and fourteen animals, including five ibexes, a horse, a hind, and two stags. Among the human figures the only certain one is of a naked woman, with a large posterior and little tresses of hair and armed with a large bow. A man bears another very large and sharply curved bow. There are two other small bows, one of which is held by an archer in the reverse position from that used for shooting. He has a feather headdress and wears a quiver. Another archer has a short-horned cap and garters on each leg.

The drawings of the fourth series have fine, red lines with some thick and thin strokes and are partially hatched in. There is a single figure of a woman with four large animals—one horse with mane flying and three stags. One of them, a very fine example with magnificent antlers in distorted perspective, is in every way similar to the Gravettian animals of the Cantabrian coast (La Pasiega).

The fifth series shows only very small figures in thin, black lines with the animal bodies partially hatched in. There are no more than five human figures, and one only is complete. Three are archers with single-curve bows; two have heads shaped like mushrooms. The animals are relatively numerous—twenty-eight—and can be recognized as including two ibexes, a boar, three horses, two hinds, and a wolf.

The figures of the sixth series are larger, in fairly dark brown, usually of fine outline and hatched in lengthwise or obliquely, but at times completely filled in with colour. The animals are fewer than the humans, numbering only thirteen: three ibexes, one very fine, two horses, one bull, and seven stags with horns in false perspective. From twenty-three human figures one can make out two very tall men and parts of two others. The former have the upper part of the body conventionalized, with arms akimbo, and both wear garters. One has two small horns on his head and carries a very small bow. Most of the others are acting a large battle scene where foreign archers with striped bodies and very large, highly curved bows[1] are attacking an unarmed group that includes a naked woman riddled with arrows.

The figures of the seventh series are drawn in reddish brown, with thicker lines and filled in with cruder hatching, sometimes with plain colour. The animals predominate. There are nineteen, including nine ibexes, five stags, and one bull, all much less artistically done and merely 'dashed off', as can be seen from the very conventionalized antlers of the stags. Only seven humans are represented—five women, in dresses, one archer, and a young man courting a girl. The two men bear on their shoulders some indeterminate package.

In the eighth series the animals are completely predominant—six stags, a hind, an elk, a roebuck, perhaps a reindeer-head, four bulls, two with horns front view, a grazing horse, seven ibexes, perhaps an izard, a feline, and a stork. The human figures, heavy in style, include three dressed women and one naked, four men, three of whom are archers and one with a stout posterior having double ornamental garters and a small single-curve bow. Fairly numerous schematic elements begin to appear. Realist art is waning.

The ninth series of polychromes is somewhat doubtful as a result of numerous restorations at different times, although they are unmistakable at other sites—Albarracin, for example. They comprise only nine animals, including one ibex, one stag, one certain elk, two bulls, a possible saiga antelope, and a fish.

The paintings of the tenth series, done in plain sepia or with broad washes and hatching, ought probably to be divided into two. Eleven animals are represented, of which four are very big: a large cow and three maneless Equidae (*Equus hydrontinus* found as an engraving in Sicily and a fossil elsewhere); seven others are small and include four stags and a bull. All are artistically inferior. The human figures number seven, including an archer with a pointed head and a small bow, one naked woman, and another in a dress, walking with a naked child she holds by the hand and providing one of the most touching scenes in all this art.

The eleventh series of small drawings in plain black, or occasionally hatched in, is dominated by animals, but the quality is so poor that their identity remains uncertain. However, it is possible to make out a fox, or wolf, two ibexes, four hinds, one lying down, and a young stag—

---

[1] These highly curved bows, found also at Alpera and elsewhere, are evidence of contact with the Neolithic people of North Africa, who were perhaps already there at the end of the Quaternary.

the two latter shown without legs—a stag with large, stylized antlers, and four or five other stags that have lost their antlers or have not yet fully developed them. The human beings are fairly numerous, being sixteen or seventeen, though only a few are good, one of them an archer with a large bow. One of the drawings is linear, and strange figures begin to appear, like the headless hermaphrodite with frog's feet, and a headless character wearing what appear to be trousers.

The red or sepia figures of the twelfth series are very bad, the animals being nearly unrecognizable. One can distinguish two composite figures with animal and human elements and a large ithyphallic man in semi-schematic style.

The thirteenth series consists of only black and entirely conventionalized figures representing characters standing or sitting and seen from the front. They are quite outside the range of Palaeolithic naturalistic art from Eastern Spain, and are certainly connected with the Neo-Eneolithic art of the Peninsula.

It is obvious that an analysis of the single rock-shelter at Minateda cannot constitute an exhaustive study of the various phases of rock art in Eastern Spain, since, indeed, several stages are missing at Minateda. For instance, nowhere there can we find the beautiful, strikingly realistic stags done in fairly bright red on the rock at Calapata, Cogul, and El Tormón, traces of which reappear at Alpera under frescoes similar to the series four to seven at Minateda.

A study of the highly diversified and complex human figures at El Barranco de Valtorta has revealed many details of style, clothing, and weapons not otherwise found at Minateda, although the drawings are related to series seven and eight. This applies also to the figures in white, or pinkish white, some outlined in colour, at Albarracin or El Tormón, where they were probably painted in that way because light colours had to be used for drawing figures on the dark rock of some of the shelters.

Moreover, at Minateda there are no scenes with the huntsman pursuing the quarry, with its tracks drawn in (as at Valorta, La Araña, and La Gasulla), belonging to a relatively late stage in the development of this art and to be placed probably at least as late as the twelfth series.

At Los Cantos de la Visera (Murcia) the stages through which the art degenerates through realism to semi-realism, then to semi-schematic and finally schematic forms, spread over several phases that are no doubt fairly close to the last three series at Minateda.

If most of these stages can easily be dated in the Leptolithic, starting from the original Aurignaco-Gravettian, it must be admitted that in its degenerative phases such art passes into the Mesolithic and joins hands with later schematic forms, Mesolithic at first, then Neo-Eneolithic.

The question also arises whether all these paintings represent the local inhabitants. It is not at all certain. In the battle scene at Mina-teda there appear tall, strapping men, gaudy with hatching-strokes, wielding great triple-curved bows known as reflex types and said by experts to be of Asiatic origin.[1] Other examples of these figures are re-produced on various rocks, at Altamira and at La Cueva Remigia (Castellón), and it is not unlikely that they represent strangers who came, perhaps by sea, to explore new territories and merely passed through.

The Minateda rock-paintings date from before the birth of the new schematic art, and in them we can watch the gradual deterioration of realist art. The animals are 'dashed off' from memory—calligraphed, so to speak, according to stylized patterns and not animated by detailed consideration of the living creature. Drawings of men cease to be realistic, becoming more or less conventionalized, and those of animals, in turn, follow the same tendency. The bounds of the Leptolithic, in-deed, of the Mesolithic, have been crossed, and strangers have come from Asia to colonize and develop a Western world they find attractive.

Excavations by L. Péricot in the shelter at El Parpalló (Valencia) have brought to light a great number of engravings and a few naturalis-tic paintings on slabs and tablets. They were found in all levels from the Upper Aurignacian (Gravettian) up to the Solutrean and the early and Middle Magdalenian of the site. This is assuredly proof of a rela-tionship with the other rock-paintings of the region, although so far these *art mobilier* objects have shown no human figures. Differences in the subjects treated also exist in French Franco-Cantabrian art, where, for example, fish, which are very common in *art mobilier*, are almost completely lacking in wall art. Conversely, the very common realistic human figures from Magdalenian III at La Marche have no counter-part in wall art of the same date.

On the other hand, the discovery at La Cocina (Valencia) during excavation work by the same prehistorian, near the base of layers con-taining microliths, of slabs with very faint painted figures, perhaps of animals, confirms the persistence of such art up to that period, but gives absolutely no basis whatever for attributing any part of it, however slight, to Neolithic times or, indeed, even later. To connect naturalistic art with the Neolithic civilization that is so completely devoid of it is a major aberration.

The fairly constant presence of a variety of microlithic flints at the

---

[1] Is the triple-curved bow, called 'Asiatic' by ethnographers, really from the East? Could it not rather be of Western origin, since the earliest representations of it are found in the Spanish Levant? This question was put to H. Breuil by Baron A. C. Blanc. The fact is that this type of bow is abundantly pictured in Africa, north of the Great Forest Belt, particularly on rock-paintings in Libya. It came down the great African lakes and spread into frescoes in Rhodesia and South-west Africa, but came only later to the eastern centre (Drakensberg, Basutoland, East Orange Free State).

approaches to the painted rock-shelters of the Spanish Levant, and at times the odd find of more recent objects, has given rise to conjectures tending to bring them all forward in date up to the Mesolithic and even later. According to Spanish authorities, the rock-painters of the Levant who carried out this work were Mesolithic and not contemporaries of the Franco-Cantabrian artists, and they are supposed to have carried on their way of life into Neolithic times and even later, thus living on in the mountain-ranges on the eastern edge of the Spanish central plateau. From the very first H. Breuil wrote that the latest work at Minateda could be contemporary with the Neolithic, precisely because it had degenerated. He had also agreed that there was a primitive schematic background connected with the art of the peoples of the Mediterranean coast and which existed prior to the penetration of Franco-Cantabrian influence of an advanced Gravettian level. As everywhere else, it would seem that this Gravettian colonization was, on the outer fringes of the Solutreo-Magdalenian world, at the root of the local post-Palaeolithic microlithic cultures, but, apart from the evidence from fauna and geology in Italy, it is impossible to say, in Spain and beyond, where the epi-Gravettian Leptolithic, and its derived Mesolithic preceding to some extent the French Mesolithic, can be considered to end. The required evidence is lacking in Spain (except for the elks noted in the paintings), even at El Parpalló, which is, however, admitted to be entirely Leptolithic and which, with La Cocina, is the only site with known fauna and verifiable painted and engraved tablets.

The theory of the Spanish writers is therefore based on a hypothetical prolongation of early Palaeolithic conditions in the eastern mountains of the *Meseta*. But one merely has to consult the map to see that Cogul, Cretas, Charco, Amargo, Alpera, Minateda, and La Visera are on the edge of the plains on routes leading from the high plateaux to the coastal lowlands, so that there is no question of the people being refugees in the hills, as may quite possibly have been the case in the western valley of Las Batuecas in a remote corner of the Sierra de Francia.[1]

In the extreme west of Spain, in the wild and picturesque valley of Las Batuecas, cutting deeply into the southern flank of the Sierra de Francia, lies a still-isolated group of painted rocks, the most famous being 'Las Cabras Pintadas.' In the sixteenth century the poet Lope de Vega had heard of this, and in the eighteenth the Spanish geographer

[1] Those who are determined to give Eastern Spanish art a more recent date at any cost have quoted the domestic horse, their sole example being the rock-painting at Villar del Huomo (Cuenca), where the style is degenerate and a man is holding a horse by a long rope, which might also be a lasso. This painting is supposed to be an example of later sub-schematic art. Elsewhere the name of 'ass' has been given to sub-schematic animals that might well be hinds. Other sub-schematic frescoes which might derive from it have been classified as part of the art of the Spanish Levant, though they are clearly of later date.

Madoz mentions it. There are several layers of small, semi-naturalistic paintings one above the other, depicting first brown ibexes, with horns seen from the front, then others in red, black, and white, with horns in profile, these latter being associated with completely schematic figures of dogs, stags, and archers, with numerous punctuations and bars. Finally comes the schema pure and simple, poor in motifs as it always remains in rock-paintings to the north of the Tagus (Serra da Estrella, Sepulveda, and the Cantabrian caves).

The earliest layer on some of the other rocks in the region of Cabeza del Buey (Badajoz), made up of minute, schematic human figures and a few curved, finely drawn geometrical signs, may be as old as the Meso-lithic, as may be some very small stags and ibexes on other rocks in the province of Almeria. This also applies to schematic rabbits and dogs at La Cueva Negra de Meca (Albacete), below which a Tardenoisian industry was discovered, and they overlie remains of naturalistic work.

But another and far more fruitful source of schematic art came and mingled with and submerged the local elements. This was the Neo-lithic influence, coming from the Eastern Mediterranean, but originat-ing even farther afield, perhaps in Eastern Asia and Siberia. We shall not deal with that here.

ROCK-PAINTING AND -ENGRAVING IN THE FOREST OF FONTAINEBLEAU

A painted rock in the valley of the Loing, at Montigny, shows, to the left of the surviving painted panel, traces of ochre in wavy, parallel lines similar to the finger-tracings known as 'macaronis' found in the shelter at La Pileta (Malaga) and at La Baume Latrone (Gard), and belonging to the beginnings of Leptolithic art.[1] To the right can be seen a sub-naturalistic figure of a cervid, with antlers in twisted perspective, painted in reddish brown, strikingly reminiscent of Eastern Spanish art in its degenerative period. Very early excavations on this shelter site, partly destroyed by quarry-workings, revealed flints classified by Gabriel de Mortillet as being Leptolithic.

A second group, in the valley of the Essonne, is characterized by black tectiforms drawn with manganese.

Among the very numerous rock-shelters decorated with incisions many have been dated thanks to the investigations of Mr James L. Baudet. At Le Puiselet (commune of Saint-Pierre-les-Nemours, Seine-et-Marne) in a passage blocked to the roof by loess, where the floor had given an archaeological level of very late Levalloisian aspect, the walls were decorated with deep vertical incisions. These are per-haps the oldest known trace of Quaternary art.

[1] It is interesting to note that a rock-shelter near Alcoy (Alicante) also shows broad panels of such 'macaronis,' associated with crude stags in the Eastern Spanish manner.

More recently, near Neuilly-la-Forêt (Seine-et-Oise), a quarryman cutting up a block coming from an ancient rock-fall in a painted cave came upon a very beautiful figure of a galloping bovid, though the head could not be found. Its connexions with Eastern Spanish art are obvious, and we are indebted to Mr J. L. Baudet for publication of the details.

Other decorations, mostly linear, mingled with a few human faces are connected with a habitat belonging certainly to the Leptolithic. Similar human faces are found in the Magdalenian at Marsoulas (Haute-Garonne) and at Les Trois Frères (Ariège), but there is no room for further doubt about two other localities, Nanteau-sur-Essonnes (Seine-et-Oise) and Lavaudoue (Seine-et-Marne), where the style is Mesolithic and the archaeological level, seemingly Tardenoisian, has provided small blocks of soft sandstone with series of parallel-line incisions in every way similar to those decorating the walls of this shelter and a great many others. Since similar engravings have been found in Luxemburg and in the Vosges, it is not unlikely that excavations carried out under them would reveal habitats of the same age as those previously mentioned. A comparison of these decorations, firstly with the geometrically ornamented Azilian pebbles reported by D. Peyrony from Dordogne and found sporadically elsewhere, and then with the older geometrical decorations in the Mediterranean area (Romanelli cave, Italy; El Parpalló, Spain) and in the Capsian and epicapsian cultures of Tunisia, brings out the Mediterranean source of the inspiration, which spread elsewhere in the wake of Mesolithic migrations. L. P. Péricot found a quantity of them at La Cocina (Huesca).

⌈16⌉

The Mesolithic

From the Mediterranean to the Atlantic: The Azilian; The Asturian; The Sauveterrian and the Tardenoisian; The Montmorencian

FROM THE MEDITERRANEAN TO THE ATLANTIC

Between the period when Leptolithic man was hunting the last reindeer herds in France and the time when half-civilized invaders were ploughing the first furrows there and grazing the first flocks of domestic cattle stretches an era known as the 'Mesolithic'—that is to say, intermediate between the Leptolithic, with animals now extinct or migrated, and the Neolithic, with the fauna of our times.

This definition, though true for regions subjected to the fierce extremes of glacial conditions and those that saw the development of the reindeer age, becomes less exact farther south, even in Southern Europe, where present-day fauna occurred from Leptolithic times. It is even more a term of mere convenience if we cross the Mediterranean and consider Africa and Asia Minor. Furthermore, if we take into account the fact that the Neolithic cultures that gradually occupied more and more of Europe from the beginning of modern times had certainly begun to develop in neighbouring continents, it must be admitted that there were already Neolithic herdsmen and farmers in those regions at the time when our [French] Leptolithic was at its height.

Thus the geological and palaeontological definition of the Mesolithic is not full enough and must be completed by sociological considerations. The peoples known as Mesolithic are, in fact, a series of Leptolithic tribes which at the beginning of our era emigrated, either into lands previously uninhabitable, or into places occupied by other indigenous Leptolithics that the newcomers either replaced or mingled with, living, like them, by hunting, fishing, and food-gathering.

That is why the term *epi-Palaeolithic* has often been applied to them, since it expresses the way in which the newcomers carried on their former mode of life (H. Obermaier).

Their migrations were, moreover, connected with the improvement in the climate of areas previously subject to glacial conditions, and this was accompanied by a corresponding drying-out of vast, formerly very rainy regions, now deserts, making them inhabitable. In effect, further drying forced the tribes already settled there at the end of the Quaternary, and practising husbandry and cattle-raising, to seek new areas for pasture and tillage. This was the reason for the pressure of proto-Neolithic emigration on the small scattered tribes living by food-gathering, on shellfish, and by hunting and fishing round the rim of the Mediterranean—a pressure which forced them in turn to overflow into lands then finally freed from the grip of glacial conditions. It is therefore possible that at one time there were Leptolithic, Mesolithic, and Neolithic peoples living contemporaneously, and these terms merely express the different stages of social development reached during the migrations—the actions and reactions of these various categories.

It is therefore an abuse of words to attempt, for instance, to bring forward in time all the pre-Neolithic stages in North Africa and Asia Minor to align them with our Western Mesolithic. In fact, those continents witnessed, much earlier than Europe, the growth of the pastoral and agricultural life that must have been lived for thousands of years by the very first civilizations that developed there prematurely according to our European time-scale. The nearer we get to these ancient centres where true civilization worked out its fundamental characteristics against a wide background of peoples already Neolithic in their way of life, the farther must what is locally termed 'Mesolithic' recede into the last stages of the Pleistocene.

The first Egyptian and Asian civilizations, contemporaneous with our Mesolithic, presuppose, at a time when the deserts now surrounding their centres were still inhabitable, the flourishing of less advanced but already Neolithic cultures that were to be their basis, and it is not only probable but quite evident that parts of such cultures survived in districts that were cut off from the centres where the rest found conditions suitable for agriculture. There have been Neolithic men in the Sahara from the end of the Quaternary, and there still are some at the stage of the European Bronze Age. In the same way, while the Neo-lithization of Europe was creeping up from the south and east towards the north and west, peoples at Leptolithic or Mesolithic stages, geo-graphically isolated to the east and the south of the great deserts and tropical forests, have lived on for thousands of years, reaching the Christian era in Arabia, the Hegira in Somaliland, and even the nineteenth century in South Africa.

In the classical areas of Leptolithic civilization, South-west France and North-west Spain, several successive waves can be discerned, all with considerable differences—the *Azilian*, the *Asturian*, and the *Sauve-terrian-Tardenoisian* complex, not to mention the *Montmorencian*, which may have started much earlier.

The Azilian

Overlying Magdalenian VI on the left bank of the Arize, in the vast tunnel-cave of Le Mas d'Azil (Ariège), come layers where the reindeer is completely absent, being replaced by *Cervus elaphus*, the roebuck, the boar, and sometimes the elk. These are Édouard Piette's Azilian layers, underlying several Neolithic and later levels. Similar horizons exist in many of the caves in the Pyrenees and Cantabrian Mountains, from the Mediterranean to Oviedo. The flints, like those of the Magdalenian, vary according to the local raw material, but always include small, short scrapers, round or square, slivers trimmed into knife-blades or more rarely into crescents. At Valle (Santander, Spain) there are some geometrical, triangular microliths. The graver, fairly rare at Le Mas d'Azil, is abundant at Valle, especially the angle graver. There are punches, polishers, bone cutters, all of simple pattern, rarely decorated with parallel lines and even more rarely with simple geometrical designs. Pierced teeth are common, as are imported, perforated shells. All these have lost the elegance and skill of Magdalenian times, but the harpoon still persists, flat and made from stag-antler, and often perforated at the base. The hole is generally spindle-shaped, but in the older ones it is round, or lacking—and then it is replaced by small lugs at each side of the base, as commonly found in Magdalenian VI.[1] The barbs are sometimes on one side, sometimes on both; some have an acute angle, a more advanced type, but many retain the blunt angles of the later Magdalenian models. Indeed, there is every kind of intermediate stage between the broad harpoons of the end of the Magdalenian and those of the early Azilian. The geographical distribution of Azilian harpoons runs, in the north, to the Lot (Reilhac), to the Dordogne (Laugerie Basse, La Madeleine, Roche-reuil), to Poitou (Chaffaud), and to the Mayenne. It passes into England (Victoria Cave) and later reaches Scotland, especially the west (Oban and the isles). In these parts, moreover, some show Maglemosean influence. To the east of this line of migration they are much rarer, though there was a typical example in the Swiss Jura and a fragment has been found in a Belgian cave.

Another category of objects that are very abundant at Le Mas d'Azil is characteristically Azilian—pebbles, either painted or engraved, or both. At this level they occur in a number of other caves in the French

---

[1] Quite a number of Magdalenian harpoons from Cantabria have a pierced lug at the base. There is only one French harpoon from the advanced Magdalenian at La Madeleine that is similar—the hole being drawn, but not perforated.

Pyrenees—Bize, La Crouzade, La Tourasse, Marsoulas, Saint-Girons, Gourdan. The painted pebbles from Sordes (Landes) and the Cantabrian hills are of plain colour; the one from Valle (Santander) is divided into four quarters of different colours. The Lot has produced some at Gramat, in a layer with harpoons. Traces have been found in the Dordogne. Those in Scotland are from the Iron Age, but there are other odd ones, perhaps of earlier date, in several caves in the Gard, including La Salpêtrière. Others have been found, without harpoons, in the Alpine Azilian of the Vercors and in the cave at Birseck, near Basle. An example has been reported from Holland, probably from a Mesolithic complex. Victoria Cave (England) has given a few traces of them, while in Bavaria painted tablets of the same type were found in the Magdalenian V layer at Neu-Essing.

It is by no means certain that with a little care they could not be found in any level of the European Leptolithic, since the painted caves have on their walls groups of points or bars and signs of this kind. The Romanelli cave (Otranto, Italy) yielded a broad slab with a row of schematic signs, from an early Grimaldian level. The little Leptolithic slabs from El Parpalló (Valencia) also bear a certain number of signs or painted decorations.

The origin of painted pebbles is thus deep-rooted in the Leptolithic, particularly in that of the Mediterranean area.

Romanelli, in its Grimaldian, has given a good many more engraved pebbles geometrically decorated with bands and hatchings entwined on both faces. The Grimaldian at Mentone has provided several with complicated decorations of the same kind; others came from El Parpalló and La Cocina; and all these are connected with others, Capsian in style, but Neolithic, from a cave near Constantine.

This sort of engraved decoration, but Azilian this time, is found in the Ariège reduced to parallel lines, but at Sordes (Landes) complicated examples of it occur on a tablet at the Dufaure shelter. It is fairly common in the Azilian at La Madeleine, and an odd specimen was picked up in the woods at Vilhonneur (Charente). Slabs from certain shelters in the forest near Étampes provided J. Baudet with abundant material of this kind.

In its art, therefore, the Azilian is connected with the Mediterranean Grimaldian. The painted motifs, mostly dots or bars in various groupings, also give more complicated designs—crosses with one or two bars, barred circles, fern-leaves, criss-crossed rectangles, centre-dotted circles, and a few rare letter-forms like E, F, M, and W. Obermaier quite rightly interpreted some of these signs in the light of the schematic rock figures in Spain, which are, moreover, of later date (Neolithic and Eneolithic). Painted pebbles are a first step in schematic art. Also Le Mas d'Azil has given rare painted, schematic, animal figures that are quite recognizable (H. Breuil).

Farther east and considerably later in date the Falkensteinhöhle, Tiergarten, and other places on the Upper Danube provided, in 1934, flat harpoons with double rows of barbs, similar to those from Mac-Arthur's Cave at Oban (Scotland), in association with triangular microliths and even with flat stone axes sharpened by rubbing, one of them fixed in a stag-horn handle. This is perhaps the source of some very large flat stag-horn harpoons that the bed of the Danube has yielded at various points, a set of which, now in the Belgrade Museum, was found in the Eneolithic village at Vinça.

The Asturian

In the caves along the coast near Oviedo (Spain) the Azilian is followed by a strange industry, from a people who lived on shellfish, and dating from a period corresponding to the post-glacial optimum. This is the 'Asturian,' a very primitive culture of pebbles chipped to a point on one face only, of hand-picks with ends worn down in scraping for molluscs along the inshore reefs; with these go rare examples of worked bones, including stag-horns perforated with an oval hole, similar to those found in certain late Leptolithic levels in the Hamburg area.

Before he found it in its stratigraphical setting Count de la Vega del Sella had connected this Asturian industry with a kind of Acheulean, whereas one of us (H. Breuil) was inclined to place these quartzite picks among similar flint picks that sometimes go with the normal Leptolithic implements at all levels, and also among certain groups of keeled, pointed scrapers of elongated shape and with a thick heel. It was thought that they represented the erratic development of some Leptolithic group. An enormous number of beach settlements were found along the north-west coast of Portugal and the littoral near Spanish Galicia, and they were often mingled with elements recalling the early Palaeolithic. Some, at least—at Serpa Pinto—seemed older than the Asturian, and Breuil gave them the name of 'Ancorian' (from the site at Ancora, Portugal). Investigations started by H. Breuil and Zbyszewski in 1942 on the beaches near Viana do Castelo show that after the fall of the Tyrrhenian sea an Acheulean group settled on this beach and were followed by Languedocian tribes who began to fashion, among other implements, broad picks made from pebbles. These tools were later mingled in the Riss-Würm period by the Grimaldian sea with underlying Acheulean specimens and with others of more and more Asturian type, and the whole formed a mass of rolled implements that it is extremely difficult to sort out. In stormy weather the sea-water still continues this churning and rolling, but at low water on the reefs the typical Asturian shapes can be found in quantity and absolutely intact, and more run out below the level of the lowest tides. Thus the more recent Asturian in Asturias seems to come from the migration of elements derived from the banks of the Minho, when the rise of the sea at the post-Würmian optimum deprived them of the reefs that supplied them.

It is well known that the Asturian has been found at Biarritz, under the beach at Moulignat, and also in Catalonia.

It is also possible that certain Neolithic flint industries with great quantities of awls found in the lower Charente (Moulin de Vent) and in the island of Yoh (Morbihan) may be more or less a continuation of this tradition, but this is only a deduction. As for the Irish flint industries to which some wished to give this name, they are probably contemporaneous, but really do not belong to the same group of industries.[1]

There is another implement made of chipped pebble, found in various forms in the Asturian sites on the northern coasts of Portugal and thought to be a weight for nets or fishing-lines because the long-shoremen use similar objects for the same purpose to this day. The oldest type, which can be associated at least with the Minho Langue-docian with broad picks, and which was rolled by the Grimaldian sea, is of fairly stout size, being an oval pebble chipped on the two edges with a very wide groove, single- or double-sided. Other types, certainly of more recent date, are smaller. In some the grooves, narrower and always on both sides, are mostly deep and double-sided. Some have certainly been rolled by the Grimaldian sea. Others have much smaller notches, usually at the ends. Some look so fresh that it is doubtful if they date from very far back, and they either belong to modern times or are contemporaneous with those discovered in large quantities in the *citanias* along the coast, going well back into barbarian times.

At Oviedo and Biarritz the Asturian has given no objects of this kind.

The Sauveterrian and the Tardenoisian

These industries are characterized by abundant microliths in geometrical shapes—triangles and crescents for the Sauveterrian, with the addition of short trapezes for the Tardenoisian. Their geographical distribution is extremely extensive, covering all the Old World and Australia. But it is particularly round the Mediterranean that they seem to have developed from local Gravettian Leptolithic phases, and then to have swarmed off in all directions as though fleeing their starting-points, now invaded by the Neolithics. At least in this Western group in the Old World the industries show certain constant features in the way their microliths were produced. The thin flakes of strips from which they were made were usually notched with a groove at the desired point of breakage, this being achieved by a light blow, with the

[1] *Cf.* H. L. Movius jun., Curran Point, Larne (County Antrim), "The Type Site of the Irish Mesolithic," in *Proc. Royal Irish Acad.*, September 1953.

weakened part resting on a small anvil. The break could be made by making an oblique facet on the underside, with a very similar splitting plane to that of the strip to be cut through. This produced at the break an obtuse, bevelled point, similar to certain Leptolithic 'plane' gravers, and these were the *Tardenoisian micro-gravers*, the product of a special chipping technique found from south of the Euphrates to India, in Kenya, in Morocco, from Palestine to the Crimea, in Poland, on the German plains, in Holland, Belgium, England, France, the Spanish Peninsula, and Italy. This micro-graver was not—at least, not usually —a tool made for its own sake, although it often shows signs of use. It persists in Europe as long as geometrical microliths were used— that is to say, during a considerable part of the Neolithic and even Eneolithic industries, which is accounted for no doubt by the fact that many of the Sauveterrian and Tardenoisian Mesolithic peoples adapted themselves to Neolithic life. Where and how was this technique born?

Microliths, some geometrical, are found in many levels of the Lepto- lithic, and it did happen that in order to shorten them a chipping process of this type was used from the Gravettian and Grimaldian periods onward, so that they could be mounted in the groove on the staff they were intended to fit into with others. However, the process did not seem to spread, and the microliths of these times did not finally come to be so specially used, so that micro-gravers are not themselves typical of microlithic industries, as was at first thought.[1]

The birth of this technique may have been detected in the group of Sebilian industries in Upper Egypt. There, towards the end of the pluvial period corresponding no doubt to our late Würm, Sebilian tribes (studied by Vignard) had pitched their encampments on the edge of a widened part of the Nile. The latter gradually receded as the dryness increased, and Sebilian II and III followed the river-bank down. Now the oldest of these people chipped short blades or flakes according to techniques that were still Levalloiso-Mousterian—it is known that these methods went on very late in East and South Africa. To remove the rather thick base of these flakes they employed, starting from a notch with a lateral edge, a kind of transverse 'graver-stroke' that removed the end, and the line of breakage was then trimmed up. This gave fairly large, geometrical tools. In the two subsequent stages

---

[1] However abundant micro-gravers may be in the microlithic levels of the Meso- lithic, their presence is not sufficient to make them characteristic of these levels, since they are met with in Southern Italy, at Romanelli, dating from fairly early in the local Grimaldian, and in Southern Spain, at El Parpalló, in several Leptolithic horizons. The same holds for Grimaldi (Riviera). Near Brive they are abundant in a Magdalenian III level with many microliths and occur again at various Gravet- tian levels. They provide, therefore, proof of the development of facies with micro- lithic tendencies in the Mediterranean area, parallel to various Leptolithic facies in Western Europe, and perhaps indicate the importation of other elements and techni- ques full into the middle of Gravettian, Solutrean, and Magdalenian milieux.

the cores are no longer Mousteroid, and the flakes are lighter and more like blades. It can be seen that notching and cutting on an anvil were coming in. The geometrical shapes are firmer and smaller, though they remain larger and heavier than in the sites with Sauveterrian and Tardenoisian facies. Was this technique therefore first produced in Egypt? In any case, it is found again in the Capsian, mainly in the advanced form in Tunisia (Négrine, Tabelbalah, Beni Abbès), in Kenya, in the Natufian in Palestine, as far afield as Kurdistan, and all the area already mentioned.

The Natufian, the last pre-Neolithic stage in Palestine, seems to have already had some notions of growing cereals. It had neither pottery nor polished stones, but used the sickle (a hollowed-out rib fitted with microlith teeth) and did artistic and fairly effective carvings of humans and animals in bone or soft stone. It might be of the same date as the later stages of the European Leptolithic, and also used the bone harpoon. Besides geometrical microliths, mainly crescents, it produced a small triangular arrow-head with a slightly concave base, found again at Helwan, near Cairo, and seems to have been the origin of the concave-based points at El Fayum and all the Saharan Neolithic in the microlith tradition. Some of the inhabitants of Southern Saharan sites in this line also chipped leaf-points and used bone harpoons with one or two rows of barbs that are very close to Upper Magdalenian work. As they caught fish and ate hippopotamus in regions that are completely dried up to-day, they must have lived there before the disappearance of the last rainy conditions.

After this broad general survey, let us return to Western Europe. Caves in the Eastern Pyrenees—La Crouzade and Bize (Aude)—contain a level with tiny triangles intercalated between the Azilian and the Neolithic. The Mocchi shelter on the Riviera has revealed, overlying the most recent Grimaldian series, a very fine layer with triangular microliths and abundant micro-gravers. The Gramat caves (Lot) yielded a series of post-Magdalenian levels with triangles, micro-gravers, and painted pebbles. At Sauveterre-la-Lémance (Lot-et-Garonne) Coulonges revealed a whole succession of levels with microliths, going from Sauveterrian triangles through pure Tardenoisian trapezes and into Neolithic types. The Sauveterrian with triangles is found again at the Barbeau shelter (Le Moustier, Dordogne), right in the centre of the Vézère sites. These different phases covered all France, with special modifications in the north-east. Only the Sauveterrian series with triangles seems to have crossed the Channel, while the sandy districts of the Paris Basin have given beautiful groups of the two types, at Piscop (Seine-et-Oise)[1] and around Fère-en-Tardenois

---

[1] With a strong admixture of Montmorencian chipped sandstone which here, in any case, is of the same period.

o

(Aisne), their eponymous site. Stations in Belgium, as in England, were preceded by the microlithic facies of the end of the Palaeolithic, and these were no doubt indigenous (Cresswellian industries) and parallel to Magdalenian VI. The reindeer was still to be found in Belgium when the true microlithic peoples, with implements quite clearly different from their predecessors, arrived there.

Among the most famous sites connected with this industrial complex are the *concheiros* at Muge and near by, in the old estuary of the Tagus. Well back from the present river-banks and 50 miles from the mouth, the hollow bank of the former estuary is strewn with considerable piles of seashells, mixed with ash and containing broken bones of large bulls, stags, boars, and, more rarely, horses and other animals. They are accompanied by a range of industrial materials—worked stag-horn unperforated axes, chisels, drifts, antler-tines cut into lengths and sharpened, awls and bone spatulae, a few of them decorated with parallel lines, pierced shells, and so on. There are fair numbers of very large bones roughly trimmed for use and a not very abundant series of stone implements, including rare chipped quartzite pebbles recalling Languedocian work, flakes of the same material, and some flints. These appear as small strips, notched blades, a few micro-gravers, and geometrical microliths, both triangular and trapezoidal, the latter of more recent date. This is indeed Sauveterrian and Tardenoisian material, and has been recognized as such as a result of investigations by Portuguese experts. It ought to have been called 'Mugian,' since it was the first great complex of this kind to be discovered and described.

These collections of shells do not mark the habitats, which have still to be discovered in the neighbourhood (the Abbé Roche discovered one recently). Bones would be lacking in such sandy soil, but the stone work should be very copious as in the rock-shelter of similar date found at Rio Maior by Dr M. Heleno, or in the hut-settlements in Germany and the Paris area (Piscop, Forest of Montmorency).

On the other hand, these collections that were mere garbage-tips have preserved not only relics of the land fauna, but also many burial-places, mainly hidden very deep down in the masses of accumulated shells.

On the islands off the coast of Morbihan, in other *concheiros* of similar date, expertly studied by M. and Mme Saint-Just Péquart, many skeletons were found buried, with extraordinary ritual, under piles of stag-antlers covering both single and multiple graves. The industries are somewhat different, the triangles being larger and micro-gravers absent. But each body was accompanied by a worked bone blade, cut off obliquely. These daggers were very skilfully made and some-times decorated with geometrical incisions.

In Northern France, Belgium, Holland, and all along the southern edge of the German plain, from Württemberg to Poland and down to the Crimea, the Tardenoisian sites are confined to sandy soils and carefully avoid loess surfaces. The same is found in South-east England.

But farther north in England (West Yorkshire and the Pennine Chain, which is over 300 metres high in places), in Franconia (Ansbach), and in the Black Forest they are found on high, sandy plateaux between 400 and 600 metres—for instance, at Hohlefels, Holzheim, and Lichtenfels. They are scattered along the ancient banks of the Federsee (Württemberg). They often occur as small villages, with huts sometimes made of reed wattles smeared with clay, forming, at Tannstock and Federseemoor, a group of thirty-eight. These dwellings measure $3\frac{1}{2}$ metres long by 1 or 2 metres wide, and are grouped in twos or threes, with a fireplace in the centre.

Some rock-shelters were also inhabited at this time—for example, at Ensdorf, where three levels were found, passing from an older one with simple triangular microliths (one single cutting edge blunted obliquely) to others mingled with warped trapezes with one side concave; later, alongside lengthened scalene triangles with two short, blunted sides, appears the micro-chopper. Everywhere the micro-graver is common. At White Hill (Yorkshire) was found a linear group of thirty-five triangles, spaced $1\frac{1}{2}$–2 centimetres apart, constituting the barbs on a wooden shaft that had rotted away. The only bone tools were found at the Hensdorf shelter (Franconia), being simple cuts from antlertines and a long, curved wand sharpened at one end. Tannstock yielded a large, spindle-shaped throwing-spear.

The fauna of the Tardenoisian level in the caves at Cresswell Crags (Manchester) is sylvan and probably still contained bison.

The peat deposits in England have provided material for interesting pollen analysis. Here the Tardenoisian with triangles comes at the end of a maximum with pines, silver birch, elms, hazels, between two maxima with oaks, and before the arrival of the lime and the alder. The level of the land was then higher than it is to-day, and this corresponds to the end of period II and the beginning of period III of the Baltic Mesolithic. Data from Württemberg give similar results.

The Tardenoisian industry went on, beyond the Mesolithic, in various parts of the Spanish Peninsula. It is associated with a Neolithic complex at El Argar (Almeria) containing polished axes, points, arrow-heads, and pottery. It reappears in Portugal and Biscay, in camp- and shelter-sites and in very archaic little dolmens, much older than the others. The Almerian and Portuguese Tardenoisian, therefore, became Neolithic. It is interesting to note that there was no use of the fish-hook made from shell, found by Miguel Such in the cave at Cantal Gordo (Malaga) in a level with geometrical prototypes that were probably much older.

The Montmorencian

Not far from the Tardenoisian village of Piscop (Seine-et-Oise) can be seen a vast work-site of chipped, quartzitic sandstone where the tools are often large and have quite a different aspect. A number of other similar deposits are scattered on the heights of the Forest of Montmorency at other points where the Fontainebleau sandstone is in evidence. They certainly are not all of the same date. On the surface, in the most recent deposits, a chipped axe of Neolithic aspect occurs, though rarely. In others can be found a few uncertain choppers looking somewhat pre-Campignian. But all contain implements, mostly made of long, trihedral pieces, similar in proportions to long picks—though they are not these, since their ends, usually undifferentiated and even fragile, have never been used. The places where they are worn are on the lateral angles, mainly in the centre where they have been sharpened time and time again until the implement was so narrowed down and worn there that it could no longer be used and finally broke through at the narrowest part. Some have been found *in situ*, mingled with hearths containing microliths (Vignard).

Such objects for wood-working are met with, though no doubt much more rarely, in Neolithic contexts—indeed, even among dolmenic articles—but they do sometimes occur in Leptolithic milieux (Valle, Santander: Magdalenian VI) and the absence in the Montmorencian deposits of any pottery and anything of expressly Neolithic form places them as prior in date. It is still too early to define the area around Paris covered by this curious culture and its connexions with others of the same period.

[17]

The Mesolithic in the
Baltic countries[1]

*The background to the end of the Leptolithic, leading to the Nordic Mesolithic;
The Maglemosean culture—Star Carr (Yorkshire)—Maglemosean art—The
Ertebölle culture*

Thanks to the combined study of glacial, marine, and lake deposits in the Baltic countries and also to research into the positive and negative movements of the earth's crust and the variations in temperature ranging from Arctic conditions to an optimum, with consequent influence on flora and fauna, no other region has had its Mesolithic better explored than Scandinavia and the neighbouring lands, nor enabled the different phases of its successive civilizations to be evaluated in periods of years.

From 10,000 to 8300 B.C. the Baltic was still covered by the Scandinavian, Göti-glacial type of glacier, in progressive retreat. Off the edge of the ice-front, round about Hamburg, in a sub-Arctic climate, stretched tundra with willow, herbaceous silver birch, and *Dryas*. Reindeer and lemmings lived there, and in the summer it was roamed by epi-Magdalenian tribes, come for the hunting and fishing.

When the glacier no longer blocked the passage into the Baltic from the North Sea salt water containing *Yoldia* flowed in, between 8300 and 8000 B.C. As the temperature rose to reach between 8° and 12° Centigrade in July and August (a pre-boreal climate) forests of silver birch, pine, and willow sprang up. The tundra fauna were increased by

---

[1] Except for the art, we have in this chapter mainly followed the excellent study by J. G. D. Clark in his book *The Mesolithic Settlement of Northern Europe.*

other forest species. The reindeer still existed, but the lemming had disappeared. That was the beginning of the Mesolithic.

Prior to the melting away of the Scandinavian glacier, around 6800 B.C., an upheaval again separated the Baltic from the North Sea, and fresh water replaced the salt water by a lake containing *Ancylus*, which disappeared only about 5000 B.C. The summer temperature went steadily up from a maximum of 12° to one of 17°, giving a dry, northern, continental climate. At first the reindeer lived on, then died out. The elk became very common, with other lake and forest animals. Woods spread, first with pines and silver birch, mingling with alder, oak, lime, and elm, and later hazels multiplied rapidly. The dog was man's companion in the second period of the Mesolithic.

The North Sea began to encroach on the continent about the year 6200, and from 5000 the Baltic became a sea bearing *Littorinae*, remaining so after 2500, when Neolithic peoples had replaced the Mesolithics of phase III. This climatic optimum, when the temperature reached 17°, was a damp period.

The reindeer had now totally vanished, being replaced by forest, marsh, and marine animals. Oak, elm, lime, and alder made up the forests. After the development of the Neolithic, about 2500, the cold set in again, with a drop in humidity, ushering in a sub-boreal phase that still persists.

THE BACKGROUND TO THE END OF THE LEPTOLITHIC, LEADING TO THE NORDIC MESOLITHIC

At the time when the glacial front stretched south of Hamburg human tribes also frequented these parts. From Poland to England the stone implements found are related to a kind of extension of the Gravettian, often mingled with weak Magdalenian elements of frequently increasing microlithic tendencies. This is the English *Cresswellian*, so similar to the Belgian *mobilier* from *Remouchamps* and *Martinrive*. It includes blades cut transversely or obliquely, only a few triangles, small knife-blades with convex blunted backs, small, short scrapers, gravers (rare), and tanged points of inferior chipping and workmanship, with pierced shells and a few bone awls. At Remouchamps a bone decorated with a band of dots arranged like a star, with a dotted rectangle or triangle in the centre, provided the oldest example of an art tending towards the Mesolithic that was soon to become Maglemosean. Similar flints have been found in Hanover, at Kirchdorf, slightly more recent in date than the culture at Ahrensburg-Lavenstedt, between Lübeck and Hamburg, where it is represented only by flint blades trimmed into ordinary gravers, as yet without any notable microlithic tendency, and some oblique-cut points, with or without tangs, associated with short, broad scrapers. This same industry reappears in the cave at

Hohlenstein, Westphalia, accompanied by reindeer, boar, roebuck, and beaver. Furthermore, a kind of small, oblique chisel was found at Ahrensburg and a concave-based, oblique-cut point at the Hohlenstein cave.

On the other side of Central Europe, at the base of the dunes of the Vistula and the Bug, on the first blown sand to cover the Baltic moraines, but outside them and underlying Tardenoisian and Neolithic humus levels, lie traces of the *Swiderian* industry, also characterized by tiny tanged points, often with inverse trimming or oblique cutting-off of the ends; by small blades with blunted backs and oblique points, flakes made into scrapers, and many 'bec-de-flûte' gravers or gravers made, perhaps, from a wedge of blade cut off crosswise. This culture also spreads over Germany and the Ukraine and seems to have influenced the Western Magdalenian VI, as regards tanged points in particular. There are no known examples of worked bones.

Such is not the case for the *Hamburgian* culture. Rüst has investigated its stations with great success on the banks of the Alster, north-east of Hamburg, and at Meiendorf, near the city. Here the production of microliths by using the micro-graver is evidence of the infiltration of southern influences from the Mediterranean.

On such sites, within sight of the very front of the glacier, men of the time of our [French] most recent Magdalenian would come and settle for the summer on moraine crests between the ice-bottomed lakes and hunt the reindeer in their thousands, as well as horses and waterfowl, throwing their rubbish into the lakes and leaving their flints on the crests. The kitchen refuse and tools have been preserved under peat bearing the pollen of pine forests from the end of the first period of the Mesolithic. They date from the very end of the Quaternary. Lemmings are absent, and the silver birch accounts for 95 per cent. of the pollen analysis, against very little pine. It is a kind of final Magdalenian.

The stone implements are made up of fine blades, not cut off crosswise, but often terminated as scrapers, as cross-cut angle gravers, or as a sort of curved awl. There are long, narrow-keeled scrapers with a very high ridged back and the ends trimmed up like hook-nosed gravers, and also notched points, but no tanged ones. All such pieces can be found in the advanced Magdalenian VI in South-west France. Nearly all the flints come from the surface of moraine crests, though some have been found under the most recent peat, among rubbish cast into the old glacial lakes, containing whole bodies of female reindeer with the bowels replaced by large stones—evidence, perhaps, of a fertility rite or an attempt to store food. The same sites have provided a rich harvest of objects in worked reindeer-horn: many antlers; long, curved wands taken off with a graver and probably 'loosened up' with the curved awls previously mentioned among the implements; fine spear-heads with double-bevelled or pointed bases, and chisel-punches, the whole

being very Magdalenian in style. Less so is, firstly, a harpoon-head
with only one set of angular barbs, similar to those appearing at odd
times at the end of Magdalenian VI, but with a different base. Its lug
is replaced, along the line of the other barbs, by a recurrent barb,
preceded by another, triangular in shape and with two points, one
directed forward, the other identical with the points of the other barbs.
Only one other harpoon from the Magdalenian world is comparable to
this, and it was found in a level corresponding to the very end of the
reindeer at Bobache (Isère). It has barbs on one side only, and they are
all angular. Bobache is situated geographically at the limit of the spread of
the Magdalenian towards the east. This fact, and the very 'provincial'
look of the harpoons from the Kesslerloch, on Lake Constance, seems to
confirm the *provincial* Magdalenian origin of the Hamburgian industry.

Another object, several examples of which were found, is even more
original. It is a kind of crooked stick or bent club of reindeer-horn,
pierced through above the bend by an oval hole in which was firmly
fixed an untrimmed, pointed flint-blade. If this unique assembly is not
the work of mere chance it is evidence of the use of this kind of handle.
Moreover, the end of the crook is hollowed out and bevelled and
certainly meant for the insertion of a bone or stone to form a pick-
head or an axe-blade. Round this termination are decorations of
parallel furrows, wavy on one side and on the other forming interlocking handles or bows. This kind of decoration was unknown in the
Magdalenian and is perhaps an ornamental reproduction of a binding
applied to this end to make fast the flint forming the working point of
the instrument. In this culture art is represented by *graffiti* on thin
tablets. They are too fragmentary to be intelligible, though the
engraving is intentional. (They were investigated by H. Breuil in
1936.) Much clearer is a figure of a pike, about 40 centimetres long,
economically fashioned from a palm of reindeer antler thinned down to
form the head from the sawn-off part, with incisions for the gills and eyes.
This pike was, indeed, part of the kitchen refuse found at Hamburg.

A little above this level stretches another, more recent horizon of
similar type, but where the graver tends to disappear.

It is tempting to compare these reindeer-horn crooked sticks with
other objects found at odd times—the handles and axes of the *Lyngby*
culture, of which they are the sole representatives, along with a few
broad, flint tanged points. The period and distribution of these
implements spreads over Poland, East Prussia, Westphalia, and
Southern Sweden at the time of the *Yoldia*-bearing sea when Denmark
was still joined to her neighbour opposite. Their age varies from
Mesolithic I to II, and, according to the region, pollen analysis has
shown an abundance of birch and pine with some willow, alder, and
hazel, or many of the latter types, but accompanied by oak, elm, and
lime.

The instrument known as a 'Lyngby axe' is a curved tine of reindeer-horn, topped by the stump of a single frontal branch with a bevelled cut so that to it can be bound a tool with a vertical cutting edge, making it an axe, or a horizontal one, making it a hoe.

Other industries developed farther north; beyond Bergen (Norway) and on the whole of the north coast of Finland came the *Komso* culture, of which we have only chipped, broad-flaked stones with little trimming, found tiered in two groups above the beach containing *Tapes* (period III). A study of these has been published by Professor Bøe. In the most recent and low level there were polished axes in green rock, arrow-heads and chisels in polished schist, and flint crescents, indicating a Neolithic stage. A higher and older horizon, at heights varying, according to the place, from 20–30 metres to 66 metres above sea-level, has revealed rocks of different kinds that had been merely chipped—quartzite, quartz, and dolerite. Broad-flake chipping predominates, but the blade, though rare, is found. The retrimmed tools are stout implements of crescent shape, with a convex, blunted back, recalling the Aurignacian Châtelperron type, or blade scrapers, 'bec-de-flûte' gravers, broad triangular tanged points,[1] and, less certainly, choppers made from flakes.

Trondhjem fjord was the centre of the *Fosna* culture, scattered over small sites about 5 metres wide (huts) at a height of 44 metres. For good pieces flint was used mainly (Kristiansund), and the industrial types consist mostly of numerous spindle-shaped points with the base tang slightly truncated, a very few scrapers, a single stout graver made from a wedge of blade cut crosswise, and a few chipped axes, indications recalling in some ways the whole range of periods II and III of the Mesolithic. The Fosna industry starts in the Littorina beach (period I) and continues in periods III and IV and then in the Megalithic age, associated with arrow-heads in polished schist or with concave base and serrated edges, and with polished axes and pottery.

In Eastern Ireland, at Island-Magee, in the diatom-bearing deposits of the river Dan, covered with peat and estuary clay, was discovered another industry with broad, tanged points made from short flakes, and this was contemporaneous with the end of the Mesolithic (periods III and IV) and has probably some connexion with certain previous groups. The short blades were chipped from large, cylindro-conical cores (see Movius, loc. cit.).

The Maglemosean Culture

The Maglemosean culture is by far the most interesting of the Mesolithic civilizations in Northern countries, where it seems to be a continuation of the Magdalenian, preserving its gravers and the rich bone

[1] It is interesting to note that a much older specimen was found in the site at Salzgitter-Lebenstedt, pre- or proto-Würm.

tooling, but adding the use of curved fish-hooks and, it would seem, a knowledge of the piercing-drill and net-making. The fish-hook was already known at various points on the Mediterranean (Cantal Gordo, Malaga, Spain). Hand-picks had been used from time to time, from the beginnings of the Leptolithic and even before, by the Ancorian tribes on the north-west coast of Portugal, but in the Mesolithic they came farther north, as did rough axes or choppers mounted on stag-horn handles that were probably the contributions of the Lyngby and Hamburg cultures.

At that time the North Sea stretched uninterruptedly from Holderness to the north of Jutland, but had no passage through to the Baltic, then a freshwater lake bearing *Ancylus*. On the other hand, part of Sweden, Western Estonia, and Finland were submerged. The Magle-mosean developed all along these coasts. The areas richest in finds from this culture are Denmark, Southern Sweden, and the modern islands of Zealand and Scania, though sporadic discoveries prove that it stretched much farther south, west, and east—to Poland, Scotland, England, Picardy and even to Paris. Off the Norfolk coast it is not uncommon for fishermen to bring up in their nets pieces of peat containing Magle-mosean objects, including harpoons used by the inhabitants of lowlands since submerged by the North Sea.

The Maglemosean tribes lived, at least in summer, in very small groups on the shores of lakes, marshes, rivers, and the sea. Being first and foremost hunters of water-fowl and fishermen, they also went after the primitive bull, the elk, the boar, the stag, and the roebuck. For the first time there is evidence that the domestic dog was their companion. They also gathered wild fruit, particularly nuts. Their summer quarters, of very limited area—nothing is known of their winter camps—were sited on crests not very high above the water's edge and submerged by the winter floods. They often strewed their floor with pine- and birch-bark.

A great part of the Maglemosean range of stone implements was derived from retouched blades and strips. Some blades have their ends cut off square; there are rare examples of awls, a very few blunt-backed blades, as well as ordinary gravers and cross-cut, blade-wedge gravers of the straight or concave kind (particularly at Duvensee, Lübeck). Other pieces were made from short, medium, or fairly small flakes, such as scrapers, and there are specimens of core-shaped scrapers.

Microliths were made from strips using the micro-graver technique with a prepared notch, giving pieces with cross-cutting of one or both ends, crescents, symmetrical, lengthened isosceles triangles with bilateral trimming, or asymmetrical scalene triangles with unilateral trimming. Even a micro-chopper with shaped, concave sides was found on Zealand.

Besides this range of objects derived from blade technique and not very different from what can be found in certain Magdalenian sites, except for the micro-chopper, there is another group of implements chipped directly from flint blocks or large flakes, giving chisels, mattocks, and chopping-axes of varying sizes and shapes, some broad, some narrow, or ovoid, trapezoid, and triangular, but all terminated at one end by a very sharp cutting edge. This was at first preserved from the original flake, the sides being knocked off, and then restored by a lateral blow when the first edge had been chipped by use. All these tools had stag-horn handles and must have been used for working on the wood that abounded in the surrounding forests at the time of the second Mesolithic period, when the climate was fairly warm and continental.

But the Maglemoseans were not only equipped with chipped flint tools. Sweden has furnished some of their pestles made from pebbles. Sometimes they made, by pricking out or gouging, other pieces such as the little mortars found at Svaerdborg. These have two small cups, one on either side, or have double conical perforations, the former being similar to Magdalenian types, the latter to Capsian specimens from North Africa or the pierced knobs of the digging-sticks used in Palestine, or by the Neolithic Egyptians, and by all the inhabitants of East, Central, and South Africa, and comparable to the 'drills' found in many other regions, including modern China.

More surprising are three long, spindle-shaped club-heads, pierced in the centre, the first two by a double conical hole and the later one by a cylindrical cavity. On this last specimen two broad lateral lobes are developed in the middle, being an exaggeration of a smaller globular swelling on the two other clubs and providing strengthening for the centre of the implement. Two examples from Kungsladugard (Göteborg) have been dated by pollen analysis as coming from the beginning of the Maglemosean and can be placed as prior to the encroachment of the Tapes sea. Two others belong to the third period. In the lower level at Sandarna, in Sweden, some long pebbles with their surfaces shaped by pricking and ends sharpened by rubbing are the first signs of what were to be polished axes.

These stone implements seem to be reproductions in the softer stones of other axes and hoes usually made of stag-horn, or at times of a long bone. These were also perforated for mounting on a wooden handle, though some were not. In period II hoes with horizontal-cutting edges are more numerous than vertical-cutting axes, but in Mesolithic III the proportion is reversed in favour of the axes.

The same perforation is found again on sections of stag-horn, hollowed out at one end for the insertion of a stone tool (mattock or small chopper) or a bone (Svaerdborg) or even another antler-tine. This type goes out with the subsequent Ertebölle culture. Wooden sticks used as handles have been found with the end swollen out wider than the diameter of the perforation, to avoid losing the tool fixed to them. Some antler-tines were also pierced at their broadest ends, and, being made from a section of main antler, carefully polished and ornamented, they recall the pierced sticks of the Western Magdalenian. Fairly small, tubular segments of bone, or cylindrical sockets, could also be used as handles. Certain small sticks or spatulae are believed to have been used for net-making.

Bone awls are abundant. Ulna-bones sharpened into daggers are rarer and disappear completely in the Ertebölle culture.

Even more important are the different ways of arming arrows that were meant to be thrown like javelins. Some are extremely simple, in the shape of smooth, cylindrical wands, sharpened into a long, slender point. Others are three-sided in section and can be divided into a three-sided pyramidical base and a broad stem with a sharp point. In Estonia and East Prussia they are slender and swell out into a pike-head at the end. Estonia has also given a type with a slender base tang, suddenly widening out above; then the stem, after two symmetrical shoulders, becomes progressively more slender and is finally edged at each side by a serrated fringe.

Many of these more elaborate arrow-heads are indiscriminately classed as harpoons, whatever their purpose, whether it was single or multiple, for hunting or fishing. It simply means that they were armed with lateral teeth, mostly in recurrent sets. These are the most characteristic objects of this culture, and many recall the shapes of Magdalenian IV, V, and VI, and even the Azilian.

In Northern Germany, Southern Sweden, and on the Thames very simple types show an edge serrated with more or less deep and frequent incisions. Harpoons with a single unilateral set of barbs or two symmetrical barbs[1] near the tip—or very near the base, forming a tang—seem peculiar to Estonia.

In most of the other countries barbs, nearly always down one side and angular, become more numerous, one exceptional shape having two at each end and on the same side. Three specimens at Mullerup, others at Kunda (Estonia), and on the Danish islands of Zealand and Bornholm, have the barbs made by a series of oblique incisions on a straight or curved stem, and in the last case the base is twisted. The kind with broad, curved barbs, but with a reversed barb at the base, can be found from Hanover to East Prussia. In the same region a related type, with straight, oblique barbs, shows a base nearer to Magdalenian VI and is accompanied by a very similar type that occurs over Pomerania and Southern Sweden.

---

[1] Several specimens of this type with long stems and double barbs were found in a dolmen-tunnel at Cuise-la-Motte (Oise), not far from Compiègne, together with beautiful polished flint axes. They were destroyed during the 1914–18 War. H. Breuil handled them, but did not make drawings of them.

Another variety that is very close to the harpoons of the Magdaleno-Azilian transition in France is cruder and thicker, with broad, slender, angular barbs and a perforated base with inversed, recurrent barbs. It is found from Poland to Sweden, through East Prussia, Pomerania, Schleswig-Holstein, and Denmark. The harpoon with a double row of alternate, angular barbs and a double bulb at the base exists in the same areas, and both replace more primitive types with only a few notched barbs. This is really an advanced shape from Magdalenian VI.

Finally, other harpoons have their barbs made, not by carving into the stem, but by fixing in two lateral grooves spaced rows of small flint blades. They are found mainly on the island of Zealand and in Southern Sweden, where they are of more recent date than the harpoons with carved barbs. The most elaborate model (from Bussjö, Scania, Sweden) has fine oblique serrations on one side at the base and the tip, and its barbs are triangular microliths. It is found again at Pernau (Estonia).

Harpoons[1] are not the only objects to have blunt-backed small blades mounted in grooves. There are also flat-stemmed bone knives in which they were fixed in grooves along the edges so as to form a continuous cutting edge along both sides. Several are magnificently decorated, like the one from Mullerup, with a lancet-shaped base, and another example from Copenhagen. No throwing-weapons or implements designed for rough work were decorated in this way. They can be found again in the Ertebölle culture.

One of the innovations peculiar to the Maglemosean is the invention of the curved bone fishing-hook, with unbarbed hook and the head broadened out for the attachment of the end of the line. In the smaller Brandenburg types this flattening is more developed or is replaced by a hole. The Estonian forms are quite different, the hook being short, the stem very flattened and often pierced by several little holes, and the mounting-lug spread into two little lobes.

Boar-tusks provided the material for various tools and were often mounted on handles. As for the teeth of other animals, some were pierced, such as the canines of the bear, otter, and cat and the incisors of the bull and the stag. These, together with a few rare amber pendants, pierced and decorated with dotted figures, constitute the only jewellery of the period.

Wood-working certainly played a very great part in the production of Maglemosean equipment, but it has been preserved only in Zealand, in the form of fire-hardened spear-heads, and of staves and paddles. In Scotland a canoe found at Perth over a peat-bed containing pine

[1] It should be noted that the Neolithic in the South-east Sahara also has para-Magdalenian bone harpoons, with one or two rows of barbs, and that harpoons occur in the Palestinian Mesolithic Natufian and the Neolithic on the Nile.

and birch dates from Mesolithic II. It had been hollowed out by fire, but unfortunately the two ends did not survive.

Among fishing-tackle we have the meshed net, like the one from Antrea (Viborg), with eighteen pine-bark floats and stone weights, dating from a quite early period of the Ancylus Lake.

STAR CARR (YORKSHIRE)

Discoveries at Star Carr (Seamer), near Scarborough, enabled J. G. D. Clark and his collaborators to apply to an encampment of the earliest Maglemosean times all the most up-to-date methods of investigation, and their results are so important that they deserve special mention.[1]

It was in the mouth of a small valley where it runs down to the North Sea, on the edge of a glacial moraine at that time surrounded by a marsh, that proto-Maglemoseans laid down a bed of brushwood faggots covering 240 square metres. The group probably numbered four or five families, living on a vegetable diet (nettles, water-lily shoots, *Chiropodium*, willow-leaves and -shoots, and rowan-berries) and what they could hunt (stag, roebuck, elk, boar, *Bos primigenius*). Wolves were about, but there were few birds, and fishing was not practised. The flora passed through various stages: from a lower zone, preceding the settlement, with mainly herbaceous vegetation still including the *Betula nana*, it passed into another where birch, willow, poplar, and several pines and hazels appear. In zone V, with the spread of hazels and a predominance of birch, pines develop. Zone IV, the time when the settlement was started, was characterized by a new rise in sea-level (near to the present-day one). This development of the flora ended in a great increase in pines and the appearance of ivy. After man had abandoned the site the pine was still increasing, elm had appeared, and hazel was spreading. An examination of the wood by the carbon-14 process gave an approximate date of 7538 (plus or minus 350) B.C. Judging by the quantities of stag and elk antlers, the place was more fully occupied from October to April.

The archaeological levels[2] reveal a sort of transition between the Baltic epi-Magdalenian (Ahrensberg, etc.), studied by Rüst near Hamburg, and flint implements, often of local origin from the moraine. Pyrites and tinder no doubt indicate fire-lighting material, and the rolls of birch-bark are perhaps the remains of a form of lighting. There are millstones. The types of flint implements, comprising only 15 per

---

[1] J. G. D. Clark, *Excavations at Star Carr: An Early Mesolithic Site at Seamer, near Scarborough (Yorkshire)*, with chapters by D. Walker, H. Goodrick, F. C. Frazer, and J. C. King, and an Appendix by J. W. Moor (Cambridge University Press, 1954).

[2] No burial-place has been found, and the race to which these people belonged is unknown.

cent. of the chipping products, include choppers mounted like adzes and used to cut down silver birch (which was brought back to the camp and its resin used for fixing tools), and angle gravers sometimes combined with scrapers, these latter occurring in large numbers.

Of the many microliths the notched strips were destined, as elsewhere, to be split by the 'micro-graver' technique. The geometrical types are micro-triangles, micro-trapezes, some of them still bearing the resin they were mounted in, but there are also serrated small blades with truncated ends and long trapezes with double, divergent truncation, and finally a few slender, stemmed points, borers, and awls.

The woodwork, in an exceptional state of preservation, has enabled handles and shafts to be identified, and a paddle reveals the use of light craft, no doubt of skins. Animal materials (hides, tendons, etc.) must have provided straps, thongs, thread, and clothing, but it is the Cervidae horns (stag and elk) that have given the most remarkable remains, by contrast with bones, which were little used. Yet there is not the slightest manifestation of any artistic activity, since no single trace of decorative engraving, either figurative or conventionalized or geometrical, has been found. There are personal ornaments, such as pierced shells and even amber beads; and several pairs of stag-horns, still attached to their frontal bones, have been adapted by perforations in the latter to be worn on the head, no doubt for ceremonial rites or as hunting-decoys. Stag-horn, which was used as a food, since the region is lacking in limestone, also provided material for making vast numbers of hunting-weapons and many tools. The horn was cut up with a graver, by the classical technique well known since Lartet first described it in 1863, using parallel, deep-cut grooves converging at their extremities. From this were made awls, trimmers, chisels, and so forth, but the most important category comprises the 'harpoons' or arrow-heads, with unilateral barbs, and here most certainly used for hunting. In dimensions they vary a good deal, between a few and 18 centimetres and occasionally reaching 35. This last size has only five stout barbs, but others have more; they seem to have been grouped in *foënes*, and the barbs are fine and close-packed. In the larger, older types they are separated and stand well out. Their unperforated base is not diamond-shaped as in the Upper Magdalenian. Only one has a median perforation. We can also note the existence of a sort of spoon. Among the larger tools a stout elk-horn pick and two types of axe are worth mentioning.

This magnificent site is well to the west of the whole Maglemosean world and is older than it (except for the site at Klosterb, which has true affinities with the English deposits). It would therefore seem that the Maglemosean developed from west to east, before the return of the North Sea into the Rhine–Thames estuary. So Star Carr and its Scandinavian counterpart belong to the lower Tardi-glacial period, an epi-Magdalenian phase. The Ahrensburgian is probably a little later, and the Hamburgian, a little earlier than Star Carr, comes in the pre-Boreal era, while the more classical deposits of the Scandinavian Maglemosean at Mullerup and Svaerdborg can be placed in the Boreal—that is to say, in the Atlantic optimum.

MAGLEMOSEAN ART

Realistic art has little place here. One single object, the pierced stick from Ystad (Sweden), shows two poor drawings of hinds, the complete one of which has four clumsily drawn feet. These animals are, moreover, associated with various geometrical motifs, triangles or rectangles in alternate groups, or in chequer-board pattern, in the purest Maglemosean style.

Other figures, highly conventionalized and perhaps partly symbolic, were executed either by generally very light incisions (which ought to be blacked over to make them more easily visible), or else by pricking out, or by dots made by a borer or drill driven by a bow. The first example of this technique, unknown to the Magdalenians, was reported from Remouchamps (Belgium), but others are known from the Leptolithic, in the Aurignacian (?) at Malta (Eastern Siberia). Groups of punctuation marks made on flint are found in the French Aurignacian and at various Magdalenian levels, and Magdalenian III is no doubt the level containing the greatest number of these purely schematic and geometrical designs, finely executed in interesting groups. A pierced stick, decorated with several double bands of punctuation marks in rows, from Svaerdborg and a net-shuttle from Jämtland are datable as from period II of the Mesolithic; other specimens from Langö, Fyn, come down into the third period. Most can be dated only by comparison. This art, then, becomes rarer and poorer, and its decadence continues into the subsequent Ertebölle culture.

Schematic representations of living creatures are not uncommon, either in isolation or more usually associated in arrangements of apparently geometrical design of bands or networks, which reduces them to the rôle of mere motifs. Among the more recognizable the human figure plays an important part, as in all other schematic arts the world over. Many of these little figures are made from a single or double axial line, to which the two pairs of limbs are attached, sometimes three, as in rock art, with rarely a vague indication of the head, which in exceptional cases is surmounted by a large pair of horns (Fyn). The arms, either together or separately, form a chevron or a bow, with the ends pointing up or down, or else are arranged like basket-handles, open or closed. The legs are similarly arranged, but may also form a diamond or oval, open at the bottom. At Fyn and at Silkeborg (Jutland) the male sex is indicated and even the female.

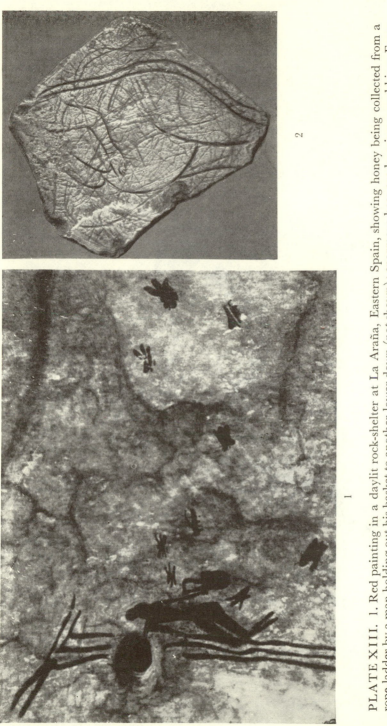

PLATE XIII. 1. Red painting in a daylit rock-shelter at La Araña, Eastern Spain, showing honey being collected from a rope-ladder by a man holding out his basket to another lower down (not shown); enormous bees are buzzing round him. From the copy by Hernandez Pacheco. 2. Nude woman, engraved on limestone tablet from the cave at La Marche, Lussac-les-Châteaux (Vienne). Magdalenian III.

PLATE XIV. The 'horned god,' a black-painted wall engraving in the Trois Frères cave (Ariège). Magdalenian IV. The perpendicular axis of the figure runs from the right of the head to the left foot. Copy by H. Breuil.

A line at the waist may signify a belt or a garment (Silkeborg Sö and Kolding Fjord, Jutland). It is also credible to interpret as female figures the fourteen double triangles ranged between two lines, at Silkeborg, and the fifteen or sixteen at Horsens Fjord (Jutland). On this latter object the two triangles are in four places separated by a lozenge, forming the bust between the head and the dress.

The wand fitted with tiny blades from Langeland Island bears a figure that is both less abstract and more doubtfully human, since it equally resembles a frog, the body being elliptical with a few wavy outlines towards the differentiated head. Two little arms (?) fixed in the base point forward, while two small legs, with bent knees and feet, are placed at the other end. The centre is criss-crossed with hatching.

Much more schematic, and only barely recognizable, is the synthetic point-drawing of a line of stags, at Kolding Fjord (Jutland), apparently facing a hunter armed with a bow (?). The first two and clearer animals in the line have bodies made of a horizontal line, carried on two pairs of vertical lines for the four legs, and topped by a vague head with flourishing antlers. A similar animal with long, straight horns and another beast have been drawn on a bone blade with many human figures from Fyn, and it recalls, except for the dotted decoration, certain disks from the Pyrenean Magdalenian IV.

Fish also play little part in this figurative art. They appear on a pierced stick from Skalstrup, in the form of a headless body, and on a very ornate net-stick from Travenhort (Holstein), associated, on the other side, with subjects that cannot be certainly identified.

On a stick from Skalstrup (Zealand) it is reasonable to interpret as snakes the little double zigzags terminating at one end in an enlarged head, and this may be a possible explanation of the decorations engraved in wavy or straight bands on the stick from Klein-Machnow (Southern Germany).

Purely geometrical decoration is very much more widespread than the above forms and is almost exclusively linear. Punctuation is the most frequently employed and of the very simplest type. There are the double bands of dots diverging from the opening on the Svaerdborg stick; the bands of multiple dots on the flat wand from Limhamn (Sweden); similar bands, parallel and alternating, on a stick fitted with flints from Copenhagen; lines terminating in a fan of strokes radiating from a centre-pierced disk or button from Havel (Northern Germany), recalling in its technique the dotted decoration of certain thin bone spindles from Magdalenian III in the Pyrenees and Cerdaña. From the same site a small stick for net-making (?) bears on its axis a triple line of dots straddled by a band of chevrons, a motif that recurs at Pernau (Estonia), with the difference that the axis has a single line of dots and the inside of the chevrons is not pricked.

P

Linear designs are considerably more common and are often taste-fully arranged. Certain objects, such as the stick from Mullerup (Zealand) and another specimen from Illebölle (Langeland Island), are decorated with broad parallel strokes and barbs on one side. On this latter object they are repeated in uninterrupted series, as they are on the stick from Mazowze (Poland), where the gaps are filled by transverse zigzags. These are found doubled on a fragment from Mullerup, where the intermediate spaces bear vertical sets of very tiny chevrons forming M's and N's and even tripled. On a stick from Mullerup and a knife with a double row of fitted bladelets from Ostro-lenka (Poland) we find again, in superposed groups of twos and fours, these vertical sets of tiny W's or M's made from two or three chevrons, running alongside a small single or double chain of dog-tooth hatchings placed side by side on a line running the whole length of the object.

Other incised designs are obtained by rectangular grouping of lines, such as the long lines with small cross-lines on the stick from Kalund-borg (Zealand), or a line with unilateral comb teeth on a wand from Travenort (Holstein); or the double lines connected by transverse streaking, making it into a scalariform, from Skalstrup (Zealand); or a rectangle with many transverse and other strokes—vertical, oblique, or in oblique, criss-cross trellis-pattern—from Kalundborg; or a motif with triple or quadruple cross-strokes, transformed into a chequer-pattern of alternate squares filled with vertical hatching, from Skalstrup and Travenort (Holstein); or a more extended chequer with five bands from the Kalundborg stick; or the lozenge-based chequer from the Ystad stick, coalescing with a hatched-in double triangle and next to two groups of alternately striped triangles. One motif on the Skalstrup stick is made up of a fairly large equilateral triangle with each angle filled equally with chequering so that the inner space is made into a hexagon; on the upper part a double chequered band continues the theme.

Reticulated motifs are often reduced to mere filling-in with a series of X's and bands with parallel lines (the amber statuette of a boar from Resen Mose, Jutland). The object also bears coalescent triangles with triple lines. More accurately reticulated is the very fine decoration of a bone tube from Bohüslan, done in single lines. In a sample from Horsens Fjord (Jutland), in which the vertical lines are quadruple or quintuple, the oblique strokes are only doubled, which is perhaps a transcription of the idea of nets with regular mesh, though the hexagonal shape of each of the sections, or alveoles, does not at first sight seem to favour such an interpretation. Might it not rather be a purely geo-metrical derivation of similar regular groupings of definite human schematic figures, as on the object from Silkeborg (Jutland), where one can see successive bands of hexagons and short lozenges, clearly reticulated, but with the lines dotted?

The decorative theme arranged on the back of the 'frog' wand with fitted flint bladelets from Langeland Island appears to be of the same sort, though at first sight its larger scale seems to invalidate the comparison: there are, in fact, three stems axially superposed, each terminating in a fork at both ends and facing the corresponding fork of the next one. The lozenge-shaped gap, taken as a decorative element, has been hatched in, and another half-lozenge is repeated at each side. The spaces to left and right are also occupied by very extended hexagons.

The very simple, small hatching marks along the edge of an accidental split in the handle of a piece from Svaerdborg were intended to give a better grip for some sort of repairing-cement, or may be a representation of surgical stitching. One might also interpret as an imitation of dressmaking stitches—as in Eskimo cultures—or as derived from net mesh, the loose zigzag with little vertical sidelines found at the top of the angles on the net-making stick from Mullerup. On the other hand, the small hatching marks emphasizing the contours of a spindle-shaped hollow in the stick from Taarback (Zealand) bear the signs of a sexual significance.

Except for the most elementary designs found in all decorations made by incision, and then not in the same context, none of these themes is found in the Western Magdalenian. Maglemosean art thus has other origins. It is not strictly true to say that at the end of the Magdalenian naturalistic art gave way to stylized art: it accompanied and inspired it. Truly schematic art hardly outlived Magdalenian III, during which it reached its peak. As for realist art, that developed independently and had no noticeable effect on it. This does not mean, however, that the Maglemosean does not come in part from the Magdalenian or even from a source common to both cultures. The use of the 'drill' in executing figures is certainly foreign to the European Leptolithic, but it concerns only rather less than a third of the objects reported in the work of J. G. D. Clark, and the ornamentation is in parts very simple.

It is interesting to note that schematic drawings of humans or animals, singly or in groups, are done more often in dots than in full lines, and yet there is only one known object with advanced dotted decoration. The contrary is to be seen in line-drawings, where the human being is rarely represented, but showing fish and snakes (?) that are absent from the other group where geometrical decoration predominates. The absence of interference between the two techniques would seem to indicate different derivations, perhaps from spontaneous strokes of genius. To explain the variety of Maglemosean harpoons we know, moreover, that some recall Magdalenian IV shapes, most of them look like Magdalenian V, and finally a few seem Magdalenian VI and even Azilian. To find the sources of Maglemosean art we shall have to wait for new discoveries to throw light on some minor problems relating to the geographical and strati-graphical distribution of the material. It is to be noted that objects of Maglemosean art remain fairly rare and are so far completely absent from the big deposit at Star Carr, apparently the oldest of all.

Let us now consider the rare figures carved in the round from this art.

The amber figure representing a boar, from Resen Mose (Jutland), cannot be an isolated case, and may be compared to other statuettes in the same material.

A very remarkable amber statuette of a horse carved in the round, but heavy in form, was discovered at Woldenberg, near Friedeberg (Brandenburg). It bears a complete resemblance to the figures from the South-western French Magdalenian IV carved on the head of a throwing-stick, with the four legs converging at their ends. A small, round-carved head in the same material was found in the same level in the Isturitz cave (Basses-Pyrénées) and has the same conven-tionalized stippling of the hide. The horse from Woldenberg belongs, in its naturalism, to the same tradition. Indeed, no Neolithic milieu has shown itself capable of such realism, truly characteristic of pure hunting peoples. The same can be said of the bear from Stolpe (Pomerania), with rudimentary legs but a fairly well-executed head, and of a few other statuettes of the same areas, the boar from Danzig among them. These are the only specimens of this very attractive art that has been called epi-Mesolithic by certain German prehistorians.

Lake Ladoga has yielded, in a level with late Maglemosean harpoons, other figures, cut out of bone blades, with the surface scattered with tiny, curved, orderly incisions: a man, seen face view, with his head developed into a broad crescent, and a seal, no less conventionalized, for both of which the term 'epi-Mesolithic' would seem suitable.

Although the great development of the Maglemosean culture took place in the second period of the Mesolithic, it still survived in the pure state at the time when the level of Central Sweden rose and the Littorina sea, in a contrary movement, invaded the Baltic. It is found at Stavanger, at Bergen, in South-west Norway, and in the rock-shelter at Viste, at a level $3\frac{1}{2}$ metres above the Tapes sea of the time, associated with bones of the elk, the boar, the beaver, birds, and fish and mingling a few potsherds and a fragment of axe in polished green rock with harpoons fitted with bladelets. Such harpoons have been found at Höilandsvandet, south of Stavanger, dating from the end of the Littorina sea, as late as the first phases of the Megalithic culture in Southern Sweden, and also at Ruskenesset (Bergen), where among the remains of domestic animals and traces of cereals came barbed harpoons, both plain and crooked fish-hooks, and arrow-heads of polished schist or flint with concave bases. This already represents the final Megalithic in Southern Scandinavia. Farther north the Magle-mosean was in the process of becoming Neolithic.

THE ERTEBÖLLE CULTURE

Farther south, particularly in Denmark and Schleswig-Holstein, another culture had developed during the maximum of the Littorina sea, which reached and slightly overshot the present water-level. This was the *Ertebölle* culture. Some of its sites are less than 8 metres above the present sea-level. It is the period of the famous Danish *kjoekken-moeddings* and *spalter* (flint chopping-blades). Except for the dog, found in all parts, domestic animals were unknown. Hunting, mainly for wild bull, and fishing were the main sources of food for these peoples, who, unlike their forerunners, lived on the coast all the year round. Molluscs such as oysters, *Littorinae*, *Cardium edule*, mussels, and *Nassa* made up a large proportion of their food.

Their stone tools contain a great number of chopping-knives, but the pick is absent. The blades are stout, and many have been trimmed up for special uses: some, retouched on all edges and pointed, have blunted backs (knives), others have straight or concave truncated ends; there are scrapers made from blade sections (except short scrapers), awls, and serrated blades. Gravers are very common, made at a single blow into plain types from broken blades and with oblique or concave cross-cuts.

Microliths are abundant as triangles and long trapezes, mainly for transverse-cutting arrow-heads, many of which have been found still attached to their shafts. The shapes show considerable variety— squares, short trapezes, triangles, some with lateral edges so steeply carved away behind the widened blade that it forms a veritable tang, some narrow from one end to the other. A few rare specimens have an oblique cutting edge. The pricking and polishing of the axe-edges, or rather the adzes, appears only in the last two-thirds of the Ertebölle period—a time when this implement, round in section and made of rock, not flint, was very common. Medium-sized pebbles with double conical perforations are also found.

The use of bone for tools was widespread, and finds include many stag-horn axes, often perforated through the base of the frontal tine, still showing the basal rosette. Adzes are lacking, and handle fittings, so frequent in the Maglemosean, have disappeared.

Harpoons are heavy and rare. Of the three harpoons found at Bloksbjerg one is straight with a cylindrical stem and weak barbs; the second, reduced to half a point with two alternate barbs, one on either side, suddenly bends below the second. The third resembles a large Azilian harpoon with two stout barbs on the right, and, being sharply curved on that side, is convex on the left; a deep notch like a counter-barb follows the last barb. Like Maglemosean and Magdalenian types, these pieces were meant to be mounted in groups ('*foënes*'), and were only rarely used singly. Another flat, curved harpoon from

Ellerbek has only two small barbs near the point. In and under the kitchen-midden at Nivaagaard were found a few harpoons with fitted bladelets and decorated flat knives, also with mounted bladelets for the cutting edge. The fish-hooks recall those of the Maglemosean, but are smaller. Only one really new bone object appears in this period—the five-toothed comb, with a bowed, perforated back or terminating in a small stem with a button.

Another novelty in the Erteböllian culture is the appearance from the beginning of low-baked pottery, generally plain, but with edges decorated with finger- or nail-prints. It comprises two types of vase, one with a pointed, conical base and sides opening out above a fairly bulbous waist, while the other is long, in the shape of a canoe.

At Braband Sö (Jutland), in a clay with *Littorinae*, several hazel-wood objects were found, about 50 centimetres long, and identified as throwing-sticks. One is flat and crescent-curved; two are bent between a pointed part and a cylindro-conical one; and the other is flat. The same clay also yielded fragments of an ash-wood bow.

The Erteböllian seems to be the continuation of the Maglemosean, but modified by a certain number of outside elements, introduced mainly in the second third of the period. A poor kind of punctuated decoration was then used in ornamental art. Transitional layers have been discovered on the deposits from the maximum of the Littorina sea.

Farther north, in Sweden, Denmark, and the island of Rügen, a few small, later groups of industries carry on the same tradition. After the retreat of the Littorina sea they increasingly take on elements from the Megalithic cultures (from Limhamn, Lihult, and Nöstvet). It would even seem that the beginnings of the Nöstvet culture were as old as the Erteböllian. The same applies, in South-east England, to the Lower Halstow group (North Kent), where the Erteböllian is represented by an industry with small chopping-knives and picks. There is no doubt that the Erteböllian occurs again in Belgium, where it is at the root of the more advanced *Campignian* culture and of many stations derived from it, up to the end of the very latest Neolithic.

The Erteböllian is a late Mesolithic culture, still without domestic animals, except for the dog, or cultivated crops, but with polished axes and pottery. It is a prelude to the general Neolithization of Europe and its colonization by shepherds and farmers.

[18]

The funeral customs of
fossil man[1]

*The cult of human skulls—The cult of animal skulls—Various methods of burial
and funeral rites*

Though we can, to a great extent, penetrate the outlook and ideas basic to the development of everyday life among fossil men, almost insurmountable obstacles arise as soon as we attempt to look into the religious past of the oldest members of the human race. During the colossal span of glacial and interglacial times many human types lived on the earth, different from one another and from us. Except for remnants of their implements, people so remote from us in time have left behind so very little material on which to base our conclusions that it was not until the discovery of cave art that we obtained a body of evidence sufficient to enlighten us on their religious outlook.

For the whole of these very early times, covering more than nine-tenths of human antiquity, the verified facts that can be interpreted as indicating supramundane beliefs are confined to the discovery of deposits of isolated skulls or animal bones buried intentionally and to skeletons laid to rest with certain rites and in particular places.

THE CULT OF HUMAN SKULLS

It is only such funeral rites that give any basis for supposing that early man had any preoccupations beyond the immediate prospects of everyday life.

[1] This and the following chapter were not given in lecture form in 1942 at Lisbon University, but were written up by R. Lantier from separate notes provided by H. Breuil.

The oldest evidence of such customs, enabling us to point to direct human intervention, is represented by the discovery in the successive levels of the cave at Chou Kow Tien (China) of about six skulls, with fragments of face- and jaw-bones, belonging to the *Sinanthropus* type of man. The remains, corresponding to six children, two adolescents, and twelve adults, had been treated in a different way from the animal remains with which they were mingled. The almost complete absence of other parts of the skeletons implies that these remains were not brought into the cave to serve as food, as were the animals, whose bones, whole or broken, make up a considerable part of the kitchen refuse. It therefore looks as if the *Sinanthropi* dwelling in the cave had carried the corpses of their relations outside and brought the skulls and jaw-bones back there, when the flesh had disappeared, to serve only as mementoes. The enlarging of the occipital orifice with a flint instrument noted on certain skulls at Chou Kow Tien does not necessarily imply cannibalistic practices. The same operation has been reported in connexion with the funeral ritual in two-stage burials. It is also present on the skulls found in the cave at Samboang, on the south coast of Celebes, before the conversion of the Bungis to Mohammedanism, as on the proto-Neanderthal skulls at Steinheim and at Weimar from the time of the interglacial periods, the former from the second, the latter from the third. It appears on the children's skulls at La Quina (Charente) and Pey de l'Aze (Dordogne), one with and the other without its jaw-bone. Isolated fragments of face-bone have been found in the Grotte des Fées at Arcy-sur-Cure (Yonne), at La Ferrassie (Dordogne), in the shelter of Le Petit Puy-Moyen (Charente), at Malarnaud (Ariège), and at Isturitz (Basses-Pyrénées). Outside France they occur at La Naulette (Belgium), at Ehringsdorf (Germany), Devil's Tower and Forbe's Quarry (Gibraltar), in the cave at Šipka (Moravia), and at Krapina (Slovenia). Outside Europe, in Indonesia, come the eleven skulls in a group in the site at Ngandong (Java), fairly old intermediaries between the *Pithecanthropus* and the Wadjak type (Java), the latter being considered as the forebear of modern Australians and their predecessors (skull at Cohuna); then in South Africa there are other fairly ancient relics of this practice, the main ones being the skulls from Broken Hill and Walfish Bay, both also found in isolation.

It would be unwise, though understandable, to extend these conclusions concerning the 'skull cult' to the discoveries of the very ancient skulls and jaw-bones at Swanscombe, Heidelberg, and Steinheim, all found in river deposits. These parts of the skeleton are, in fact, more resistant than the others to erosion, and the accidental discovery of long bones is far less striking to the imagination of the untrained observer.

The most conclusive proof of the practice of the skull cult by Neanderthal man comes from discoveries in Italy—in the Saccopastore quarry, at the very gates of Rome, where a deposit contained two skulls, less their jaw-bones, dating from the last interglacial (or 180–120,000 B.C.), and in the tiny cave at San Felice de Circeo, where a skull from the last glaciation (about 120,000 B.C.), with an enlarged occipital hole, had been laid, together with a jaw-bone not belonging to it, in a circle of stones near other groups of stones surrounding a few animal bones, perhaps intended as offerings.

On the other side of Europe, at Kiik-Koba (Crimea), a grave containing only the feet of a skeleton is evidence of two-stage burial.

The skull cult continued during the Leptolithic. Human skeletons without their skulls have been found at Předmost (Moravia). This absence of the 'noble' part of the remains must be seen in relation to the discovery of single skulls at Předmost, in the Prince Jean cave at Lautsch (Moravia), at the Vogelhard, at Stetten-ob-Lonetal (Württemberg), at the Röthekopf and at Fühlingen (Germany), at Willendorf (Austria), at Freudenthal (Switzerland), at El Castillo and Camargo (Spain), and at Oborzysko (U.S.S.R.). But it is in France that the finds have been most numerous: skulls appear at Laugerie Basse (Dordogne), Le Placard (Charente), and the Grotte des Hommes at Saint-Moré (Yonne). More numerous still are isolated finds of fragments of skulls and whole or broken jaw-bones: at La Madeleine, at Les Eyzies, at the Lachaud shelter (Dordogne), at Lussac-les-Châteaux (Vienne), at Les Forges de Bruniquel (Tarn-et-Garonne), at Pair-non-Pair and the Grotte des Fées at Marcamps (Gironde), at Aurensan and Lourdes (Hautes-Pyrénées), at Le Mas d'Azil, Gourdan, and Lorthet (Ariège), at La Balme (Savoy), and so on.

The arrangements found at Le Placard and in the Grotte des Hommes, where the skulls had been placed on a ledge or on flat stones, and sometimes decked out with shells, a bone pin, a lignite pendant, and fragments of a round lamp, leave no room for doubt about the existence of rites connected with the skull cult.

A whole body of further evidence throws a strange light on the part played by the skull in the beliefs of Leptolithic man. A certain number of brain-pans were made into cups, and the place allotted to them in the ritual sites is a clear indication of the part they were intended to play. At Dolni-Vistonice they were deposited in an artificial cavity made in the loess or set side by side, on their convex surfaces, flanked by a femur and a humerus in the cave at Le Placard. One of the cups had contained red ochre. Other examples were found at Solutré (Saône-et-Loire), at Laugerie Basse and La Madeleine (Dordogne), and at El Castillo (Spain).

The Mesolithic also has such deposits of skulls. There are those from Kaufertsberg, painted with red ochre and hidden in a little grave dug out of the underlying Magdalenian level; others, from the Hohlestein cave in the Lone valley (Germany), with their jaws and cervical vertebrae close beside them, laid in a funnel-shaped cavity, it too dug in the under-lying Magdalenian layer. There are the twenty-seven skulls from the first deposit and the six from the second at Ofnet near Nördlingen, laid concentrically in two graves a yard apart and hidden in a thick bed of red ochre, nearly all accompanied by their jaw-bones and cervical vertebrae, with traces of cutting by flint instruments (decapitation) and all with the marks of the mortal blows that shattered them. Then comes a child's jaw-bone from the peat-bog at Mullerup (Denmark), fragments of a single skull from Le Cuzoul de Gramat (Lot), and a single brain-pan from the hiding-place in the burial-site at Le Trou-Violet at Montardit (Ariège).

In view of the multiplicity of these discoveries, there can be no doubt that in the different regions of Eurasia that skull was the object of a cult, and that, indeed, from the earliest times in prehistory. However, over the many thousands of years it is possible to detect a development in the ideas behind the elaboration of these beliefs.

It seems difficult to see, at the source of such practices, evidence of a head-hunting rite. The custom observed in the Chou Kow Tien site is much closer to those noted among the Andamans in the Indian Ocean, where the bones of a buried corpse are at the proper time ceremoniously exhumed, washed in the sea, and brought back to the village to a wel-come of wailing women. The skulls and jaw-bones of relatives, pre-served in this way, are worn by their kinsfolk round their necks, though the other parts of the skeleton are not given such loving care and are often lost or broken. In certain cases these relics play a part in family feasts and are anointed with grease or oil for the occasion. Some Australian tribes have a similar custom: when the flesh has gone from the corpse after its exposure on a platform built in a tree the bones are often broken and scattered, but the jaw-bone is frequently worn by a relative as a memento of the dead person.

These human remains do not all represent battle trophies, since, ex-cept at Ofnet, no neck-vertebrae have been found, and they would have adhered to a head cut from a recently dead body. We are, in fact, faced with the remains of a peaceful cult of the skull, as something friendly, a relic to be venerated because of the bonds of affection between the worlds of the living and the dead. The existence of this cult pre-supposes the notion of continuity between the community of the living and its dead, and by coming back to take their places among their kith and kin these dead again form part of the family group. Being too illustrious or too powerful to be lost in the legions of the dead, they are given a place of honour among the living.

However, from the time of Neanderthal man a development in the nature of these links can be detected. A new factor is to be seen in the ritual burial at Monte-Circeo (Italy), where the skull shows a gaping mutilation in the temporal region near the eye-socket. The bonds of affection linking ancestors to descendants was tending to be replaced by other feelings, to be found fully expressed in the sites at Hohlestein and Ofnet, where the skulls are, indeed, true trophies. In the main grave of the two at Ofnet twenty-two skulls of young men or women had been carefully laid in a bed of ochre and covered with adornments made of shells and pierced teeth. They had been severed from the bodies and still retained the top cervical vertebrae, which bore signs on their inner surfaces of decapitation by flint knife. Most of them showed signs of fractures by a blunt instrument like an axe, proving that these people had been massacred.

Evidence of ritual cannibalism of young men or women found in the cave at Krapina (Croatia) is connected with the same preoccupations. By such means the living could absorb into themselves the vitality and special powers residing in the flesh of the dead, who, moreover, were spared the horror of slow, degrading decomposition and assured of a more honourable burial for their earthly remains.

Either in the very old family ritual of the earliest times or in the more recent practices of head-hunting the outstanding factor is the importance attached by Palaeolithic man to the noblest and most characteristic part of the human body—the head. Consciously or not, he considered that it contained the centre and principle of the life-force, as well as of mental and physical power, and its possession, besides providing him with a relic of the departed, gave him at the same time an afflux of his life and powers—these ideas being, apparently, common to primitive men.

THE CULT OF ANIMAL SKULLS

Connected with these beliefs are curious discoveries made in high-altitude caves (1200, 1700, and 2400 metres) revealing the existence of strange rituals involving the bones of the cave bear and dating from the last interglacial period. In the floor of the cave on the Drachenloch, in Switzerland, half a dozen rectangular containers made of dry stone and covered by great slabs were full of bear-skulls, several placed together and all pointing in the same direction. Outside and against the walls of these little shrines were piled sorted groups of the long bones from the same animal. Similar tabernacles containing bear-skulls were found again at Petershöhle (Bavaria), where ten other skulls of the same species had been laid on a rough platform. Other and no less spectacular finds were made in caves in the Pyrenees and the Mâcon district. Inside the cave at Les Furtins (Saône-et-Loire) eight bear-skulls had been placed, all except one facing the same way. Six of them were resting on lime-stone slabs, spaced separately in the gravel. A bundle of long bones, similarly protected, had been laid against the north-west wall, recalling not only the arrangements in the Alpine caves, but also the bundles of long bones found near the wall on the Mousterian floor of the cave at San Felice de Circeo, in Italy.

It is perhaps not too far-fetched to compare these arrangements with the piled-up remains of slaughtered ibexes, Bovidae, and Cervidae reported from the lower layer of the Prince cave at Grimaldi (Italy). In the open-air Palaeolithic sites at Cannstatt (Germany), Předmost and Dolni-Vistonice (Moravia), and Honci (Ukraine) heaps of mammoth-tusks and molars had been grouped in a particular order. At Předmost (Moravia) twelve wolf-skulls had received similar treatment.

What is the meaning of such deposits? It is impossible not to think of the Alaskan Eskimo custom of hiding the unbroken bones of their animal quarry under stones, to prevent the dogs from gnawing them and also to assist the reincarnation of the souls of the animals, so vital to their existence. Such a likely interpretation could be given to some extraordinary deposits of animal bones dating from the very end of the Leptolithic. At Meiendorf, in the bottom of a glacial lake, were found the bodies of several female reindeer. These were about two years old, the age for reproduction, and had been purposely sunk, the entrails having been replaced by large stones; a stag skull had been fixed on a pinewood pole.

VARIOUS METHODS OF BURIAL AND FUNERAL RITES

At one time nobody would believe in the existence of graves, and therefore of funeral rites, dating from the Mousterian. This was a serious error, for Mousterian man of the last Ice Age left his burial-places in the caves where he set up his homes. Even the Neanderthal man, found when a small cave was being cleared near Düsseldorf, must have been properly buried, since at that time only interment could have saved a body from being eaten by hyenas.

When two Neanderthalians were found side by side at Spy (Belgium) what had been a probability became a certainty, although at that time (1886) it was considered unscientific to talk of fossil man's burial-places. The facts could no longer be ignored when the Dordogne valley produced the successive finds of Le Moustier, La Chapelle-aux-Saints, and La Ferrassie, all belonging, like Spy, to an advanced phase of the Mousterian and dating from the first third of the last Ice Age (about 100,000 B.C.).

In the rock-shelter at Le Moustier, Hauser and Klaatsch, working in the Upper Mousterian horizon of Acheulean tradition, exhumed in 1908 the remains of a young Neanderthal adult, lying on its side, the right hand supporting the head and the left arm extended. Near by D. Peyrony discovered, shortly after, three truncated-cone graves, two containing the bones of very young infants and the third with animal bones, covered by flat stones. At La Chapelle-aux-Saints (Corrèze) the

Abbés A. and J. Bouyssonie excavated in the same year (1908), at the base of a Mousterian deposit, a grave dug in the marl subsoil 30 centimetres down, containing the skeleton of a fairly old adult, with the head to the west, the feet to the east, the legs bent to the right, the left arm extended, and the right raised towards the head, which was protected by large animal bones and had near it a bison-hoof. A short distance away, in a small grave, had been buried a horn and the frontal bone of a bison. D. Peyrony and Dr Capitan, working in the shelter at La Ferrassie (Dordogne), came upon the graves of two adults and several children—these latter buried in conical cavities—near others containing offerings of food. The first adult was in a hollow in the subsoil, probably deepened for the purpose, and had the same position and orientation as the skeletons at Le Moustier and La Chapelle-aux-Saints. A flat stone had been put on the head and another on each shoulder. Bone splinters and some very fine flint tools were sprinkled over it. The remains of the wife, pointing in the opposite direction, had had the skull destroyed by the trampling of later Mousterians and was separated from the man's skeleton by 50 centimetres. It lay on the right side, with the arms brought down over the legs that were sharply bent up against the body and the hands resting on the knees. At other places in the shelter there came to light the remains of two very young infants, buried in a conical grave, and of two others in an oval cavity, over whom three fine pieces of flint had been laid. In a fourth, food offerings had been placed. In a large rectangular excavation lay a child's skeleton, without the head, laid out east–west. The separated skull had been placed at the south side of the tomb and covered by a large slab, chipped with cupules grouped in twos. Another large stone with artificial cupules covered the face of a child buried in an irregular grave. Thus La Ferrassie contained a veritable cemetery of Neanderthal people, and no further doubt was possible about the existence of funeral rites in Mousterian times.[1]

Palestine revealed an even more important burial-place, discovered by D. Garrod and MacCown, in a shelter of fairly old Mousterian content. This gave ten Neanderthaloid skeletons, much nearer *Homo sapiens* in physical characteristics, from the Mugharet-es-Sukhul cave on Mount Carmel; one classical Neanderthal woman from the neighbouring cave of Mugharet-et-Tabun; and three other graves similar to the Mugharet-es-Sukhul type in the cave at Djebel Kafsa, near Nazareth, excavated by R. Neuville.

In the Leptolithic (40,000–9000 B.C.) burial-places are very numerous. The oldest, found by Buckland in 1823 in the cave at Paviland (South Wales), contained the skeleton of a man, covered with ochre and with a mammoth-skull behind the head. To this same Aurignacian era belongs the famous Cro-Magnon find at Les Eyzies (Dor-

[1] I was present at these exhumations. (H. B.)

dogne) in 1868, in a collapsed shelter covered by a thick bank of rubble. On the surface of the Aurignacian hearths lay five skeletons, accompanied by many shells and pierced teeth. Among the occupants of this common grave were a fairly old man and a pregnant woman. In the same district of Les Eyzies, at Le Roc de Combe-Capelle, under a Lower Aurignacian horizon covered by a more advanced typical Aurignacian, the skeleton of a man lay flat on its back, stretched out on a slab forming part of the floor and hollowed out in the middle to take the pelvis, with the head pointing north slightly inclined to the right, and surrounded by numerous shells of the *Littorina littorea* and *Nassa reticulata*. A shell was placed on the right tibia, a *Littorina* at the level of the third dorsal vertebra. The right arm was laid along the body, the hand against the thigh, while the left arm, bent at right angles, had the hand on the pelvis. The right leg was bent outward, the left had been considerably disturbed since the knee was in contact with the pelvis, whereas the head of the femur was some way to one side. A few Mousterian flints and three small bifaces, one of Micoquian type, were found at the feet. One incomplete skeleton—skull, ribs, vertebrae, and a single arm—lay in the grave at Les Cottés (Vienne). In the loess near Strasbourg (Bas-Rhine) the skeleton of a man had been covered with thick red ochre and adorned with a necklet made of the pierced canine teeth of a stag.

Near the Franco-Italian frontier the sea cliffs at Grimaldi are full of caves that have revealed a great number of burial-places dating from the local reindeer age. The most famous was found by E. Rivière, in 1872, in the Cavillon cave. It contained the skeleton of a man, lying on the left side and covered with ochre, the two arms folded against the chest, the hands up to the chin, and the legs bent. A bonnet embroidered with more than two hundred *Nassa* shells covered the head, along with a crown of pierced teeth of stag. A long bone dagger was placed against the forehead and two fine flint knives at the nape of the neck. At the left knee was fixed a garter made of forty-one *Nassa* shells. In the near-by Grotte des Enfants the same investigator found the remains of two children, one of about five or six, the other at least four years old, lying side by side, the two heads towards the west. They had been dressed in a sort of petticoat running from the navel to the upper third of the thighs and completely covering the pelvis and the loins, all embroidered with small *Nassa reticulata* shells. In 1884 Barma Grande was found to contain a skeleton, lying on its back along the axis of the cave, with the head to the north, wedged between two flat stones and sprinkled with a thick layer of red ochre; the remains were partially covered by a massive block and rested on a bed of stones. Three flint strips had been laid, one on the skull, the two others on the shoulders. 1892 saw the discovery of a triple burial-site containing, side by side on a bed of ochre, a tall man (1·9 metres), a young woman, and a boy, with no sign of a dug-out grave. The man was laid on his back, with the woman and the boy, lying on their sides, facing him, their arms raised and folded. Round the man's neck was hung a necklace of fish vertebrae and stag canines; similar ornaments were placed on the skull and thorax, and to the knees were fixed two large *Cypraea*. A magnificent flint knife rested in the left hand. The young woman's head was propped on a bovid femur. Her adornment was not so rich, but she too held a large flint blade in her left hand. Another such blade was found near the young boy's head, his forehead being adorned with several pendants and his skull covered with two rows of trout vertebrae and shells. A necklace, still in place, was made up of two rows of these vertebrae enclosing a string of shells, interspersed at regular intervals by stag canines. Still at Barma Grande, Abbo discovered under three flat stones a skeleton with headdress and necklet similar to the preceding ones. Another skeleton lay on a hearth that had partially burnt it. The neighbouring cave, Baousso da Torre, gave three other tombs: one, of an adult, also laid out over a fire, had shell adornments, arms, and flints; to his right and slightly forward, on a bed of ochre, head resting on the left side, lay a skeleton, with the lower limbs partly disturbed by a hyena and replaced in more or less their proper position by the survivors, and wearing a crown on the back of the cranium and bracelets on both elbows, all these being made of shells. Parallel to this latter and orientated towards the cave entrance was the skeleton of a boy of about fifteen, lying face down, with no trace of funeral adornments.

Excavations by Prince Albert of Monaco, following up those by E. Rivière, in the Grotte des Enfants brought to light further discoveries: the burial-place of a man of Cro-Magnon type, lying on his back with the legs stretched out, the hands on a level with the throat, the head turned to the left, and resting on a sandstone slab painted with red ochre. On the left side, up by the ribs and under the jaw-bone, lay the remains of a necklet of *Nassa* and pierced canines of stag. A broad, heavy stone had been placed over the body. At the very bottom of the Leptolithic layer came a double tomb of a very different kind, containing in a shallow grave the remains of two fairly short Negroids. The first—a man, still young—lay on his right side, the body being sprinkled with ochre, the legs bent back horizontally, heels under the buttocks, arms slightly bent along the trunk. On this body had been deposited, in an unnatural position, the body of an old woman, with the occiput touching the young man's face, knees drawn up under the chin, arms folded on the chest. Shell bracelets encircled the arms.

A remarkable burial of the same type as those at Grimaldi was found in the Leptolithic layers in the cave at Arene Candide (Finale Marina, Italy) on this same Mediterranean littoral, but nearer to Genoa. The skeleton of a youth was lying, head to the south, with the left arm along the body, the other arm bent at right angles, and the hand grasping a very large flint blade. The body and face had been sprinkled with ochre, while piles of tiny pierced *Nassa* shells ran down from the left shoulder to the middle of the arm and were massed near the head. Four extraordinary objects of elk-horn, with conical stems and broad, rounded palettes with a circular hole in the middle, had been laid in pairs, one on the left shoulder and arm, point downward, the other symmetrically on the right flank, but point upward. A shell bracelet and garter had been fixed to the left wrist and knee. Arrangements had been made to ensure that the body did not move: large stones stood at the feet and hands, others protected the head and right side.

In Central Europe the funeral sites at Předmost (Moravia), associated with the habitat of mammoth-hunters discovered in 1894 by Maška, are among the most important collections of burial-places in existence. Under the archaeological layer an elliptical hearth, dug out to 2·60 metres and covered with a layer of stones 40 centimetres thick, with mammoth shoulder-blades flanking either side, was crammed with skeletons—eight adults and twelve youths or children, mostly in a crouching position. Although a surround of large stones formed a kind of rampart, the tomb had been visited by wolves. One child wore a necklet of fourteen ivory pearls shaped like double buttons. The skull of a polar fox lay isolated among the other skeletons. A further six deposits of separate bones were found—among them a child's skull and three jaw-bones—piously sheltered under mammoth shoulder-blades.

In Moravia, in September 1891, three individual burial-places were laid open at Brno, 4·50 metres deep in the loess under the surface of the Franz-Josefstrasse. In the middle of a pile of animal bones (containing several rhinoceros ribs and a skull, two large mammoth-tusks, and a few horse and bovid teeth) came a dug grave containing an adult male skeleton smeared with a layer of ochre, the head against a mammoth shoulder-blade and a necklace of six hundred *Dentalae* round the neck. Further funeral *mobilier* consisted of two large centre-pierced disks, three flattened roundels of limestone, five others of ivory, three of them cut from mammoth teeth, then three others cut from a rib of the same animal. Some of these objects are decorated with small marginal incisions, only one being pierced and the rest slightly hollowed in the centre. On one specimen deep grooving radiating from centre to edges recalls the sexual engravings on Aurignacian blocks in the Périgord. The most extraordinary object is a sturdy ivory statuette of a man with no legs and only a single arm.

In the Aurignacian level at Malta (Siberia) the skeleton of a child of three was laid on a slab, reclining on its left side, with legs bent and arms extended along the body. Traces of red ochre were found, mainly on the left side. On the neck had been placed a large bone disk and a necklace of 112 threaded beads, enhanced by pendants, one in the form of a cross. On the arm was an ivory bracelet and near it a flint knife.

PLATE XV. Burial-site K, at Téviec, Morbihan. Mesolithic. After M.
and Mme Saint-Just Péquart.

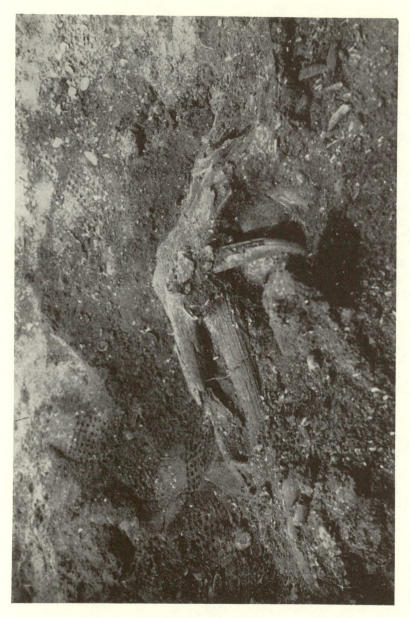

PLATE XVI. Burial-site D, Téviec, Morbihan. Mesolithic, showing skull under its crown of stag-antlers. After M. and Mme Saint-Just Péquart.

On a level with the first lumbar vertebrae lay the ivory tip of a hunting-spear and near the feet another, with an awl and two flint implements.

Solutrean burial-places are represented by discoveries made at Solutré (Saône-et-Loire) at the Labattut shelter at Sergeac (Dordogne), at Le Roc de Sers (Charente), and at Mittlere Klause, Neu-Essing (Bavaria).

The Solutré site has yielded many skeletons, but in the early days they were not always dealt with scientifically. The oldest burials, underlying the layer with horse-bones from the last part of the first third of the reindeer age, the Gravettian, are in the three tombs investigated in 1923 by Dr F. Arcelin. Eighty centimetres down in the magma two vertical slabs stood up like tombstones, and at their feet lay the head of a female skeleton, with, near by, the remains of two children and a foetus. At the same level a second hearth burial was marked by two other slabs, raised head-high. The skeleton, affected by fire, was laid on its back, arms extended over the lap, head resting on the left side. Also marked by two raised slabs was a third grave containing a skeleton with a crushed skull. Two other graves without stones were a continuation of the same line.

The skeleton at La Terre Sève, found in 1869 by the Abbé Ducrost, lay inside an oval hut of dry stones opening to the west; it was laid on its back, head to the east, and had rich funeral trappings. Near the right hand were two laurel-leaf points and a series of smaller ones, one pierced half-shell of a *Pecten Jacobeus* with fragments of shells from the shell-marls of the Bordeaux region, two roundels of stone pierced with double holes, another in serpentine marble, and two small limestone figures, one of a reindeer in bas-relief, the other of a bison. Against the outer wall of the hut were piled about eighty reindeer antlers, a nearly complete reindeer skull, and a mammoth jaw and tibia.

In the Labattut rock-shelter the skull and body of a child were found in a compact Solutrean breccia, together with large *Cypraea* shells and perforated teeth of stag.

A few metres below the cave at Le Roc de Sers enormous blocks that probably collapsed at some time prior to the Upper Solutrean formed a kind of shelter, inside which Dr Henri-Martin found a burial place containing three skeletons—a man of fifty, a woman of forty, and a youth of eighteen, all buried at the same time, covered with stones and belonging to the Chancelade group. They rested—at least, in the case of one body—in a crouching position on the Solutrean hearth and separated from it only by a thin layer of sand. Some atypical flints and animal bones accompanied the bodies. This collective burial at Le Roc probably belongs to the final Solutrean or the early Magdalenian found in the neighbouring cave.

In the level with the Solutrean layers at Mittlere Klause (Bavaria) the skeleton of a thirty-year-old man was laid in a burial-site prepared

Q

by the local Solutreans: the legs were stretched out, the pelvis flat, the head slightly offset to the left and entirely surrounded by a pile of mammoth-tusks, and the whole body nearly submerged in a mass of red ochre.

Discoveries of Magdalenian burial have been even more numerous. In France the so-called 'crushed man' at Laugerie Basse lay on his left side in a crouching position, head towards the north-west in the direction of the line of the Vézère, feet to the south-east towards the rock and brought up to the level of the pelvis, arms with elbows bent and touching the femurs, the right hand on the neck, the other on the left parietal bone. Twelve *Cypraea* shells of Mediterranean origin were grouped in pairs, two couples on the forehead, one near each humerus, four at the knees, and two at the feet. At La Madeleine (Dordogne), in 1926, D. Peyrony discovered a child's skeleton stretched on its back in a hollow in the ground, arms along the body, head to the south, and protected by three stones in a semicircle. Pierced teeth and many small shells were found on a level with the head, the neck, the wrists, the knees, and the ankles. In 1888, in the Raymonden rock-shelter at Chancelade (Dordogne), at the bottom of an early Magdalenian hearth and occupying a space only 40 by 67 centimetres, there came to light the body of a fifty-year-old man who had been tightly bound in a forcibly bent position; lying on the left side with the right hand brought over the head on a level with the lower jaw, it had the legs bent up so sharply that the feet were as high as the lower pelvis and the knees in contact with the dental arch, the knee-cap adhering to the nose. A thick layer of ochre had been spread all over the body, mainly behind the skull, the left side of which lay against the rock, with the right side slightly raised. Another body, also bound, was found in 1914 in the Cap-Blanc shelter near Les Eyzies (Dordogne), at the very bottom of the layers under a deposit of Magdalenian III, in a grave to the left of the shelter, surrounded by a mass of small stones. Three large stones had been laid, one on the head, the two others at the feet. It was lying on the left side, the arm bent and raised, the right elbow on the right knee, the hand on the face; the legs, bent as far as they would go, were tightly pressed together, the heels almost touching the pelvis, the face turned to the left and level with the chest. Also bound was the skeleton, so mesocephalic as to be almost brachycephalic, found in a very old Magdalenian at Saint-Germain-la-Rivière, between Libourne and Saint-André-de-Cubzac (Gironde), lying on the left side, and orientated east–west, with the head to the east. The bones, entirely covered in red ochre, were protected by several horizontal slabs propped on smaller stones, forming a miniature dolmen. The funeral trappings consisted of two reindeer-horn daggers laid on the body, a split cervid rib, flint tools comprising gravers, scrapers, blades, and needles, and a necklet of shells mixed with Cervidae teeth, pierced and engraved with geometrical motifs. Food offerings had been laid near the tomb, and there remained a bison skull and horns, horse jaw-bones, and reindeer antlers.

On the sixth hearth in the cave at Les Hoteaux (Ain), in a Magdalenian level with no harpoons and settled in the stone rubble at the base of the habitat, lay stretched on its back the skeleton of a youth, in an ochre bed that was particularly thick over the head and brow. The feet were towards the cave entrance, the arms extended, the femurs apart beyond the pelvic axis and their places exchanged; level with the legs lay a pierced stick, decorated with an engraved stag, and a flint knife on a level with the shoulder-blade; a flint point was near the humerus and stag canines to the left of the remains. A large stone was placed behind the head.

In the Magdalenian IV layer, lower than the level with double-barbed harpoons, in the Duruthy cave at Sordes (Landes) an incomplete skeleton was associated with a necklet of forty bear canines and three others of lion, all decorated with engravings—of seal, pike, bear-heads, and many arrow-shaped signs. The knuckles were placed near the skull, on which were laid several blocks of stone.

In Germany, at Obercassel near Bonn (Hanover), in a layer impregnated with ochre, under the lehm, but not topped with loess (early Magdalenian ?), workmen brought to light the skeletons of a man and a woman covered by broad basalt slabs and accompanied by the bones of reindeer, bear, and bull, by a dagger with the pommel decorated with an animal's head, and by a decorated pendant.

In Hungary, at Ballahöhle, near Repashuta, the skeleton of a child one year old was found in an undisturbed Quaternary layer containing the remains of reindeer and Arctic rodents.

In Great Britain the skeleton, associated with Magdalenian objects and a pierced stick, found in Gough's Cave had the legs bent and one arm and hand placed behind the head.

A certain number of burial-sites belong to the Mesolithic. At Les Mas d'Azil (Ariège) E. Piette discovered on the left bank of the Ariège river two skeletons that had been buried after the flesh had been removed with flint knives and the bones coloured with red ochre. The long bones were not in anatomical connexion, and the other bones were not present. At the base of Azilian hearths at Soussac (Ain), in a grave dug in the underlying tufaceous sand, lay a skeleton with feet directed outward and sharply bent legs. The arms were missing.

The two Azilian burials at Le Trou-Violet, Montardit (Ariège), date from the time when Azilian deposits had completely blocked up the cave and there only remained room, between the arch of the roof and the floor of the main chamber, for a body to be slid inside with its funeral trappings. Then all that remained was to roll up large stones to seal the tomb. The two bodies had been carefully laid over the site of old hearths, together with their funeral *mobilier*. The first skeleton— that of a man—was stretched out with the head raised, leaning against the wall, to the right, the feet pointing to the back of the cave and a little lower. A large flat stone had been placed on the legs. The reddish bones were complete, except for most of the bones from the hands and feet. All round the skeleton had been set eighteen pebbles, the biggest decorated with marks traced by a finger dipped in ochre. The second burial-place, situated 50 centimetres lower than the first, contained the skeleton of a young man, stretched out in the same position and also surrounded by pebbles, some bearing traces of red stain. The funeral trappings, very similar in each tomb, but more abundant in the second, were made up of granite hammer-stones with traces of colour, small rectangular slabs, lamps or make-up palettes, an anvil in red sandstone, chipped fragments of quartz and steatite, crude flint scrapers, and a thin boar-tusk blade.

Twenty centimetres down in the thickness of the Azilian layer inside the Rochereuil cave in the Grand-Brassac district (Dordogne), three metres from the roof and under two metres of earth, lay the skeleton of a man, orientated east–west, lying on its back in a crouched position with the head resting on the right hand, the upper part covered by a layer of ashes with a touch of ochre in them. In a tomb at Le Chaix, near Besse-en-Chandesse (Puy-de-Dôme), the body, bent up on itself, had been covered with red ochre.

The Sauveterrian phase gave two burial-spots; one, containing the skeleton of a child with a skull similar to the Negroid type from Grimaldi, was found in the rock-shelter at La Genière, Serrières-sur-Ain (Ain). The other, at Le Roc du Barbeau, Tursac (Dordogne), showed the skeleton of a man, reclining on its back, slightly inclined to the south, along the axis of the south-facing shelter. The bent legs were brought up on the right side, feet together, left arm resting on the chest, hand open, fingers stretched, while the right arm pointed up towards the head, hand closed. A triangular stone had been placed behind the head to the right. Two others, fixed in the ground, protected the right side. A layer of ash 10 millimetres thick covered the burial-place, which was sealed by a limestone slab dented with cupules. The preparation of the tomb had been carried out with some care: all the hearths used before the Sauveterrian occupation had been thrown out forward of the habitat, the floor cleaned down to the limestone brash, on which the first occupants of the cave had settled, and a layer of red sand sprinkled on it, taken from the neighbouring plateau and mixed with red ochre of similar tint.

Since the tomb opens four metres from the rock wall, it must be supposed that there was some sort of wooden construction, covered with branches, to form an extension of the shelter and protect the grave. The funeral furnishings included an important collection of points, core-shaped scrapers, flint triangles and micro-gravers, two bone awls, two red-coloured pebbles, a red-ochre tablet, and a few pierced snail-shells. The remains of stag-bones found over the tomb represent food offerings.

In the typical Tardenoisian, making up the second level in the rock-shelter of Le Curgoul de Gramat (Lot), a male skeleton was laid on its back, arms extended, hands on thighs, and the femurs slightly convergent. The skull, placed on a block of flinty limestone and adorned with a circlet of pierced shells, was resting on the left side, with the face turned to the east.

Two important Tardenoisian cemeteries were found by M. and Mme Saint-Just Péquart on the islands of Téviec and Hoëdic, off the Morbihan coast. On a raised beach of the west coast of Téviec twenty-four burial-places had been made, either over the hearths or near them, in random order. The graves are shallow, being a mere hollow in the ground in which the body was placed in a crooked position, lying on the right side, legs drawn up, arms along the body, hands on thighs. Two of the tombs were unusual in that they were covered with stag-antlers arranged to form a kind of open-work hut. In another grave a man was holding on his arm the skeleton of a small child, with the feet resting on his right hand. A woman's grave showed the same association of adult and child, the latter being crowned with stag-antlers.

A few of the graves had been used again, one of them having seen as many as six successive interments. After filling in with earth from the same deposit large blocks had been piled on the tomb. The funeral equipment consisted of adornments such as necklaces, hair-nets, bracelets, loin-cloths (?) with shells, stylets, pins for fastening clothes, and a few bone and flint implements, including some oblique-cut blades. Traces of red ochre were to be noticed on the skeletons, mainly in the region of the chest. Food offerings in the form of stag or boar jaws had been placed near most of the bodies, either in the hearth lit above the burial-place or directly against the skull.

The cemetery on Hoëdic, 30 kilometres by sea in a direct line from Téviec, revealed nine burial-places containing the remains of thirteen people. The same ritual had been followed as in the preceding case: the grave, sometimes making use of a hollow in the rock, was surrounded by a cordon of small stones and covered with slabs to keep the bodies in place. Two tombs side by side were separated by a tiny wall. When the grave was used for several successive interments the remains of the preceding occupant were pushed aside and piled up without much ceremony. Some bodies were also buried in a sitting position, orientated north-west–south-east, with the legs forcibly bent. Four of these graves have the decorative trappings of stag-horn surrounding the remains:

> The skull rests on two antler branches, one standing out to the left, the
> other to the right, both forming a halo round the face with their tines and

enveloping the shoulders. Two other branches arranged along the torso complete this strange framework. Finally, in the angle formed by the thigh and the leg came a fifth branch, with the peculiarity that its tines had been cut off. (M. and S.-J. Péquart.)

But the arrangements were not the same as in the cemetery at Téviec. The antlers were not placed so as to overhang the bodies, but to frame them as closely as possible, by means of pieces laid flat alongside them. Nor were hearths often found above the tombs. The composition of the funeral equipment was not notably different from that found in the Téviec cemetery, giving hair-nets, necklets, wrist- and ankle-bracelets, bone stylets, and so on.

In Portugal, at Muge, at the head of the former estuary of the Tagus, now some 50 miles inland, more than two hundred skeletons, mostly of women and children, were scattered among the piles of Mesolithic kitchen refuse, most of them laid out on their backs. These vast cemeteries are not unlike the less extensive ones found on the islands off the Morbihan coast.

In Spain, deep in the cave of El Aven del Rabasso (Tarragona), a burial had been accompanied by the deposit of an equipment of flint bladelets, triangles and trapezes, a small awl, and the remains of colouring materials. The tomb at Axpeca (Alava) gave four skeletons and was laid under a small tumulus 60 centimetres high. Near the bodies were laid parts of necklaces, and pierced shells with schist beads and a piece of ochre. A tiny dolmen occupied the centre of the tumulus.

In Belgium the second burial-place at Engis, which had contained the remains of three individuals, as well as the bones found at Aveline's Hole, near Bristol, in Great Britain, all date from the Mesolithic. At Arene Candide (Italy), at the bottom of Mesolithic layers, the skeletons laid in fifteen burial-sites were resting on their backs in a bed of ochre and had at their feet an abundant collection of shells and pierced teeth. In the same horizon a pair of elk antlers was resting on a stone.

In Palestine, in the vast funeral deposits of Mugharet-el-Oued and Shoukbah (Mount Carmel), in the Natufian level, lay the skeletons of ninety-two adult men and women and forty children. Some of these corpses had been trussed up, some lying on their sides, others face downwards. The women had usually had their incisors removed in their youth (a feature also common to the Tardenoisian burials at Muge and Téviec). All the bodies had been decked in rich adornments of seashells and teeth, tastefully arranged as follows: on the back of the head a hair-net or a diadem of *Dentalae*; around the neck strings, as of beads; bracelets on the legs; and garters at the knees. One child's skull was topped by a hat decorated with bone beads.

The sheer number of these finds leaves no possibility of doubt about the existence of the practice of intentional burial from Mousterian times.

However, interment in a tomb was not the only means used by Palaeolithic men to dispose of a corpse. In the deposits at La Quina (Charente) human bones were scattered in the Mousterian horizons in small, broken pieces, none of which fitted together, and yet too thinly spread to suggest that they had been broken in rock-falls by mechanical means. As for explaining these remains as indications of regular cannibalism, their very limited number argues against it. These bones were broken before being fossilized, and there is no doubt that it was deliberate and they were scattered of set purpose. Such a custom could be connected with the relatively frequent discovery of isolated fragments of face-bones noted in the skull cult. Just as among the Australians, when the corpse had been exposed on a platform or tree, the bones were probably collected and some ritually broken, while others were kept as mementoes. The discoveries at La Quina and elsewhere are in no way inconsistent with well-defined funeral practices, and may well be explained by customs still in use among modern primitive communities.

The same site at La Quina has revealed another form of burial, also dating from the Mousterian. The skeleton of the 'drowned' woman, lying in a layer of mud subjacent to levels which yielded fragments of human bones, is not evidence of a tragedy or an accident. The corpse was probably thrown into the river to get rid of it. Such practices connected with the abandonment or exposure of bodies may have existed prior to the periods for which we have evidence, at a time when interment was not general. Acting thus, man was not motivated so much by feelings of affection as by self-interest. For him death is still far from being considered as the inevitable end of life. It is the result of magic or an evil spell, whose conscious or involuntary authors he will seek to discover. It is not surprising that the dead person should seem to wish to seek vengeance on the one he may incline to consider as his murderer, and to hold collectively responsible for his demise all those lucky enough still to be enjoying the life he has been unjustly deprived of. All funeral customs are, basically, controlled by man's attitude to death and contain the tangible expression of the precautions taken by the living either to dispose of the corpse and appease the wrath of the dead or to make sure of his co-operation.

Interment in a grave must have seemed far more effective than abandonment, for it is not only a shelter, it is also a prison. Such ideas imply that the dead retain some sort of existence, conceived like life on earth, with the same necessities to be met by the same means.

The digging of the grave, or the intentional arrangement of a natural cavity, to receive the body, the precautions taken to protect it from the fangs of wild animals, and the often touching care taken over the arrangement of the corpse in its last resting-place that was frequently sited over places the departed had known during life—all this is evidence of pious, intentional funeral ritual from Mousterian times on.

Burial did not necessarily imply the laying of the corpse in a grave specially dug through the mounting layers of the habitat. Palaeolithic man often interred his dead in open ground or in a slightly deeper hollow (La Ferrassie, Dordogne), or on a slab, scooped out to accommodate the pelvis (Roc de Combe-Capelle, Dordogne), or using a natural hiding-place among roughly trimmed rocks (Mittlere Klause, Bavaria). The graves he dug had no particular shape, being truncated cones at Le Moustier (Dordogne), conical or oval at La Ferrassie, and always irregular in outline. Special attention was given to protection of the head rather than the feet or the trunk of the dead body, where the stomach only was covered by a stone, while the head was guarded, sometimes by a box of stone slabs (Předmost, Grimaldi, Solutré) and sometimes flanked by the bones of large animals (La Chapelle-aux-Saints, San Felice de Circeo).

In the Leptolithic, piles of mammoth-tusks protected the dead (Mittlere Klause), and the body was often laid out on the family hearth while it was still burning, so that it was partly incinerated (Barma Grande, Le Roc de Sers, Les Hoteaux). The burial also became more complicated; there was a dry-stone funeral hut at La Terre Sève, Solutré, and a miniature dolmen protecting the head at Saint-Germain-la-Rivière. The site is indicated by stones raised like tombstones at the head and feet (Solutré). The grouping of some collections of graves formed, from Mousterian times, veritable cemeteries, in Dordogne (La Ferrassie) as well as in Palestine (Sukhul, Djebel Kafsa).

Sometimes a single body, sometimes two or three (Barma Grande, Le Roc de Sers), would be laid in the same grave. Others are true communal tombs, with five skeletons on a single Aurignacian hearth at Cro-Magnon and twenty in the hunters' ossuary at Předmost, resting on a great oval hearth covered with a layer of stones and flanked on either side by mammoth shoulder-blades.

There were no fixed rules for orientation or for the position of the body in the grave. This does not mean, however, that Palaeolithic man was unconcerned with such matters, since it is possible to detect certain common features which denote at least usages or a kind of tradition.

According to the burial-site, the body might either be placed along the main axis of the cave or aligned with its entrance. Positioning by the compass-points was variable: facing north (Barma Grande), west (Grotte des Enfants), south (Arene Candide), north-west with feet to the east (Laugerie Basse). At Solutré five skeletons were laid out strictly east–west, with the feet to the west.

The body was laid in a position of rest, sometimes on a bed of stones, maybe on its back or on either side, with the legs extended, or bent to take up less room. The position of the arms varies: bent against the chest, hands towards the chin or folded on the chest or in the lap; or else one arm stretched along the body, the other bent at right angles across the trunk. The head was often bent to one side, or raised, or resting on a pillow of chipped flints (Le Moustier), or propped against a mammoth-skull or shoulder-blade (Paviland, Brno).

A change occurred during the Leptolithic in the relations between the living and the dead. To the ideas of respect and even affection expressed in the arrangements found up to then was added a feeling of fear shown in the precautions taken to keep the dead person safely inside the tomb. The first sign of such changes can be detected—and that from Mousterian times—in the contracted position of the skeleton of a woman found at La Ferrassie. This ritual reaches its peak in the trussed-up bodies at the Raymonden shelter at Chancelade, at Cap-Blanc, and Saint-Germain-la-Rivière, bent by sheer force until the knees came in contact with the jaws, elbows bent and hands brought up to the face. Similar preoccupations may well have dictated the positioning of bodies face downward (Grimaldi, Laugerie Haute, Cro-Magnon) and the mutilations of certain skeletons (decapitated child at La Ferrassie).

Other means were designed to prevent the dead from leaving the tomb: on the upper slab of the micro-dolmen at Saint-Germain-la-Rivière a fire had been lit, and the existence of other fireplaces has been noted above other tombs or very near them. Like the family hearth on which some bodies were laid, the flame lit at funeral feasts was also supposed to help to retain the spirit of the dead person in the places where his earthly life had been spent. The dead fear the cold, and the heat thus produced may please them and ward off evil spirits.

The statuette found in the burial-place at Brno sprang from such concepts. Legless and without a right arm, it was no doubt intended to serve the double of the dead man, who, deprived of means of moving and acting, was thus confined to the inside of his last resting place.

For these redoubtable dead, still living a life similar to their earthly one and subject to the same needs, steps had to be taken to ensure their means of survival beyond the grave. By minutely discharging this debt, might one not also render them, if not favourable, at least harmless?

Such a belief in an after-life is already manifest in the Mousterian burials at Le Moustier, La Ferrassie, and La Chapelle-aux-Saints in the shape of deposits, as funeral offerings, of quarters of venison placed in small neighbouring graves or in the tomb itself. The same applies to the mammoth-skulls (Paviland), the rhinoceros-head (Brno), the boar-jaw found in one of the graves in the Grotte des Enfants at Grimaldi, and the reindeer-head, together with the mammoth-jaw and tibia, laid outside and against the wall of the burial hut at La Terre Sève (Solutré).

The very widespread Leptolithic custom of sprinkling all or part of the body with red ochre which left traces on the skeletons and near-by objects was intended, like the food, to help the dead to find the strength to carry on life beyond the grave. Primitive man's way of likening red colouring to blood conferred on it the powers of a source of life and strength. The laying of small animal figures in the grave (Solutré and Předmost) was a sign of similar intentions.

Yet the food offerings, the sprinkling with red ochre, and the provision of animal images would have been insufficient if the dead man had not also had the arms and implements to help him in the next world to hunt successfully as he had done in this, and thus procure the venison he required to sustain him. This is why some of these everyday objects were laid beside the body.

This funeral equipment, though usually not very abundant, consists of high-quality flints, more rarely accompanied by bone and stag-horn pieces. There was no rule about the way these should be arranged in the tomb; at times they were laid at the feet of the body (Roc de Combe-Capelle),[1] at others on the skull and the shoulder (Baoussé-Roussé), near the humerus (Les Hoteaux), or else held in one or other of the hands (Baousso da Torre, Arene Candide). Blades predominate, but some coups-de-poing and points have also been found (earlier objects imported) (Roc de Combe-Capelle), and even a whole range of tools, with blades, scrapers, and gravers (Saint-Germain-la-Rivière). Rarer still are works of art belonging to funeral trappings, like the pierced stick with the stag at Les Hoteaux and the awl with the animal's head from Obercassel.

Finally, to complete the resemblance to earthly life the dead person was dressed in his best finery—loin-cloths embroidered with shells, diadems, hair-nets, bonnets, or at least necklaces, bracelets, and garters (Grimaldi, Duruthy, Les Hoteaux).

The Mesolithic funeral practices seem in the Palaeolithic tradition. Examples are in the isolated burial-places in the small cave at Le Barbeau, at Le Moustier, and at Le Cuzoul de Gramat, during the Sauveterrian; still more in the shell-heaps at Muge (Portugal) and on the Morbihan islands of Téviec and Hoëdic. Some bodies are extended in the position of rest, others are bound up tight, or crouching and bearing a small child in their arms. Piles of stag-horn cover the tomb.

Such customs, varying from one group to another but universally practised, are grounds for deducing the existence of a variable funeral ritual. Many of the details of burial still escape us, but we now possess a certain stock of archaeological data about the rôle of the family hearth and the funeral feast. Rock art has preserved a memory of one of the ceremonies accompanying funerals. An engraving on the roof of the Pech-Merle cave (Cabrerets), showing women near a prostrate man, might be interpreted as a scene of funeral lamentations.

These Palaeolithic and Leptolithic funeral customs were the starting-point of all the care men accord to their deceased; and in them is the germ of all higher concepts connected with the cult of the dead.

---

[1] This grave having been dug in the underlying Mousterian by Châtelperronians, it would appear that the deposit of Mousterian flints was not intentional

[19]

The religious practices of
Leptolithic man

Leptolithic amulets—The abode of the gods—Magicians or gods?

The 'gods,' the authors and organizers of the world and dispensers of all good things, have, in one form or another, always been the objects of a cult ever since man first began to reflect upon the mystery of life and things. Like all primitives, the reindeer-hunters lived in a world to which they attributed a living principle and a soul. They placed the source of the innumerable dangers that threatened them in elements they did not understand, such as the spirits of sickness and death and hostile animals and other men. To combat these they had recourse to charms and amulets, perhaps first used out of a desire for adornment, but later considered to have powers of protection.[1] In the Leptolithic this new source of information provided by the countless artistic decorations on such talismans gives us the first body of material about the religious ideas and practices of Quaternary man.

Without wishing to express any preconceived notions about the purposes for which the Aurignacians and Gravettians carved statuettes of buxom women in advanced stages of maternity, or about conventionalized derivatives from them (group at Mezine, Ukraine), one can say that some of these—for instance the 'lady of Sireuil,' obviously a young girl with budding breasts—were meant to be worn and that most probably their purpose was to favour amorous enterprises and fertility.

In Magdalenian IV we find the idea of the male pursuit of the female

[1] The bone decorated with an engraving of a viper from Les Rideaux (Haute-Garonne) also shows the two imprints of its bite.

in the engraving on a bone knife from Isturitz (Basses-Pyrénées), where a man is closely following a woman, her thigh stabbed by a no doubt symbolic arrow, as it might be Cupid's(?). On the other side can be seen a bison wounded by a similar arrow in its vital organs. At La Madeleine D. Peyrony found a small pebble engraved on one side with the figure of a slim young woman and on the other with an ithyphallic man, both having their heads hooded by a ceremonial mask. The (Magdalenian level at Teyjat gave a half-round wand on which the organs of the two sexes, reduced to ornamental form, are associated with the head of a bear. A phallic stick from Le Placard (there are others of this kind) also bears the carved representation of a vulva (Magdalenian II). There is also the well-known cut-away carving at Laugerie Basse (Magdalenian IV) showing the strange association of a male reindeer and the silhouette of a pregnant woman lying on her back between its legs.

In animal *art mobilier* the choice of engraved or carved figures was directed as much towards favouring the reproduction and capture of the species on which the life of the group depended as towards the destruction of dangerous predators. Among these pieces it can be noted that the decoration of those intended to be worn is less advanced than it is on others that may have had a ceremonial character. The former were pendants, as can be seen from the suspension eyelet bored in them. One of these, from Le Mas d'Azil, with a picture of three ibexes in high relief, has been much worn down by prolonged rubbing and must have been a talisman worn for the hunting of these animals. It would be too long to list the engravings of animals wounded by arrows. A famous engraving from Laugerie Basse shows a hunter in an extended position pursuing a bison and hurling after it a dart from a throwing-stick. Very numerous, but found only in Aquitaine, are the thin, hyoid bones of large Herbivora and from the gills of large fish, cut into the shape of horse-heads and often finely detailed. Such pieces have been found in the Magdalenian IV levels from the Indre (Saint-Marcel) to the Pyrenees. In the cave at Labastide (Hautes-Pyrénées) a whole necklet of twenty small heads of ibex and one of bison was found under a great stone.

THE ABODE OF THE GODS

A second source of information is at the same time provided by the recesses decorated with engravings and paintings hidden in the depths of dark caverns. Access is sometimes dangerous, and man did not live there, but only came, whether often or rarely, to these secret places where in such remote ages the rites and ceremonies of magic and religion were performed. In each Western region containing caves there are a certain number of sacred places dating from early times— veritable shrines open only to the initiated.

The first group is located in the valleys of the Dordogne and the Vézère and in the Charente and Poitou areas. These are high places set up, during the Aurignacian, Gravettian, Solutrean, and Magdalenian periods, on rock terraces. The most typical have been investigated at Laussel (Dordogne), at Le Roc de Sers (Charente), the Fourneau du Diable (Dordogne), Cap-Blanc (Dordogne), Angles-sur-Anglin (Vienne), and Penne (Tarn). Traces of other shrines indicated by the remains of carvings in which animal figures predominate have also been met with in material excavated from various deposits of similar date: a bison in relief from Les Jean-Blancs (Dordogne); a musk-ox head from Laugerie Haute (Dordogne); bison from the Reverdit shelter at Sergeac (Dordogne); horses from the Papeterie shelter (Charente).

The excavations at Laussel and Le Roc de Sers enable us to reconstruct to some extent the general arrangement of these shrines, since they were the work of communities with the same ideas and at the same stage of culture.

At Laussel, where human figures predominate, the Perigordians used the space inside the shelter between the rock overhang and the scree, thus forming a kind of 'chapel' where, on one of the larger blocks that could not be moved, the image of the 'horned woman' presided. All the other bas-reliefs, done on easily movable slabs, were found on the floor of the *cella* in the following order, starting from the large fixed pedestal—woman with cross-shaded hair; man with belt; hind; horsehead; third female figure. The last carvings were near limestone fragments with strong red tinting, and the 'horned woman' had been rubbed with ochre.

The shrine at Le Roc de Sers with its back to the cliff-face, opens up below the caves of the Virgin and of Le Roc. The cult images, having collapsed at the foot of the stone pedestals that had borne them, were lined up along the rock-wall. From left to right they were: bison; a fine ibex; figures of a small person fleeing before a charge of musk ox; two superposed horses; a mare in foal; and a bison with a boar's head. Other fragments not found in place were decorated with representations of reindeer, Bovidae, two ibexes head to head, and a bird. Some of these figures had undergone transformations: the head of a bison had been changed into that of a swine, and several small horses had been carved in relief encroaching on the mass of bisons' bodies, of earlier date and larger, of which other parts could still be seen.

At the Fourneau du Diable the large bas-relief with little cows carved on an irregular pyramidal block had been placed 4·50 metres from the entrance and facing it, with one of the decorated sides towards the east, the other towards the west, the whole being propped on three large stones to keep it at an angle with the floor.

At Cap-Blanc, as at Angles-sur-Anglin (Vienne), although both were set up under a rock-shelter, the shrines can be added to the list of Leptolithic open-air sanctuaries.

There may have been no very definite rules, but a certain number of common features seem to have controlled the general arrangement of this first group, where the cult images were, at the time they had to be abandoned, purposely mutilated and thrown face down on the ground. By reason of the place reserved for them, they form the vital element in the sanctuary, being set in full daylight, where they can easily be seen by the faithful, either one above the other (Le Roc de Sers), or sometimes raised on individual pedestals, or again standing out on a sort of specially orientated monolith (Fourneau du Diable). Elsewhere they unfold in long friezes as on the walls of the shelter at the Penne cave (Tarn) and at Angles-sur-Anglin. With a few exceptions like the men at Laussel, Angles-sur-Anglin, and Le Roc de Sers, and the women at Laussel, Angles-sur-Anglin, and Penne, all the other figures are from the animal world: horses, Bovidae, ibexes, and reindeer predominate in the representations, all done in high relief, probably for reasons of lighting. They seem all to have been based on a general idea, since all these animals are shown at rest or grazing, like the horses at Le Roc de Sers, Cap-Blanc, and Angles. However, at Le Roc there are reindeer, horses, bison, and a musk ox in a running position.

The nature of the walls, the absence of surfaces suitable for supporting cult images, and questions of lighting all had an influence on the arrangement of some of these sanctuaries, where the religious furnishings are represented by slabs and movable, engraved stone tablets brought from outside and arranged as changeable panels (La Marche, at Lussac-les-Châteaux, Vienne), equivalent to walls decorated with painting or carving.

If the painted rock-shelters of Eastern Spain, often covered with scenes containing human figures, can be connected with this first group of Palaeolithic sanctuaries this is not true of the shrines set up inside deep caverns. These shelters do not generally have outside their entrances the enormous accumulations of debris testifying to long human occupation, whereas at Le Roc de Sers, the Fourneau-du-Diable, La Marche, Cap-Blanc, and Penne the habitats existed side by side with the shrines. Another feature contrary to what has been noted in the first groups is the position occupied by the engravings and sometimes the paintings: they are barely visible, hidden in recesses, difficult to get at, down long passages and at the end of dark chambers, where they could be seen only with the aid of fat or resin lamps or torches, and this shows a desire to create an atmosphere of mystery in a secret place forbidden to the uninitiated. Certain nooks of the sanctuary-cave were given a specially sacred character. There, in spite of the presence of free surfaces and easier access, can be noted the repeated re-utilization of the same positions on which figures were superposed in successive layers, the older ones being destroyed even at the cost of spoiling work of greater artistic merit. Preference was also given to a cave situated on a steep slope, where the opening was narrow and protected inside by a series of natural obstacles. Thus at Niaux the Black Chamber is 800 metres from the entrance and at Rouffignac (Dordogne) farther still. Access to holy places is guarded by the labyrinths of old underground rivers, by steep drops at La Pasiega (Spain), by difficult scree at Salitré (Spain), by a cat-trap, a narrow corridor, and stalagmites at La Clotilde (Spain). At Font-de-Gaume, in Dordogne, a narrow tunnel seems to come to a dead end, yet two small gaps open off it, one to the right at ground level behind calcite hangings, the other to the left and 1·70 metres up, a cat-hole that is extremely hard to get through and forms a real 'Rubicon,' though the Palaeolithic men did not hesitate to cross it; these openings lead to numerous friezes beyond. At Le Tuc d'Audoubert (Ariège) it would seem that men again accumulated obstacles to preserve the mystery of the shrine. The entrance to the cave is protected by a mill-race formed by the resurgent Volp; 160 metres from the opening there rises a small cliff, forming the edge of a vast chamber. From here a chimney rises, at first straight and then in a corkscrew, leading to a long corridor that eventually widens out into the final chamber concealing the 'clay bison.' A small stream also protects the sanctuary of the clay bear, in the Hountaou cave at Montespan (Ariège). The same desire for mystery is found again in the Trois Frères cave at Montesquieu-Avantès (Ariège). There a series of passages ends in a wide, winding tunnel, and then, on the right, a crack in the wall gives on to a small round chamber, a kind of chapel, where a clearly visible stalagmitic fall has been engraved with a black-painted lioness with an arrow on her flank. Beyond stretches the largest chamber in the cave, partly divided by a great roof-fall of clay filled with the bones of animals that fell in through the hole in the vault. The right wall is filled by two large lion-heads, face view, guarding the shrine. Farther on still an uneven passage ends in a cascade of stalagmites, after which access can be gained, lower down, to the oblong chamber with the walls covered in engraving. There, more than 400 metres from the entrance, is a real sanctuary, where every nook and cranny is loaded with drawings of different sizes and styles, belonging to two distinct periods—the Gravettian and Magdalenian IV. In a narrow corridor, followed by another rise and a sharp right turn, the walls are entirely covered with figures of all periods, especially from Magdalenian IV, and all over-drawn with fine *graffiti* of bison, horses, small reindeer, and several kinds of animals of mixed characteristics. One group contains reindeer hidden on a vast surface like a lower ceiling, visible to the visitor only if he slides in and lies flat on his back. At the top of the climb anybody with a good sense of balance can mount a spur of rock and, through a kind of window in the back of the shrine, just manage to insert himself into a cavity 3·50 metres above the floor. There, in a position visible from the shrine, is a picture of a bearded, horned figure with a long, hairy tail. It is the only painted engraving in the place, and represents not so much a magician as the god that presides over the fertilization of the animal species present, among which females, often in foal, predominate. Farther on still, but after coming back a little and crossing, instead of coming down, the stalagmite cascade (at the risk of a dangerous slide down it), leaving the 'sanctuary' on the right, one steps across a well-shaft and comes to a high gallery ending in a low crossways with decorative stalagmites. Beyond this is a fine Magdalenian bison, the engraving accentuated by black, coming between two chambers, and then a clay-floored gallery on the right where earlier Aurignacians delighted in making a host of *graffiti*, difficult to decipher and preceded or accompanied by 'macaronis.' Engraved over these and picked out in black are two Magdalenian bison. At the entrance, on the left, spread a pair of snow owls and their owlet.[1]

In regions where there are no deep caves small sanctuaries are found hidden, for secrecy, in remote corners of rock-shelters. At Laugerie Haute (Dordogne) access to the tiny chapel is gained by following a narrow passage running west along the rock-wall.

The presence of 'guardians,' watching at the threshold of the most secret chambers of these holy places, emphasizes the mystery attached to them and the fact that the profane were not admitted. At Les Trois Frères (Ariège) a lioness and lion cub, engraved and painted, are followed a considerable distance farther in by two enormous felines, their eyes glaring at the intruder to forbid him further access. A few hundred yards away, at Le Tuc d'Audoubert, guard is mounted by strange half-feline, half-bovid monsters. At Montesquieu two modelled felines guard the entrance to the clay-bear chamber, and there are modelled horses on the floor.

These seem to be the main lines of the framework within which Leptolithic man performed his magic or religious ceremonies when the groups came together for the winter.[2] Some definite traces of their ritual have come down to us, proving that early man tried to intervene

---

[1] Le Tuc d'Audoubert and Les Trois Frères are so close that the two caves probably communicated in former times at their extreme ends, which converge and cross in plan. In any case, they were both part of the underground fossil bed of the river Volp which hollowed them out.

[2] Lascaux seems to have been used for summer rites, since cold air penetrating there in the winter has given spells of frost and made it uncomfortable. Moreover, though it is Gravettian, the fauna shown contains neither reindeer (apart from some rare *graffiti* of slightly later date than the other figures) nor even mammoth. But in the new cave of Le Cro de Granville, at Rouffignac (Dordogne), the absence of bulls and any Cervidae (reindeer or stags) and the rarity of bison and horses, as well as the great preponderance of mammoths, seems to be due not to any question of season or era, but to a deliberate choice of certain species to the exclusion of others.

in the natural order of things by acting on the principles controlling it. However, we are in contact not with the religious beliefs themselves, but with the material vestiges of what seems to represent religious practice. These take the form of a series of arrangements designed to ensure that the celebrations were secret; footsteps marked in clay; ceremonial objects, pictorial representations, either engraved or painted, and carvings, which shed a little light and, with the help of parallels from ethnography, enable us to see into the religious life of these peoples. The hypothetical, though very rational, nature of conclusions based on such evidence cannot be too strongly emphasized.

The first set of facts relates to customs directly connected with the hunt, which, it is hardly necessary to mention, was the exclusive source of food for man in Palaeolithic times. Even better than the products of *art mobilier*, the palimpsests of superposed drawings of differing techniques enable the main lines of development to be traced by close observation of the successive layers. Firstly there can be noted an apparent contrast in the general arrangement of the figures in wall-engravings and paintings according to whether they were done inside dark caves or in shelters more or less open to daylight. Animals, usually shown as isolated individuals, are followed, mainly and especially in the rock-shelters of Eastern Spain, by scenes in which man plays a part as well as the animals, whether it be hunting, fighting, dancing, or episodes from daily life.

Prehistoric men thus expressed their fierce desire to meet the herds of stags or ibexes or the swarm of bees they sought, or to conquer their enemies, and so they projected into the future hunting and warlike expeditions still to come. We are therefore led, in spite of the different styles in which they materialized their hopes, to see in such representations the same magic motives that inspired the paintings and engravings in dark caverns where the predominating animal figures are normally independent one of the other. They are nearly always pictures of the species man used for food—mammoths, horses, reindeer, stags, ibexes, all with plenty of flesh on their bones. Females in foal are commonly shown also. Certain animals were modelled in clay, like the two bison at Le Tuc d'Audoubert, a male following a female. This motif is found again in paintings at Lascaux and at Font-de-Gaume, where a stallion sniffs at a mare, at Les Combarelles and elsewhere, as on the bone blade from Isturitz, the man pursuing a woman—a scene that occurs at Les Combarelles as well. No less significant is the fact that it was not considered necessary to draw fresh figures, and often the artist was content to modify previous ones when, according to the needs of the moment, the reproduction of different species was desired. At Le Roc de Sers and at Mas d'en Josep at Valtorta (Spain) Bovidae were transformed into Suidae; at La Vieja de Alpera (Spain) the mere addition of horns changed bulls into stags, these being pictorial transcriptions of rituals

R

designed to favour the reproduction of species required by man. Other groups are connected with the magic of destruction intended to annihilate harmful animals. Examples are the bear statue at Montespan, which had been given a real head and a soft pelt and riddled with spear-wounds, and the two lions nearby shattered by Magdalenian men. Later, by a gradual transition, the wounds were drawn or merely suggested by the simple representation of the weapons supposed to have caused them: the bear at Les Trois Frères has its body strewn with arrows and wounds, and in the same cave the body of one of the horses is surrounded by clubs.

All these figures were drawn with a very precise feeling for the true shapes of the living creatures, yet a few—the unicorn at Lascaux and the bear at Les Trois Frères, to take specific examples—so far from being treated with the representational realism characteristic of Magdalenian art, seem to have been purposely distorted and disfigured by the addition of the physical attributes of other species. The general shape is that of a bear, but one has been given a wolf's head, and the other, with a quite definite bear's head, has a bison's tail. Such intentional deformations[1] or disguises were probably the result of some interdict, as in modern primitive communities. Perhaps the tribe using the Trois Frères cave in Magdalenian times feared to upset the spirit of the bear by too faithful a likeness and portrayed him in a disguised form.

All these figures represent elements in ritual ceremonies for the magic of reproduction and destruction. The animal, even the man, was reproduced in effigy and then symbolically killed either by real wounds, by showing weapons on the body, or by imitating the impact of arrows.

The main basis of this ritual was mimicry, as is seen in the processions of figures, one holding a kind of palm, round a head and two hooves of a bison, at Chancelade and at Le Château des Eyzies, or the masked figures at Hornos de la Peña, Altamira, and other places, or the scenes of spirit-raising or exorcism at La Marche and Lussac-les-Châteaux (Vienne).

Along with these graphic records, two types of implement—throwing-sticks and pierced sticks—may also be part of the equipment used in these religious mimes. The decorations produced on them give them great artistic value, but also increase their fragility to the point where it is doubtful if they were ever used for hunting as the simple throwing-sticks of Magdalenian III no doubt were. Whatever may have been their real uses, pierced sticks interest us here only in so far as they were decorated, as occurred from Magdalenian IV onwards. Some of the

---

[1] At Les Trois Frères, in a strange scene where a man with a bison's head and hide seems to be playing a musical instrument, the two animals preceding him have had their special characteristics purposely changed: the nearest one has the body of a female cervid running into the head of a bison looking backward, while the animal in front of it has webbed front feet.

subjects portrayed—a series of *Cervus elaphus* heads (Laugerie Haute), *Cervi elaphi* and salmon rising (Lorthet), a seal (Montgaudier), and swans (Teyjat)—would seem to bear an interpretation connected with the sequence of the seasons. The regular passage at certain times of particular species of animals, migrating before the frosts and returning to the same spots with the better weather, may have created associations in the minds of Leptolithic men, symbolizing the successive death and resurrection of seasonal life. This leads us on to look farther into the interpretation of animal symbolism and glimpse the cyclic nature of the feasts and ceremonies, in which music also played a part (musical bow of the disguised figure at Les Trois Frères and other flutes and musical bows).

Certain highly decorated fusiform bone blades resemble the rhomboids, or vibrating plates, which, when swirled about on the end of a string, make buzzing noises recognized by most modern primitives as ancestral voices. They also use them to produce rain or direct swarms of bees towards a particular spot.

Some pebbles, engraved or painted with schematic or geometrical signs, have been compared to the Australian *churingas* in which the spirits of the ancestors are thought to reside. Similar objects are used by the Tasmanians for contacting the dead or for communicating over a distance. They are particularly numerous in Mesolithic levels.

The seasonal character of these practices is also brought out by other observed facts: Lascaux, which can only be occupied in the summer, was a seasonal sanctuary. The discovery in the engraved cave at Bernifal (Dordogne)[1] of a barrier of quarried stones covered with silt completely blocking the original entrance also supports this conclusion. Before they went the faithful had walled up the entrance to their sacred place to prevent it from being profaned.

Mimicry also played a very important part in the seasonal ceremonies held in the Leptolithic shrines. The idea of creating in this way the likeness of a particular animal must certainly have occurred very early in the minds of early men. Then, for the keenly observant Leptolithic hunters, it was but an easy step to find the artistry to express this likeness in movement.

Even to-day the Negrilloes, and more so the Bushmen, are experts in performing mimetic dances of magic intent, imitating the behaviour not only of animals but of men, during the ceremonies preceding great hunting expeditions. They begin with a chant and end with an offering to the spirit of the animal. The movements of the quarry and the adventures and episodes of the chase are reproduced with scrupulous exactness, and such mimicry is a form of painting, a prefiguration of reality.

As far as the testimony of Leo Frobenius can be relied on, his account

---

[1] D. Peyrony discovered Bernifal via the collapsed roof, to the right of the real entrance used during the Leptolithic occupation of the cave and found later by this investigator.

of preparations for an antelope-hunt in the Kongour forest throws some light on this ritual. At dawn, accompanied by a woman, the pygmies climbed to the top of a hill, where they cleared and flattened a small patch of ground. When this had been done one of the hunters drew with his finger on the ground the outline of an antelope, while his companions murmured incantations. Then came an expectant silence, and at the moment when the sun rose over the horizon one of the men, bending his bow, came up to the bare patch. A few minutes more and the sun's rays touched the drawing. At that very moment the following extremely rapid scene took place: the woman raised her hands as if to seize the sun, muttering words, while the bowman shot his arrow into the silhouette traced on the ground. Again the woman muttered, and then the hunters, with their weapons, bounded off into the undergrowth. The woman remained a few moments longer and then went back to their camp. When she had gone Leo Frobenius noticed that the arrow had been shot into the neck of the animal drawing. When evening came the pygmies brought back an antelope, killed by an arrow through its jugular vein. On their return they had run to the site of the morning's ceremony to lay there some tufts of the victim's hair, pour out a cup of his blood, and pull out the arrow. At dawn next day the drawing had been effaced, and the hunters asked Leo Frobenius not to speak about the scene he had witnessed.[1]

Though it may be fruitless to try to reconstruct with the aid of the available contemporary evidence religious ceremonies from the Upper Palaeolithic, it is not, however, without interest to draw attention to the fact that there is not much difference between graphical representations of this kind by Leptolithic men and those by pygmies. In Frobenius's account we can detect the elements of a ritual: the secret nature of the ceremony, to be celebrated at a precise moment of time, the ephemeral nature of the representation, destined to be effaced as soon as the event it prefigured had taken place, the final act of appeasing the spirit of the victim and of lifting the blood-curse from the killer.

Parallel to these temporary manifestations designed to have an effect on the animal, we can find traces of tendencies towards a more permanent form. The pre-Mousterian rite of orientating the bear skulls piled in the little tabernacles in the Drachenhöhle might be rooted in a mimetism intended to produce the desired results by constant repetition of the same act. In these high-altitude lairs the bears were invited, even forced, to follow the direction set by the skulls of their dead predecessors, and thus become in their turn an easy prey for the hunters.

Of all these hunts, these dances, and these mimed combats, no trace

[1] At Montespan, at the entrance to the gallery with the models where the statue of the crouching bear presides over the bas-reliefs of the horses on the floor, can be seen the remains of clay statues of two large felines, which may be old traces of ritually destroyed animal figures.

remained, and it seems that by fixing them in pictures on the rock-walls of sanctuaries an attempt was made by visual means to increase their spiritual effect still further. Hence also the intentional exaggeration of certain human figures, sometimes endowed with enormous, powerful legs, sometimes rendered in filiform lines and, as though freed from gravity, seeming endowed with wild movement, whereas no distortion appears in the animal's body, an effect certainly not due to mere chance.

Then the barrier separating man from animal was vague. We have noted substitutions and parallels (engraved bone from Isturitz with, on one side, figures of a man pursuing a woman and, on the other, two bison), or associations (woman and reindeer at Laugerie Basse), or humans mingled with animals (Les Combarelles), as well as the drawing of hybrid silhouettes combining both human and animal characteristics. His head topped by antlers of a *Megaceros* stag with two long, hairy ears, the horned god from Les Trois Frères has the eyes of an owl that can see at night and a vast beard. Leaning forward like a dancer, his body has purely human members and sex, but a bushy tail hangs from his loins. In the same cave, on the panel on the right wall of the narrow, low recess through which one must crawl on all-fours to climb up to the 'magician,' rises a figure with a bison's head connected to a vertical, human body. The bison's hair seems to come down on to the shoulders and even lower, for the small of the back is prolonged into a long brush of a tail clinging to the hindquarters, its line coming forward again to cut the legs. The saddle-backed line of the spine is indeed human, as is the left leg, bent and marking time. The front legs are not, and one of them holds a long spindle-shaped object, a flute or musical bow, one end of which touches the bison mouth. Forward of this personage, an equally strange figure has cervid characteristics, both in the shape of its rear legs and its rudimentary tail, and it should be noted in what careful detail the artist has drawn the anus and the vulva. The forelegs are those of a bison, as is the head, turned and looking back— always a rare attitude in Leptolithic animal figures. It is crowned by a mass of hair joining on to the trunk. At the head of this group of figures arranged in files moves a reindeer, abnormal only in its forelegs ending in hastily drawn feet, similar in general shape to a duck's. Given the perfect anatomical detail of the drawings in this part of the Trois Frères cave, such distortions are certainly not due to any lack of skill in the artist, but to intentional alteration of the natural shapes, similar to those found in other engravings, in particular the bodies of bears with a wolf's head and a bison's tail.

MAGICIANS OR GODS?

What we know about religious life among primitive peoples will perhaps enable us to attempt an explanation of the associations and substitutions found in ceremonies performed to ensure the fertility of game animals, where the parts are played by men acting as intermediaries. Can we therefore see in these drawings and paintings a graphical transcription of these religious mimes? Such an interpretation seems very attractive, since what glimpses we get of the religious life of primitives show constant examples of integration. The 'bear ceremonialism' of polar peoples cannot be reduced to a simple matter of relations between man and the animal. It constitutes a system of ritual, myth, and belief, connected with the mythology of ancestors and the renewal of cosmic life. The initiation ceremonies performed in certain Leptolithic sanctuaries, the heel imprints at Le Tuc d'Audoubert, the footprints at Niaux, and sinuous lines printed in clay, are all related to the existence of a supreme being, or the mythical figure substituted for him, be he demiurge, civilizing hero, or ancestor. The relations between man and the animal are never simple, but imply a well-organized mythico-religious system, from which the presence of supra-terrestrial beings can not be excluded *a priori*.

The use of the mask itself presupposes community life. Moreover, it is made to surprise some one else and absolutely must have a witness. It also argues the roots of a belief. In its complexity and under its conventionalization, it is charged with religious meaning and its symbols with power. Masks are worn in battle to terrify, and in sacred ceremonies to inspire obedience and respect, to give the wearer the appearance of a mantle of supernatural powers and to impress the beholders with the idea of the powers inherent in the image. The mask becomes a means of participation. It is itself endowed with a terrible reality. Such are the powers that the mask gives the wearer. The result is an association of ideas between his aspect, at the same time both human and animal, as celebrant of the rite and the power of magic itself. It therefore becomes possible to imagine the existence, in the same hybrid forms, of supernatural beings with similar powers. The personification of such beings during religious mimes creates a visual image that reappears as well in the magician's trance as in the dreams of the onlookers, and all the more forcefully since the ceremonies are of capital importance for the existence of the community. In the minds of primitives, as in those of Leptolithic men, the barrier between true perception and hallucination becomes blurred, and for them such hybrid personages as bison-men, goat-men, or bear-men seen in their dreams are living creatures, but, not being men, they can only be supernatural.

We are therefore led to attribute to these graphical transcripts of sacred mimes that may have been used as models by Leptolithic artists —though they did not need to borrow them from masked dances—a meaning quite different from magic. In his book on the mythical world of Australian aborigines and Papuans, Lucien Lévy-Bruhl emphasizes our tendency to attribute to prehistoric men the same ideas as we have about animals. As long as it is only a question of observing the shapes, of a feeling for movement and skill in portraying it, there is no difference. But what we learn from these primitives and their reactions is something very different: it is not the physical strength of the animal, nor its visible characteristics, but rather its invisible and mysterious powers that must have deeply concerned Leptolithic man, as it does these primitives.

Though the Leptolithic believed in the effectiveness of the pictures he drew or painted or the images he carved, he was, however, far from being certain of making the animals fall into his hands by this magic means. There is a connexion between the mystical power of these images and that of the ceremonies. It assures the fertility, growth, and permanence of the animal species through the presence and help of their mythical creators. "It is only a consequence of the action of the image. It is not its immediate purpose. Here the mystical plane controls the utilitarian. It does not merge with it" (L. Lévy-Bruhl). Consequently, composite half-animal, half-human figures do not necessarily represent masks and costumes used in dances and ceremonies. "Like the masks themselves, and for the same reasons, these are probably direct 'creations' of mythical beings, for they have also the same purpose no doubt as the dances and ceremonies: to ensure the presence and the action of these mythical beings and the communion of the group with the ancestor whose name and essence it shares" (L. Lévy-Bruhl).

The parallelism noted between the composite Leptolithic figures and the masks used in certain dances by the Eskimos of the Bering Strait corresponds to the identical desire to bring out the dual nature of the mythical being which is represented. There is, for example, the bird's-head mask which at a particular moment in the ceremony opens mobile shutters to allow a human face to appear, expressing ingeniously the consubstantial unity of animal and man, or the animal heads on the engraved stone at La Madeleine, under which appear, as in a transparency, human features.

If we accept the interpretation suggested by L. Lévy-Bruhl we cannot see in the 'magician' from Les Trois Frères, the hybrids from the same cave, the dancer with the bear's head from Le Mas d'Azil, the masked figure from La Madeleine, or the 'imps' from Teyjat mere figures of hunters in full panoply or magicians in their ceremonial costume. These composite forms created by Leptolithic men would then represent a plastic transcript of half-human, half-animal beings, masters both of animals and men. These are mythical pictures. Man only appears in them masked, as in the ceremonies where the mask mimes the totem, and we may suppose that in these myths were shown the adventures and creations of these superior beings with a nature at once human and animal. Perhaps they were considered as ancestors.

It does not appear, however, that these myths were of the nature of totems, for it is very difficult to establish a totemic connexion with the wall art of the Leptolithic. If such contact could be made we should find ourselves in the presence of communities with a strangely restricted number of totems. Now, a totemic group must necessarily be subdivided into several clans, and the necessity for this subdivision is in the law on marriage outside the clan to which the individual belongs. Moreover, the Palaeolithics would then be supposed to have gone to the strange length of choosing their totems among their game animals, and only among them.

In the last analysis, we are once again led to seek points of contact in the communities of Melanesia and North America. Among these peoples who, like the Leptolithics, aim at hunting certain species of animals the ceremonies, whatever place they may occupy in the social organization, are secret and mysterious, and this secrecy is one of the bases of their ritual.

Told by word of mouth, or represented in dramatic or plastic form, the myth is an assurance of the real presence of the ancestor and, by the same token, of his effective action. His image occupies a place of honour in the shrine: the horned god at Les Trois Frères dominates the animal population he controls; at La Pasiega (Spain) he was enthroned perhaps in a kind of stone stall. And this ancestor cult appears again on another series of graphic records: a human (?) bone at Péchialet, with the representation of a man's face; the conventionalized human faces (?) on the wands at Isturitz, or the subcircular *graffiti* with indications of the eyes at Les Trois Frères. With such beliefs are also connected the tectiform signs hidden in the recesses of certain Cantabrian caves and representing perhaps the resting-places where the spirits of these mysterious beings came to take shelter.

If we admit that Leptolithic men had myths and that they made artistic representations of some of their protagonists it is no longer wrong to ascribe to them belief in a complex of supernatural forces, or the experience of a supernature, both distinct yet inseparable from the visible world, representing a mythical period.

In a more general way, we are led to note how far the reindeer age was from the origins of human society. The Leptolithics seem to us like very advanced peoples, as complex as hunting peoples living in our own times. But while these latter, defeated and banished to the less desirable parts of the world, are now but the shadow of their former selves, when we think of what men were in the reindeer age we see human groups filled with strength to expand, to discover, and to progress, possessing a moral culture far more highly developed than might be supposed from the remains of their material civilization.

Select Bibliography

GENERAL WORKS

BLANC, A. C.: *Origine e sviluppo dei populi cacciatori e raccoglitori*. Rome, Scienza, 1945.

BREUIL, H.: *La Préhistoire. Leçon d'ouverture de la chaire de Préhistoire au Collège de France*. 2nd ed., de Lagny, 1937.

BURKITT, M. C.: *Prehistory. A Study of Early Cultures in Europe and the Mediterranean Basin*. 2nd ed., Cambridge University Press, 1925.

——*The Old Stone Age of Palaeolithic Times*. Cambridge University Press, 1933.

DÉCHELETTE, J.: *Manuel d'archéologie préhistorique, celtique et galloromaine*. Vol. I. Paris, A. J. Picard, 1908.

EBERT, M.: *Reallexikon der Vorgeschichte*. Berlin, W. de Gruyter, 1924–32.

GOURY, G.: *Précis d'archéologie préhistorique. Origine et évolution de l'Homme*. Vol. I., *Paléolithique*. 2nd ed., A. J. Picard, 1948.

MENGHIN, O.: *Weltgeschichte der Steinzeit*. Vienna, A. Schroll, 1931.

OBERMAIER, H.: *El Hombre fosil*. Comisión de Investigaciones paleontológicas y prehistóricas, mem. No. 9. Madrid, Museo de Ciencasnaturales, 2nd ed., 1925.

——*Urgeschichte der Menschheit*. Geschichte der führenden Völker, Vol. I. Freiburg-im-Breisgau, Herder, 1931.

——*El Hombre prehistorico y los origines de la Humanidad*. 3rd ed., Madrid, 1942.

HISTORY OF PREHISTORIC RESEARCH

AUFRÈRE, L.: *Figures de préhistoriens. I. Boucher de Perthes*, in Préhistoire, Vol. VII, 1940.

——*Le mouvement scientifique à Abbeville dans la première moitié du XIXᵉ siècle et les origines de la Préhistoire (1795–1840)*, in Sciences, No. 4, 1936, pp. 175–195.

——*Le Musée des origines de la Préhistoire*, in Sciences, No. 23, 1938, pp. 119–133.

BÉGOUËN, COMTE: *La Préhistoire à la Société archéologique du Midi de la France*, in Mémoires de la Société archéologique du Midi de la France, 1932.

BREUIL, H.: *La conquête de la notion de la très haute antiquité de l'Homme*, in Anthropos, Vols. XXXVIII–XL, 1942–45, pp. 667–687.

——*Les découvertes paléolithiques en France et la conservation des grottes et gisements* in Congrès archéologique de France, XCVIIth session, Paris, 1934, pp. 323–340.

CARTAILHAC, E., ANGLADE, J., and LECLERC DU SABLON: *Un chapitre de l'histoire intellectuelle de Toulouse. Le professeur J.-B. Noulet* (1802–90), in Mémoires de l'Académie des Sciences, Inscriptions et Belles-Lettres de Toulouse, XIth series, Vol. VI, 1919, pp. 421–483.

CHEYNIER, DR A.: *Jouannet, grand-père de la Préhistorique.* Brive, Chastrusse, Praudel, 1936.

GUMMEL, H.: *Forschungsgeschichte in Deutschland. Die Urgeschichtsforschung und ihre historische Entwicklung in den Kulturstaaten der Erde*, edited by Karl Hermann Jacob-Friesen, Vol. I. Berlin, Walter de Gruyter, 1938.

GUYÉNOT, E.: *L'évolution de la pensée scientifique. Les sciences de la vie aux XVIIe et XVIIIe siècles. L'idée d'évolution.* L'Evolution de l'Humanité, No. 68, Paris, 1949.

ANTHROPOLOGY

ARAMBOURG, C.: *La genèse de l'Humanité.* Paris, 1943.

BLANC, A. C.: *L'Uomo fossile del Monte Circeo: un cranio neandertaliano nella Grotta Guattari a San Felice Circeo.* Rendiconti. Accad. naz. dei Lincei, S. 6 a, 1st sem., 5, 1939.

BOULE, M.: *Les Hommes fossiles.* 3rd ed. Paris. Masson, 1943.

BREUIL, H. and BLANC, A. C.: *Rinvenimento in situ di un nuovo cranio di Homo neanderthalensis nel giacimento di Saccopastore (Roma).* Rendiconti R. Accad. dei Lincei XXII, S 6 a 2nd sem., 3–4, 1935.

BROOM, R.: *Australopithecus and its Affinities.* Early Man, Philadelphia, 1937.

GIESELER, W.: *Die Fossilgeschichte des Menschen.* Die Evolution der Organismen. Jena, 1943.

KEITH, A. and McCOWN: *The Stone Age of Mount Carmel.* Vol. II. Oxford, 1939.

NEUVILLE, R. and RUHLMANN, A.: *L'âge de l'Homme fossile de Rabat*, Bull. Soc. Anthropol. Paris, 9th series, III, 1942.

PEI WAN CHUNG: *Report of the Excavation of the Locality 13 in Choukoutien*, Bull. Geol. Soc. of China, XIII, 3, 1934.

SERGI, S.: *Gli ominidi fossili di forme estinte*, in Le Razza e popoli della terra. Vol. I. Turin, 1940.

WEINERT, H.: *Entstehung der Menschenrassen.* Stuttgart, 1941.

GEOLOGICAL EVIDENCE OF THE ANTIQUITY OF MAN

BLANC, A. C.: *La curva di Milankovich e la sua applicazione alla datazione assoluta dei Neandertaliani d' Italia*, Atti. Soc. Tosc. di Sc. Nat. Mem. XLVIII, Pisa, 1939.

——*Variazioni climatiche ed oscillazioni della linea di riva nel Mediterraneo centrale durante l'era glaciale.* Geolog. der. Meere und Binnengewasser, 5, 12, Berlin, 1942.

BREUIL, H.: *De l'importance de la solifluxion dans l'étude des terrains quaternaires de la France.* Revue de géographie physique et de géologie dynamique, VII, 4, Paris, 1934.

BREUIL, H.: *Terrasses et quartzites taillées de la Haute Vallée de la Garonne.* Bulletin de la Société préhistorique française, 1937.

BREUIL, H. and KOSLOWKI: *Études de stratigraphie paléolithique dans le Nord de la France.* L'Anthropologie, 1931–32.

MILANCKOVICH, M.: *Mathematische Klimatlehre und astronomische Theorie der Klimatschwankungen.* Handb. der Klimatologie, I. Berlin, 1910.

——*Astronomische Mittel zur Erforschung der erdschichtlichen Klimate.* Handb. der Geophysik, 9. Berlin, 1938.

NEUVILLE, R. and RUHLMANN, A.: *La place du Paléolithique ancien dans le Quaternaire marocain.* Institut des Hautes Études Marocaines, Vol. VIII. Casablanca, 1941.

LES GROTTES DE GRIMALDI: Vol. I. *Historique et description,* by Canon de Villeneuve. *Géologie et paléontologie,* by M. Boule. Vol. II. *Anthropologie,* by Dr Verneau. *Archéologie,* by E. Cartailhac, Monaco, 1908–10.

ZEUNER, F. E.: *The Pleistocene Chronology of Central Europe.* Geolog. Mag., LXXII, London, 1935.

——*The Pleistocene Period. Its Climate, Chronology, and Faunal Successions.* London, 1945.

——*Dating the Past. An Introduction to Geochronology.* 2nd ed., London, 1950.

PALAEOLITHIC AND LEPTOLITHIC INDUSTRIES

BREUIL, H.: *Les industries à éclats du Paléolithique ancien. I. Le Clactonien.* Préhistoire, Vol. I, 2, 1932.

——*Les subdivisions du Paléolithique supérieur et leur signification.* 2nd ed., Paris, 1937.

——*Le feu et l'industrie de la pierre dans le gisement du Sinanthropus à Chou-Kou-Tien.* L'Anthropologie, 1932.

——*État actuel de nos connaissances sur les industries paléolithiques de Chou-Kou-Tien,* L'Anthropologie, 1937.

BREUIL, H. and ZBYSZEWSKI, G.: *Contribution à l'étude des industries paléolithiques du Portugal et de leurs rapports avec la géologie du Quaternaire. Les principaux gisements des deux rives de l'ancien estuaire du Tage.* Comunicaçãos dos Serviços geologicos de Portugal. Vol. XXIII. Lisbon, 1942.

GARROD, D. A. E.: *The Upper Palaeolithic in the Light of Recent Discovery.* Presid. Address. British Assoc. for Adv. of Science. London, 1936.

HENRI-MARTIN, G.: *La grotte de Fontéchevade.* Part I: *Archéologie.* Archives de l'Institut de Paléontologie Humaine, mem. No. 28. Paris, 1957.

PEI WAN CHUNG: *Le rôle des animaux et des causes naturelles dans la cassure des os.* Palaeontologia sinica, new series D, No. 10, whole series No. 118. Peking, 1938.

See also the collections of the principal periodicals for accounts of research on Palaeolithic industries and sites: *L'Anthropologie, Association française pour l'avancement des sciences, Bulletin de la Société préhistorique française, Congrès préhistoriques de France, L'Homme préhistorique, Congrès international d'Anthropologie, Congrès international des Sciences préhistoriques et protohistoriques, Préhistoire, Quartär, IPEK, Revue anthropologique, Revue préhistorique, Quaternaria.*

THE ACTIVITIES OF PALAEOLITHIC MAN

LEONHARD, F.: *Jäger, Bauern, Händler*. Leipzig, 1939.

LINDNER, K.: *La chasse préhistorique*. Translated into French by G. Montandon. Paris, Payot, 1941.

OBERMAIER, H.: *La vida de nuestros antepasados cuaternarios en Europa*. Paper read before the Real Academia de la Historia at the reception of Don Hugo Obermaier, May 2, 1926. Madrid, 1926.

VALLOIS, H.-V.: *La durée de la vie chez l'Homme fossile*. L'Anthropologie, 1937–39.

MESOLITHIC

BAUDET, J.-L.: *Le continent immergé de la région Sud de la Mer du Nord*. L'Ethnographie, 1957.

CLARK, J. G. D.: *The Mesolithic Settlement of Northern Europe. A Study of the Food-gathering Peoples of Northern Europe during the Early Post-glacial Period*. Cambridge, 1936.

COULONGES, L.: *Les gisements préhistoriques de Sauveterre-la-Lémance*. Archives de l'Institut de Paléontologie Humaine, mem. 14.

LACAM, R., NIEDERLANDER, A., and VALLOIS, H.: *Le gisement mésolithique du Cuzoul de Gramat*. Archives de l'Institut de Paléontologie humaine, mem. 21, 1944.

PÉQUART, M. and SAINT-JUST: *Nouvelles fouilles au Mas d'Azil*. Préhistoire, Vol. VIII, 1941.

RUST, A.: *Das altsteinzeitliche Rentierjägerlager Meiendorf*. Neumünster-in-H., 1937.

——*Die alt- und mittelsteinzeitlichen Funde von Stellmoor*. Neumünster-in-H., 1943.

LEPTOLITHIC ART

BREUIL, H.: *Les origines de l'art*. Journal de Psychologie, XXII, 1925; XXIII, 1926.

——*L'évolution de l'art pariétal dans les cavernes et abris ornés de France*. XIth Congrès préhistorique de France, Paris, 1934.

——*Una Altamira francesa. La caverna de Lascaux en Montignac (Dordogne)*. Archivo español de arqueologia, 1942.

——*400 siècles d'art pariétal*. Montignac-sur-Vézère, 1952.

BREUIL, H. and BÉGOUËN, H.: *Nouvelle gravure d'Homme masqué de la caverne des Trois-Frères (Montesquieu-Avantès, Ariège)*. Proceedings of the Acad. des Inscriptions et Belles-Lettres, 1920.

BREUIL, H. and OBERMAIER, H.: *The Cave of Altamira*. Madrid, 1935.

KÜHN, H.: *Kunst, und Kultur der Vorzeit Europas. I. Das Palaeolithikum*. Berlin, W. de Gruyter, 1929.

LANTIER, R.: *Les origines de l'art français*. Paris, G. Le Prat, 1947.

MORIN-JEAN: *Les artistes préhistoriques*. Les grands artistes. Paris, Laurens, 1933.

OBERMAIER, H.: *Las pinturas rupestres de la cueva Remigia (Castellón)*, in collaboration with H. Breuil and J. B. Porcar, Madrid, 1946.

——*Nouvelles études sur l'art rupestre du Levant espagnol.* L'Anthropologie, Vol. 47, 1937.

PASSEMARD, E.: *La Caverne d'Isturitz en Pays Basque.* Préhistoire, Vol. IX, 1944.

PÉRICARD, L. and LWOFF, ST.: *La Marche, commune de Lussac-les-Châteaux (Vienne). Premier atelier du Magdalénien III à dalles gravées mobiles.* Bull. Soc. Préhist. Fr., XXVII, 1940; XXXIX, 1942; XL, 1943.

SAINT-PÉRIER, R. DE: *L'art préhistorique.* Maîtres de l'art ancien, Paris, Rieder, 1932.

WINDELS, F.: *Lascaux, Chapelle Sixtine de la Préhistoire.* Montignac-sur-Vézère, 1948.

Many of these works give a detailed bibliography on the discoveries concerning Palaeolithic art. See also the publications of the Institut de Paléontologie Humaine: *Peintures et gravures murales des cavernes paléolithiques* and *Archives de l'Institut de Paléontologie Humaine*, and the procedures of the Council for the Pursuit of Scientific Studies and Investigations in Madrid, *Comisión de Investigaciones paleontológicas y prehistóricas.*

RELIGIOUS PRACTICES

1. *General Works*

BLANC, A. C.: *Il sacro presso i Primitivi.* Rome, Partena, 1945.

CLEMEN, C.: *Urgeschichtliche Religion.* Unters. z. allgem. Religions-geschichte, Book 4, 1932.

LEVY-BRUHL, L.: *La mythologie primitive. Le monde mythique des Australiens et des Papous.* 3rd ed. Paris, Alcan, 1935.

LUQUET, G.: *L'art et la religion des Hommes Fossiles*, Paris, Masson, 1926.

MAINAGE, Th.: *Les religions de la Préhistoire. L'age paléolithique.* Paris, Desclée, de Brouwer, A. Picard, 1921.

SCHMIDT, R. R.: *L'aurore de l'esprit humain.* Paris, Payot, 1936.

WERNERT, P.: *Les Hommes de l'âge de la Pierre représentaient-ils les esprits des défunts et des ancêtres?*

——*La signification des cavernes d'art paléolithique.* Histoire générale des religions, sous la direction de M. Gorce et R. Mortier, Vol. I. Paris, A. Quillet, 1948.

2. *The Skull Cult*

ANDRÉE, R.: *Schädelkultus. Ethnographische Parallelen.* 1878.

——*Menschen Schädel als Trinkgefässe.* Vehr. Volkste., 1912.

BALFOUR, H.: *Note on the Use of Human Skulls as Drinking and Libation Vessels.* Journ. Anthrop. Inst., XXVI, 1897, pp. 347 et seq.

BREUIL, H. and OBERMAIER, H.: *Crânes paléolithiques faconnés en coupes.* L'Anthropologie, XX, 1909, pp. 523 et seq.

SCHMIDT, R. R.: *Die altsteinzeitlichen Schädelgräber der Ofnet.* 1913.

WERNERT, P.: *Le culte des crânes à l'époque paléolithique*. Histoire générale des religions, sous la direction de M. Gorce and R. Mortier, Vol. I. Paris, A. Quillet, 1948.

3. *Palaeolithic Burial-places*

BOUYSSONNIE, A. and J. and BARDON, A.: *Découverte d'un squelette humain moustérien à La Bouffia de la Chapelle-aux-Saints*. L'Anthropologie, Vol. 24, 1913.

BREUIL, H.: *Remarques sur les sépultures moustériennes (affirmation d'un témoin)*. Inst. Français d'Anthropologie, 1921.

BREUIL, H. and BLANC, A. C.: *Le nouveau crâne de Saccopastore*. L'Anthropologie, 1936.

CAPITAN, L., and PEYRONY: *Deux squelettes humains au milieu de foyers de l'époque moustérienne*. Revue de l'École d'Anthropologie de Paris, 1909.

PEYRONY, D.: *Les Moustériens inhumaient-ils leurs morts?* Bulletin de la Société Historique et Archéologique du Périgord, 1921.

—— *Le Moustier. Ses gisements. Ses industries. Ses couches archéologiques.* Revue Anthropologique, 1930.

4. *Leptolithic Burial-places*

BLANCHARD, R. B.: *Note sur le fossile humain de Saint-Germain-la-Rivière*. S. 1., n. d.

CARDINI, L.: *Nuovi documenti sull'antichità dell'Uomo in Italia. Reperto humano del Paleolitico superiore nella grotta delle Arene Candide.* Razza e Civiltè, 1942, n. 1–4.

PEYRONY, D.: *Découverte d'un squelette humain à La Madeleine*. Institut Intern. d'Anthropologie, 3rd session, Amsterdam, 1928.

5. *Mesolithic Burial-places*

JUDE, DR, and CRUVELLER, J.: *La grotte de l'Homme de Rochereuil*. Bull. Soc. Hist. et Archéol., Périgord, 1938.

PÉQUART, M. and SAINT-JUST, BOULE, M., and VALLOIS, H. V.: *Téviec, station nécropole mésolithique du Morbihan*. Archives de l'Institut de Paléontologie Humaine, mém. 18, 1937.

PÉQUART, M. and SAINT-JUST, and BOULE, M.: *Hoëdic. Deuxième station nécropole du Mésolithique côtier armoricain.* Antwerp, 1954.

Index